03

09 10
1   1

GAYLORD MG

THE FIGHTING FORTIETH

In War and Peace

by

James D. Delk

Library of Congress Cataloging-in-Publication Data

Delk, James D., 1932-
    The Fighting Fortieth in war and peace / by James. D. Delk
    p.   cm.
    Includes bibliographical references (p.   ) and index.
    ISBN 0-88280-140-6 (hardcover)
    1. United States. Army. Armored Division, 40th--History
I. Title
UA93.5.40th.D45   1998
358'.183'0973--dc21

                                                     97-41814
                                                 CIP

****

Published by ETC Publications
         Palm Springs
         California 92262

Published in the United States of America.

This history is dedicated to the many thousands of soldiers who wore or wear "The Patch," and most especially, those who never returned.

TABLE OF CONTENTS

CONTENTS

MAPS

PHOTOS

CONTENTS

PREFACE

The 40th Division, like many other divisions, has a distinguished combat record. The entire division was mobilized for three wars, with selected units and individuals called or volunteering for others.

In addition, the 40th Division has always been headquartered in the most disaster-prone state in the nation. There have been many disasterous earthquakes, just the most recent being the Northridge earthquake. There have been innumerable forest fires and floods. And there have been the many riots in prisons, at the docks, and in the cities, including the most destructive rioting in our nation's history. The 40th Division was involved in all of them, with unquestionably the most active peacetime record of any National Guard division.

When assuming command of the division in 1986, the first thing I asked for was a copy of the division history. I don't know of any division with a combat record that has not had at least one comprehensive history published. I was therefore more than a little surprised when told that none had been published for the 40th Division. That served as the initial impetus for this work, which eventually became a labor of love. It took too long, but there were many tips, tales, myths, and legends to follow up.

* * * * * * * * * *

Writing a history of this magnitude would have been impossible without the encouragement of veterans and members of the division, plus the direct help of many individuals and institutions.

Great soldiers and military historians like Colonel David A. "Gus" Gustafson repeatedly sent information and leads. Colonel William G. "Bill" Hamilton provided many resources from his invaluable collection, which fills his garage as well as much of his home. Kenneth E. "Ken" Camozzi provided key leads, especially to his grandfather (Captain Bob Munyon), and processed outstanding photographs on his computer. Norman R. Zehr of Colorado has an incomparable library covering all aspects of the Korean War. His bibliography is the most complete I've seen.

When I needed to find individuals who witnessed particular actions in combat, the contacts for various alumni associations of the division were always helpful. These included Sid Sultzbaugh of Ohio, secretary of the Association of 40th Infantry Division Korean War Veterans, and Ed Lown in New York, contact for a similar group headquartered there. Richard C. Fette and Norman L. Hackler of the 223rd, and Ron Gorrell of the 224th Infantry Regimental Associations were always responsive.

The patience of archivists in the various museums and archives never ceases to amaze me. Brigadier General (SMR) Donald E. Mattson and Bill Davies of the California Military Museum in Sacramento endured literally dozens of my visits. Richard J. "Dick" Summers of the United States Army Military History Institute in Carlisle, Pennsylvania was especially helpful in the World War II phases of my research. The Center for Military History in Washington, DC had key pieces of the puzzle.

The archivists at Duke University were fast and efficient. I flew out to review the Eichelberger Papers from World War II. Janie Morris had the papers beautifully catalogued, along with his photographs, so I was able to go through them all in a single day.

Every historian must spend time in the National Archives in Washington, DC. The archivists at College Park and Suitland have a tough time keeping a tight grip on literally mountains of material, but they provided much valuable input and great photographs.

Lieutenant Colonel Leonid E. "Len" Kondratiuk, Historian of the National Guard Bureau, several times provided me archival material including old units histories and general orders.

Many veterans were helpful in adding details to sometimes obscure records. Major Generals Thomas O. Lawson and Donald N. Moore, Colonel Donald P. Reece and Major Robert H. Rogers provided a great deal of material, much of which was sent on to the California Military Museum for future researchers. Colonel Arthur L. Belknap provided key insights regarding the rescue of Peter Tolputt. Valuable insights on Medal of Honor actions were provided by former lieutenants Richard S. Agnew and Richard C. Wagner, both survivors of severe wounds. Many others provided important information, and are listed in Appendix 9, under Sources.

The encouragement of former commanders like Major General Thomas K. Turnage kept my nose to the grindstone. My helpful proof readers and critics were my father (himself published), James H. Delk, along with his wife Winnie, plus my youngest son Jack, along with his beautiful wife, Debbie. My toughest critic and proof reader, as always, is also the one who endures my funks...my high school sweetheart, Edna. Thank you, hon.

Finally, if any errors remain in this history, it is my fault, not the editors. I also hope I haven't added credibility to myths. There are still many convinced the locomotive bell of the 184th Infantry never existed. I followed every lead, and *think* the account in this history is factual. Regardless, it is important and interesting military lore.

SHOULDER PATCH

Approved by the Commanding General of the American Expeditionary Force, November 23, 1918. Amended March 17, 1931 to wear point up. Described as: On a blue square, 2-1/2 inches on a side, with yellow sun in splendor, the disk 13/16 inches in diameter, twelve rays within a circle 1-7/8 inches in diameter. The square to be worn point up.

UNIT CREST OF THE 40TH INFANTRY DIVISION (MECHANIZED)

On a gold background, at the top, a blue triangular area bearing a gold semi-sunburst representing the Division's home of Southern California. In base, a blue Torii Gate (representing the division's award of the Republic of Korea Presidential Unit Citation), surmounted by a red arrowhead (alluding to the fire-power of the division and representing the division's assault landing at Luzon in World War II), all over a gold Philippine sun (refers to the Philippine Presidential Unit Citation Award) with a demi fleur-de-lis (symbolizing service in France during World War I), at the top. A gold scroll with the motto DUTY - HONOR - COUNTRY in red letters. This crest was approved for the 40th Infantry Brigade on January 13, 1970, and was redesignated for the 40th Infantry Division (Mechanized) on January 31, 1974.

CHAPTER ONE

FORMATION OF THE 40TH DIVISION

He paused as he worked his fields, enjoying the crisp morning. He was warmed, not only by the sun, but with the glow of self-satisfaction as he studied what he had accomplished. Some of the largest tree stumps remained...but he told himself that with the help of Jesperson, his neighbor, they could be pulled after rotting for another year or two. He listened to the singing of the birds, noted the few sparklets of dew that remained, and rested his horse Handy for a few moments.

He resumed plowing, being particularly alert for hostiles as he approached the trees at the end of each furrow, and kept an eye on Handy's ears. He thought he heard something, and quickly reined in the horse. He waited until the harness and traces quieted, while cocking an ear toward the settlement's tiny church and meeting hall. Sure enough, the bell was pealing. He quickly removed the tack from Handy, grabbed his musket, and raced to the cabin to drop off Handy and tell his wife he was leaving. He then ran over the low ridge towards Jesperson's in the next valley, too far away to hear the bell, before they both dashed to join the other minutemen.

Every able-bodied man in the colonies was a minuteman, and expected to keep his weapon handy and respond immediately when called to protect his community. The minutemen could afford little time for formal drill, and relied heavily on the former professional soldiers schooled in European warfare that were scattered throughout the settlements. Those veterans leavened the volunteers, strengthening the militia force while providing a teaching base. Most settlers already knew how to shoot so they could put meat on the table, but the former professionals were needed to teach the basics in soldier skills and tactics. Continental tactics were revised to accommodate the heavily forested terrain, rather than the comparatively open terrain found in Europe. The tactics were also adjusted to best take advantage of the minuteman's strong character and lack of training time.

The militia in America came of age when it served as the core of George Washington's forces in winning our independence in 1776. George Washington was himself a member of the Virginia militia, and knew the militia well. The militia grew in size and experience over the years, but was not adequately supported by the Federal government until passage of the Dick Act in 1903. The Dick Act was sponsored by Senator Charles Dick, a Major General in the Ohio National Guard, and was triggered by the nearly disastrous mobilization for and prosecution of the Spanish-American War.

The new law ensured there was Federal support for the National Guard, and provided for Regular Army officers to be detailed to help train the Guardsmen. The Dick Act and legislation that followed modernized the National Guard and was the first of several seminal pieces of legislation that eventually ensured the National Guard would be combat ready when needed.

One of the many modern forebears of the 40th Division can be found in a Los Angeles area unit that traces its contemporary history to 1890. The unit was organized then as Company F, Ninth Infantry, and a few years later was redesignated as Company L, Seventh Infantry. California National Guard units in those days saw their domestic role as responding to civil emergencies and banditry. However, the unit was mustered in for the Spanish-American War on May 9, 1898, returning to the California National Guard on April 13, 1899.

The next call for the unit was in 1916. On March 9th there was a cross-border raid on Columbus, New Mexico by Mexico's Francisco "Pancho" Villa. A few days later, a 5,000-man expedition under Brigadier General John J. Pershing went chasing after Villa. The Mexican government protested and the U. S. troops were pulled out of Mexico. There was concern along the border regarding possible Mexican retaliation for Pershing's incursions into Mexico, so in May, National Guard troops from Arizona, New Mexico and Texas were mobilized for duty along the border.

Governor Hiram W. Johnson of California received a request for troops from the President on June 18. 1916. Many western units, including Company L, Seventh Infantry, were mustered for duty on June 29th. Troops around California were mobilized in their armories within twelve hours, and were to be sent to the State Fairgrounds in Sacramento. When the fairgrounds were ready, 4,600 troops assembled there. Some were then sent to Nogales, Arizona to protect the border against incursions by Pancho Villa's troops. Most of the service by Guardsmen during the Mexican War involved little or no action, and was extremely boring for the troops.

The threat of war in Europe had been real ever since the turn of the century. The assassination of Austrian Crown Prince Franz Ferdinand in Serbia on June 28, 1914 merely provided the spark. America's leaders kept an eye cocked across the Atlantic as they considered our own preparedness for conflict. The U. S. Navy was much better prepared than the Army. The Great White Fleet was becoming somewhat obsolescent, having been constructed some years before, but still gave the Navy considerable punch. Although ship construction had stagnated in the interim, Congress greatly expanded shipbuilding in 1916. This had little effect on the construction of capital ships by the time America entered the war. Nonetheless hundreds of smaller ships; especially destroyers, submarine chasers, minelayers and submarines; were later added to the 197 ships in commission when war was declared.

There were more serious weaknesses in our ground forces. Soldiers in the Regular Army of those days had inadequate equipment and were poorly paid, enlisting for three years at $15.00 per month. National Guardsmen were paid much less, so usually joined for reasons other than remuneration. Many felt the pull of

3

patriotism, and among the many other motives, some joined for social reasons, or simply for the camaraderie they found with their buddies. The National Guard was the first line of defense behind the Regular Army, but had only about 150,000 men, and they were poorly equipped, organized, and trained.

In the years just prior to World War I, the National Guard had "Camps of Instruction" conducted during the summer. In California, troops usually gathered at Fort Winfield Scott near San Francisco, and Camp Gigling near Monterey. There was comparatively little of what the military now calls "battle focus" during the training, as no one really expected to get involved in large scale warfare. When senior War Department planners started to get serious about expanding the Army, it was realized that the National Guard did not have the infrastructure required for rapid expansion. There were no infantry units organized higher than battalions and regiments in the National Guard, and those organizations only had rifle companies. The problems had to be corrected, and a fix was legislated in 1916.

The National Defense Act of 1916 provided a detailed plan for a peace time army designed for expansion in the event of war to a force adequate for national defense. In the same legislation, corps areas were created. There were nine corps areas in this decentralization, the intent being to give the Corps Commanders the authority and discretion previously reserved to Washington.

The numbering designations for the divisions and their organic elements in the National Guard and the National Army (primarily draftees, but later the Organized Reserve Corps as well as the Army Reserve), were logical and symmetrical. The Regular Army Divisions were to be numbered up through 25, National Guard Divisions were to be numbered starting from 26, and the National Army (later Army Reserve) Divisions to be numbered starting with 76. Each division was to have two infantry brigades, with those brigade numbers based on the highest being twice the division number. In the Fortieth, they therefore were to be the 79th and 80th Brigades.

Regimental numbers were based on the highest being quadruple the division number. In the Fortieth they were to be the 157th, 158th, 159th and 160th. Ambulance companies and field hospitals in the division had the same numbers.

Special units were numbered sequentially starting with 101 for the 26th Division. For the Fortieth therefore, 115 was the designation to be used for the trains elements, plus the engineer, signal and military police units. Machine gun battalions and artillery regiments were numbered sequentially starting with 101 for the 26th division, going up by threes. For example, the 27th had 104, the 28th had 107, up to the 40th which had 143. The Fortieth therefore was to have the 143rd through the 145th Artillery Regiments and Machine Gun Battalions. Artillery brigades were numbered sequentially starting with 51 for the 26th Division. The Fortieth Division therefore was to have the 65th Artillery Brigade.

This obviously symmetrical numbering system didn't survive for long. After World War I, exceptions were made until the system was almost unrecognizable by World War II.

The commitment of troops along the Mexican border in 1916, consequences of the passage of The National Defense Act of 1916, and war news emanating from Europe, resulted in cancellation of the Camps of Instruction. This permitted the initial steps in reorganization to meet the intent of the Act.

Each corps area was supposed to have one Regular Army division complete with all its elements and ready to take the field as a mobile force as part of the first line of defense. Two National Guard divisions were to be in each corps area, fully organized and maintained at peacetime strength, but with sufficient arms and equipment on hand to form the nuclei around which a full division could be formed. Under this plan the 40th (California and Utah) and 41st Divisions (Idaho, Montana, Oregon, Washington, and Wyoming) were eventually assigned to the Western or 9th Corps.

The plan was good in principle, but there was not enough money, and there were only three Regular Army divisions in the entire contiguous United States. Of those three, the only one even close to being fully organized was the Second Division with its headquarters at Fort Sam Houston in San Antonio, Texas. This forced a change in plans, so the National Guard was made the largest element in the Army of the United States. It, with the Regular Army, constituted the first line of defense.

When tensions began rising as a consequence of World War I, the Secretary of War telegraphed the governors to federalize the National Guard. Then, for example, Governor William D. Stevens of California ordered the Second, Fifth and Seventh Infantry Regiments to assemble at their armories and actively begin recruiting. The actual order; General Order #10 from The Adjutant General's Office in Sacramento was dated March 26, 1917 and read:

> The following orders received from the commanding general, Western Department, United States Army, will be carefully obeyed by all concerned:
>
> 1. The 2d, 5th, and 7th California Infantry will be promptly assembled at their company rendezvous.
> 2. Descriptive lists (Forms No. 29, A.G.O., W.D.) for each man will be started from date of assembly.
> 3. The morning report, sick report, and guard report will be kept from date of assembly.
> 4. Organizations will begin recruiting to war strength.
> 5. A recruiting party of one officer and three enlisted men will be established at each rendezvous.
> 6. If no National Guard medical officer is present at rendezvous the enlistment will be completed at mobilization camp. The physical examination at the rendezvous must, however, be thorough, and conducted in accordance with previous instructions, before the recruit is accepted for enlistment.
> 7. Training the recruit will begin at once, also the training of the company. Frequent drills daily in setting-up exercises, school of the soldier, and school of the squad will begin at once.
> 8. The Articles of War enumerated in Bulletin No. 32, War Department, 1916, will be read and explained to each recruit and soldier.

9. All arms, ammunition, equipment, clothing, animals, and wheel transportation will accompany organizations to mobilization camp, and all property belonging to the United States and pertaining to the military service thereof will be taken or shipped to the mobilization camp.

10. All United States property not in possession of troops or needed en route should at once be prepared for shipment to mobilization camp.

11. Allowances for subsistence not exceeding 75 cents per day for each enlisted man is authorized while company is at rendezvous and en route to mobilization camp.

12. Supply officers and company commanders can obtain meals by contract.

13. Give the contractor receipts each day for the meals furnished by him on that day.

14. The receipts must show (a) organization, (b) the numbers of men furnished meals each day, (c) the number of meals furnished, (d) the signature of the company commander. The contractor will present these receipts to the camp quartermaster of the mobilization camp for settlement.

15. Officers will be held strictly accountable for exceeding the allowance of 75 cents per day for each man actually present as shown by the morning report.

16. If means for shelter at company rendezvous are inadequate, commanding officers are authorized to permit men to sleep at home, but such men must report promptly for duty each day.

17. Supply officers and organization commanders are authorized to hire the necessary means of transportation to haul baggage from armory to depot. Give the contractor receipts for such transportation and instruct him to present the same to the camp quartermaster of the mobilization camp for settlement.

18. Organizations when assembled at rendezvous will await the orders of the commanding general, Western Department.

19. The sanitary personnel of the regiments should furnish the necessary medical attendance at the company rendezvous. If such medical attendance is not practicable then paragraph 1476, Army Regulations, will govern.

20. Regimental commanders will report by telegraph to the commanding general, Western Department, at 10 o'clock, p.m. each day the strength of each company.

War clouds continued to gather. The unrestricted submarine war-fare had cost many American lives, especially in the sinking of the Lusitania on May 7, 1915. The sinking of that British ship cost 124 American lives, and inflamed public opinion. In February of 1917, America's Secret Service intercepted a secret letter from Germany's Secretary of Foreign Affairs to Germany's Minister (Ambassador) in Mexico. The letter requested assistance in uniting Mexico and Japan with Germany in prosecuting war against the United States. The President publicly revealed contents of the letter on February 28th. These were merely two in a series of less serious German provocations

On April 2, 1917, the President in an address delivered to a joint session of Congress announced that war would be necessary. Congress then quickly supported the President on April 6th, voting to declare war on Germany. Shortly afterward, units of what became the 40th Division were assigned to guard duty protecting key sites from sabotage. These included such installations as bridges, tunnels, dams, piers and munitions plants in California, Nevada and Utah.

In April of 1917, the National Guard was to consist of sixteen tactical divisions, organized under Tables of Organization furnished the states three months before. They were understrength, so additional units to fill out the divisions were authorized over the next several months. Two additional divisions were also authorized and later organized. The Regular Army didn't have any combat ready troops, and there wasn't enough sea transport for even a small force when war was declared on Germany. Mobilization of the Army was slowed by lack of supplies, changes in the tables of organization which couldn't have come at a worse time, and slow construction of cantonments to house and train the men.

The British and French pressed to get at least one tactical division overseas. However, the Army War College prepared a memorandum on May 10, 1917 which advised against sending any troops to Europe. The confidential memorandum concluded "the War College is of the opinion from a purely military point of view, that the early dispatch of any expeditionary force to France is inadvisable because of lack of organization and training, and because the trained personnel contained therein will be needed for the expansion and training of the national forces." In spite of the above, it was decided to send a division overseas to bolster morale of the allies.

All 11,581 members of the California National Guard and the Naval Militia had been called into Federal service by August 5th, based on a Presidential Proclamation dated July 3, 1917. As had been the case in the days of the first minutemen, the ranks of the militia were again leavened by veterans. Many of the Guardsmen who reported for service had experience gained during smaller conflicts. Thousands had served in Federal service along the border with Mexico from mid-1916 through late 1916 or early 1917. Some of the older Guardsmen had seen service in the Spanish-American War of 1898 and the Philippine Insurrection of 1899.

Two thirds of the National Guard had already been federalized before the entire National Guard was federalized on August 5, 1917. While not formally a division, the elements of what were to become the 40th Division were identified and inducted on that date. Troops were authorized from California, Colorado, Arizona, Utah, New Mexico and Nevada, although there was no National Guard organized in Nevada at that time.

The elements that were to become the Fortieth Division mobilized in several western posts. An example of the odyssey followed by many Guardsmen of the day may be found in the diary of Corporal Howard O. Derby. Corporal Derby was a member of Company M, 5th California Regiment, with its armory in Ione. Ione was right in the middle of California's fabled gold country of Amador County. Typical of many, Corporal Derby, who lived in Jackson, received a telegram on March 26th directing him to report to the armory in Ione. He maintained a detailed scrapbook during the early part of his mobilization and training. It reads:

"*March 26: Papa brought it* (the telegram) *to stamp mill. I drew my time, went home, cleaned up and Papa and the rest went with me to Ione in the car.*

"*March 27: Reached San Jose at 1:20 a.m.*

"*March 28: Visited around town.*

"*March 29: Two squads organized, I have first. Camp made at 6th and Santa Clara Streets   (near gas station). I have charge of quarters that night.*

"*March 30 and 31: Drilled.*

"*April 1: Had charge of quarters that night.*

"*April 2: We packed up and went to Frisco on the 2:30 p.m. local.*"

The unit stayed at the Presidio of San Francisco until April 14th, then dropped off detachments throughout central California. Derby and a detachment of about twenty men guarded railroad installations around Calwa, about three miles south of Fresno. This type of duty continued for several months, although sometimes at different locations, while Corporal Derby was promoted to Sergeant in September. The unit arrived at Camp Kearny, near San Diego, the evening of September 27th. There the unit put up cots on tent floors under the open sky. The next day they got their tents up, and were told they were now a part of the 159th Infantry Regiment.

Finally Camp Kearny was completed, and the division was organized there on August 25, 1917 using existing units. The 40th Division was then organized:

	Previous Designation	Redesignated in 40th ID
Arizona	1st Infantry (-)	158th Inf
California	2nd Infantry (-)	159th Inf
	2nd Bn & Co L, 2nd Inf	160th Inf
	5th Infantry	159th Inf
	7th Infantry	160th Inf
	Machine Gun Troop, Cavalry	145th MG Bn

	1st Separate Squadron Cavalry (-)	145th MG Bn
	Troop D, 1st Sep Sqdn Cav	40th Div Hqs Trp
	1st Regiment Field Artillery	143rd F.A.
	2nd Regiment Field Artillery	144th F.A.
	Co. B (Wire) Signal Co	115th Fld Sig Bn
	1st & 2nd Ambulance Co	115th Sanitation Train
	1st & 2nd Field Hospitals	115th Sanitation Train
Colorado	1st Infantry	157th Inf
	2nd Infantry (-)	115th Ammo Train
	Band/A/B/C/D/MG/Sup 2nd Inf	115th Supply Train
	Machine Gun Company 2nd Inf	115th Trench Mort Btry
	1st Regimental Cavalry (-)	157th Inf
	Troop E, 1st Regiment Cavalry	115th Engineers
	1st Battalion, Engineers	115th Engineers
	Co. B (Wire) Signal Co	115th Fld Sig Bn
	1st Engineer Train	115th Engineer Train
New Mexico	3rd Bn & MG Co, 1st Inf	144th MG Bn
	1st & 2nd Bn, 1st Inf	143rd MG Bn
	HHC & Sup Co, 1st Inf	115th Hq & MP
Utah	1st Regiment Field Artillery	145th F.A.
	F Hospital Company No. 1	115th Sanitation Train

Camp Kearny was built near the town of Linda Vista about 11½ miles north of San Diego. The camp was named in honor of Brigadier General Stephen W. Kearny, who led an expedition to California during the war with Mexico, and later was appointed governor of the California territory from March to June 1847.

Camp Kearny was officially established July 18, 1917, specifically to serve as the training camp for the new 40th Infantry Division. The camp had 12,721 acres, of which about 8000 acres were devoted to the camp proper. The camp was designed to be temporary. Nonetheless, in addition to the tent city, a program to build 848 buildings was started on July 24, 1917 at a cost of over $4 million. The temporary buildings included not only the mess buildings for each unit, but Y.M.C.A., guest house, telephone exchange, infirmary, library, canteen, and post office buildings. The eventual troop capacity was 32,066 troops.

About 5,000 former Guardsmen from Arizona, California, Colorado, New Mexico and Utah arrived in camp during the month of September, 1917. The units were increased to full war strength, which in the case of infantry companies was six officers and two hundred fifty men. The camp rapidly filled, having over 24,000 troops by the end of November.

The regimental headquarters and all billets were in tents. The "mess house" was a wooden frame building. Derby's scrapbook continued:

"October 24: I have been drilling men from American Lake in school of the soldier without arms this week. Today is Liberty Loan day. No drill.

"October 26: The regiment dug trenches today.

"November 3: Recruit drill without arms this week.

"November 10: Recruit drill, manual of arms this week.

"November 17: Division review, school of the soldier, squad, and company and sighting and aiming drill this past week.

"November 18: Hard wind and clouds of dust. Fire call for brush fire north of camp.

"November 23: Battalion dug trenches at west end of parade ground.

"December 4: At target range. (Much of the firing was done from trenches).

"January 1 (1918): 159th Infantry placed in quarantine due to outbreak of scarlet fever in "I" Co.

"January 2: Quarantine did not prevent us from drilling.

"January 7: Quarantine lifted. Night march and problem tonight. (this continued for several days and nights)

"During January the weather was unsettled. The drilling was steady and hard. It included close order drill, bomb (grenade) throwing, bayonet work, signal practice, many hikes and field work, and a good many regimental reviews and parades. Work was begun on trench drill.

"In March (Derby was on detached duty as a Military Police Sergeant in San Diego for a month and a half) *we had gas school. Poison gas. One man gassed. Sham battles..."*

Entertainment was provided to break up the tedium of training. There was no United Services Organization at Camp Kearny, but various troupes visited and provided similar entertainment for the troops. One well-remembered group were the Liberty Belle Minstrels, two dozen ladies who gave fourteen free performances for troops of the division.

The Y.M.C.A. played a huge role in the early life of the division. The Y.M.C.A. set up eight facilities to serve the troops. Here the troops could borrow a book, or watch one of the movies normally scheduled about three times a week. They could join bible classes, participate in Y.M.C.A.-sponsored athletic events; play checkers, chess or dominos; or just sit in front of the fireplace. Guest speakers and other entertainments were furnished. Classes were taught in such subjects as French and mathematics, as well as English to literally hundreds of men with foreign backgrounds. Once a week the "Mending Mothers" came in to help the soldiers by sewing on patches, mending holes, or making alterations. The attendance at each of the eight Y.M.C.A. buildings was estimated as high as 5,000 per day, supported by several "Y.M.C.A. Secretaries." Over a hundred secretaries, ninety-eight men and three women, served in that role at Camp Kearny.

The Knights of Columbus had five facilities, including the most imposing building on the post. Knights of Columbus Building Number One even had an open air concert shell behind the building. The facilities were open to soldiers of all faiths. Entertainment of all sorts was provided, from violinists and pianists to band concerts, from classic dancers to famous singers. The Jewish Welfare Board also had a facility to serve at least twenty-five officers and between five and six hundred enlisted soldiers of the Jewish faith in the division. They conducted dances, social visits and other entertainments for the soldiers, and visited Jewish soldiers in the hospital.

Branch libraries were set up in all of the above facilities. The Central Library had 13,317 volumes, with 15,883 volumes scattered throughout the post in various branches. The American Red Cross had a facility at Camp Kearny, under the charge of a field director. They focussed on morale issues among the soldiers, provided such comforts as sweaters, and augmented supplies in the infirmaries.

A woman from La Jolla underwrote construction of a large Y.W.C.A. building centrally located in Camp Kearny. It opened on Thanksgiving Day in 1917, serving doughnuts and cider to the troops. It had a huge fireplace, the first in the camp, and was the site of many talent shows involving the division's soldiers. Called the "Hostess House," the building was primarily designed to accommodate women who visited the post.

The first division commander was Major General Frederick S. Strong, who was born in Michigan, November 12, 1855. He began his military career in 1876, entering West Point as a cadet in that year and graduating in 1880, when he was assigned to the artillery. He participated in the last Sioux Indian Campaign, 1890-1891. During the war with Spain he served as Adjutant General of the First Division, Second Army Corps, U.S. Volunteers. In 1904 he was promoted to Major in the Artillery Corps and in 1907, to Colonel. He attained the rank of Brigadier General in 1915, and was assigned as Commanding General of the Hawaiian Department. He was promoted to Major General on August 5, 1917. Major General Strong commanded the 40th Division from its initial organization through the division's service in France.

Sports played a big role in the early life of the National Guard. These included team contests such as tugs of war, team races, grenade throws and similar events. The San Diego Stadium, built for the 1915 San Diego Exposition and seating 39,000 spectators, was used quite often for the larger athletic events. The division fielded football and basketball teams, track and field teams, and had an aggressive boxing program.

There were many obvious advantages in being stationed near the beach. There were however, some minor irritants. One Sergeant George Price of a 115th Ammunition Train Truck Company had attended a beach party at La Jolla with a party of young people. When he came back he was covered with sand fleas, and eventually had to be sent to the hospital where he spent three days in bed under observation for measles. The sergeant later told his buddies it was a case of "fleasles being mistaken for measles."

Elements of the division made practice marches in full field gear to San Dieguito Rancho to conduct field exercises. For example, the 80th Brigade left Camp Kearny on March 30, 1918 for a ten day exercise that included a total of about sixty miles marched. Another training area was at Cuyamaca Lake, about seventy-five road miles away from Camp Kearny. The 115th Engineers culminated their training at Camp Kearny with a march to Cuyamaca Lake, and exercises and return march that totalled three weeks.

The division was handicapped in its training by a lack of equipment, horses, and materiel. The nation simply was not ready for a general mobilization in World War I. The depots were short of everything, including small arms ammunition.

The National Guard divisions were particularly short of equipment. One example serves to illustrate the problem. The World War became the war of the machine gun. In a report prepared by the War College, it was found that the National Guard was woefully short of machine guns. The National Guard prior to the war had fifty-four machine gun organizations with four Lewis guns each. Of those, fifty units had to turn in their machine guns (a total of 200) to the Signal Corps so they could be used to equip aircraft. There were no machine guns on hand to replace them.

Eventually the problem was partially solved with assistance from the allies. France and Great Britain furnished surplus machine guns, and both furnished large quantities of artillery. Nonetheless, soldiers were seen training for many months mounted on saw horses instead of live animals, with wooden guns and howitzers.

The 144th and 145th Field Artillery Regiments were temporarily equipped with 4.7 inch guns early in January, 1918. This permitted gun drills and limited service practice which included live firing, but only for a short time. The guns were sent on to Fort Sill a short time later. A fleet of twenty aircraft were sent to the division, along with aviators and mechanics, in December. The artillery then sent observers for flights to practice reconnaissance.

CHAPTER TWO

WORLD WAR I

The war had been triggered by the assassination of Austrian Crown Prince Franz Ferdinand in Serbia on June 28, 1914. The war rapidly spread through Europe, and by the end of 1914, was already a world war. Austria-Hungary, Belgium, the British Empire, France, Germany, Italy, Japan, Poland, Russia, Serbia, Turkey and several smaller countries were quickly embroiled. The war soon spread to the rest of the globe, including Asia, Africa, the Middle East, and South America.

The war was incredibly expensive in both human and materiel costs. The war saw projectiles from thousands of machine guns and artillery pieces slamming into bodies and terrain. Gas was used in quantity for the first time. Total casualties were horrendous. The Battle of the Marne, lasting less than a week in September of 1914, cost over a million casualties. Losses that year in the east were almost as bad, crippling Russian effectiveness for the rest of the war.

As the war spread, Europe settled into trench warfare that stretched from the Swiss Alps in the south to the North Sea. The bloody fighting escalated, with literally millions of casualties from all fronts, including a half million in the Dardanelles alone.

The contending sides were almost evenly matched, with both sides at close the same strength as 1916 dawned. The use of aircraft for offensive operations expanded that year, and the tank made its first appearance. It was the year the great naval battle of Jutland was fought. There the British and Germans fought to a bloody draw, with the loss of almost 10,000 seamen and a total of 25 vessels.

By 1917, while the strength of the allies grew with the spread of compulsory service and maturation of mobilization efforts, the terrible losses in manpower were being sorely felt. Appeals for help were being increasingly directed towards America, made more urgent by Russian political instability which made it possible for Germany to move more troops west. America responded when they declared war in April, but as previously described, was poorly prepared. General John J. Pershing led the first American military contingent to France in mid-June. However, it would be several months before sizeable contingents of American soldiers and marines would arrive in significant numbers. It would be a year before total allied strength in the west surpassed the numbers representing the Triple Entente.

In late June of 1917, the 1st Division (the "Big Red One") landed in France. They were to be the one American division to see combat before the year was over. As American troop strength grew to over 170,000 by the end of the year, the allies brought increasing pressure to use those soldiers as replacements for the British and French. General Pershing refused, insisting that the Americans be given a portion of the line and used as a single entity. In France, five divisions were either en route or had arrived by the end of 1917.

In the meantime, America was mobilizing. The Selective Service law was passed on May 19, 1917, and was invaluable in expanding the small American Army from less than 200,00 to about 4,000,000 by war's end. The first draftees reported to the 40th Division in October and November, 1917 when 9,000 fillers were received from Camp Funston and Camp Lewis. This brought the division to full war strength, however, levies on the division's personnel began to be received shortly thereafter. In January 1918, the division was levied for 1,200 engineers. Fully trained engineers were sent to Washington Barracks in response, and designated as the 20th Engineers and the 534th Pontoon Train. This was followed in April with a request for 1,500 trained infantrymen. Those troops were sent to join the 42nd "Rainbow" Division, most being Guardsmen who had seen service on the Mexican border. In May and June, every division in the continental United States was asked to furnish every qualified infantry and artillery soldier available to fill the ranks of other divisions. The 40th Division furnished 4,000 infantrymen and 1,100 artillerymen who had at least eight months of training.

The training of the division was assisted by the attachment of combat veterans from both the British and French armies. The French mission was headed by Lieutenant Colonel Jules Amiot, with a total of twenty officers and fifty-eight enlisted men on site at various times. The British mission was headed by Major V.E.C. Dashwood, M.C., and had a total of eight officers and eleven enlisted, to include a Regimental Sergeant Major. They instructed the troops in trench warfare and other combat training based on their experiences fighting on the continent.

The troops were constantly reminded that they were to be involved in coalition warfare. One significant review of troops was conducted at the parade ground at Camp Kearny to honor Allied Countries. The distinguished guests who attended included General Henri Cloudon, Commanding the French Mission to America; Major V.E.C. Dashwood of the British Mission at Camp Kearny; Rear Admiral Edward W. Eberle, U.S. Navy; Rear Admiral William F. Fullam, U.S. Navy; and Admiral Susuki, Commander of the Japanese Squadron visiting San Diego Harbor.

By June of 1918 the 1st, 2nd, 3rd, 5th, 26th, 32nd, 35th, 42nd, 77th and 82nd Divisions were either entering the line or actively serving. In May 1918 the U.S. offensive saw American troops take Cantigny. In June, troops reached the front at Château-Thierry, and marines took Belleau Wood.

American divisions in 1918 were extraordinarily large, about twice the size of European divisions. They were authorized 979 officers and 27,080 enlisted soldiers, for a total of over 28,000 soldiers. They were also authorized 3,936 horses, 2700 mules, 238 bicycles, 319 motorcycles, and 800 motorized vehicles in addition to the horse and mule-drawn vehicles. Weapons authorized in addition to rifles and pistols included 24 howitzers (6" or 155mm), 62 guns (fifty 3" or 75mm, and twelve 1 pounders) 36 antiaircraft machine guns, 224 heavy machine guns, and 36 trench mortars.

The American divisions were not only larger, they were much better trained than their European allies, who had to expedite training to make up combat losses. In general, American soldiers received about six months training in the United States, followed by an average of two months training in Europe. They then were usually sent into a comparatively quiet sector of the front for their initiation to combat.

The route followed in reaching the combat zone in France taken by the Headquarters Troop, 40th Infantry Division, was similar to that taken by all elements of the division. The unit entrained at Camp Kearny on July 26, 1918, and arrived at Camp Mills, Long Island on the first of August. They embarked at the Port of New York on August 8th, arriving August 20th at Liverpool, England. The next day they proceeded to Winchester, England. On August 23rd they entrained for Southampton. They immediately boarded a ship camouflaged with the huge angular patterns used in those days. They moved at night and arrived at Cherbourg, France the morning of August 24th.

When they arrived in France, many of the soldiers saw their first German prisoners of war. Local veterans of the war told their blood-chilling tales to the newly arrived soldiers of the Sunshine Division. The next day, division soldiers entrained on the boxcars built for forty men or eight horses to La Guerche, France, arriving on August 28th. They remained on duty with the division headquarters until October 31, 1918, when they were transported by train to Revigny, France.

The 40th Division arrived in France just as the Germans completed a series of powerful drives, smashing the allies back several miles in three sectors. Ludendorff's three drives had started in March, and did not run out of steam until July 18, 1918. There had been appalling casualties. The cost to the allies was measured in the hundreds of thousands, including many lost by the Americans who had recently assumed responsibility for a sector of the line. As a consequence, the Americans were in dire need of replacements as the allies prepared for the offensives that ended the war.

The 40th Division had expected to play a role in France as a combat division. Instead, they found that they were to provide replacements for divisions that had arrived in the theater earlier. The bloodbath involved in the World War was sucking in replacements for casualties much faster than originally anticipated. Depot Divisions were formed from six infantry divisions to provide replacements. The divisions selected, with dates corresponding to the arrival of the division headquarters in France:

41st Division - Dec 27, 1917, becoming the 1st Depot Division
83rd Division - Jun 17, 1918, becoming the 2nd Depot Division
76th Division - Jul 20, 1918, becoming the 3rd Depot Division
85th Division - Aug 10, 1918, becoming the 4th Depot Division
39th Division - Aug 18, 1918, becoming the 5th Depot Division
40th Division - Aug 20, 1918, becoming the 6th Depot Division

In addition, the 31st, 34th, 38th, 84th, 86th, and 87th divisions, all arriving in September and October 1918, were "skeletonized" for replacements.

The conversion to a depot division required the 40th Division to reorganize under a different table of organization. The division kept only two officers and thirty enlisted men in each company as training cadre, and sent all of their infantry and machine gun officers and men to other units. The replacements included:

1,500 to the 32nd Division furnished from La Guerche,
September 1918.
2,000 to the 28th Division furnished from La Guerche,
September 1918.

21

4,000 to the 77th Division furnished from La Guerche, September 1918.

1,000 to the 81st Division furnished from La Guerche, September 1918.

2,100 to the 80th, 82nd, and 89th Divisions from La Guerche in September 1918.

900 specialists were sent to the 1st Depot Division, St. Aignan in October 1918.

146 officers sent to various divisions from La Guerche.

In preparation for the Meuse-Argonne offensive, which commenced on September 26, 1918, there was a particularly heavy levy for the 77th Division. When the 6th Depot Division was tapped for replacements, they quite often were sent off as groups of individuals. However, in this instance, Captain Nelson M. Holderman led his Company L, 160th Infantry as a unit into service with the 77th Division. Company L, 160th Infantry, redesignated from Company L, Seventh Infantry when the division was formed at Camp Kearny, was originally in Santa Ana, California. However, by the time the unit arrived in France, many of the original troops had been siphoned off as fillers and replacements in other divisions.

Captain Holderman had been the company commander from the start. He was one of the company commanders of what came to be known as the "Lost Battalion," along with Captain Leo A. Stromee, formerly of Company K, 160th Infantry. Captain Holderman was wounded on four successive days, October 4, 5, 6, and 7, 1918. He was awarded the Medal of Honor as well as the Purple Heart, and received decorations for valor from Belgium and France. Captain Stromee was awarded the Silver Star and the Purple Heart Medal.

The division furnished 12,000 of its soldiers as replacements to other divisions, and later processed many tens of thousands through its camps and depots while serving as a depot division. As an example of how our soldiers were spread far and wide as replacements, one regiment had its soldiers sent off to six different divisions, the 1st, 2nd, 3rd, 26th, 77th and 79th.

The 40th Division Commander and Staff in France
(Photo: Colonel William G. Hamilton)

Some elements of the division were detached and sent else-where. The division's 69th Field Artillery Brigade, along with its ammunition train, was sent to the training camp at De Souge, Geronde (near Bordeaux). The 143rd Field Artillery Regiment was scheduled to join the First Army as Army Artillery, and trained on the French 75mm gun. The 144th Field Artillery Regiment finally ended up at Clarmont, Ferrand, a training center for heavy artillery. The 144th had positions assigned prior to the battle in the Argonne Forest. The 115th Trench Mortar Battery trained at Vitry-le-Francois. However, the armistice was declared before any of the division's artillery saw combat. The 145th Machine Gun Battalion did see combat, supporting the First Army in the Meuse-Argonne offensive.

The 115th Engineers initially were used to build the Classification Camp for 8,000 casuals at La Guerche. Their commander,

Colonel George P. Pillsbury, was a Regular Army officer who had been with the regiment since it was first formed at Camp Kearny. Shortly after the organization arrived at La Guerche, he was sent to command the 102nd Engineers at the front. Work continued at La Guerche, but before it was completed, the 115th was detached to serve as Corps Engineers. The 115th Engineers were transferred to Chattillon sur Seine for additional training, and then on to the Toul sector in Second Army's area.

The 115th Field Signal Battalion was also sent the Second Army as Army troops. The Signal Battalion left one officer and a small detachment with the division to provide signal support, while the bulk of the battalion worked for Second Army in the Toul sector. Company A (Radio) took responsibility for operation of the Army Net Control Station on October 18th. Before they completed their duty, they had suffered enemy air raids, some long range artillery interdiction, and had even experienced a gas attack in the area of Dieulouard. Details from the unit also supported the 2nd French Colonial Corps and the French Metro Station at Troyon.

Company B of the Signal Battalion was primarily kept in reserve, but did perform various signal details. Company C (Outpost) was given the mission of improving the Toul telephone system. They replaced much of the previous system, a great deal of which was a tangled mess. They installed and operated many switchboards, including the Western Electric Telephone Tractor with five operators manning the switchboards, and a similar Western Electric tractor for telegraph operations.

The Signal Battalion was particularly pleased with two facts at the end of the war. One was that none of eight hundred soldiers of the battalion had lost their lives from any cause. The other was that only seven venereal disease cases were reported among the 756 enlisted men in the battalion. No statistics were furnished on the commissioned officers.

Elements of the 115th Sanitary Train also saw service. The 157th and 158th Field Hospitals, along with the same numbered ambulance companies, were assigned to the Sixth Army Corps on October 29, 1918. Initially at Rosiere en Haye, on November 17, 1918 they were transferred to the Second Army and established hospitals and dressing stations at Mars La Tour. They provided medical support there until starting home on May 24, 1919.

The Sixth Depot Division established a Classification Camp at La Guerche, Department of Cher. A hundred buildings were requested and constructed, along with supporting utilities and a road network. The construction was supervised by division engineers and assisted by a company of the 512th Engineers. Troops were provided by the 115th Engineer Regiment, the 115th Supply Train and details from elsewhere in the division. There were about six hundred troops working each day. Interestingly, the construction was completed extraordinarily fast in spite of a severe shortage of tools and equipment. They were short of saws and hammers, had to quarry rock without explosives, and rolled macadam with a road roller pulled by teams of men because no tractors or horses were available.

Operations began on October 16, 1918. For the next fifteen days, 11,000 soldiers released from hospitals were processed. They were administratively serviced, provided gas masks and chemical training, fully equipped, and then sent on to their organizations.

The Sixth Depot Division was notified on October 22, 1918, that it was transferred to the First Army as a regional replacement depot. On November 1st the division left for its new station at Revigny (Meuse), where it was to establish another camp to handle casuals. Casuals were those soldiers in a temporary status awaiting permanent assignments. They included replacements entering the theater, stragglers, and most especially, former patients awaiting reassignment.

The division found itself in trouble before it could get fully organized. Medical units in the region had been directed to empty out their hospitals as much as possible for casualties of the renewed Meuse-Argonne offensive of November 1st and an upcoming drive on Metz planned in the Second Army sector. The flow of recovering and recovered patients into the division's area quickly overwhelmed what few facilities were available. The division was in an area that had been devastated during the war, and buildings suitable for billeting were extremely limited. It had been estimated that a hundred barracks would be required to meet the division's needs, and that number were planned for construction, but only seven buildings in a military camp near the town of Contrisson were immediately available.

The Classification Camp deloused, reequipped, and updated the personnel records of those soldiers who moved through their facility. The camp had a maximum capacity of about seven hundred, about a tenth of the capacity they had enjoyed in La Guerche, but several hundred casuals arrived at the camp every day. The hundred barracks never were constructed, so considerable improvisation was required.

The situation was complicated after the armistice of November 11th, when the division found itself caught in the midst of heavy traffic. Troops along the front were being sent to training areas in the rear and home as quickly as possible, while divisions of the Third Army were being sent forward to replace them. Transportation was then embargoed to assist demobilization of the French Army. As a consequence, following processing, the Classification Camp at Revigny was forced to march soldiers up to twenty kilometers to various divisions chosen because they could properly feed and house the soldiers.

The one Classification Camp handled over 20,000 soldiers between November 9th and January 1, 1919. Most of them were processed during the first two weeks of that period.

There were other elements of the division performing work similar to that handled by the Classification Camp at Revigny: A Corps Provisional Replacement Battalion at Chelles (Seine et Marne) was taken over by the 158th Infantry and the 144th Machine Gun Battalion. The Second Corps Provisional

Replacement Battalion at Saleux (Somme) was taken over by the 159th Infantry and the 143rd Machine Gun Battalion. Finally, the Fifth Corps Provisional Replacement Battalion at Froidos (Meuse) was consolidated into the Third Corps Provisional Replacement Battalion at Grange le Comte (Meuse) and operated by the Division Personnel Adjutant.

The war ended with the signing of the armistice on November 11, 1918. A total of 42 American divisions reached France before the armistice. Twenty-nine of those divisions saw combat. The balance of the divisions, including the Fortieth, were used for replacements or arrived too late in the theater to have a mission assigned.

The 6th Depot (40th Division) continued processing casuals until early January, when the division was asked to move still again. They made the short move to billeting area No. 3, Base Section No. 2, where 8,800 casuals were received for transport back to the United States.

Elements of the division were shipped back to the United States for demobilization. The 145th Field Artillery Regiment was demobilized at Logan, Utah in January of 1919. The 143rd and 144th Field Artillery Regiments were demobilized by the end of January at the Presidio of San Francisco.

When the units of the 40th Infantry Division returned to California, they were discharged at Camp Kearny and the Presidio of San Francisco. New Mexico's 144th Machine Gun Battalion was demobilized at Fort Bliss, Texas in April. The 157th Infantry Regiment from Colorado was demobilized at Fort D. A. Russell, Wyoming, and the 158th Infantry Regiment of Arizona was demobilized at Fort Bliss, Texas. Both were demobilized in the month of May, 1919. Most of the other elements of the division were demobilized at Camp Kearny, California.

The division had not had an opportunity to fight as a division. However, the American Army could take pride in fighting well, and in tipping the balance in favor of the allies. The materiel contributed to the allies more than made up for the weapons provided the American Army. Before the war ended, America had shipped the allies almost 30,000 freight cars and hundreds of locomotives. There were 47,018 trucks sent over, as well as 68,694 horses and mules.

There also was a considerable cost in blood. From a mere 2,500 Americans engaged at Cambrai in 1917, the numbers had grown to 1,200,000 engaged during the Meuse-Argonne offensive in 1918. Before the war was over, seven Regular Army, eleven National Guard, and eleven National Army divisions saw combat of the forty-two American divisions sent overseas. That cost Americans 50,280 battle deaths and 205,690 wounded.

CHAPTER THREE

BETWEEN WORLD WARS

The shoulder insignia for the division was officially adopted by order of the Commanding General, American Expeditionary Forces in France, on November 23, 1918. When the National Guard was reorganized following the World War, the shoulder patch was authorized by the Secretary of War as the official insignia of the reorganized 40th Division. The description of the division's shoulder patch: "On a blue square two and one-half inches on a side, a sun in splendor in yellow, the disc thirteen-sixteenths of an inch in diameter, twelve rays within a circle one and seven-eighths inches in diameter."

The wearing of the insignia was not specified, but the official drawing of the patch indicated that the top (flat) of the square was to be worn uppermost. However, during the war, most units of the division set a precedent by wearing the patch with one point up. The Commanding General of the division wrote to Washington for an official ruling. The reply of the War Department stated that the top of the square was to be worn uppermost, but that favorable consideration would be given a request for a change, if concurred in by the interested states, and upon presentation of proof that such was the practice in the 40th Division of the World War. There was considerable correspondence, plus some photos of the patch being worn point up, provided to the War Department. On March 17, 1931, authority was granted by the War Department to wear the shoulder sleeve insignia point up, the point of the square to be one-half inch below the shoulder seam.

After the Great War, the National Guard was again organized and grew slowly over the years. In 1920, the California National

Guard had 303 officers and men attend annual training. The attendance grew each year, exceeding 2000 by 1922, 3000 by 1924, 4000 by 1926, 5000 by 1929, and 6000 by 1931.

Patriotism was rampant as citizens celebrated the United States' role in winning the war. On Armistice Day, November 11, 1921, the 160th Infantry participated in what was called a "monster parade" in Los Angeles. It was merely one part of a three day celebration sponsored by the American Legion. In the evening, the regiment held a military ball in the Exposition Park armory. The next year there were similar celebrations. They were followed on December 2, 1921, by a reception involving the 160th Infantry that was held for Marshal Ferdinand Foch, the Frenchman who commanded allied forces during the World War.

The annual encampment for 1923 was held at Camp Gigling, near Monterey and Salinas, California. The Federal government budgeted $1.00 per day per soldier but the state failed to match the allotted amount. Public spirited citizens provided funding so that each soldier was paid up to $1.00 per day for his participation during the encampment. The summer camp of 1923 held at Giggling was described as one of the most unhappy training periods ever conducted by the peace-time National Guard. There was sand everywhere, inadequate transportation infrastructures (especially rail), and poor accommodations. The Gigling reservation, with the acquisition of additional real estate, later became Fort Ord.

A short time after that camp, Captain Frank C. Tillson of Company I, 160th wrote a poem which was adopted by that Regiment:

FOLLOW THROUGH
When your pack is getting heavy and the road seems long
and rough,
When you're weary, tired and footsore, and a soldier's life
seems tough,
Then remember that your buddy may be just as tired as
you.

*So raise your chin and grin a bit--a soldier "Follows
     Through."*

*When the bullets clip the grass tops and your wounded
     comrades moan,*
*When you're crawling out to God-knows-where and feel
     you're all alone*
*When your cartridges are finished--then your bayonet will
     do,*
*For the testing of a soldier is the way he "Follows
     Through."*

*When you get a bullet through the arm and you're feeling
     sort o' sick,*
*It's a good excuse for lying down--are you going to quit or
     stick?*
*The enemy are still in front--then what are you going to
     do?*
*You will never know your limit unless you "Follow
     Through."*

*When Brotherhood of Adventure meets, the lodge of the
     Men at Arms,*
*When the Strong Men sit by the great god Mars, and talk of
     War's alarms,*
*When the sentry stops you at the gate--what will you say
     and do?*
*For the only question he will ask you is, "Did you "Follow
     Through?"*

In 1924 the 40th Tank Company of Salinas received eight light
"Whippet" tanks. One was a radio tank, fully equipped with "receiving and transmitting apparatus." The six-ton tanks were armed
with either 37mm cannons or machine guns, had a crew of two, and

moved about six miles per hour. There was great excitement when these Renault light tanks were received, and they were in constant demand for military demonstrations and displays. The tradition of having armor stationed in Salinas continues to this day.

Other units that became elements of the reestablished division were organized, slowly but surely. There remained a large social component involved in joining the National Guard of those days, as units spent a great deal of time and energy in sports and social activities. Units sponsored such social events as smokers (stag parties), vaudeville and minstrel shows. Many units built club rooms, with such improvements as a pool table, card tables, and a radio set with loudspeaker.

Sports teams included basketball, football, baseball, swimming, wrestling, and boxing teams, plus teams in such military pursuits as shooting, riding (equestrian) and close order drill.

In 1925 the annual Training Camp of Instruction was held at Del Monte, as it was in 1924. The artillery trained at Camp Lewis in Washington state. The terrain at Del Monte was much better than Camp Gigling, but had inadequate space for maneuver training of large units. About this time the drums started beating for the acquisition of a state-owned camp.

The training tempo was much slower in those days. The troops would arrive by train on Saturday, and set up camp. Sunday would be spent at church services and in recreation. Saturday morning of the middle weekend would involve an inspection, with the troops having the rest of Saturday and all of Sunday off. The last Friday afternoon would be devoted to show-down inspections and packing, with the troops entraining for home. The training days were comparatively short, with little or no night training. A typical encampment might include a day and a half in the field.

Training for the balance of the year involved drills conducted for one evening each week. There was additional training. For instance, officers in one regiment were required to attend a special training program for two hours on the second and fourth Friday night of each month. The subjects included Drill and Command, Military Law, Bayonet Training, Map Reading, Estimate of the Situation, Combat orders, Marksmanship and Musketry, Scouting and Patrolling.

There was considerable emphasis on recruiting. The Adjutant General offered a new Pershing Cap or leather waist belt to the first 250 men of the California National Guard to bring in a recruit during the first three months of 1926. Feelings about membership were captured in a poem written by soldiers of Company B, 160th Infantry and published in 1925. Hardly world class poetry, but it captured the feelings of the time:

BE'IN IN THE GUARD

There's many a man that likes it--This be'in in the Guard,
And many a man that hates it, and says the life's too hard.

Oh, it's a helluva job, I'll grant you--that it's tough,
Takes all of one hour in one-sixty-eight, we all agree, that's
        rough.
A woeful drain on one's time, one in one-sixty-eight,
Business or life can't last long, while squandering time at
        this rate.
But think, fellows, why do we do it, we re-up again and
        again.
It's first the association, with real red-blooded men.

It's shootin' on the ranges, the summer camp's bill-o-fare,
We like it all, tho' when ordered out, we swear we'll not be
        there.
The cussin' of the sergeants, the ballin' outs and such.
These things get next to your heart, boy, you can't deny it,
        not much.
It's creepin' and a crawlin', and using a parry stick,

*From all of these, we know full well, we get the proverbial
    "kick."*

*It's been absent drill and two months later explainin',
And then, Old Boy, when a warrant's out, we know damn
    well it's rainin'.
Then there's a stronger attraction, tho' I know it's not the
    best,
It's when the pay roll's out and the company clerk gets a
    rest.
Some have a hard time making drill --getting away from
    work,
But it's done of our own free will, and it's what most other
    men shirk.*

*It's the pride we have in our country, that's why we're in it
    now,
And we hope the whole World knows it, --we're here when
    she gets in a row.*

The 143rd Field Artillery was scheduled for firing during their 1925 encampment at Camp Lewis, Washington. The train started at 9:00 p.m. Thursday, July 2, 1925 in the bay area, and picked up other batteries on the way in Livermore, Stockton and Lodi. The two battalions, totalling 357 officers and men, arrived at Camp Lewis at 5 p.m. on July 4th. They had stopped en route at Shasta Springs, where they detrained for exercises. They also stopped in Portland, Oregon early on July 4th, where they paraded.

At Camp Lewis they took over the horses and materiel from the Army's 10th and 146th Field Artillery Battalions. On Sunday, mounted passes were issued, and troops rode "their" new horses around the reservation to become familiar with the new mounts. On Monday, training started under supervision of the officers of the regiment, assisted by commissioned and non-commissioned officers loaned by the 10th Field Artillery. The training:

Monday - Orientation and Training
Tue-Wed - Maneuvers limbered and reconnaissance and occupation of positions in mornings, tactical situations with the solution of a tactical problem each afternoon
Thursday, Friday and the following Monday - Service practice with shrapnel
   (Saturday a.m. - Inspection and mounted Regimental review. Troops were off on Saturday p.m. and Sunday, with most going to either Seattle or Tacoma.)
Tuesday - The Regiment started a three day maneuver. The three day maneuver was concluded with firing that was controlled by aircraft. They used both shrapnel and high explosive shell.
Friday - Regimental field day was held with section, communications, and rescue races, plus baseball.
Saturday - Entrained for home Saturday morning.

On May 4, 1926, the War Department granted authority to organize the 40th Division of the National Guard. After conferences with the Militia Bureau, the 9th Corps Area, and National Guard officers; the State of Utah and the State of California agreed on the allotment of Division Staff Officers.

There were many social and special events sponsored by the National Guard. When reviewing activities of those days, it is important to remember that the "war to end all wars" had been fought. An example of one such event was the "Military Concert and Exhibition" sponsored by the 184th Infantry Regiment (the "Valley Regiment," with units from Chico to Visalia) in Sacramento's State Theater on Tuesday evening, June 1, 1926. The activities not only served as a morale raiser for the Guardsmen, but also as a recruiting vehicle.

The printed program included a description of the American Flag and rules regarding its display, the history of the 184th, and photos of senior leaders of the regiment. Entertainers from the civilian community joined the Guardsmen in presenting the program. The program included:

> Act One - Concert by the 184th Infantry Regimental Band
> Act Two - Three tunes sung by a guest soprano
> Act Three - Machine Gun demonstration by Company H of Yuba City
> Act Four - "East is West." Comedy skit.
> Act Five - Comedy Drill by "Hindoo Awkward Squad" of Service Company, Sacramento.
> Act Six - "Parlevouz Francais." Comedy skit.
> Act Seven - Rifle Drill performed by Headquarters Company, Sacramento.
> Act Eight - "Hell, Heaven or Hoboken by Christmas." A dramatic interpretation of the front line.
> Act Nine - Music and song with a piano, violin, and other artists.
> Act Ten - Baritone accompanied by a pianist.
> Finale - "Songs and Jokes of the War."

On June 18, 1926, the 40th Division was officially organized with headquarters in Berkeley under command of Major General David P. Barrows. General Barrows had a very interesting background. Highly educated, he was selected to be the city superintendent of schools in Manila, P.I. in 1900, when he was only thirty years old. Ten years later he was a professor at the University of California, and was immediately advanced to Dean of the Graduate School. In 1913 he was named Dean of the faculty. When war clouds rose over Europe, he enrolled in the first officers training camp, and was commissioned as a major.

Major Barrows was sent to the Philippines, where he worked in the G-2 section. He later served as a Lieutenant Colonel, and G-2 of the Siberian Expeditionary Force. When he returned home after the war, he was elected in 1919 the First Department Commander of the American Legion for California. The same year he was named President of the University of California. In 1921 he helped form units of the 159th Infantry in the bay area. As the senior battalion commander, he became the first post war regimental commander.

The 40th Division in 1926 was composed of the 40th Division Air Service; the 40th Tank Company; the 40th Signal Company; the 79th Infantry Brigade comprising the 159th, 160th and 184th Infantry Regiments; and the 143rd Field Artillery with horse-drawn 75mm guns, all units being part of the California National Guard.

Units of the 40th Division were allocated even if there was insufficient structure in each state to man the units. For example, California was allocated the initially unmanned 185th Infantry Regiment, 80th Infantry Brigade Headquarters, 115th Ammunition Train, most of the 115th Medical Regiment, the 115th Motorcycle Company, and the 40th Division Service Company.

The National Guard of Utah had always been strong in artillery. During the Spanish-American War, Utah contributed a battery which took an active role in actions around Manila. When the 40th Division was formed, Utah was allocated not only the 145th Field Artillery but the 65th Field Artillery Brigade headquarters to which the California field artillery regiment also belonged.

Utah was also allocated the Engineer Regiment of the division, although nothing had been done to create such an organization. This also applied to the 115th Ordnance Company, and a battalion in the medical regiment. However, Utah had the only medical unit in the 40th Division that was functioning, a hospital company that had been organized for some years.

None of the units allocated to Nevada had been established due to the limited population and resources of that state. The units allocated to Nevada were the 138th Motor Transport Company, 130th Wagon Company, 130th Motor Repair Section, 144th Hospital Company, and the 40th Military Police Company. The 40th Military Police Company was the first unit organized, mustered into service at Reno on June 21, 1928. The first commanding officer was Captain J. E. Martie, who had a brilliant record during World War I. He had been a captain in the First Division ("Big Red One"), and had won the Distinguished Service Cross and several foreign decorations. His was the first National Guard unit to be organized in Nevada since the Spanish-American War.

The 40th Division's Air Corps was located at Griffith Park in Los Angeles. The airport at Griffith Park was leased to the state by the City of Los Angeles at no cost. Two hangars were erected using materials furnished by the Federal government. The 115th Observation squadron was organized June 16, 1924, followed by the 115th Photo Section and the Medical Department Detachment of the 40th's Air Service Organization on May 3, 1926. By then the division was equipped with eight J. N. Curtiss aircraft.

The division trained at Camp Del Monte July 31st through August 7th, 1926. The Adjutant General, Brigadier General R. E. Mittelstaedt, was commander of troops so that General Barrows could concentrate on training his new staff. General Barrows took his staff to the Presidio of San Francisco for the first week, and then to the Presidio of Monterey where they conducted tactical rides in the Monterey area during the second week. Brigadier General Walter P. Story, the new commander of the 79th Brigade, also participated along with members of his staff.

General Mittelstaedt made it clear he believed "a good athletic program will develop better 'doughboys' and make the fellows more able to stand the rigors of the 1926 Polo Field Campaign." The chaplains put together a program that included four track meets. Indoor baseball was a requirement for every soldier in camp not otherwise engaged in athletics. They were required to play baseball for 45 minutes every afternoon commencing at 2:30 p.m.

There was also outdoor baseball. Each company was to have a team for competitions leading up to regimental champions. Other competitions included swimming, boxing, wrestling, and golf, and various special contests. Those included various mounted contests, including artillery section contests, mounted rescue races, a communications race, and separate jumping contests for officers and enlisted men. Appropriate medals and trophies were provided for all.

The schedule of bugle calls illustrates the tempo of training.

Reveille	5:45 a.m.
Assembly (work call)	7:30 a.m.
Recall	11:30 a.m.
Lunch call	12:00 p.m.
Assembly (work call)	1:10 p.m.
Recall	2:30 p.m.
Guard mount	4:25 p.m.
Taps	10:00 p.m.

When the units returned to home stations after their annual training, they resumed their weekly drills. A couple of examples serve to illustrate activities of the militia in the mid-twenties. The band of the 160th Infantry played band concerts for as many as 10,000 people every Sunday in Los Angeles' Exposition Park from 2:30 to 4:30 p.m. The music was provided free of charge, and led by a famous bandmaster. The expenses of the band were underwritten by the Regimental Commander at the time, Colonel (later Major General) Walter P. Story. Colonel Story paid for some instruments and the band uniforms out of his own pocket, and saw to it that an outstanding bandmaster was appointed to head the band. Colonel Story wrote a personal check to pay for rehearsals and the Sunday concerts.

The other example shows how recruits were trained in those days. Training of the recruits was a burden on each of the units that recruited new Guardsmen, so an innovation was introduced immediately following the summer encampment of 1926. All the new soldiers in the 160th were brought together in one "Recruit Company." An experienced captain was given command. Soldiers in the Officer Candidate School were used as instructors. The California Guardsman for November, 1926 said "It relieved the company commanders of the bugbear of recruit training."

Units routinely sponsored horse shows and presented entertainments during the year. Some presented "Smokers". They were open to the public, and sometimes involved boxing and wrestling matches. Others presented soldier entertainment such as singing, magic shows, and comedy acts. Others presented military acts including marching units, weapons drills, and band playing.

By 1927, units were sprouting up all over California. Some small towns had surprisingly large units:

Hanford, 66 Guardsmen from a population of 7,000
Gilroy, 64 Guardsmen from a population of 3,650
Livermore, 64 Guardsmen from a population of 3,100
Maxwell, 22 Guardsmen from a population of only 500
Oakdale, 27 Guardsmen from a population of 1,740

Pay during these years was $1 for a private who attended drill, up to $2.80 for a first sergeant. Annual training in 1927 was conducted for the last time at Camp Del Monte, as training was eventually moved to Camp San Luis Obispo on the "beautiful Morro Beach Highway."

On Thanksgiving morning, November 24, 1927, over a thousand Folsom Prison inmates rioted and took possession of the prison library. Shortly before 11:00 a.m., the warden notified the Governor that 1400 prisoners were rioting. At 11:30 a.m., the Governor authorized the mobilization of ten National Guard companies totalling over 500 men from five communities to quell the riot and attempted prison break.

The first troops reported by 1:00 p.m., under the command of Colonel Wallace A. Mason of the 184th Infantry. Troops from his regiment were augmented by artillerymen from the 143rd Field Artillery in Stockton and Lodi. They were four units from Sacramento, three from Stockton, and one each from Woodland, Marysville and Yuba City. They were quickly transported to Folsom. In addition, two airplanes from the 40th Division Air Service flew up from Los Angeles "just in case."

Two tanks from the 40th Tank Company in Salinas were trucked over. The company got the word at 7:00 p.m. Thursday night. Before light the next morning, the tanks requested by the Governor were at the prison. They had made the move in less than thirteen hours from the time they were called. The tanks weren't used, although the prisoners may have been intimidated by their presence.

Two companies were immediately deployed around the prison while negotiations continued with the convicts. At dawn on Friday, when no significant progress had been made, Guardsmen entered the prison grounds with fixed bayonets. At the same time, tear gas was hurled through the windows of the building where the mutinous convicts were crowded together. Officers noted the grim look on the faces of the men, when, with fixed bayonets, in the cold gray dawn, they entered the prison walls. The Guardsmen were told not to fire unless they received orders otherwise. Under the stress of those times, the law enforcement officers were said to have poured about two thousand rounds into the library where the convicts were barricaded. The Guardsmen didn't fire a shot.

Most of the convicts immediately surrendered at 7:00 a.m., and crossed into the main cell house. There was a standoff with some hard core holdouts, who refused to surrender most of the night. Finally, they also accepted the warden's ultimatum. The troops were relieved from duty at 10:00 a.m. on Saturday the 26th. They returned home pleased with their deportment. They especially took pride in holding fire, as ordered, even though the prison guards fired the estimated two thousand rounds into the library.

On Sunday, March 25, 1928, the American River overflowed its banks. Members of Battery D, 143rd Field Artillery of Sacramento and the 184th Infantry Regiment assisted in the rescue work and in protecting property from looters. Two officers and fifty-two enlisted soldiers under command of Captain A. E. Waite of the 184th reported and remained on duty until April 1st. Blankets and cots were furnished refugees and the North Sacramento armory was used as a relief station.

The training of the division had been problematic over the years. The division had never had a training camp to call their own. Regular Army Instructors had repeatedly commented on the inadequacy of such training sites as Del Monte and Camp Gigling, which had too much sand and not enough training area.

The search started for a training site, and quickly centered on a site four and a half miles from the City of San Luis Obispo. The original 1,982 acres could not be leased from the owners, so the site was purchased by a committee of citizens. The War Department detailed a board of officers, headed by a Colonel W. N. Caldwell, to examine the site. The report they produced included the following quotations:

> "There is everything here needed for an ideal military camp site.
> "A wide plateau with just enough slope to make efficient drainage; wide and clear for maneuvers.
> "There is a clear, level space for an aviation field facing the direction of the prevailing winds.
> "There is a real artillery range...(and) an ample supply of water.
> "It will be a very simple matter to run a spur track on the property.
> "Weather conditions, as taken from the U.S. Weather Bureau reports, indicate that the climate is ideal.
> "With a deep water harbor only a day's march from the camp, where troops could embark or disembark in event of an emergency, the site is ideal."

The Federal government allotted $134,969 for the first year's construction work including complete water, sewer and electric systems, two warehouses and one regimental unit. The regimental unit included sixteen mess halls, four lavatories, sixty officers' and two enlisted mens' tent floors. Contracts were signed for the next unit, with the total planned to cost about $500,000. Signs were posted reading "National Guard Training Camp, 40th Division."

A total of $25,000 was raised in contributions from the troops, profits of post exchanges, entertainments and public subscriptions for recreation purposes. As a consequence, a fifty by one hundred foot swimming pool and a post exchange building were constructed the first year, with plans for recreation buildings later.

1928 was the first year that troops trained at their new Camp San Luis Obispo (CSLO). There was considerable anticipation by both the soldiers and local residents, and July 4th was scheduled for the official dedication. The streets of San Luis Obispo were decorated by the city for the occasion. The 184th Infantry paraded in the city in the morning along with the American Legion and other groups that normally paraded on Independence Day. The camp was opened up and about 10,000 citizens came to CSLO for a huge luncheon put together by the Citizen's Committee in charge of the celebration. They also provided ice cream and cake to all of the enlisted messes.

In the afternoon there was a review by the regiment in front of the Adjutant General and other dignitaries, and the post was formally dedicated. This was immediately followed by a field day. The troops participating in the field day were exempted from the review so the games and races could start immediately following the review.

The activities in the afternoon also included a forty-eight gun salute, followed by daytime fireworks furnished by the Celebration Committee. That night there were two dances in town sponsored for the men, which lasted past midnight, as well as a memorable fireworks display.

Camp San Luis Obispo had 2,989.67 acres owned by the state plus an additional 1,200 leased acres when the post was officially dedicated. In the early thirties, $142,500 was appropriated by the California legislature to purchase an additional 1,557 acres of land, making a total of 4,427 acres. It was felt that this was enough property to house a brigade of infantry, a regiment of field artillery, a signal company, a military police company, an engineer company, and division aviation.

Progress was made each year in the late twenties and early thirties as more buildings were constructed. By 1934, Public Works Administration monies ($16,609) were expended at CSLO for several new buildings.

On April 1, 1929, the 185th Infantry was organized and again added to California's troop list. The headquarters was established in Fresno, with units organized from new and existing companies transferred from the 160th and 184th Infantry Regiments. The new regiment ended up with units from as far north as Oakdale, and as far south as Santa Ana. The 40th Division then became the last of the National Guard divisions to attain recognition, all the others having progressed more rapidly than the 40th, and had attained a satisfactory status at an earlier date.

The annual training encampment at CSLO included routine bugle calls at 11:00 a.m. (Stable Call), and 4:30 p.m. (Water Call). Sports competitions continued to play a major role in the life of the division. There were competitions in basketball, marksmanship and equestrian events. There also were competitions in boxing, wrestling, track & field, baseball (both indoor and outdoor), and swimming. Such competitions were routine between the world wars.

In 1930 the 185th Infantry Regiment established a Breakfast Club in Fresno. Each Sunday morning the members would arise at dawn, proceed to the riding academy, and draw their mounts. They would ride for about two hours along the bridal path before eating a hearty breakfast. Those officers who did not have the luck of the draw might not know their mounts, and have some difficulty in "retaining the poise and dignity" becoming to an officer.

In 1930 and 1931, the division attended their annual encampment at CSLO in two halves. The organizations in those days were not fully structured, so the small post met the needs of the division.

The Fortieth Infantry Division, while under-structured, also had units in Nevada and Utah. In his annual report written in 1930, the Adjutant General noted that the California National Guard was at its full strength of 6,589 Guardsmen authorized by the War Department, and his office had applications on file from more than forty cities that wanted a National Guard unit.

The National Guard was and is territorial. Units were quite proud of their home town, and the name that applied (e.g. "Salinas' own" tank company, later a tank battalion). Prior to World War II, the great majority of armories were leased, often with a sharing arrangement. There were very few vehicles, so the greatest need was for an exclusive-use strong room for weapons and other equipment. The Masons or other organizations might use the building on nights the National Guard company didn't meet.

As explained before, soldiers were expected to train one night a week and during a two week summer encampment. However, successful units had soldiers who spent additional evenings plus weekends for rifle marksmanship and military schooling. Units met on different nights of the week, Monday through Friday, for several reasons. In multi-unit armories, though in the old days there were very few large armories (only four in California early in the Twentieth Century), limited space on the drill floor and in classrooms forced units to meet on different nights. The only unit in the division that did not meet one night a week was the Division Aviation. The aviators met on "Sunday morning and Monday night, alternating."

In 1931, as budget constraints of the depression were beginning to be felt, troops were directed to use .22 calibre rifles for preliminary rifle instruction. However, the full allowance for .30 calibre ammunition was available for combat firing courses.

The National Guard was beginning to receive attendance quotas for training at Regular Army Service Schools. In 1932, California was allotted slots for six officers and two enlisted men for the training year. The depression-driven budget cuts were being felt, as the annual training pay of officers and warrant officers was reduced 8 1/3%, same as the Regular Army.

The City of Long Beach was hit by a devastating earthquake at 5:45 p.m. on March 10, 1933. Buildings were flattened, fires started, and all telephone communications knocked out in this worst of all earthquakes to ever strike Southern California. The earthquake was felt from San Diego to Santa Barbara, but the worst damage was experienced in the area bounded by Los Angeles, Newport Beach, and Anaheim.

Radio station W6JFQ, the radio call letters for headquarters of the National Guard's non-divisional Second Battalion, 251st Coast Artillery Regiment, provided the first news of the earthquake. At 6:14 p.m., Radio Station KGER broadcast the message (repeated at 10-minute intervals for two hours): "All National Guardsmen in Long Beach and San Pedro report at their respective armories immediately." By 6:40 p.m. a first aid station had been established in the Long Beach armory, and the Guard had sent out seven six-man first aid squads. They took care of fractures, abrasions and similar problems until people could be moved to hospitals.

By 7:10 p.m. the first battalion had been mobilized, and a second emergency surgery was established at 8:50 p.m. The first telephone communications out of Long Beach were established by the National Guard from the Long Beach armory within about three hours of the earthquake. Tentage, cots and blankets were used to shelter people who lost their homes.

The division provided troops from a battalion of the 185th Infantry, who were stationed in Santa Ana and Anaheim from March 10th through 13th. The troops assisted the Chiefs of Police in those two cities by guarding installations and businesses, controlling traffic, and patrolling the streets to prevent looting. A detachment of ten officers and 175 enlisted troops from the 160th Infantry was in Long Beach from March 11 until March 28. They established four field kitchens which fed refugees a total of approximately 242,000 meals.

When searches for survivors were completed, it was announced that more than a hundred people died, and over a thousand were injured by the earthquake. The greatest number killed were about seventy-five in Long beach, followed in turn by Compton, Huntington Park, and San Pedro.

The depression was continuing to be felt, as the allowance of ammunition was again reduced. As was often the case then (and is still true to some degree as this is written, regardless of economics), some types of ammunition were simply not available. There was another 15% pay cut in 1933. In addition, the number of paid drills was reduced from 48 to 36, even though most of the Guardsmen attended all 48. The attendance was gratifying in spite of reduced pay and paid drills.

Attendance at Camp San Luis Obispo in July of 1933 was way up, as was drill attendance. For instance, camp attendance for the major commands ranged from 94.06% to 99.27%. A series of 14-car trains delivered troops on July 9th, arriving in half hour intervals. Division reviews were conducted, as were the first large ceremonies of the division employing the new "Infantry Drill Formations." There was an exercise that started on the weekend of that annual training with mounted soldiers commanded by General Barrows versus motorized troops. The mounted troops set up camp south of San Luis Obispo with the mission of destroying rail communications between Arroyo Grande and Santa Margarita. The motorized troops defended against their raids, with the exercises called a draw at 5 a.m. on Monday.

On August 6th, the 143rd Artillery, which was horse drawn, was redesignated as motorized. Each battery was then authorized six 1½ ton Chevrolet trucks and two station wagons. The gun carriage wheels were converted to pneumatic tires so the guns could travel at a high rate of speed.

Major General David P. Barrows departed shortly after annual training for extensive traveling in Europe. Brigadier General Walter P. Story, commander of the 80th Brigade, assumed command of the division during the nine months General Barrows was gone. General Barrows returned to Berkeley on April 10, 1934.

The pay situation improved somewhat in 1934, with the number of paid drills for the training year from July 1934 through June 1935 increased to 42 of 48. There had been no .45 calibre pistol ammunition for years, so it was solved by providing .22 calibre ammunition to be used with adaptors that fit into the barrels of the .45 calibre pistols.

A strike was called in early May of 1934 among the 12,000 longshoremen who worked in ports along the Pacific Coast. The strike caused operations to slow down considerably in Seattle and Portland, though they had little impact in Los Angeles. However, it was worst of all in San Francisco, where maritime operations came to a complete stop.

In July the strike of San Francisco longshoremen grew violent for the first time. Two citizens were killed, while twenty-two were wounded. On July fifth, Governor Frank F. Merriam ordered out the National Guard. His proclamation:

Whereas there exists in the City and County of San Francisco, State of California, a state of tumult, riot, and other emergencies, or imminent danger thereof, and there are present therein tumultuous, riotous and unlawful assemblies with intent to do violence to persons and property therein, and to resist the laws of the State of California and the United States of America; now, therefore, I, Frank F. Merriam, Governor of the State of California and by virtue thereof commander-in-chief of the militia of the State of California, do hereby call and order, and authorize the Adjutant General of the State of California to forthwith call and order into active service such portion of the active militia as may be necessary to protect life and property and to maintain peace and order in said city and county, and said Adjutant General is hereby authorized and ordered to forthwith take such action or actions as may be necessary for the protection and preservation of peace and order in said City and County of San Francisco.

The Adjutant General of the State of California will provide all transportation and services and furnish all rations and other supplies necessary for the proper performance of the duties hereby authorized and ordered, and for each and all of said purposes I do hereby suspend all provisions of the laws of the State of California which require advertisement for bids for purchases of supplies or employment of services.

This proclamation to be and continuing forth uninterruptedly until revoked by me as Governor of the State of California.

Done under my hand and the great seal of California at the State Capitol, Sacramento, California, this 5th day of July,

Brigadier General Seth E. Howard, the Adjutant General, called General Barrows shortly after noon on July 5th, and authorized mobilization of the 250th Coast Artillery; the 159th Infantry Regiment; and Company D of the 184th Infantry Regiment, a machine gun company to be attached to the 250th. All units were on duty on San Francisco's Embarcadero shortly after 5:00 p.m. Shortly after the initial call, General Barrows determined that additional units would be needed, and called in Companies K and L of the 184th Infantry. Steel helmeted Guardsmen were on guard in front of every dock from Fisherman's Wharf to China Basin by midnight.

The dock strike was followed by a general strike, which also was violent. It was clear a great many more troops would be required. The 160th Infantry Regiment in Los Angeles was alerted Saturday afternoon, July 14th. That regiment had assembled at the Exposition Park armory by 2:00 a.m., and entrained by 8:00 a.m. The 160th detrained in San Francisco at about 9:00 p.m. on Sunday night.

While fellow Guardsmen were focussed on the strike in San Francisco, the 185th Infantry Regiment and the 143rd Field Artillery were in camp at San Luis Obispo. This was the first annual training encampment where the artillerymen got to use their motorized equipment. As was usual for those years, there were shortages of many common types of ammunition. This was particularly obvious in salute ammunition, when the Governor attended the annual review. Two salutes had been fired for the division commander, one on opening day, and one the day after he passed over the camp en route to Los Angeles. That left no salute ammunition for the annual review.

The day was balmy at Camp San Luis Obispo on Sunday, July 15, 1934. Guardsmen were lazily following whatever pursuits attracted their fancy on that day off when a bugle call at 2:00 p.m. sounded officers call. The regimental commander told the officers they were to depart at 6:30 p.m. that night for San Francisco. Most of the troops entrained, and arrived at the Third Street Station in San Francisco at 2:00 a.m. Monday morning. They detrained under cover of the Port Command Gas and Riot Detachment, and moved to the vicinity of Pier 50B. In the meantime, the 143rd moved by truck convoy.

Wherever the National Guardsmen arrived at the port, violence immediately ceased except for isolated incidents. An exception occurred on Saturday night, July 21st. That night, Company C, 185th Infantry was stationed at an outpost several miles from the rest of the regiment, in a potential trouble spot. Three men in an automobile suddenly fired at two sentries from Company C. The sentries returned the fire, but instead of firing to kill, fired to disable the car. When the car stopped, the Guardsmen took the offenders into custody.

That was the most potentially dangerous of the various incidents that occurred during the strike. Shortly afterwards, the troops began to be released for return to civilian status.

Range firing and shooting competitions between commands grew during the thirties. There were competitions between units in each regiment, as well as competitions with other regiments in the division. In 1935, a .22 calibre pistol competition was conducted between Company H, 185th Infantry and the 11th United States Infantry from Fort Benjamin Harrison, Indiana. The match was 25 shots at 20 yards by a ten-man team, with the five high scores counting. Company H defeated their Regular Army competitors by thirteen points. This was especially telling because many commanders in 1935 didn't have enough rifle ammunition to qualify some of their troops, and were unable to conduct any pistol marksmanship at all.

More comparatively modern equipment was being issued to the National Guard. Receipt of trucks by divisional units in other states permitted closer associations and combined training. The 145th Field Artillery of Utah, along with the 145th Hospital Company, undertook a particularly arduous convoy to annual training in California in 1935.

The movement of the 145th Field Artillery (one of the division's three artillery regiments) from Utah to CSLO and return received national attention. The regiment, with its twenty-four 75mm guns, made the move west with 101 vehicles over the 972 miles one way in four days. The return trip was by way of San Diego, where they visited the San Diego Exposition, with a total length of 2,200 miles for the round trip. The long trip was made so the Utah troops could train with California and Nevada elements of the division. Parallels quite naturally were drawn with the march of the Mormon Battalion to San Diego during the Mexican War.

Annual training in 1935 involved most elements of the division in war maneuvers at Guadalupe near Santa Maria. The exercises involved Red attacking forces from the Southern California brigade against Blue defending forces from the Northern California brigade. About six thousand Guardsmen from divisional units in California, Nevada and Utah participated in these largest maneuvers seen in the area since 1918. In addition to the maneuvers during annual training, the Fourth Army conducted Command Post Exercises at Fort Lewis that year. Staff officers from the 34th, 40th, and 41st National Guard Divisions trained with Regular Army staff officers there.

The 196th Field Artillery Regiment, a non-divisional organization, was disbanded on June 18, 1936. This facilitated organization of the "Grizzlies" of the 144th Field Artillery, who were part of the division when the division departed for World War One. The headquarters were established in the City of Santa Barbara, an action considered especially propitious, as much was made of the fact that Saint Barbara was the patron saint of artillerymen everywhere. The organization was completed by 1940.

Annual training in 1936 started, as it did with many of the units, following going-away dinners for the Guardsmen. These were often sponsored by the local Elks or American Legion Post, and were gala affairs, many with entertainment furnished either by the hosts or the Guardsmen.

Maneuvers designed by General Barrows "to meet a hostile threat coming by way of the Pacific Ocean, that is, a mobile defense of a sector of the Pacific Coast." were conducted by the division (less the 159th Infantry). That was an interesting portent of exactly what the division was asked to do in 1941. Elements of the division, with the 250th and 251st Coast Artillery attached, organized themselves and practiced defending the coast of California in the vicinity of San Luis Obispo.

The 159th Infantry, playing the role of the "Maroon" (invading) force, made two landings. The main landing at the Standard Oil Company's pier at Cayucos was observed by a Japanese Naval Tanker, whose captain visited Regimental Headquarters. The First Battalion, less Company C, landed on the rough coast of Spooner's Cove the night of July 20th. One boat went on the rocks. Major Leonard Dunkel, the battalion commander, later received the Soldier's Medal for rescuing two soldiers from drowning.

General Barrows was scheduled to reach his statutory retirement age before the normal annual training date in 1937, so a big review to honor him was conducted on the afternoon of July 25th, the middle Saturday of annual training in 1936. The ceremony was described in the division's new newspaper, first published that year, called the *Bear State Defender*. Governor Frank M. Merriam attended, with more than 10,000 citizens observing the ceremonies.

A study conducted that year again showed that small towns in California were much more supportive of their National Guard units than larger cities. Woodland, with a population of only 5,542 people, supported a unit of 71 soldiers, or the equivalent of 1,281 per 100,000. A sampling:

City	Guardsmen per 100,000
Woodland	1281
Auburn	1278
Yuba City	1193
Marysville	1123
- -	
Los Angeles	89
Burbank	37
Hollywood	22
Santa Monica	12

Annual training in 1937 was typical for those days. The first Sunday was spent setting up camp. Each work day started at 7:00 a.m. with pack rolling. The bugler's school started at 7:15 a.m. Training included squad and section drill, scouting and patrolling, combat principles for the squad and section, and advance guard. Later there was training in combat principles for the platoon and company, and defense against aircraft. Each morning there was a foot inspection from 10:30 a.m. to 11:00 a.m. There were division problems on Thursday and Friday of the first week, with the

Governor's Review on Saturday. Governor Merriam again took the review, with more than 30,000 civilians there to watch.

There were more than 8,500 National Guardsmen from California, Nevada and Utah to participate in Fourth Army maneuvers from Monday through Thursday under Major General George S. Simonds. This pitted the entire 40th Infantry Division, with non-division artillery attached, against Regular Army troops in Fourth Army maneuvers. The entire 65th Field Artillery Brigade was assembled for the first time. Again, the 145th Field Artillery conducted a long convoy from Utah, as did the 222nd Field artillery. Those two organizations drove almost a thousand miles, and brought 155mm howitzers with them. The 2nd Battalion, 115th Engineer Regiment of Nevada also attended annual training with the Division.

The maneuvers were followed by a critique on Friday. This was the first time since World War I that all of the Fourth Army was in the field. The maneuvers assumed the enemy landed at Monterey and were moving northward against San Francisco. The mission given to the 40th Division was to protect railroad facilities and oil shipping installations north of Morro Bay. The maneuvers provided an excellent shakedown, as participants gained valuable experience while needs for additional training were exposed.

On 27 June 1937, a retirement ceremony was conducted to honor Major General David P. Barrows, mandatorily retired at sixty-four years of age, after eleven years commanding the division. The 160th Infantry invited the general to mess with them on his last day in the field. The 159th Infantry Regiment (he had previously commanded both the 159th and the 79th Brigade) lined the road while carrying field packs and fixed bayonets, along with all the officers of the division. The 159th Infantry band led the way, playing "The Old Gray Mare." As the general passed, each company presented arms, bayonets flashing in what was described as "a sincere and moving tribute to a great leader."

General Barrows was a dashing cavalryman of great vigor. Even years later, when celebrating his 76th birthday with some National Guard officers, he jumped into an icy pool in his BVDs. Only two other (much younger) officers were willing to take that plunge during his birthday celebration. He had his own string of horses, and would lead his staff on tactical rides. His chest was covered with decorations, including several from foreign countries. Greatly respected as well as genuinely liked by his soldiers, he was a hard act to follow.

General Barrows' place was taken by the senior brigade commander in the division, Brigadier General Walter P. Story. General Story, son of a Montana banker, was born 18 December 1883. He graduated from Shattuck Military Academy in Minnesota. After graduating from Eastman College in New York, he spent a short time in one of his father's banks. He was unhappy with banking, however, and followed the gold rush to Nevada. There he organized a trucking company before selling out and engaging in the real estate business in Los Angeles.

In 1914, he helped father an artillery battery, recruiting Battery A of the California Field Artillery, later Battery A, 143rd Field Artillery. He also raised funds to build an armory and stables in Exposition Park, Los Angeles. He served in World War I as a captain of artillery, although his only Federal decoration from that war was a Victory Medal. He was active in organizing the National Guard immediately following the war. He organized the first separate infantry company, then later a separate infantry battalion, and eventually the 160th Infantry Regiment which he commanded for several years. General Story later commanded the 80th Brigade, and graduated from the Army War College's Class of 1932-33 in Washington.

He initiated and published the 160th Infantry Guardsman, which later became the state-wide California Guardsman. He introduced and had all officers of the 160th equipped with blue mess jackets. The regiment, perhaps because of the foregoing as well as the meticulous discipline maintained by the organization, became known as "The Imperial Guard."

General Story assumed command of the division on July 1, 1937. The division headquarters was moved to Los Angeles on October 1, 1937, with Federal recognition of the move received effective October 18, 1937.

Later that year, the National Guard was able to procure space at the California State Fair. A lot of equipment and weaponry was put on display, including a tank and a howitzer. The display received a great deal of attention from the visitors.

Southern California suffered disastrous floods in March of 1938. On March 2nd, Brigadier General Harcourt Hervey put his 80th Brigade on alert. The Mayor of Anaheim requested assistance from the commander of the 3rd Battalion, 185th Infantry Regiment on March 4th. The flooded town was congested with sightseers, telephone lines were dead, and looting had begun. Not waiting for orders, Major Donald Winans notified General Hervey, and directed Lieutenants Leonard E. Echols and Kermit H. McCoy to assemble the Headquarters Company. Orders arrived at 1:50 p.m., and by 3:15 p.m. troops were on duty. Traffic was controlled, anti-looting patrols were established, and trucks, ambulances and rolling field kitchens were sent into the affected area. The unit provided first aid, food and shelter to the refugees. Several years later, Echols was in command of the 185th Infantry in the Philippines, while McCoy commanded the battalion.

In addition to routine subjects like first aid, marksmanship, interior guard duty and map reading, riot control was taught in 1938. That was also the year that the National Guard Association of the United States met at the Fairmont Hotel in San Francisco.

Military units, especially National Guard units where many soldiers remain in the same unit for their entire careers, develop more than their share of famous characters. One of the most famous during these years was "Whispering Ed" Gentry. He was the first sergeant of Company F, 160th Infantry, located for many years in the huge Exposition Park armory in Los Angeles. "Whispering Ed" had such a loud voice, that occasionally when he yelled "Company F, FALL IN," the entire regiment responded. It was said that his voice was so loud he made the steel rafters vibrate.

As tensions increased due to Germany's activities in Europe, war jitters were beginning to be felt in the United States. There were several consequences felt in the National Guard. One was an authorization in 1939 for an increase in strength of units, which immediately triggered a big recruiting campaign. Drill periods authorized for National Guard units were doubled to two per week, and additional periods of field training were prescribed.

In March of 1940, when some of the troops got to Camp San Luis Obispo, they wondered if they were there to help with the construction. There were unfinished mess halls and tent frames, and stacks of pipe, lumber and wire. Most structures that were up hadn't been painted yet. Worse, there was mud everywhere. Summer camp for 1940 was extended to three weeks. This precedent created problems with employers for some of the troops.

In October, the division was authorized to start enlisting people for one year enlistments, rather than the normal three year commitments. In December, some of the noncommissioned officers with dependents were discharged. There was no longer any question that Guardsmen faced the possibility of war, and most of them became much more battle-focussed in their training.

Division soldiers with 38mm gun in field maneuvers at Fort Lewis,
Washington in August, 1941
(Photo: California Military Museum)

CHAPTER FOUR

TRAINING FOR WORLD WAR II

As World War II in Europe heated up, the United States Army consisted of ten Regular Army and eighteen National Guard divisions. The ground forces were clearly not large enough, and the Army's total strength of 264,118 on June 30, 1940 was to be expanded to a total of 1,455,565 on June 30, 1941. To handle the tremendous training challenges that would result, General Headquarters, U. S. Army was activated at the Army War College in Washington on July 26, 1940. General Marshall designated Brigadier General (later Lieutenant General) Lesley J. McNair to run General Headquarters.

They immediately ran into problems with the confusing command structure of the Army. The relationships between the armies, corps areas, Air Corps, and the War Department General Staff were extremely convoluted.

The mobilization of the National Guard was further complicated by other factors, facing some of the same problems encountered prior to fighting in World War I. Divisions were to be reorganized from square to triangular, a reorganization which couldn't have come at a worse time. In addition, while a great deal of money had been appropriated for equipment, there was considerable delay between ordering and receiving the millions of pieces of equipment and ordnance required to equip and train a large army. As a consequence, Guardsmen found themselves again training with make-believe equipment, including mock tanks, mortars made out of pipe, machine guns fabricated of wood, and artillery made out of sheet metal.

Camps and training areas were needed to accommodate the large Army, but the construction program was lagging behind schedule. The Army was extremely short of troop housing, having facilities for only about 124,000 officers and men when action to fix the problem started. However, by the end of the year, shelter had been prepared for about 1,500,000 men. This prodigious effort was coordinated by a newly created Cantonment Division (later the Construction Division) of the Quartermaster Corps.

President Franklin D. Roosevelt had been trying to obtain authority to mobilize the National Guard for many months. After a series of hearings in Congress, he was finally given the authority. While some units of the division were mobilized in February, most of the 40th Division was inducted on March 3, 1941:

GENERAL ORDERS INDUCTING UNITS FOR FEDERAL SERVICE WWII:

GO 4 Hqs, California National Guard dated January 20, 1941.

Under instructions received from the Governor, State of California, from the Secretary of War, pursuant to and in compliance with the provisions of Executive Order 8633, January 14, 1941, the following units of the California National Guard are hereby ordered into active military service of the United States, effective dates set opposite unit designations:

144th Field Artillery...............3 Feb 41
Co C, 194th Tank Bn...........10 Feb 41

General Order #16 dated February 18, 1941 inducted the bulk of the division. The general order was based on a radiogram, dated February 7, 1941, and ordered the California units of the division and the 115th Observation Squadron into active military service on March 3, 1941. All were told that they were to be mobilized for one year of Federal service.

Units assembled in their armories, undergoing administrative processing and some training. The 160th Infantry Regiment went to the Coliseum where they were scheduled to remain for a couple of weeks. They stayed in the tunnels of the Coliseum while undergoing administrative processing at the Exposition Park Armory. After about three days of the dampness, exacerbated by the rains outside, they moved into the Exposition Park Armory. The troops that were within a short commute distance of their homes were permitted to go home each night because of the shortage of space.

Units paraded, or had going away ceremonies before leaving for Camp San Luis Obispo, which had been inundated with rain. When each train arrived at Camp San Luis Obispo, the troops found that it was still unfinished, and extremely muddy. As a consequence of the rains, mud, and soldiers always being wet, the post's hospital was full of troops laid low with pulmonary problems. The troops started training with their makeshift weapons. Eventually these were exchanged for the real thing, although the division didn't receive its full allowance of weaponry.

The division was not notified until twenty-one days after the induction date as to which Table of Organization and Equipment it would be organized under. There were literally thousands of man days expended because the National Guard systems differed from the Active Army. The Guardsmen lacked administrative and supply regulations, publications and blank forms. This was a frustrating experience for the Guardsmen, a lesson not remembered, and destined to be repeated to some degree in every call-up until Desert Shield/Desert Storm in the early nineties.

All four regimental commanders were sent off to Fort Benning for three months of schooling. This couldn't have come at a worse time, with their commands suffering the turmoil of mobilization. To complicate matters, the regimental commanders were switched, so they all had to become familiar with units that were new to them. The three brigadiers in the division were switched also. Officers were told that the switches were made to break up pre-war relationships. There was some concern expressed behind closed doors that some of the switching may have been an effort to make National Guard senior officers look bad to open up positions for Regular Army officers.

The division was given several tests by Fourth Army while training at Camp San Luis Obispo. Maneuvers were scheduled at Hunter Liggett Military Reservation (HLMR) in Central California. The Army had activated III Corps at the Presidio of Monterey in December of 1940. That command, under the command of Major General Joseph W. ("Vinegar Joe") Stilwell, served as the Maneuver Headquarters during what later came to be called the "HLMR Massacre." As a result of those maneuvers, a number of senior commanders were relieved.

General Story retained command until June of 1941. It was announced that he was going to have to leave the division due to serious illness. Many senior officers felt that was a cover story. At least one heard him criticized by a senior general officer for not knowing how to properly utilize his artillery. This was particularly damaging when remembering that Story claimed, based on his World War I experience, to be an artilleryman.

The details of General Story's relief are rather obscure. His physical condition was given as the reason, although like most National Guard commanders, his supporters felt he was removed simply because he was a Guardsman. Most National Guard Division Commanders were eased out, with the exception of a couple. Their replacements often had World War I experience, and most ended up later in the war as Corps or Army Commanders.

Among his own senior officers, General Story's reputation was somewhat clouded. They felt he tried to surround himself with former regular officers to offset his own lack of knowledge, and was said to help them find civilian jobs. Whatever the full truth, Brigadier General E. J. Dawley assumed command on June 23, 1941. Dawley was a West Point graduate, and another artilleryman who served in World War I. General Dawley had been with

Pershing in World War I, and was considered close to such senior officers as Leslie McNair.

The division was scheduled in August of 1941 for maneuvers in the state of Washington, south of Fort Lewis. They were billed as the largest military games in Western (US) history, and involved about 100,000 troops.

In mid August, the division traveled to Southwestern Washington State by both rail and motor convoy. There were seventeen troop trains, each consisting of fifteen coaches and baggage cars. The trucks traveled in eight convoys totalling about 2,000 vehicles, which took about five days to reach Washington, averaging about 235 miles a day. The troops stopped at small towns like Turlock, Mount Shasta, and tiny villages in Oregon. All commented on the friendliness of the townspeople, who couldn't seem to do enough for the soldiers. All of the division arrived in Washington on schedule and without a major accident.

The troops were divided into blue and red forces, as was traditional in those days. The Blue Force consisted of the 7th and 40th Infantry Divisions in Major General Stilwell's III Corps, plus the 3rd and 41st Infantry Divisions in Ninth Corps commanded by Major General Kenyon A. Joyce. The Blue Force had the mission of defending against an invading Red Force. Half of the Blue Force was already in Washington. Their mission was to hold off the invaders until reinforcements, including the Fortieth Division, could arrive and help drive the invaders back.

On August 24th, the division participated in a counter offensive, when the 79th Brigade's 159th and 184th Infantry Regiments attacked in conjunction with the 7th Infantry Division. They quickly captured the small towns of Pe Ell, Doty, and Dryad.

One of the toughest assignments was given to the Second Battalion, 185th Infantry. They were sent a hundred miles southwest into the wild timbered country of Pacific County. They then detrucked to march an additional twenty miles. The battalion, commanded by Major Daniel H. Hudelson, who was a future division commander from Los Angeles, carried their machine guns and mortars with them. Supplies couldn't reach them, so they ate wild berries and crawfish, and drank from the streams in the area. They walked out of the wild country two days later, tired and drenched.

All but two battalions of the Fortieth had seen action before the maneuvers were called to a halt on Monday, August 25, about five days before the scheduled conclusion. The exercise was terminated because the Red Force was trapped after getting to the edge of the maneuver area well before the maneuvers were scheduled to be terminated. The troops maneuvered better than expected in spite of a great deal of rain during the exercise.

The troops started convoying the vehicles south on August 28th, with the last convoy leaving on September 1st. Shortly after all troops had returned to Camp San Luis Obispo, General Dawley conducted a series of maneuver critiques. Most were held in No Name Creek Amphitheater, a natural amphitheater with the Santa Lucia mountains as a backdrop, which would hold up to three thousand troops.

The 159th Infantry Regiment was detached from the division on September 29, 1941 and assigned to the 7th Infantry Division. This left the division with the three regiments normal in a triangular division of that day. The 159th was motorized in late October, and was transferred to Fort Ord on December 3, 1941.

Major General Stilwell was a rising star, although he was considered somewhat of a "hatchet man," who had recently activated the 7th Infantry Division at Fort Ord, General Stilwell directed maneuvers to be conducted at Hunter Liggett Military Reservation. Hunter Liggett, formerly part of William Randolph Hearst's huge ranch, at that time consisted of 154,000 acres.

The exercise had the 80th ("Blue Force") Brigade maneuvering against the 79th ("Red Force") Brigade, clashing near Jolon. The exercise was temporarily halted when the company mascot ("Duke") of Company D, 160th Infantry took off after a large jackrabbit, with a mad chase across much of the field of battle into the river bed of the San Antonio River. The troops "cheered lustily" until settling down and resuming the battle.

The 40th Division had been federalized later than other National Guard divisions, and there were the many personnel changes alluded to earlier. Almost inevitably, mistakes were made, and some heads rolled. Also inevitably, there was some bitterness and resentment. This surrounded what was perceived as discrimination against Guardsmen, at least partially attributed to the craving of some regular officers for senior billets in National Guard organizations.

When Pearl Harbor was attacked by the Japanese on December 7, 1941, things immediately changed. All posts and camps went on full war footing. Leaves and furloughs were cancelled, and a recall was broadcast to all troops. All troops were to be in uniform at all times. Visitors were only allowed on posts for business purposes and with a special pass.

Commanders were concerned about the Japanese-American soldiers in their units, most of whom were exceptionally good soldiers. They were afraid some of their Japanese-Americans could be mistaken for enemy infiltrators and shot by someone with an itchy trigger finger. There was also concern they could start a panic, as there was a great deal of hysteria early in the war.

A typical solution was exercised by Colonel Curtis H. O'Sullivan of the 184th. He made the Japanese-Americans his Palace Guard, forming them into a security detachment. They did cause consternation for some visitors. Shortly they all were transferred out. However, some of the commanders were concerned their Japanese-American soldiers might end up discharged and be sent to relocation camps. Some almost certainly went on to serve in the all-Nisei 442nd Regimental Combat Team which later distinguished itself in the Italian campaign.

On December 8th, elements of the division were scattered to defend strategic areas of Southern California. The first Field Order of the Division read:

FO No. 1   Hq San Pedro Sub Section
                                        8 Dec 41 4:45P

MAPS: Road Map State of Calif. -- Los Angeles and Vic. San Luis   Obispo Calif

    1. a. A state of war exists between the United Sates and Japan.
       b. The provisions of Rainbow 5 are put into effect.

    2. SAN PEDRO SUB SECTOR: Troops of the San Pedro Sub Sector will organize and defend the area indicated by "Defensive-offensive" action. They will defeat and destroy any invading force before it lands or while attempting to gain a foothold either by boats or airplanes. Occupation of position on order from Section Headquarters, (opn map)

    3. a. 185 Inf (less 1st Bn and 3rd Bn) attached, Co C 115th Eng. Organize and defend area (opn map). Beach to be defended by beach guard detachments and connecting motor patrols not to exceed one battalion. Observation to be provided for all portions of beach, minimum once hourly. Reserve (opn map) committed on Sub Sector orders only.
      b. 1st Bn 185th (attached Btry A 145 FA and Det 115th Engrs) prepared to provide local protection for Harbor defenses of San Pedro.
      c. 115th Engineers (less Cos A B C and Det with 1st Bn 185th Inf) prepared to place guarded demolitions on existing wharves, critical railroad and road bridges. Prepare tank obstructions on defiles in area. Prepare underwater Obstacles at critical beaches indicated (opn map). Assist Infantry and Artillery in organization of the ground to defend critical beaches.
      d. 1st Bn 145th FA (less Btry A) from a position of readiness, prepare to support units of subsector. Priority of beaches on which artillery will be prepared to fire (see Par. X).
      e. Reserves: 3rd Bn 185th Inf (opn map). Committed on Sub Sector Command only. Motors attached for movement of entire battalion. Plans: Prepared to counter attack any force that effects a landing

either by boat, parachute or airplane. Priority of preparations to follow priority of Par. X.

   f. Headquarters and Headquarters Btry 65th FA Brig to be attached to 40th Inf. Div. Hq.

X. 1. All units, forces and installations are responsible for own interior guard and anti-sabotage defense and local defense against low flying aircraft and parachute troops.

     2. Use of toxic agents is prohibited. Smoke and non-toxic agents may be used.

     3. Priority of areas to be defended:
     a. Los Angeles and vicinity
     b. El Segundo
     c. Beaches
        1. Long Beach to New Port Bay
        2. Santa Monica to Malaga Cove
        3. Ventura to Mugu Lagoon
        4. Dume Cove
        5. Santa Barbara

     4. Within each of the areas indicated, defense priorities are:
     a. Vital industrial plants when damage to or cessation of work threat would seriously interfere with national defense.
     b. Oil storage and loading facilities for the fleet.
     c. Permanent fortifications and naval establishment.
     d. Important airdromes and other military establishments.
     e. Other important commercial and transportation centers and public utilities.

     5. Liaison officers are to be exchanged as follows:
        Monterey Sub Sector
        San Diego Sub Sector
        Southern California Sector
        Commander San Pedro Sector, 11th Naval District

     6. March Plan Annex No. 1

     7. Administrative Instruction Annex No. 2

8. Signal Instruction Annex No. 3
Command Post San Pedro Sub Sector, Exposition Park Open
2:30 P.M. 9 Dec 41. Remaining units (opn map)

By command of Major General DAWLEY

M.C. BRADLEY,
Lt. Col. G. S. C.
Actg. Chief of Staff

OFFICIAL:

(signed)
EUGENE W. RIDEOUT
Major, 184th Inf.
Actg. Asst ACof S G-3

ANNEXES:
No. 1   March Plan, accompanied by Overlay No. 1 and No. 2
No. 2   Administrative Instructions
No. 3   Signal Instructions

- -

While the above order was dated December 8th, some battalions were on the move by the evening of December 7th. There was a great sense of urgency as the division headed out in response to these new orders. Truck drivers in support of the troops worked extraordinarily long hours in getting the division's logistical tail in place. The move was assisted by the Greyhound Bus Company and escorts from the California Highway Patrol and local police departments. Camp San Luis Obispo very quickly became a ghost camp.

Thomas O. Lawson was a lieutenant (he later retired with the rank of major general) during these days, and kept a detailed diary. His diary for 1942 gives a good sense of what was happening as the division adjusted to a wartime footing. At that time he was a platoon leader in Company M, 160th Infantry. The entry for January 1, 1942: *"I moved from Gaviota to Santa Barbara...stayed there 10 minutes* (when I) *received emergency orders to move out to Newhall Battery Headquarters - took over tunnel guard from AT Co* (Anti-Tank Company) *- out all night - took over guard this morning at 5:45 a.m."*

His entry for January 3rd: *"Went to Wayside Prison farm today and had first hot shower since last Saturday. Made tour of guard - no excitement."* His entry for January 5th: *"Still here at Bouquet Canyon. Things in a rut. Men going stale on this guard duty."*

In January the division established an officer's school in an old Civilian Conservation Corps camp in Griffith Park, Los Angeles. The school, dubbed "Dawley Tech," operated for about six weeks under the direction of Lieutenant Colonel Daniel Hudelson. It served as a refresher course for the many officers inducted into the division immediately after war was declared. Griffith Park was so large that machine guns and artillery could be fired inside the park as part of the training.

Japanese-Americans were moved into relocation camps starting in early February. There was particular concern about the large fishing colony of Japanese on Terminal Island in Los Angeles Harbor. Two of the camps Japanese-Americans were moved into were at Arvin and Delano. The 40th Division was tasked with moving these unfortunate civilians, and for guarding their possessions. They were forced to quickly liquidate their homes, or arrange for non-Japanese friends to act as caretakers. Most liquidated homes and furnishings at great losses, and were permitted to take into the relocation camps only that which they could carry with them.

On February 18, 1942, the division was formally reorganized from a square to triangular division. The 2nd Battalion, 144th Field Artillery was redesignated as the 981st Field Artillery Battalion. The 159th Infantry had already been sent to the 7th Infantry Division in Alaska for use in the defense of the Aleutian Islands.

The revised organization of the division:

New Designation	Former Organization
Hqs, and Hqs Company and 40th MP Co	
40th Signal Company	
40th Cavalry Reconnaissance Troop	Hqs Co, 80th Infantry Brigade
160th Infantry	
184th Infantry	
185th Infantry	
Hqs and Hqs Battery, 40th Div. Artillery	Hqs, 65th F. A. Brigade
143rd F. A. Bn (105mm Howitzer)	1st Bn, 143rd F. A. Regiment
164th F. A. Bn (105mm Howitzer)	2nd Bn, 143rd F. A. Regiment
213th F. A. Bn (105mm Howitzer)	1st Bn, 145th F. A. Regiment
222nd F. A. Bn (155mm Howitzer)	1st Bn, 222nd F. A. Regiment
115th Engineer Bn	1st Bn, 115th Engr. Regiment
115th Medical Bn	Hq, Hq & Svc Co, A, B, E, H 115th Medical Regiment
115th Quartermaster Bn	HHC, A, B, E 115th QM Regiment
640th Tank Destroyer Bn	Batteries G & H 222nd F. A. Regt and other elements.

Any false sense of security was shattered on February 28th, 1942, when a radio station interrupted its broadcast schedule to announce that a Japanese submarine had shelled the city of Santa Barbara. It turned out that the I-17, a very large Japanese submarine commanded by Commander Kozo Nishino, surfaced above Santa Barbara (near Goleta) to repair an engine. The engine had been repaired by shortly after 7:00 p.m., when the captain directed his gunnery officer to open fire with the 5.5-inch deck gun as they closed to within less than a mile of the Bankline Oil Company's Ellwood oil fields. Over the next half hour they fired about two dozen rounds, most of which turned out to be duds. They slightly damaged a pier and one oil rig.

As the submarine sailed away, the alarm was spreading, with cities blacked out from San Diego all the way up to Monterey Bay. Battery A, 1-143rd Field Artillery was sent to Ellwood and arrived on the scene about 10:00 p.m. They located the many duds over the next few days, including several brought in by farmers in that area, and disposed of them. Things returned to normal after a couple of weeks, but the full story wasn't revealed until after the war.

A Replacement Training Center was established in late February at Camp Haan, near Riverside. The training center was organized as a provisional regiment under the command of Lieutenant Colonel William B. Zeller to train replacements as they reported in for assignment to the division.

The troops had been scattered all over Southern California. A listing for March shows how widely the command posts were dispersed:

40th Div Hqs (San Pedro Sub Sector)	Exposition Park, Los Angeles
40th Cavalry Reconnaissance Troop	La Mesa
40th Military Police Company	Exposition Park, Los Angeles
40th Division Finance	Exposition Park, Los Angeles
40th Division Signal Company	Exposition Park, Los Angeles
115th Engineer Battalion	Hollywood Track, Inglewood, Camp Cooke, National City
40th Division Artillery	Exposition Park
143rd FA Bn	Santa Barbara, Ellwood, Capitan, Summerland, Carpenteria, Gardena
164th FA Bn	Gardena, El Segundo, Ft. MacArthur, Aliso, Dana Point
222nd FA Bn	Escondido, Carlsbad
160th Infantry Hq & Spec Units	Houghton Park, Long Beach
1st Bn, 160th	Municipal Airport, Long Beach
2nd Bn, 160th	Banning Park, Wilmington
3rd Bn, 160th	Recreation Park, Long Beach
184th Infantry Hqs & Spec Units	Del Mar
1st Bn, 184th Inf (-)	La Mesa
(Co. A)	San Clemente Island
2nd Bn, 184th Inf	Lindberg Field, San Diego
185th Infantry Hqs & Spec Units	Centinela Park, Inglewood

1st Bn, 185th Inf (-)	Centinela Park
(Co A)	Catalina Island
2nd Bn, 185th Inf	Recreation Park, Santa Monica
3rd Bn, 185th Inf	Ventura
115th Medical Bn	Sawtelle, Compton, Santa Barbara
115th Quartermaster Bn	Van Nuys
640th Tank Destroyer Bn	Griffith Park, Los Angeles

Units were scattered even further from these command posts. As an example, the 160th Infantry at various times had elements as far away as Phoenix, Arizona and Salt Lake City, Utah. One rifle company, using a combination of strong points and motorized patrols, was responsible for 150 miles of coastline. Tension was high, with persistent rumors about saboteurs and penetrations by enemy aircraft. The news accounts of overwhelming odds faced by our troops at Wake Island and on Bataan exacerbated the tension.

On April 16, 1942, Brigadier General Rapp Brush assumed command of the division. He was an ROTC graduate of the University of Illinois who knew General MacArthur well, and had served with the 8th Infantry in the Philippines from 1912 to 1915. He had been a distinguished graduate of the Army's Command and General Staff School. He was a mild-mannered, soft spoken officer who rarely displayed emotion publicly even when quite angry. Highly competent, and a commander who spent a great deal of time up front with the troops, he remained in command of the division through all of its World War II combat.

General Brush replaced General Dawley, who was reassigned to command of the VI Corps when he left the division. Dawley went on to command the VI Corps as part of Lieutenant General Mark Clark's Fifth Army during the invasion of Italy, termed "Operation Avalanche." General Dawley was put to the test around Salerno, and unfortunately didn't do very well. He was visited by General Eisenhower, who noted the mess things were in, and was relieved from command a few days later. He was reduced in rank and ended up commanding a replacement depot.

On April 22, 1942, the division was ordered to Fort Lewis, Washington for advanced training after being relieved of its mission in California by the 35th Infantry Division of Kansas. Training of the division focused on night operations, forced marches, and close supporting fires. General Brush personally supervised the training, and could be seen anywhere and everywhere. The division trained both at Fort Lewis and Yakima's Rattlesnake Range from May through July. The troops quickly found out why the range at Yakima received its name, as they found the area infested with rattlesnakes.

The division artillery traveled to Yakima in June, and passed their gunnery tests. They returned to support provisional Regimental Combat Teams as they maneuvered. The 160th Regimental Combat Team was actually formed in preparation for departure on a special mission until the orders were cancelled.

Also in June, the 184th Infantry left the division, reporting to the Western Defense Command on June 14th for coastal defense duties. Later the 184th was assigned to the 7th Infantry Division, and saw some of the heaviest fighting in the Pacific. Loss of the 184th left the division with just two infantry regiments until the 108th Infantry Regiment joined the division in September.

In July of 1942 the division started its move to Hawaii. Most of the division started moving in August from Fort Lewis to a staging area at Camp Stoneman, California. The bulk of the troops arrived on August 13, 1942. Almost immediately, units started loading at the Oakland Army Base and shipping out for Hawaii. The 185th Infantry Regiment shipped out on August 23, 1942, arriving at the island of Kauai on September 1st.

The experience of the 160th was typical of those who shipped out. The regiment loaded up in Oakland, and left after most of the division had already shipped out. They passed under the Golden Gate Bridge shortly after noon on September 26th. Troops aboard the ships lost sight of land in the haze about 2:30 p.m. The next day they had a submarine scare, which turned out to be a false alarm.

They participated in the shipboard routine of those days. That included fire, gun, and abandon ship drills, plus the constant rumors and speculation about course changes. That routine activity was punctuated by occasional submarine scares. On October 2nd, ships in the 160th's convoy sounded the general alarm at 8:00 p.m. A submarine had been sighted, and depth charges dropped. When the convoys approached Hawaii, the troops on board would see birds, and then friendly aircraft. Finally, one or more warships would meet and escort them into port.

The 27th Infantry Division, formerly of the New York National Guard, had responsibility for defense of about half of the Hawaiian Islands. On September 1st, the 27th Division's 108th Infantry Regiment was assigned to the 40th Division to replace the 184th. This was part of an effort to avoid having all three regiments from the same geographic area, thereby spreading the impact if a division should be decimated by casualties. It was also in September that the division received its new helmets, replacing the World War I-style helmets.

By October the division had assumed responsibility for the island defense mission formerly assigned to the 27th Infantry Division. 40th Infantry Division headquarters was at Kalaheo, Kauai with General Brush acting as commander of the Kauai District. Units assigned were the 185th Infantry Regiment, 213th Field Artillery Battalion, 222nd Field Artillery Battalion, 115th Medical Battalion, 40th Signal Company, 40th Military Police Platoon, and the 640th Tank Destroyer Battalion (less Company C).

There was considerable tension in the air when the division arrived to assist with the defense of Hawaii. There was constant talk about a possible invasion of the islands, concern that remained until well after the Battle of Midway in early June 1942. It was some time before everyone realized what that battle had done to the Japanese Navy. From that time on the Japanese appeared much more tentative, and were never a serious threat that far east again. All of that must be considered in retrospect, as tension was rife until well into 1943.

Defences were improved around the islands. On Kauai, two-thirds of the coast line was encircled with strongly fortified reinforced concrete pillboxes. These were constructed in mutually supporting pairs reinforced by the small gauge railroad rails normally used in the cane fields by the sugar mills on the island. Concrete was then poured, with roofs 12-14" thick, and machine gun embrasures out the front and both sides. Access was through a tunnel dug to the rear. Barbed wire entanglements were established, varying in depth from ten to thirty feet.

The First Battalion of the 185th Regiment was particularly successful in getting their portion of the coast fortified. They cut dozens of truckloads of lumber from large eucalyptus tree groves, with logs about 10' long. They would spend the week organizing the effort, ensuring they had enough gloves, barbed wire and other needed supplies. They then had all of the students from the local high school assigned to them each Friday. They were then able to get the fortifications up much faster than even the engineers could.

The remainder of the coastline was impractical for amphibious landings, forming a natural barrier. Mobile reserves, called "assault groups," were established around the island. They consisted of mobile infantry, tank destroyers and other elements, and were designed to rapidly deliver intense firepower and shock action wherever they were needed.

There was one isolated, beautiful beach on the north shore of Kauai that the 185th felt should have an observation post to preclude any enemy landings. The cliffs behind the beach were all but unscalable, but there was one steep, narrow trail down to the beach. The 1-185th put together an ad hoc detachment consisting of troops such as radiomen from Headquarters Company, a squad or two of infantrymen, and some machine guns from Company D, the Heavy Weapons Company. It was considered good duty, as the troops got to fish and swim in the beautiful waters when not on duty.

Resupply of the detachment was accomplished using rented mules. Unfortunately (or fortunately depending on your view), a mule slipped and fell on one resupply trip, falling end over end before smashing on the rocks below in a spot that was almost impossible to reach. It was decided to not attempt to recover the equipment.

This was a bonanza for the battalion's supply sergeants. They immediately wrote up Reports of Survey (a document to explain losses of equipment) to cover the equipment on that mule so they could get the equipment written off and obtain replacements. It was some time later that leaders carefully reviewed the surveys and estimated that one mule fell with about two tons of equipment.

Some of the support elements of the division were reorganized in October. The 115th Quartermaster Battalion became the 40th Quartermaster Company, and the 115th Ordnance Platoon became the 740th Ordnance Company. These units were also assigned to the Kauai District.

The 160th Infantry Regiment, 143rd Field Artillery Battalion, one company of the 115th Engineers, and a detachment of the 40th Signal Company were located on the big island of Hawaii. They were under command of the Hawaii District.

On Maui were the 108th Infantry Regiment (less 2nd Battalion), Battery C of the 164th Field Artillery Battalion, the 115th Engineer Battalion (less one company), 40th Reconnaissance Troop, and detachments from the 40th Division Headquarters, 40th Division Artillery Headquarters, 40th Signal Company, and the 40th Military Police Platoon. The Maui District was commanded by Brigadier General Mittelstaedt. The 2nd Battalion of the 108th Infantry and the 164th Field Artillery Battalion (less Battery C) were assigned to defend Molokai and Lanai.

Spare time early in their tour there was spent exploring what to most of the soldiers was a very exotic area. One soldier, Sergeant

David L. Hendricks of the 164th Field Artillery, writing to his mother via V-Mail said:

"I have been eating all kinds of tropical fruits and nuts, pineapples, coconuts, berries and what have you. I started out Monday and went to the beach and caught crabs, then started roaming the timber and mountains around the island. We robbed a wild bee's nest which was my first, nothing but honey. We saw mountain goats and wild boar. Yesterday we explored a cave, and today I'm taking it easy."

It became obvious later that the troops were getting less spare time. The same Sergeant Hendricks complained in December that they were even having problems finding time to write.

All units of the division had arrived in Hawaii by early October. Units continued to work at improving existing defenses and developing alternate and supplemental defensive fortifications. Patrols were initiated, and strict blackout conditions enforced. Barbed wire was restrung, trails and fields of fire improved, and communications wire laid. Troops rehearsed reacting to various contingencies, and daily "stand-to," the early morning demonstration of combat readiness, was required of all units.

After each organization had ensured they were prepared to defend their portion of Hawaii, the focus shifted to training. Most initiated 52-hour weekly training schedules, with the leaders working even longer hours preparing classes, rehearsing, setting up ranges, and all of the other details involved in training their troops. There was a great deal of weapons firing, much of it done on small "mini-ranges."

Command Post Exercises were conducted at every level from battalion up through district and division. There was training in chemical warfare, jungle warfare, commando tactics, and long marches and bivouacs. As the months went by, there were amphibious landings and night problems.

While the division was in Hawaii, orders were received to send the 160th Infantry, and the 143rd and 164th Field Artillery Battalions to the 27th Infantry Division. That order was later revoked.

There were routine exercises as the troops dispersed to defensive positions in practicing to repel a Japanese invasion. On occasion, there would be alerts. One diary entry for an officer in a unit out in a tactical exercise on December 5th, 1942: *"Marched until 10:00 a.m. when received a radio message to return to battalion area. We immediately entrucked and were back about 11:30 a.m. Big naval battle of the Islands last night, a Jap task force apparently trying to land. We have cleaned up, equipment handy and are waiting for the little b------- to arrive. Company L has left already for the saddle and ammo dump I hope they try!!!!"* As time went by, the troops often didn't know which were exercises and which were genuine alerts.

Tom Lawson, by now a young commander of Company H, 160th Infantry, was sometimes spending a couple of hours per day censoring mail. His diary entry for January 4, 1943: *"Went around to the five Ammunition Supply Points the company is guarding and looked them over. Also got acquainted with a few more of the men. It has been raining steadily here for the last two weeks off and on. Also covered the one O.P. we have down near Kona - a wonderful view from there. They eat better on these small outposts than we do here in the main camp. I even had some french fried potatoes this morning.*

"They are taking another cadre out of this regiment - this time 14 officers and 190-some odd men. I understand they are going to form three new regiments, two here and one on the mainland...Excellent chance for promotion for anyone getting transferred."

Many experienced men from the division were also sent off to Officer Candidate School. In one company alone (Company L, 160th Infantry) over seventy percent of the ninety-six enlisted men mobilized with the unit were promoted to commissioned ranks before the war was over.

Lawson's diary for January 5th read: *"Had charge of amphibious training today - not bad because everyone could swim a little bit. Worked on the road again this afternoon.* (He had been cutting a road near Parker Beach on the big island) *A lot of fun as far as I'm concerned, but the mosquitos are as big as cows. Went to slap one, and 3 knocked me down before I could swing the axe. The road is a tough job because of the large trees that must be moved and removed. They have huge tap roots. We have been moving them with dynamite and TNT, and then using a winch to pull them out. Broke two axes, a shovel, shear pin on winch (twice), 3 snatch-block chains, a screwdriver, and had 2 flat tires - so we aren't without our little troubles."*

On January 12th, Lawson's unit had Kawaihae added to their responsibilities. This included some old three and six-pounder naval guns from the U.S.S. Oklahoma. This firepower was in addition to the 75's he already had. He and his lieutenants spent their days inspecting weapons, ammunition dumps, range finders and other equipment. They also spent considerable time training the "Hawaiian Rifles," on crew-served weapons. A typical entry: *"I had the Hawaiian Rifles again this morning in machine gun drill and marksmanship. They try hard, and given enough time should make good soldiers."*

The Hawaiian Rifles were more formally called the Civilian Defense Corps. They were a form of militia formed into military units, and given Army training. Many of these Hawaiians were plantation personnel of Filipino extraction, with treatment by Japanese of their relatives in the Philippines very much on their minds. The Hawaiian Rifles were officered by "responsible citizens of the Hawaiian Islands," and were trained hard by personnel of the division.

Lawson's January 29th entry: *"I am duty officer tonight. Everyone has been seeing flares at sea. At 1930, Bill* (code name) *called and told me to have the skippers of two unidentified boats in*

Kanaihae Harbor call and tell Bill what their business was. At 2130 Captain Pancook called from district and said OP #16 had reported a red light blinking for the third night in a row. Turned out to be an automobile. At 2300 Beaver (another code name) *called - OP #13 had seen a green flare one mile at sea, that rose from the sea and returned to the sea at 2246. At 2248 OP #16 called Beaver and reported a blue flare at an angle of 305 degrees land to sea. I reported all these to Major Jones, Battalion Commander. They plotted all these things in the S-3 office and found where they were and sent the Navy to investigate. I wish I knew what they found."*

Rumors were rife, and every light at sea was suspected to be Japanese. Rarely did the troops actually see the enemy. An exception occurred about a mile off the beach in Nawiliwili Bay near Lihue on Kauai. A Japanese submarine surfaced while troops of the 185th were lined up for mess. The submarine started shelling right over their heads at large storage tanks on the hillside above the pineapple fields. These were the first shots the troops heard fired in anger. After a dozen or so shells, and no serious damage, the submarine left.

Some of the most important training was not on the formal curriculum. That included trying to make swimmers out of as many of the non-swimmers as possible. Many of the troops from California had been swimming from the time they were youngsters. That was not the case for many of the troops from other states. So there were many training sessions where accomplished swimmers would take twenty or so non-swimmers to any of the beautiful beaches all around the islands, and teach them basic survival swimming.

The troops put in long days preparing for combat. Up at 5:00 or 5:30 a.m. followed by "stand to," the leaders often didn't finish work until ten or eleven at night. The training was arduous, as reflected in Lieutenant Lawson's diary entry for March 12th: *"Left here at 0730 and went in trucks to the Halapani Trail. Detrucked*

80

at 1000 and started out hand carrying all weapons. I have never in all my life and all my marches been on a tougher one - not even the ten mile forced marches at Fort Lewis could compare with this one. The trail started at sea level and ends - from where we started, 13 miles further and 3000 feet higher - almost straight up. This was bad enough, but add to that the rolling lava rock and mud almost knee deep and there you have something. It took us seven and a half hours and we didn't lose a single man. That is good in any man's language or army. I carried some part of a mortar every step of the way for the last five hours. I took turns relieving men and they certainly liked that, the colonel was very pleased too - but right now I'm so tired I can hardly sit up. That leaves me just one thing to do, and I'm half way in bed right now!"

The troops were beginning to get an introduction to what would become one of the more vivid memories of many troops who trained or fought in the Pacific. That was the rain and humidity. It rained incessantly, spawning mosquitos and leeches. The troops fought mud, mold, rot and rust.

In late June and early July of 1943, the 143rd Field Artillery was moved to Oahu to replace the 52nd Field Artillery Battalion of the 35th Division in defending the north sector of the island of Oahu. The 143rd found highly developed gun positions already prepared by the 52nd, complete with circular steel tracks of small gauge rail. These supported a camouflage framework which could be quickly rolled aside to service the guns. There were deep ammunition pits, plus personnel shelters dug into the sides of the embankments. The command post and fire direction center were dug in and well ventilated.

In July of 1943 the division was concentrated on the island of Oahu, relieving the 24th Infantry Division of its mission of defense for the North Sector. Because of the large military installations all over Oahu, the fortifications were comparatively sophisticated and permanent. There were very senior headquarters on the island, and units of the division were constantly reminded they were now stationed "near the flag pole." Staff officers of the Hawaiian Department were constantly inspecting defenses around the island, and observing reactions to alerts.

On Kauai, the 185th Infantry was relieved of its duties by the 123rd Infantry Regiment of the 33rd Division of the Illinois National Guard on July 14, 1943. The 185th then moved to Oahu, relieving the 19th Regiment in defense of the Pupukea sector. In September, the 185th was relieved of its mission of defense so it could concentrate on advanced training.

When the 185th Infantry moved to Schofield Barracks, General Brush asked Captain Robert W. Munyon to be his aide-de-camp. Captain Munyon, commander of Headquarters Company, 1-185th Infantry, had come to Brush's attention when he organized much of the effort to get the fortifications built so quickly on Kauai. Munyon was to serve as his aide through almost all of the division's combat in World War II.

Typical of the training on Oahu was that outlined for the 185th Infantry. Each battalion combat team (reinforced battalion) spent one week at Waianae Amphibious Training Center, three weeks at the Pali Training Center and a week at the Waimanalo Advance Amphibious Training Center. Picked men from each unit were sent to Lieutenant Colonel D-Elisou's Ranger and Combat Training School for special training. Training was focused on jungle and amphibious training throughout this period.

All troops went through amphibious training, starting at a large grassy area in the residential area of Schofield Barracks. There were endless loading drills, and a great deal of practice on cargo nets. They started with mock-up ships built by the division engineers, climbing down to mock-up landing craft. There was practice in knot tying. This was followed by practice in tying and lowering equipment, ammunition boxes, mortars and machine guns. Leaders learned to organize units into boat parties, divisions and waves.

When the troops had completed basic amphibious training, they traveled to the Amphibious Training Center at Waianae on the west coast of Oahu for the second phase of training. This involved actual loading and landing from Landing Craft, Vehicle and Personnel (LCVP) and Landing Craft, Mechanized (LCM). Troops practiced loading trucks, tanks and bulldozers on landing craft, first from a pier to landing craft, and then from a barge to landing craft about two miles off shore.

From there units graduated to advanced amphibious training at Waimanalo, also under supervision of the Waianae Amphibious Training Center, on the windy east coast. There the amphibious craft bucked through breakers as the troops were tossed about in the small craft struggling through to the beaches.

The training graduated into live fire exercises using live ammunition. By this time, relationships had been established that would survive for most or all of the combat that followed. The 164th Field Artillery Battalion was paired with the 108th Infantry to form the 108th Regimental Combat Team, the 143rd Field Artillery Battalion with the 160th Infantry Regiment to form the 160th RCT, and the 213th Field Artillery Battalion with the 185th Infantry Regiment to form the 185th RCT. Each Regimental Combat Team also had a company from the 115th Engineer Battalion and another from the 115th Medical Battalion.

In October of 1943 the 6th Infantry Division took over responsibility for the North Sector, permitting the 40th to centralize units at Schofield Barracks. Some units, such as the 160th RCT with the 143rd Field Artillery moved into a hut city at Schofield Barracks. These huts were hastily built out of pine boards, two feet from each other and with about twenty foot wide company streets. The huts held ten men each, had an entrance at each end, screening completely around, and tar paper roofs.

While at Schofield, soldiers authorized carbines finally got them to replace their old Springfield rifles. The troops also had an opportunity to see Japanese weapons captured on Attu by the 32nd Infantry. They were particularly impressed with the Japanese air cooled heavy machine gun, which was equipped with effective control devices and a heavy tripod, as well as a telescopic sight for long range sniping.

In November and December of 1943, Army Ground Force Tests were administered to units to ensure they were ready for combat. This contributed to one of the favorite activities of the troops, speculating about where they were to be sent. Some of the strongest rumors involved India, Wake Island, and Australia or New Zealand. By this time the Hawaiian Islands were crowded with troops from all services. The Army divisions included the 6th, 7th, 27th and 33rd as well as the 40th. As the actual time for movement got closer, the speculation grew more accurate, generally narrowing down to either Australia or Guadalcanal.

In early December, divisional units were alerted for movement to Guadalcanal in the British Solomon Islands. In preparation for the movement to Guadalcanal, shots were administered for Smallpox, Typhoid Fever, Typhus, Yellow Fever, Tetanus and Cholera for those soldiers who needed them. Units filled out their Unit Personnel and Tonnage Tables. Finally, they crated and marked their equipment, and finalized load lists. Troops were told that December 16th was the last day for mail. Those who kept diaries took them to the theater censor.

The division started its move to Guadalcanal on December 20th. When time came for elements on the opposite side of Oahu from Pearl Harbor to actually make the movement, troops loaded up in the narrow gauge railway that followed the shoreline of the western side of Oahu to the tip of Barber's Point. From there the route cut through the mountains in a winding trip that ended up at Pearl Harbor. The troops loaded on ships in Honolulu Harbor.

Many were loaded on the U.S.S. Lurline, formerly a palatial liner of the Matson Steamship Company. It didn't seem so palatial to the troops, most of whom were berthed at the maximum of ten to twelve soldiers per compartment unless they were senior sergeants. The senior sergeants in some cases were assigned at only four per compartment.

There were the usual very long lines for messing which formed on the main deck and wound down to the dining room entrance. It took at least three hours per feeding on the ship, so only two meals were served each day. No complaints were heard, as the quality was excellent. In addition, the troops were able to sit down at tables with chairs. In fact, the Lurline was much more comfortable than the troop transports previously experienced by the Fortieth.

The artillerymen took over the many anti-aircraft artillery and machine guns all over the ship, while the infantry took responsibility for inner guard of the lower decks. There was little work for the approximately 7,500 passengers. The first sergeants handled what few details there were by using their duty rosters. Most of the ten days was spent in what the troops called "bunk fatigue" (sleeping).

The tedium of sleeping, reading, or standing in the long lines was broken by drills. Fire is always a great concern at sea, so Fire and Abandon Ship Drills were held regularly. They were some-times held twice a day until the troops could reach their stations on the main decks in four minutes or less.

The Lurline was so fast that it safely traveled without an escort. Several days out of Honolulu, the ship's loudspeaker told everyone that the ship would be traveling by way of the Fiji Islands in taking the troops close to their destination near Henderson Field, Guadalcanal.

Christmas day found the ship about 600 miles at sea. The sea was a beautiful blue, and the weather matched. Christmas carols were sung during services conducted on the main deck by the Navy chaplain aboard.

The equator was crossed at 1:30 p.m. on December 27th. The lack of space precluded the normal initiation into the "Mysteries of the Royal Order of the Deep," and Davy Jones. So everyone was issued a certificate or card instead. On other ships there were the traditional ceremonies to convert landlubbers to "shellbacks" when the ships crossed the equator.

Late the evening of December 28th, the Lurline's system picked up an unidentified "undersea watercraft." All guards were immediately doubled, and gun crews were on full alert all night. Everyone kept their life jacket handy, as few troops slept well that night.

The ship arrived at Pago Pago, American Samoa just before 6:00 p.m. on December 29, 1943. The ship remained there overnight for two reasons. One was to take on fresh water. The other was to allow time for the transport Matsonia to finish unloading troops at the one pier at Guadalcanal large enough to handle the Lurline. Troops were surprised to see that Pago Pago acted as though no war was on. Lights were blazing everywhere, a sight the troops hadn't seen at night for a very long time.

The Lurline left Pago Pago mid afternoon the next day, this time accompanied by destroyer escorts equipped with radar. The ship was heading into more dangerous waters, so unloading ladders were slung over the ships sides, along with life lines that hung down to the water's edge. Double blackout restrictions were placed on all personnel on board. Canteens were filled with fresh water and the men were ordered to wear them on the belt in addition to the life preserver during fire and abandon ship drills.

The weather was getting so hot that the accepted uniform of the day became life preserver, shorts, and shoes - - nothing else. On December 31st the Lurline crossed the International Date Line, making it January 1st. On that day the Lurline's captain ordered all guns on the ship to be test fired. Targets were dropped over the side for gunners to shoot at, none of which floated for long after the troops opened fire.

On the first day of 1944, the ship passed to the north of the Fiji Islands. The destroyer escorts were joined shortly before dark by a B-25 bomber, which remained until the ships were in the vicinity of the New Hebrides Islands.

The small convoy entered the Coral Sea on January 2, 1944. The troops began to anticipate landing and getting on firm ground again. In the meantime, the ship had to be cleaned from top to bottom because the ship was to be immediately reloaded with some 3,000 wounded soldiers, sailors and marines who had been hospitalized on Guadalcanal for a long time.

On January 3rd a Navy destroyer joined the escort group as the convoy passed well south of the Santa Cruz Islands. After midnight on January 4th the troops could see San Cristobal Island, so they knew they were close to their final destination. Later in the day the Lurline dropped anchor near Lunga Point. When the troops got a look at Guadalcanal, they were struck by the sight of coconut trees stretching for miles in each direction. They looked like strange telephone poles because the tops had been shot off. The troops began the unloading process via small craft of all description. When the troops had been discharged, the Lurline moved twelve miles to the docks at Kukum Pier, where it unloaded the balance of the cargo. Much equipment was lost in the process, as the ship was unloaded as fast as possible with all equipment placed in a common pile regardless of markings.

The troops established bivouac areas, but not without incident. Some Japanese casualties had been buried in shallow common graves, so often the troops would hit a recently buried body when digging slit trenches or latrines. There had also been a catastrophic explosion of the Hell's Point ammunition dump, caused by a grass fire early in December 1943. Ammunition worth $143 million was destroyed, with shells and fragments scattered all over the island. Troops had to be careful around the duds they kept finding everywhere, and which occasionally would explode.

The troops greatest problem, however, was the weather. It rained and rained even though it was hot. Mud was everywhere. Troops were finally provided pyramidal tents to replace their pup tents. Most men wore pants with the legs cut off, and complained about huge rats, plus lice and mosquitos. In the evening they would button up their clothes, tuck their trousers inside their socks and wear a head net over their helmets regardless of the heat in order to protect themselves from malarial mosquitos.

By the middle of January, the movement of the division from Oahu had been completed. Troops were ordered to always wear their helmets. Not to protect themselves from the enemy, but from the very real danger of coconuts falling on their heads. There were coconuts everywhere, planted primarily by the Procter and Gamble Company, and the heavy coconuts falling 60 or 70 feet could be deadly.

The natives were very friendly. The Japanese had treated them poorly, especially the women. The natives were small, wiry, strong, and willing to work for 16¢ per day or two sticks of trade tobacco. On Tuesday, March 1st, word came down that some Japanese had attacked the natives on the north part of the island, and attempted to rape the women. The division sent out patrols to wipe them out.

Master Sergeant Walter E. Newman, Sergeant Major of the 143rd Field Artillery described the natives:

"Natives are ferocious looking. Some of the men wear bones in their noses, and both men and women embroider their black skins with a lacework stitched in blue. The women sometimes paint their faces red and white and green under the eyes, but blue paint seems most popular.

"The troops enjoyed the natives, but tended to tell outrageous tales about their cannibalism and head-hunting. The natives actually eat a lot of yams, which are much less tasty than those we are used to.

"Native houses have no walls. Families all sleep very closely together. However, when they wake up in the morning, men and women who have been snoring into one another's ears all night greet each other with the same reserve as if they had slept behind walls all night.

"You are required to knock before entering a hut. There is no door to knock on, and hardly anything to come into when you enter, but you knock on the closest pole anyhow. The head of the household says very graciously, "Okay fellah makem quicken come along in?" To lock up an unwalled house, the natives hang from the edge of the roof a dried gourd or cocoanut (sic) on which a spell has been cast. Anyone who passes under it in the absence of the owner is convinced that he will have bad luck.

"When the war came to Guadalcanal, most householders hung up gourds and retired to the inland bush. When they returned some eight months later, many discovered that the Japs had shot their houses out from under the gourds. Witch doctors had a tough time explaining that.

"Native women wear nothing but scanty grass skirts, but one "ogle" at a South Sea belle usually satisfied our men. Women do most of the work, although men join the women when they are so inclined, which is quite often.

"Natives have little sense of time, and will do things "byemby." Their "kai-kai," or barbecue, is something else. A number of cows wander around Guadalcanal. No one is expected to pay for one killed by the Japanese. So the natives put a cow out where they expect it to get bombed by the Japs. When it hits, whoever ends up with a piece of the cow, it is his. After it is cooked and eaten, the troops would often treat the natives to a movie.

"The natives enjoy them greatly, but their eyes become round over things that upset them. For instance, when a man walks alongside of a girl, and when the hero kisses a girl, they always look shyly away and peek out of the corners of their eyes."

Artillerymen from the division were tasked to train in directing naval gunfire, which would be used in support of landings at least until organic artillery became operational. The troops selected for this duty were sent to schools run on the island by Marines. Later they accompanied navy ships to nearby islands still occupied by the Japanese. There they observed and directed naval gunfire, generally surprised at how accurate it could be.

On March 25th, the 40th Division was transferred to General MacArthur's command, along with the 25th, 37th, 43rd, 93rd and Americal Divisions. The Americal had been created based on National Guard regiments from Illinois, North Dakota, and Massachusetts. The 40th was subsequently assigned to Lieutenant General Oscar W. Griswold's XIV Corps of Lieutenant General Walter Krueger's Sixth Army.

The division continued its practice in amphibious operations. The word came down that the division was to form part of the 1st Marine Amphibious Corps, and land on New Ireland April 1st to secure Kavieng and the big Japanese airfield there. New Ireland was the second largest island (about 190 miles long), of the Bismarck Archipelago. Kavieng was a heavily fortified enemy stronghold on the northern tip of New Ireland. The plan, code-named "Fore-Arm," called for the 160th to make a diversionary landing at Lossuk Bay on D minus one. The rest of the division was to hit Kavieng on D and D plus one.

The size of the force the division would face on New Ireland was initially estimated at 12,000. The estimates were later raised to 14,000, and then to 15,000. Two practice landings were made, with the transports actually combat loaded. However, on March 24th, the word came down that the landings on New Ireland were cancelled. Transports which had been loaded were then unloaded, much to the disappointment of the troops. The reason was simple. The Navy and Air Corps had significantly neutralized the enemy on New Ireland. General MacArthur decided to leapfrog New Ireland, so ground troops weren't required.

Morale had slipped after the invasion of New Ireland was cancelled. Those spirits soared again when word came that the division was to move to New Britain and relieve the 1st Marine Division at Cape Gloucester and the Army forces at Arawe. Advance elements of the division left early in April.

CHAPTER FIVE

INTRODUCTION TO COMBAT

In April, the troops loaded up again into transports preparatory to moving from Guadalcanal to Cape Gloucester on New Britain, part of the Bismarck Archipelago. At 5:00 p.m. on April 22nd, troops aboard the transports off Lunga Point were informed that an undetermined number of Japanese submarines had been contacted in the Sealark Channel that leads to Lunga Point. General Quarters was sounded and all lights aboard the vessels were immediately extinguished. All personnel donned life jackets while several destroyers from the convoy raced towards an area just off the Florida Islands near Tulagi. It wasn't long before the troops could hear and feel the concussions from depth charges even though they were several miles away. At 7:50 p.m., the order to secure from General Quarters was sounded. The destroyers continued to move back and forth, searching with searchlights. They did spot some oil slicks on the surface, indicating that one or more submarines may have at least been damaged.

The troops remained aboard the ships in port until late the evening of April 25th, when that convoy weighed anchor and moved out under the protection of nine escorts. The seas were exceptionally rough, and the rain poured.

Each morning the troops would be ordered on deck with life jackets for the seaborne version of "stand to" to stand "dawn alert" at 5:00 a.m. This was considered the most vulnerable time for the convoy.

On April 28th, one of the convoys was subjected to an air attack by about ten planes, probably from Rabaul. Two were shot down, and the rest chased away by anti-aircraft fire, heading back towards the north of New Britain.

Finchaven on New Guinea was passed by the convoy. It was lit up at night, looking like a cluster of jewels off in the distance, with apparently no blackout restrictions. By 11:00 a.m. on April 29th the last of the ships carrying the division dropped anchor at Borgen Bay. Small craft unloaded the troops and equipment.

Advance elements of the Fortieth Division had already landed on 23 April to assume responsibility for New Britain from the 1st Marine Division and the other troops that were part of the Backhander Task Force. Backhander was the name given to the holding and security troops on the island of New Britain. The troops found that the Marines had little opportunity to make improvements to their positions. There was a lot of rainfall, with heavy winds, lightning and thunder.

New Britain is a very rugged island, oblong in shape, and running generally northeast and southwest. Rabaul, occupied by the Japanese for the duration of the war, was the largest city and located at the northern tip. Cape Gloucester was at the southern end, with Talasea on a short peninsula jutting northward from the center of the island. Mountainous ridges and dense jungle domi-nated the interior. The main communications and transportation routes were via trails running along the coasts on either side of the island.

The heavy rain muddied the trails and made them all but impassable. There were no roads as such. Much of the resupply had to be handled by LCM's which shuttled supplies up and down the coast. Emergency evacuations were quite often accomplished by Navy PBY amphibious aircraft.

The troops also found a great many rats carrying typhus on the island. They were told the rats had been brought in on Japanese transports, and had since multiplied by the thousands in the tall kunai grass. The kunai grass also held poisonous insects and large tropical snakes, so the troops were told to stay out. Unfortunately, a large number of the natives had died from typhus.

Shortly after he landed in the Cape Gloucester area, Major General Rapp Brush announced he was assuming command of the Backhander Task Force. It was about this time that the division's leadership began to experience frustration with General Krueger, commanding Sixth Army. Headquarters units routinely experience some frustration with higher headquarters, especially when they feel they are being micro-managed. The frustration seems to have been especially virulent in the relationship between General Krueger and the 40th Division. General Krueger was seen as a tight-lipped, un-smiling micro-manager who never got along well with senior leadership in the division.

The 40th had a series of increasingly serious problems with General Krueger. Many were convinced that General Krueger had phase lines (but only in his head) with estimated rates of advance. General Brush was particularly frustrated by General Krueger's propensity to measure "scheduled advances" against actual personnel losses. If your casualties weren't very heavy, General Krueger tended to assume you weren't fighting hard enough. Everyone was happier when the 40th was eventually transferred to General Eichelberger's command.

The division was given the mission of neutralizing all enemy forces outside of the area of Rabaul, while containing the large force of Japanese in Rabaul itself. The lower half of New Britain was in the hands of American troops, from Arawe on the south, to Talasea on the north. The 108th RCT was placed at Arawe, while the 160th RCT was placed at Cape Gloucester near the western end of the island, along with division headquarters and special troops of the division. The 185th RCT, supported by the 213th Field Artillery Battalion, was placed at Talasea. At Kimbe Bay, the 185th was in constant contact with large Japanese patrols and reconnaissance parties. Survivors of these contacts were brought in to be questioned by the Division G-2. They revealed that there were about 37,000 partially equipped Japanese troops on the island. They were preparing for a last stand in the vicinity of Rabaul, on the Gazelle Peninsula at the extreme northeast tip of the island. Most of the Japanese seemed to be half starved.

Much of the friendly patrolling was conducted by using small boats and moving along the shore to designated spots, disembarking, and moving inland on foot. Australian coast watchers and the natives were also very helpful in providing intelligence on enemy activities.

185th Intelligence and Reconnaissance Platoon, with the help of natives, surveys jungle for evidence of Japanese activity on New Britain. May 2, 1944 (Photo: National Archives)

One of the grim tragedies of war occurred on April 29th. There was a flotilla of Patrol Torpedo (PT) boats on New Britain that would routinely send out three boats to raid Japanese shipping trying to resupply Rabaul. They would make the runs at night, making sure they were back behind the bomb line by daylight. On this night, a small group of soldiers from the 185th Infantry went along for the ride. Unfortunately, their boat got hung up on a reef near Cape Pomas, on the enemy side of the bomb line, when returning from Rabaul. The other boats were attempting to pull the stranded boat off the reef when dawn broke. U.S. Navy aircraft returning from Rabaul and the torpedo boats mistook each other for the enemy. Two of the planes were shot down, and two of the boats were hit. The popular Executive Officer of the 185th, Lieutenant Colonel James B. Pettit, was killed, with several others seriously wounded. Pettit, along with others, had jumped overboard when they were being strafed. His body was never found, and he was the first officer in the regiment killed during the war.

Natives, called Fiji Scouts, were put to good use on New Britain. About a dozen of these fierce fighters would often be seen around the division headquarters. Their appearance did not meet our soldierly standards, with their fuzzy hair, bare feet and lap-lap cloth. However, they proved extremely valuable. They were sent out to perform reconnaissance, usually at night, and were apparently fearless. They claimed they could smell the Japanese before they could see them, and on occasion would kill a Japanese or two even though that wasn't their primary mission. They also helped by carrying supplies to the Australian coast watchers, who maintained constant watch on Rabaul.

New Britain was administered by the Australians, so all traffic drove on the left side. Americans had trouble getting used to this, and some bad accidents resulted. However, when the island was completely inundated with Americans, traffic naturally evolved to the right-hand side.

The heavy jungle made movement extremely difficult. The pouring rain and mud were constant problems as patrols went out to locate and neutralize the enemy. Short roads were constructed by the engineers, but travel on the roads was a challenge due to the heavy rain and deep mud a great deal of the time. Much of the resupply was performed by aircraft and LCM's. Emergency medical evacuations were made by Navy PBY's and Army Air Corps L-5's. The division artillery spotter aircraft flew daily liaison schedules when weather permitted.

Another patrol cruising along the coast lines in Navy PT boats killed 20 Japanese in a fire fight at the mouth of the Mevelo River. These were apparently stragglers from Gasmata, a Japanese outpost in a village on the southern coast of New Britain, who were trying to get to the Japanese enclave at Rabaul. During the course of the fight, the Japanese threw a number of rifles into the river, along with ammunition and supplies. Six more were killed on the Dagi River attempting to reach Rabaul. By May of 1944, 4,300 Japanese had been killed and 300 taken prisoner by American troops.

The 143rd Field Artillery moved its gun positions to the beach lines at Cape Gloucester. There small parties of Japanese attempted landing and sortie raids on the artillery battalion. Ten Japanese were killed and one landing barge was destroyed by direct fire from the 105mm howitzers.

There was little time for recreation, but the troops did enjoy swimming out to the coral reefs several hundred yards off shore. There they found shallow, clear water where they could collect sea shells. They would dig the shells out with their trench knives, with many of them stringing the shells into necklaces. However, they had to be careful of the electric eels that inhabited the reefs.

There was very little else in the way of entertainment to provide relief from the tedium. There was some fishing (usually the "hand grenade" method). In the rear areas there were athletic programs, and movies available three times a week. Occasionally there would be U. S. O. shows, which could always count on a large and enthusiastic audience.

One troupe consisted of Jack Benny, Larry Adler (considered the world's greatest harmonica player), singer Martha Tilton, film beauty Carole Landis, and others. They were supposed to be with the division only a couple of days, but the Japanese started making threatening moves just when it was time for the troupe to leave.

They were forced to stay on the island for a few extra days, and the troops lucky enough to eat in the headquarters mess tent got to know the celebrities rather well.

Unfortunately, Jack Benny's famous violin was coming apart in the dampness and high humidity. General Brush's aide was sent out to find a violin repairman. Jack Benny was beside himself, but as is typical in any National Guard division, almost any kind of specialist can be found. The violin repairman took glue and clamps and quickly mended Mr. Benny's venerable violin before the troupe left the island.

On May 6, 1944 Company E, 2-185th was reinforced with a gun section from the 213th Field Artillery and departed San Remo by boat for a point on the northwest coast. Commanded by Major Albert J. Muhic, the mission of the unit was to retake Hoskins airstrip. This was accomplished around noon on May 7th, the Japanese having withdrawn before the unit arrived. The airstrip was overgrown with underbrush, and was booby trapped and mined with aerial bombs. The airstrip itself was prepared for use by 5:00 p.m., although it took additional time to clear the surrounding areas of booby traps. Unfortunately, three men were killed and a howitzer completely destroyed by a mine.

There was an imposing hill mass adjacent to the air strip, but no activity was observed on the hills. About three weeks after Hoskins air strip had been occupied, a group of fourteen Japanese was captured in a nearby village. Captured documents and reports showed that these Japanese were in a stay-behind detachment left to establish an observation post on the hill mass overlooking Hoskins. They were provided rations for thirty days and a radio to report American activities to Rabaul. Their supplies ran out and their batteries were depleted, so they evacuated their position to make contact with a Japanese submarine along the coast. The submarine never picked them up, and the party was stranded. Those that were not captured ended up being killed when caught on the few trails in the area.

The battle for New Britain evolved into a new strategy of containing the enemy without unduly arousing their ire, which minimized casualties to friendly forces. The Japanese around Arawe on the southern coast had been quickly defeated, and the remnants scrambled to reach enemy enclaves. These remnants eventually dried up through attrition, as it became impossible for the Japanese at Rabaul to resupply the widely scattered remnants around the island. They tried, but every time they sent a boat or barge down the coast, they were intercepted by allied aircraft or PT boats. The thousands of well armed Japanese at Rabaul, on the other hand, would have been a tough nut to crack. Yet they were not a problem for allied forces, as Japanese ships no longer tried to berth there, and aircraft were destroyed almost as fast as they arrived.

Rabaul had five excellent air strips, and was adjacent to a superior harbor, so would have made an outstanding logistical base for the allies. That need was obviated, however, when the allies captured excellent facilities in the Admiralties.

On the 26th of July, the 143rd Field Artillery Battalion sent Master Sergeant Walter E. Newman and five other enlisted men to the vicinity of Hoskins Bay to search for possible gun positions. Master Sergeant Newman's account:

"Leaving the battalion area before daybreak in a 3/4 ton weapons carrier and a jeep we followed the coast line past Borgen Bay and the Famous Hill 660 (where Marines fought a terrific battle) to where the road ended. Continuing along the beach sands crossing 7 small streams outlets (sic) *into the ocean. Before attempting to cross these streams with the vehicles we would send a man across first to measure the depth. If safe, would send the jeep over first followed by the weapons carrier. If the jeep failed to make the trip the weapons carrier would go over, pay out the cable and tow it to the opposite bank - wait for the motor to dry out and continue on. Further on up the coast line we passed many abandoned Japanese positions and Command Post installations with the beaches strewn for several miles with abandoned Japanese*

landing barges and ammunition of all descriptions - some in excellent condition. In one place we located a large quantity of rifles, helmets and miscellaneous pieces of new Japanese equipment and clothing.

"In one foxhole we found a dead Jap, only he was minus his entire skin, the ants and insects had done their work very nicely. What a mess! A mile beyond this point in an open area surrounded by a thick heavy growth of jungle vines and brush we discovered some 450 bodies of dead Japs. These were not shot but had starved to death! Many of them still remained in good state of preservation and some of them were still in their foxholes, cramped or in a sitting position. The reconnaissance at this point was decided terminated (sic) *due to the small number of personnel in our party and in close proximity to "country" occupied by the Japs we immediately returned to base camp."*

Division patrols located two Japanese Zero's near Baluma. Both planes had the cockpits burned out but were apparently untouched otherwise. Some Japanese were killed by shelling from divisional artillery near the Malim on August 12th, 1944 that was placed on houses and installations. North of Keip, with the help of dogs, six Japanese were surprised and killed.

Natives reported that there were sixty Japanese near the gardens at the northeast corner of Pondo Plantation and at an observation post on a hill in the same area. A mile and a quarter east of the Pondo Plantation, another ninety Japanese were reported in bivouac near the Tawanokoko River. A later report indicated another 300 mixed group of Japanese Navy and Army troops in tunnels along the coast just north of Pondo. Further north near Pomas several observation posts were located, as well as a rice dump of approximately 2000 bags of rice with the gardens being worked by small parties of Japanese. Total Japanese killed by mid-August on New Britain was 4,317. This was only a slight increase over the number that had been killed by late Spring, reflecting the containment policy that had been instituted earlier.

Cape Gloucester for several months a year featured incredible wind storms. When these occurred, almost daily during two months of the dry season, the troops fought both the lava dust and wind damage. The damage ranged from shredded tents and damaged buildings, to felled trees. Falling trees killed at least one soldier and injured several others. The dust was everywhere, and shower facilities were almost nonexistent, so the creeks and ocean got a lot of visitors.

Only a few men could get furloughs, so their names were usually drawn by lot. The lucky winners would get their fifteen day furloughs in Australia, which turned out to be a delightful experience. A soldier with two hundred dollars could have a great time in the land down under, where "the Yanks" were always welcome.

On September 4th, a terrific tropical storm hit the area located at the north end of the Cape Gloucester. The air strips at Cape Gloucester particularly suffered as the runways consisted more or less of loose dirt and dust. With high velocity winds running between 90 and 110 miles per hour sweeping down from the slopes of Mount Talawae across the loose runways and through the 143rd Field Artillery Battalion area, night was created from the broiling hot day. Tons of dirt and dust disappeared into the sea, carrying many communications lines and light items of equipment. Kitchens were wrecked, tents damaged and, along with some personal equipment, blown away. There also were personal injuries to several men. To complicate the situation, a "red alert" was sounded which meant everybody into their foxholes to stay no matter what happened.

Troops were increasingly becoming acclimated to jungle warfare and fighting the highly experienced Japanese soldiers. They were learning to advance cautiously, as the Japanese were masters of camouflage. In one instance, soldiers knew there was a small anti-tank gun in front of them, but were within four feet of the weapon before they spotted it.

At night, noise and light discipline had to be strictly enforced, or the Japanese would take advantage of the oversight. Our troops were getting used to the weird noises at night. Those noises ranged from those made by land crabs and lizards to the sounds of monkeys and birds. Some of the sounds were so strange that the men found it hard to believe they came from birds. One species of bird had a call that resembled a dog barking. Another sounded like blocks of wood banging together.

The 185th RCT was relieved by the 1st Australian Division on October 19th. During the first week in November, the 108th RCT joined the rest of the division in the vicinity of Cape Gloucester. The units then received replacements and much new equipment. The division also practiced amphibious landings from several types of amphibious craft.

As the division prepared for its landing on Luzon, they got word that another field artillery battalion would be joining them for the invasion. It turned out that the division already had a special tie to this battalion. The tie went back to the arrival of the division in Hawaii two years before. The 143rd had been asked to provide a cadre of soldiers to form a new field artillery battalion in the United States. Sixty-one soldiers said their good-byes, and headed east to help form the 757th 155mm Howitzer Battalion. Almost two years were spent in getting organized and training in California, Oklahoma, Kansas and Louisiana. On November 28, 1944, three LST's sailed into Borgen Bay, New Britain with that same 757th Field Artillery Battalion.

No major battles were fought by the division on New Britain, and the division was relieved on November 27th, 1944. The division returned to amphibious training on Lae, New Guinea, in preparation for the invasion of Luzon. The staffs had worked on preparing detailed plans for the invasion, with the plans then briefed all the way down to company level. There were briefs, brief-backs and rehearsals until all of the troops were comfortable with the role they were to play during the invasion. On December 1st, 1944, as the first major combat faced the 40th, Major General Brush sent a message to all soldiers of the division -

> "We are now entering the most important period in our lives and in the history of our division. The operation in which we are about to participate constitutes the culmination of three long years of war in the Pacific. I am sure that every member of the division is proud that we have been selected to participate in the spearhead attack on this vital objective.

> "Through long periods of rigorous training we have molded and hardened ourselves into a highly efficient combat team. Those periods are now behind us. We are about to receive the real test. I feel that we are fully prepared to meet this test and bring the operation to a speedy and successful conclusion. I have the utmost confidence in you.

> "Good luck and God bless you. THIS IS IT!"

The troops loaded on ships in Borgen Bay on December 9th using small craft and lighters. The next day, the convoy began moving, and by late that night dropped anchor at the Manos Island Navy Base, 120 miles from Borgen Bay. Lights were on, both on shore and aboard the ships, as normal blackout restrictions were generally ignored. Movies were shown on the main decks of some of the troop ships. The convoy was there for some time, while waiting for the convoy carrying the 37th Infantry Division. "Liberty" was enjoyed by some of the troops at the Navy base there. The Navy Chief Petty Officers' Club sold beer for ten cents a can or bottle to Army sergeants.

On December 16th, the convoy moved out. The convoy arrived off Lae, New Guinea late the evening of December 17th, where it remained at anchor for several days. Landing parties went ashore to select sites for practice amphibious landings. The units practiced for several days before returning to the Admiralties. The troops were getting tired of the constant drilling and practices. As a consequence, their trepidation was slightly offset by the anticipation of being on firm ground again. Sergeant Newman's description of life aboard a transport:

"Troops on board a transport are crowded most of the time, therefore are not as active as on shore. You begin to get "crabby and cross." Everything is run by "lines." You line up for this, and you line up for that, until it becomes monotonous and there is no outlet. You'll probably stand in line at the Ship's Post Exchange for two hours and wind up getting a tube of toothpaste. In the washrooms it is a case of shaving yourself or somebody else, there is very little room. To use the "throne" one must be an acrobat...the seats are some three feet off the deck and are slightly slanted - you roll with the ship while in process of relieving yourself, and you need a ladder to get down afterwards."

The heavily fortified island of Luzon was key to liberation of the Philippines. First, however, control of the southern flank of Luzon had to be wrested from the Japanese through invasion of the islands of Leyte, Samar and Mindoro. Luzon, the most northern of the many Philippine Islands, was only two hundred miles from Formosa (Taiwan), which was heavily fortified and considered Japan's "unsinkable aircraft carrier."

The liberation of Luzon was the object of the M-1 operation. Intelligence estimated the enemy strength on Luzon as 250,000. About half of that figure were considered mobile combat troops. The Lingayen Gulf area, north of the urbanized area of Manila Bay, was selected for the initial landings. Unlike the heavy concentrations of troops in the area of Manila, it was estimated there were only about 1,500 troops in the Lingayen area, although the excellent road network on Luzon would facilitate rapid reinforcement.

The tactical plan was to quickly establish a stronghold on Luzon, complete with airfields for use by our air forces. The objective was then to assault Manila, with support of the air force, through the "back door" over the Central Plain of Luzon.

The assault landing was to be conducted with two corps abreast, using the 6th and 43rd Divisions of Major General Innis P. Swift's I Corps, and the 37th and 40th Divisions of Major General Oscar W. Griswold's XIV Corps. General Griswold's corps was to be arrayed with the 37th on the left, adjacent to I Corps, and the 40th on the right. In the 40th Division sector, the 160th was to land on the left, and the 185th on the right, with the 108th afloat in corps reserve. Each assault regiment would land with two battalions abreast, the 160th RCT at Green Beach on the left flank, and the 185th RCT at Orange Beach on the right.

The invasion had been delayed for several reasons. There were delays caused by waiting for essential supplies and changes in priorities. In addition, the loading beach and lighterage conditions were less than ideal. To add to the delays, the invasion was put off for another twenty days due to strategic reasons. Leyte was taking longer to secure than anticipated, because the Japanese had heavily reinforced there. Diversion of transports and escort ships to support Leyte and land an additional division there (the 77th), in addition to such factors as moon phasing, forced General MacArthur to delay the invasion of Luzon.

On Christmas Eve the troops were fed sauerkraut and weiners. On Christmas they had pork chops for supper. A rehearsal of the Luzon assault landing was conducted at Lae, New Guinea. After problems were identified and corrections initiated, the ships returned to Manus, the largest of the Admiralty Islands.

Taking advantage of the delays, a rehearsal was conducted at Huon Gulf, eastern New Guinea. The troops felt they were over trained. They not only had completed formal amphibious training in Hawaii, but had participated in several practice landings. Their latest rehearsal in New Guinea reflected considerable lack of ardor. General Griswold was unhappy with the 40th's "general failure to observe the spirit of the rehearsal." This failure to enthusiastically rehearse was undoubtedly due to the many amphibious and assault landing courses and rehearsals they had previously participated in.

Nonetheless, the division was forced to conduct further training at Manus Island in the Admiralties.

The convoy formed up at the end of the year. There were over 800 ships of all sizes, including Vice Admiral Jesse B. Oldendorf's large warships. His fleet of carriers, battleships, cruisers and smaller vessels were to arrive off Luzon three days ahead of the troop ships so they could bombard the Lingayen shoreline prior to the assault waves going in. The troops were loaded in Vice Admiral Theodore S. Wilkinson's Lingayen Task Force. All got under way on December 31st.

Troops by now had been on board the crowded troop ships three weeks. When the convoy got underway, travel thoughts were interrupted by reports of submarine and aircraft sightings. Shortly after daylight on the morning of January 6, 1945, enemy airplanes attacked the convoy. No damage was suffered by the ships, although one plane was shot down and four others dispersed. Reports that midget submarines had been spotted resulted in a constant barrage of depth charges most of the night.

The convoy entered the Sulu Sea, between the northwestern tip of Mindanao and the southern part of Negros Island, subsequently passing to the westward side of Panay to cut between Panay and the Cuyo Island group. The islands of Mindanao, Negros and Panay were still strongly occupied by Japanese forces and aggressive enemy attacks were expected, but they didn't come until the next day.

At 9:00 p.m. the convoy had entered Mindoro Strait, bordered by the Calamian Group, and the Island of Mindoro. A night raid was in progress by allied forces on the island of Mindoro, and the burst of bombs on Japanese positions could plainly be seen by troops on the transports. A Japanese oil tanker, which had been hit and was beached, was burning furiously at the water's edge.

The convoy entered the China Sea at 4:00 a.m. on January 8, 1945 and headed for Luzon. At 5:00 p.m., General Quarters was sounded, as Japanese aircraft had been sighted. They attacked but were driven off by anti-aircraft fire from the ships before they caused any damage.

Six planes returned in about fifteen minutes, and commenced kamikaze attacks. All but one plane were shot down by anti-aircraft fire or carrier planes. The one aircraft slipped through, and hit the escort carrier U.S.S. Liscombe Bay at the water line on the port side of its stern. The ship quickly began to list, and within about ten minutes, several of the planes slipped off its flight deck into the sea. The planes in the air had no place to land, and some had to ditch in the sea also. The small carrier was forced to withdraw from the convoy, and eventually had to be sunk by our own destroyers.

The Navy had worked hard to smooth the way for the assault teams. Minesweepers and Underwater Demolition Teams had done their work. Then the entire fleet in the area had bombarded the City of Lingayen and beach installations for three days. They fired inland for several thousand yards. The capitol building, plainly visible from the sea, was to be spared as it was to be used later as headquarters. Some return fire was seen coming from the capitol building, so the small arms fire was answered with the fleet's big guns. Smoke sometimes obscured the targets, so the big guns would occasionally be silent to allow the heavy pall of smoke to drift away. The sickening smell of powder was everywhere.

The assault landing, as always, was disseminated in detailed operations orders. Operations Order BLT (Battalion Landing Team) 160-1 was typical.

BLT 160-1 will destroy all enemy in zone of action, advance to DBHL (Division Beachhead Line) and secure:

(1) That portion of LINGAYEN AIRFIELD in BLT zone of advance.

(2) The CALMAY RIVER crossing on the LINGAYEN-BAAY ROAD (Objective No. 1)

(3) The AGNO RIVER crossing on the BAAY-SALASA ROAD. (Objective No. 2) and establishing strong roadblocks protecting road junction in SALASA (Objective No. 3).

(4) Maintain contact with BLT 160-3 on left.

The various battalion landing teams were augmented as appropriate. BLT 160-1 consisted of:

1st Battalion 160th Infantry
1st Platoon Cannon Company, 160th Infantry
1st Platoon Antitank Company, 160th Infantry
Mine Platoon, Antitank Company, 160th Infantry
Company B 115th Engineer Battalion (less 2nd & 3rd Platoons)
1st Platoon Company C 82nd Chemical Battalion (Heavy Mortars)
1st Platoon Company C 640th Tank Destroyer Battalion
1st Platoon 40th Cavalry Reconnaissance Troop
593rd JASCO A.L.P. (Air Liaison Party)
593rd JASCO S.F.C.P. (Shore Fire Control Party)
1/2 Company A, 115th Medical Battalion
Detachment, 658th Amphibious Tractor Battalion (20 LVTs)

The BLT 160-1 operations order was five mimeographed pages. Attached were five annexes. Annex One was the operations overlay, which consisted of one hand-drawn page. Annex Two was the Intelligence Annex, and consisted of five pages. Appendix One to Annex Two covered the enemy situation, which admittedly was rather obscure, and based on nebulous information. Appendix Two was a Situation Map, and Appendix Three was a Reconnaissance Map.

The Intelligence Annex described an estimated 24,000 troops facing the division in the general area of the Lingayen Gulf, of an estimated total of 116,500 Japanese troops on Luzon. It was further estimated that enemy ground forces were supported by 205 fighter aircraft and 140 bombers. Specific enemy capabilities described for the division:

Defend the LINGAYEN area with approximately eight (8) battalions supported by artillery and light tanks, plus naval base forces, from successive defense lines (a) along the beach, (b) along the CALMAY and/or AGNO RIVERS, and (c) along the general line AGUILAR-SAN CARLOS.

Annex Three had the Boat Assignment Tables, filling thirteen pages. The first two waves had the assault troops, loaded in ten

Landing Vehicle, Tracked (LVT) in each wave. The LVTs were to land the troops and support them by fire (they were generally armed with .50 calibre machine-guns). The LVTs were then to haul supplies from the beach and assist in crossing rivers. Another seven waves included thirty-two LCMs, and twenty-three LVCPs. There was another wave (the third), which consisted of a single LCVP. It held the battalion commander and his party, and was free to roam at his command. All infantrymen were ashore by wave five. The engineers and chemical (heavy mortar) troops first appeared in wave six. Antitank capability and artillerymen first appeared in wave seven. Medical personnel were scattered throughout, with aidmen in the initial waves, and the medical platoon on wave nine.

Annex Four was the Wave Diagram and Landing Schedule. The single page displayed the ten waves, and scheduled them for landing in three minute intervals. The six pages of Annex Five covered communications. The Administrative Order consisted of eleven pages appended to the Operations Order. It included the Medical Plan, a Civil Affairs Plan, and listings of equipment and supplies to accompany individuals.

The troops had detailed plans, and were thoroughly oriented. Amphibious techniques had been practiced, and practiced again. The troops had the normal pre-invasion jitters, but felt they were as ready as they ever would be.

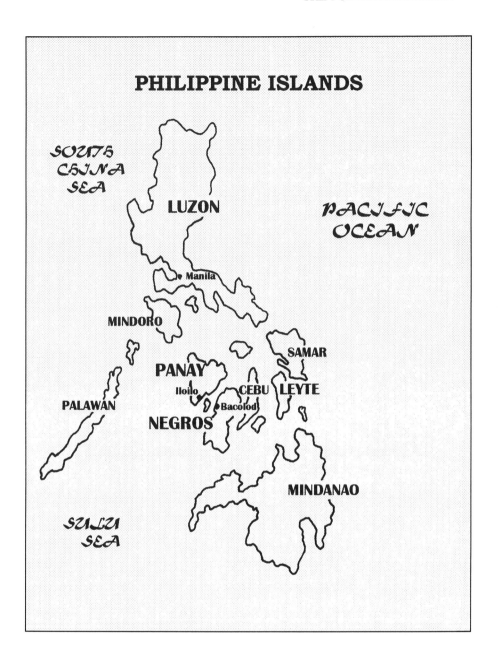

PHILIPPINE ISLANDS

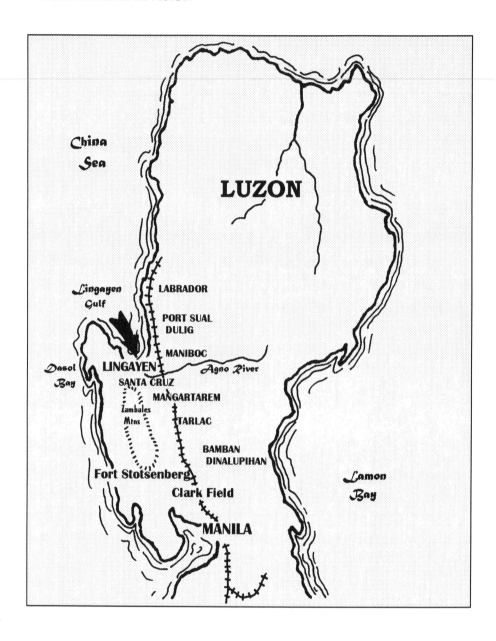

China
Sea

LUZON

Lingayen
Gulf

LABRADOR

PORT SUAL
DULIG

MANIBOC

Dasol
Bay

LINGAYEN

Agno River

SANTA CRUZ

MANGARTAREM

Zambales
Mtns

TARLAC

BAMBAN
DINALUPIHAN

Fort Stotsenberg

Lamon
Bay

Clark Field

MANILA

CHAPTER SIX

THE INVASION OF LUZON

The event the troops had trained for so long and hard, and anticipated with great trepidation, dawned on January 9, 1945. The heavy firing of the big naval guns reached a crescendo at about 8:45 a.m. No enemy artillery fire was received in return. A group of Filipino guerrillas flagged a destroyer and were picked up. They reported that the Japanese had evacuated the Lingayen area when the bombardment started on January 6th. On the basis of this report, the bombardment of Lingayen town was suspended shortly before it was supposed to.

A white star cluster was fired about 9:00 a.m. as a signal to suspend all fires so the troops could land. Landing craft had loaded the assault wave troops, and moved to their line of departure 4000 yards from shore. There they were waiting for the signal to move towards the beach in time to arrive at "H" hour, 9:30 a.m. The first wave actually hit the beach at 9:36 a.m. in what turned out to be an unopposed landing, with the second wave landing three minutes later.

It was fortunate that there was no enemy fire to greet the initial waves of landing craft, because the waters were so shallow that many of the landing craft grounded far out on a shelf. The most visible sign of enemy opposition turned out to be the many aircraft, including kamikazes, which hit several large warships.

The 160th, commanded by Colonel Edward J. Murray of Sacramento, landed on the left (in touch with the 37th [Ohio] Division). Elements of the 185th Infantry under the command of Colonel John B. Maloney, also of Sacramento, landed on the right. The 108th RCT was held in division and corps reserve. When the assault waves landed, the effects of the shelling were immediately obvious. Most coconut trees had their tops shot off. Coconuts and Japanese bodies were everywhere. There were some Japanese snipers who managed to survive the initial shelling, but there were comparatively few enemy troops encountered during the first 24 hours.

The troops advanced through the shell-torn areas, and wove their way very carefully between ponds and paddies. The troops were especially careful because it had been strongly rumored that the Japanese had planted large poisonous Cobra snakes in the area. The troops had been prepared for the worse, whether Japanese or serpents. Fortunately, the reality was less than anticipated.

The commander of the 143rd Field Artillery ordered his guns ashore at 11:00 a.m. on January 9th, 1945. They came ashore without mishap. The Japanese had destroyed everything they could not carry when they left three days earlier, and headed in the general direction of the Bataan Peninsula and the City of Manila.

Opposition was light, so the primary reliance was on gun support from the ships. The first skirmishes resulted in seven Japanese killed, plus one Formosan and three Chinese laborers captured. The bridges had been destroyed by the Japanese, so DUKW amphibious trucks were used to transport guns and personnel across the Calmay and Agno Rivers. The beachheads were secured by 4:00 p.m.

By the time darkness was falling, most units were on the Division Beachhead Line (DBHL), and some were on the Corps Beachhead Line (CBHL). The build- up of supplies on the beach was expedited, with the only harassment being Japanese suicide planes. The infantry dug in for the night, but the supply operations continued around the clock.

The 222nd Field Artillery Battalion had it tougher than their brothers in the 143rd. They were embarked on the 14,000 ton troop ship U.S.S. Warhawk (AP168), loaded with several units. The Japanese launched a suicidal seaborne attack with small motor torpedo boats late the night of 9-10 January. Troop ships around the Warhawk heard a muffled thump at 4:27 a.m. January 10th, followed by the sound of steel buckling. The Warhawk was hit at the waterline in number three hold near the bow, instantly killing troops in their bunks there. Fortunately, as many troops as possible were sleeping on deck to get away from the stifling heat. Nonetheless, the explosion resulted in the loss of 61 lives. The explosion was followed by strafing from at least one Japanese Zero, but the Zero was shot down by a soldier manning a .50 calibre machine gun. Destroyers supported the action by firing illuminating shells in what was a rather confusing action. The survivors of the battalion were landed without a single additional loss of life, as the Warhawk limped off for repairs. The Japanese boats also damaged two LST's that night.

The 160th captured the Lingayen Airstrip and the City of Lingayen (Capitol of Pangasinan Province) and rolled across the Agno-Calmay River delta before nightfall.

The 185th RCT made a rapid swing westward in a drive which eventually brought Port Saul, Labrador and Aliminos under American control. January 10th was a day of slow advances because of swamps and rivers and lack of transportation. The 115th Engineers constructed pontoon bridges, and built many small bridges, fills, approaches and bypasses as the troops moved inland. The Japanese reaction increased from snipers to occasional machine guns and mortar fire, but the supporting artillery helped quickly squelch any serious opposition. By the end of the day, enemy casualties were still only being counted in the dozens.

As the assault regiments rapidly advanced and the front line lengthened, a gap developed. General Brush requested the 108th RCT be released from Corps Reserve on the tenth, and immediately deployed the 108th on line to the right of the 160th. The division having seized the Lingayen airfield, went on to occupy the Bolineo Peninsula and San Miguel.

While the 160th and 108th RCT's were advancing through Bugallon and Aguilar, the 185th RCT and the 40th Reconnaissance Troop were cleaning out and securing Port Sual and Alaminos to the northwest. Shortly after noon on the 12th, elements of the 185th along with the 40th Reconnaissance Troop, swept into Port Sual. The 2-185th killed several Japanese in their sector, and captured ten pack horses that were already saddled. They immediately converted them to their own use.

By January 13th, some of the troops were filthy, and wanted to bathe in the rivers. The water was dirty, and kept that way because of the carabao that had appropriated the best pools. They didn't want to leave their favorite spots, but the troops persisted. The water then settled down, and the men got on with their baths.

An extraordinarily heavy rainfall hit the troops very early the morning of January 14th. Communications was disrupted, and movement was all but impossible. One battalion fire direction center (FDC) had been dug in and covered with a pyramidal tent for blackout purposes. Very quickly the FDC crew found themselves working in five feet of water. They took off their shoes and clothing and continued the mission while equipment floated around and in the tent mixed with debris raised by the flooding.

Patrolling for many days was aggressive, but routine. Small groups of Japanese were encountered, but there were no sizeable fire fights. Guerrillas were helpful in pointing out where Japanese could be found, and in several cases were holding captured Formosans. One battalion patrol brought in 154 Formosans who were being held by the guerrillas. In addition to help from the organized guerrilla units, pygmy natives were aggressive "Jap hunters," and killed quite a few.

Guerrillas and civilians reported a thousand Japanese in the mountains south of Alimanos. It turned out these were stranded labor troops from a sunken coastal craft. They were more interested in avoiding contact with our troops and reaching Japanese enclaves in the south than they were in fighting.

On January 17th, troops from the 143rd Field Artillery had a typical exchange with the natives in Mangatarem. The native girls approached the troops with packages wrapped in banana leaves on the end of poles. Those turned out to be fried chicken on a spit, with the leaves around the chicken to keep them hot. The troops quickly bartered some cigarettes for the chicken dinners.

Guerrillas guided a twelve-man patrol from 1-185th RCT to Agno Bay where 16 Japanese were killed in a stiff fire fight. On January 19th, the 13th Air Force began bombing Tarlac, which was occupied by an estimated 6000 Japanese. That night the Japanese torched the city as they prepared to evacuate. As troops of the division approached Tarlac, they passed through Mangatarem, Camiling, and Santa Ignacia.

On January 21st, only 11 days after the invasion, the 160th had advanced twenty-one miles and entered flaming Tarlac. Tarlac was a provincial capitol and strategic road and railway junction. The troops found the city a shambles, with much of the city burnt and property strewn everywhere in the hurried Japanese flight from the city.

Most of the homes in Tarlac were built off the ground to allow ventilation from the heat. They were built of lumber and bamboo, and the better homes had modern plumbing and toilet facilities. This was easy to spot since those homes had large pipes (usually of cement) running up to the toilet. The troops quickly understood this feature of Filipino houses because some had burned down, with nothing left but a toilet sitting on top of a six foot high cement pipe. From a distance, one was reminded of a bunch of bird baths.

Major Donald N. Moore, S-3 of the 1st Battalion, 160th Infantry, put together a task force consisting of Company A plus two sections of Company D. They marched into Camp O'Donnell, a detention camp where hundreds of prisoners from Bataan and Corregidor had died. Unfortunately, the survivors of the Bataan Death March had already been moved. Troops were struck by the crude burial grounds, and the many inscriptions left by American prisoners on the walls of the stables. It was clear they desperately hoped to be rescued before it was too late, and wanted everyone to know they had been there regardless of their ultimate fate. Major Moore left Company A to outpost the camp, while he returned to the battalion with the rest of the troops.

At Tarlac, 115th Engineers under Lieutenant Colonel John K. Wright of Redding put the first railroad on Luzon into operation. An advance of seventy miles was made over rough terrain against delaying forces in 16 days. During this time the 40th Cavalry Reconnaissance Troop was cited for its bold, aggressive action. The Troop had fought south of Bamban on the 21st. They advanced further and killed more Japanese than any other unit their size. The 160th entered the ruins of Bamban on January 23rd, receiving fire from the direction of Fort Stotsenburg. That post had been the home station of the 26th U.S. Cavalry Regiment, a unit annihilated while fighting a rear-guard action to cover the withdrawal of U.S. troops to Bataan at the beginning of the war.

After San Miguel and Capas were occupied, enemy contacts became more numerous, and engineer and infantry perimeters received small attacks during the night. The 40th Reconnaissance Troop had a skirmish south of Bamban and the 640th Tank Destroyer Reconnaissance Company had a stiff engagement at Magalang. The 640th Tank Destroyer Battalion had been attached to the division from the time of its organization effective February 18th, 1942 until completion of the division's campaign on Luzon. While their employment was hampered by restrictions of the terrain, the M-10 3" tank destroyers of the unit played a key role in supporting the division in every way except destroying Japanese tanks. There simply weren't that many Japanese tanks left on Luzon to harass friendly troops.

The Japanese launched a surprise night attack at 4:30 a.m. early the morning of January 23rd. They hit elements of Company A, 115th Engineers who were working on a bridge below the village of Capas. The Japanese had crossed the Cutcut River in trucks, quickly routing the small engineer force. Six men were killed and ten wounded, one of whom hid under a truck while the Japanese were burning and looting. After sunrise, an artillery air observer spotted the Japanese and spread the alarm.

The Japanese were setting up dual purpose guns in Capas as they reinforced the south end of the town, and Americans were bringing more troops down in their attack from the north. The Japanese fired a few artillery rounds before a forward observer spotted the source of medium artillery fire. The 143rd fired 48 rounds of high explosive at the battery of three Japanese 120mm Dual Purpose guns. They were silenced and abandoned by their crews.

On this same day, the 143rd received fire from 320mm guns. These huge guns were emplaced on rails in mountainside tunnels with steel doors. The doors would swing open, the gun would be rolled into position, and several rounds would then be fired at high elevation before the gun was rolled back inside the mountain. These guns were extremely tough to hit with counterbattery fire.

Meanwhile, elements of the 185th pushed southward on the west coast and reached Santa Cruz on January 23rd. They continued patrolling on the peninsula as well as along the eastern foothills of the Zambales Mountains as far south as Camiling to protect against any possible enemy threat from that flank.

Early in the battle, General MacArthur visited the division. He was friendly with General Brush, some feeling that relationship was based on General MacArthur considering General Brush an "old Philippine Islands hand." In one case, he was visiting an airfield just inland from the landing beaches at Lingayen. The Navy's Seabees had quickly made the airfield operable, and Generals MacArthur, Brush, Sutherland (MacArthur's Intelligence Chief) and others were talking in a coconut grove beside the runway. A P-38 fighter aircraft landed on the runway and the pilot lost control, perhaps because of wounds or damage to the aircraft. In any event, the plane came ripping through the coconut trees, and went right through a field kitchen towards the command group. MacArthur ignored the plane and the racket it created, including field stoves, pots and pans thrown everywhere. Others in the group were hardly so relaxed, and wanted to run for cover.

General MacArthur and Major General Rapp Brush (40th Div) reviewing advances made on Luzon.
(Source: Captain Robert W. Munyon)

General MacArthur was seen up front several times in the division area, where the troops were often concerned about his personal safety. His behavior belied the "Dugout Doug" tag he was given by others. Many troops in the division admired him, and felt he tended to go much farther forward than he should have.

The division had faced comparatively light opposition, primarily scattered enemy rear guards, after landing on Luzon. While there were large pockets of enemy soldiers, such as the estimated 6000 in Tarlac, they generally withdrew before becoming decisively engaged. There were comparatively few friendly casualties as the division advanced eighty-seven miles in two weeks before facing the Japanese troops defending Bamban on January 23rd.

The mere delaying actions and lack of determined opposition had to end, and reports to that effect were beginning to accumulate from the guerrillas as well as our own aerial observations. Every indication was that the Japanese intended to stand and fight in the hills west of Fort Stotsenburg and Clark Field.

The enemy commander in the Clark Field area was Major General Rikichi Tsukada. He decided not to attempt an all-out defense of the airfields themselves, which were on a flat plain with little or no cover. General Tsukada told his soldiers, "Against the attacks of the materially well equipped enemy, we will not offer resistance." Instead, he decided to fight from the more defensible steep mountains, especially to the west, that surrounded much of the area. He felt they could preclude allied use of Clark Field by using artillery fires and infiltration attacks from enclaves in the hills.

Major General Tsukada's troops included an airborne infantry unit designated the 1st Airborne Raiding Group, elements of the 2nd Tank Division, and other miscellaneous army and navy combat and service troops. Called the *Tembu Butai*, they totalled about 30,000 troops. He started their construction of fortifications in the hills some weeks, if not months, before the Fortieth Division arrived on the scene.

The fortifications the Fortieth Division faced along a front of 12,000 yards, and to a depth of 16,000 yards, constituted what a War Department Intelligence Bulletin (Vol. III, No. 9, May 1945) described as "probably the most elaborate and extensive system of caves and tunnel defenses yet encountered in the Southwest Pacific." The bulletin went on to say "caves in the Fort Stotsenburg-Bamban River area represent the most extensive system of cave defenses, organized in depth and supported by excellent secondary positions..."

Major General Tsukada's *Tembu Butai* was lightly armed for a force of its size. It had less than a battalion of 47mm antitank guns, two or three batteries of 70mm and 75mm guns, about a battalion of 100mm to 150mm medium artillery, and the equivalent of two battalions of naval 120mm antiaircraft guns employed for ground support. It suffered from a shortage of automatic weapons of all calibres. However, that deficiency was at least partially alleviated by stripping various damaged Japanese aircraft of their weapons. Aerial bombs small enough to be moved were also hauled into the hills and used in various ways as makeshift mines and explosive charges.

The terrain fanning out from Mount Pinatubo, and running in a northeasterly direction behind Fort Stotsenburg, included a series of steep, broken ridges, separated by steep, interlocking ravines and canyons. The rocky ground was covered with cogon grass, cane-brake, and scattered timber on the higher elevations. There was heavy jungle growth along watercourses and in ravines.

Some months before, large caves and tunnels had been carved in the rock, to protect supplies and personnel against U.S. air attacks. As the American forces island-hopped towards Luzon, bulk stores in huge quantities were transferred from Fort Stotsenburg to the less vulnerable tunnels. The anti-aircraft guns (ranging in size from 20mm to 120mm) that surrounded the field were moved to new positions blasted in the rocky hill slopes and laid for terrestrial fires. In some cases these guns were broken down into components and then laboriously manhandled up almost vertical slopes. Literally hundreds of aircraft machine guns had been removed from the battered planes that littered the Clark airfields, and carried up into the hills. The unusual number of machine guns was illustrated in the fact that twenty-six aircraft machine guns were found in positions on a single small knoll. Individual tunnels had been well stocked with food, ammunition, and other supplies so that each small group of Japanese could continue to fight regardless of the fate of other groups.

Gun positions had been planned to provide mutual support and to cover the barren approaches. In many instances the guns had

2000 to 4000-yard fields of plunging and grazing fire. The entire series of improved caves and tunnels that stretched for many miles in the mountains were supplemented by concrete pillboxes, trenches, dugouts and spider holes. The term "spider hole" came from their resemblance to the homes of trap-door spiders, who build their homes in the ground with a removable lid. The Japanese often used cunning camouflage in hiding holes they dug, making it extremely difficult to locate them until the Japanese soldiers raised the lids to their holes in order to fight.

As troops began to approach the Zambales Mountains, resistance began to stiffen. Occasionally hand grenade duels would erupt in the hours of darkness as the Japanese probed the division's lines. Those that succeeded in penetrating the division's lines cut communications wires to disrupt command and control. Approach marches were hindered by machine gun as well as sniper fire from well camouflaged positions, and minefields were increasingly being encountered.

Early the morning of January 23rd, advance elements of the 160th Infantry ran into increasing enemy resistance as they approached Bamban. Bamban was the northwestern anchor point of the Japanese plan for the defense of Luzon that was previously described. Bamban, in Tarlac Province, was a large industrial and agricultural city located at the base of the Zambales Mountains. At the northern outskirts of the city, 3-160th deployed with Company L on the left, and Company K on the right. The enemy's outpost line was quickly overwhelmed, after which the units paused before assaulting the city proper.

Soldiers quickly penetrated the first two blocks into the city, using fire and movement to eliminate pockets of enemy infantrymen. The troops then ran into a line of heavy automatic fires in a system of concrete pillboxes and trenches. The troops aggressively penetrated the system using hand grenades and bayonets supported by automatic fires from Browning Automatic Rifles and Tommy guns. Company K alone lost three killed and three wounded in penetrating that far into the city.

The battalion continued to fight its way through the city until running into intense automatic fire from caves and pillboxes in the hills overlooking the far side of the city. Help was brought to bear using M-10 3" tank destroyers and M-7 105mm self-propelled howitzers added to the regiment's 60mm, 81mm and 4.2" mortars. The direct fire of these larger weapons destroyed the pillboxes and sealed some of the caves. Many enemy soldiers were seen fleeing to prepared defense systems higher in the mountains.

Darkness began to fall as soldiers established a new defensive perimeter, either digging in or occupying enemy positions. They found large numbers of automatic weapons and sizeable stocks of fuel, ammunition, food and clothing abandoned by the Japanese. The troops settled in for the night, but continued to suffer losses from artillery fire. The incoming artillery fire was heaviest on the 24th, but continued for some days thereafter.

South of Bamban the Bamban River runs in an eastward direction, fed by a series of tributaries from the east-west gorges of the Zambales Mountains. These streams are separated by high, steep ridges which end in abrupt cliffs. The ridges and cliffs were honey-combed with caves and tunnels. Approaches were strewn with land mines.

Final elimination of the Japanese hiding in the cave recesses had to be accomplished by assaulting infantry. This agonizing work began as soon as Clark Field was neutralized. It was then - - and before the Japanese had suffered significant losses - - that the Japanese shifted their defenses from the open plain to the rugged hills and mountain ridges that had been so well fortified.

The division had fought against rear-guard delaying forces for sixteen days. They had pushed seventy miles down the highway to Manila before reaching the Bamban River. South of the river and west of the highway the large flat plain to Clark Field extended westward several thousand yards to Fort Stotsenburg. North of the river and west of the main highway, a series of east-west ridges emanating from the Zambales end abruptly in sharp cliffs overlooking the town of Bamban and the highway. Near the base of these cliffs a series of huge supply tunnels dug deep into the rocky sides and connected by a vehicular road faced to the east. In these jagged Bamban Hills - - some barren, some matted with jungle thicket, and all bristling with fortified tunnels or caves - - the enemy was found and fixed on ground of his own choosing. To continue the direction of attack southward against these ridges was impracticable. Troops could not be supplied or supported by artillery in this broken and roadless terrain. Accordingly, the division was forced to change its direction of attack.

The 40th faced westward, parallel to its supply line, and headed up the cliffs and ridges. The mission was to capture and secure Clark Field while rendering the routes to Manila free from enemy infiltration and harassing artillery fire. Guerrilla and civilian estimates of enemy strength in the Stotsenburg-Bamban area varied considerably, and insufficient enemy order of battle information precluded arrival at any conclusive figure. However, at the beginning of the operation, it was estimated that approximately 3000 Japanese occupied positions in the Zambales foothills to an undetermined depth along a front approximately 6000 yards wide.

On January 24th, the 1st and 2d Battalions, 160th Infantry, prepared to attack the caves and tunnels on a sheer cliff protected from air bombardment. This was the opening salvo of the bitter battle of the Zambales Mountains. Artillery set fire to brush on the hillsides, burned the enemy's camouflage and revealed hidden positions. Six-inch naval guns were located and silenced. Aided by fire from tanks and self-propelled guns, the infantry went to work with rifles, grenades, demolition charges and flame throwers. Under fire from the enemy's dominating positions, the battalions attacked up the steep slopes of separate ridges later named Stratta Hill and Stout Hill after the respective battalion commanders.

The 3-185th Infantry was moved to division reserve at Santo Domingo near Capas on January 24th. Later, the entire regiment, having completed operations in the Northern Zambales, was moved into the Bamban area. In view of possible employment on the enemy's rear, the battalion initiated reconnaissance of routes leading southeast from O'Donnell. Trails were found to be poorly developed and unsuitable for supply and evacuation needs.

On January 25th, the 108th Infantry, turning west at Susuba and Caupo, began its move into the hills on the right of the 160th. Troops moving up the high ground west of Hill 5, 3500 yards northwest of Bamban, received intense machine gun and rifle fire in the beginning of a vicious four-day fight. They were fighting to take this and Thrall Hill, 1000 yards to the south, named in tribute to Major Norman E. Thrall, battalion commander, who was killed during the action. His troops had seen Major Thrall reconnoitering through field glasses along with a couple of junior officers. They could see P-38's, P-51's and larger aircraft attacking the enemy to their front. Major Thrall apparently could not see enough from so far back, and said something like "I've got to get in there" as they jumped into the jeep to move closer to the front. Major Thrall was shot on a hillside, directly under enemy fire. He occasionally screamed in pain, and called for help. But anyone who attempted it was himself killed. Thrall died a short time afterwards.

From the bushy crevices and reverse slopes of the hills, the enemy delivered short range fire against infantrymen clinging to the barren precipitous slopes. So close were the opposing forces that in some instances hand grenades were traded by tossing them over the pointed crests of hills. Heavy mortar concentrations from unknown positions hit within perimeters the troops established each night.

Concurrent with the above operations, mechanized reconnaissance continued to the south and east in the direction of Mount Arayat and into the outskirts of Angeles, which was found lightly held.

On the 26th the reconnaissance company of the 640th Tank Destroyer Battalion, with one platoon of tanks and one platoon of M-10 3" tank destroyers attached, conducted a reconnaissance in force of Clark Field. Heavy enemy fire revealed the location of his well concealed artillery positions, enabling our artillery to execute effective counter-battery fire. Several pillboxes and machine gun positions were destroyed. The reconnaissance confirmed the presence of minefields, and determined the type and strength of the enemy defenses in that area.

The strongest enemy resistance was almost always based on high ground, so practically all objectives were designated as hills. The hills were initially designated with numbers based on their elevation, or names based on their physical characteristics. Hills were also named after officers who had been killed, often while attacking to take that particular objective.

The division had heard reports of remote-controlled mines in the area of Clark Field and Fort Stotsenburg. On January 26th a letter confirming the rumors was received from Second Lieutenant H. C. Conner, Jr. Conner was a downed aviator who served with Lieutenant Colonel Edgar Wright's guerrilla forces on Luzon. His letter in part read: "In the first tunnel, which lies to the east side of Top of the World, approximately 400 feet from the base of the hill, there is a control fuze box for all mines throughout the Fort Stotsenburg-Clark Field area." The presence of these buried mines was also confirmed when an untouched, buried mine was suddenly exploded very close to vehicles and troops of the 640th Tank Destroyer Battalion.

By the close of the 26th, both the 108th and the 160th regiments were in position to begin the final assaults. The division reported the latest count in enemy casualties in the G-2 report for the period ending at 1700 hours on January 27th. A total of 530 Japanese had been killed. In addition, 28 Japanese, 174 Formosans, and 27 Chinese had been captured.

On the 27th, the 160th reached the crest of Stratta Hill in the face of artillery, mortar and small arms fire. The following day, the 108th Infantry secured Hill 5 after overcoming three days of desperate enemy resistance from positions on Thrall Hill, 1000 yards south. After another day's reduction of caves and gun positions there, our troops gained possession.

During the struggle for Hill 5 and Thrall Hill, the Japanese *Kamii Butai* had been destroyed as an effective unit and its remnants driven into the mountains. By January 27th the 2nd Battalion, 2nd Mobile Infantry Regiment, of the Imperial Japanese Army was no more. The major element of the butai, this battalion had been destroyed completely with its threat and mission buried in the numerous caves and tunnels in and about the hills. The annihilation of this battalion began the slow swinging back of the enemy's left flank to an eventual dissolution in the suicidal defenses of Hills 1500 and 1700, 12,000 yards southwest. The 160th then began the long and desperate struggle up the steep and densely wooded ridges to Storm King Mountain.

Meanwhile, the 129th Infantry of the 37th Division, then attached to the 40th Division, had overrun Clark Field and Fort Stotsenburg and were on the way up the slopes of the Top of the World in the face of heavy artillery, mortar, machine gun and rifle fire.

Mute testimony to the effectiveness of the air force's all-out effort to neutralize enemy air bases prior to the landing on Luzon were the hundreds of destroyed enemy aircraft which littered the Clark Field area. In addition, they found the remains of one American fighter pilot who landed on Clark in error. He evidently had assumed the airfield was already in American hands. He was beheaded before he got very far, and the remains were left to be found by divisional infantrymen shortly after.

As the end of January approached, the troops were across the plains on which Clark Field's runways had been constructed, and ready to assault into the steep hills that overlooked the plains.

Attacks were stopped on the 27th by the heavy fire coming from the hills, looking right down the throats of the infantrymen. One unit of the 108th RCT was of particular concern to the division commander, having been described as pinned down in their hastily dug foxholes, and without any radio communication. They hadn't been heard from for hours.

The general's aide, Captain Robert W. Munyon, volunteered to see what the situation was and report back. The division headquarters was in an abandoned mansion, with a dried up rice field beside it that was used for a landing strip. Captain Munyon looked up Major James A. Williams, who headed up the division artillery aviation section, and had just landed. Munyon often flew with Williams, who had even taught Munyon the basics of flying the two-place L-4 observation (often described as a "cub liaison") plane, and let him land the small airplane over a dozen times. When Munyon explained that they had a unit lost, and the general was concerned, Williams immediately agreed to go.

They took off, and almost immediately spotted the besieged unit. The infantry on the ground had established a perimeter defense, and were hunkered down. Williams and Munyon agreed to "shoot them in for the night," establishing artillery concentrations around the unit to be called for if needed. They took about an hour to register the artillery, and established a system of flares to be shot, based on color, for the infantry to signal where they needed the artillery. As Williams and Munyon accomplished this, they observed what they thought were mortar rounds impacting in and around the infantry. Williams said to Munyon, "Bob, let's go get those bastards."

They flew back a ridge line or two, but could see no mortar positions. Suddenly there were three flak bursts right in front of their aircraft. Neither saw where they came from, so they circled around until the Japanese antiaircraft gunners fired again. Luckily the four rounds missed, but that time the source was spotted on the forward slope of the third ridge back. Munyon requested marker rounds from the divisional artillery, and when they had the artillery adjusted, were told to fly out of the way of the gun-target line. The division used a battalion "fire for effect," and the mountainside where the Japanese guns were spotted erupted with high explosive shells. When they flew over for a battle damage assessment, they clearly saw five guns destroyed and bodies everywhere. They surmised those guns had been firing like mortars because the unit trapped on the plains no longer received "mortar" fire.

The mountains where the guns were destroyed were in an area that higher headquarters had assured the division was devoid of any Japanese in large numbers. The area had been repeatedly photographed, but no enemy had been spotted. The fact that they had located Japanese antiaircraft batteries was an indicator of bigger things, so Williams and Munyon decided to look farther.

They headed up one of the many river valleys, flying about 200 feet above the dry river bed, weaving as they followed the course of the river between the hills. They almost immediately started seeing hundreds of vehicles, huge stacks of materiel concealed by camouflage nets, and countless tunnels and caves dug into the hillsides. They didn't see a single enemy soldier as Captain Munyon quickly sketched what they were observing.

They flew up the valley for several miles, and grew increasingly nervous. Finally Major Williams decided they had better get back and report what they had spotted. He turned the plane around and began flying back down the valley. When they did, the Japanese came pouring out of the caves and tunnels and shot at them with everything they had. In spite of their slow speed, they were a fleeting target at that elevation. Nonetheless, they were peppered with small arms fire. Though nothing vital was hit, the pilot received one round through his boot heel. They finally got back with their riddled aircraft, and reported what they had seen. They were particularly struck by the impressive discipline of the Japanese, who kept completely hidden when they flew by the first time.

General Brush immediately convened a staff meeting, including all key players on the division staff. One of the participants was described as a "wet-behind-the-ears" Air Force Lieutenant Colonel. Another was a reporter from the Chicago Tribune. The reporter later had his story converted to a radio play, following which Munyon received a scathing letter from his wife because he had volunteered for the mission. The Air Force officer was instrumental in scheduling a series of B-24 heavy bomber attacks over the next two days, which resulted in the heaviest bomber attacks in the Pacific up to that time.

Both Williams and Munyon received Air Medals for their contributions. Unfortunately, Williams was later killed when his aircraft was hit by antiaircraft fire and crashed.

Early the morning of January 30th, troops of 3-160th Infantry had been ordered to take a strategic hill that overlooked Clark Field and the vital road to Manila southwest of Bamban. The company commander of Company K immediately took his platoon leaders forward for a reconnaissance as the enemy's sporadic fires hindered preparations for the attack. Two of the platoon leaders were wounded as they conducted their reconnaissance from the company's forward observation post. New leaders had to be appointed and oriented before the company attacked.

Artillery plus heavy and light mortars supported the attack, opening with a heavy barrage on the objective ten minutes before the troops were to cross the line of departure. The attack commenced at 1:00 p.m. with Company K on the left, Company I on the right, and Company L in reserve. Machine guns of the Heavy Weapons Company (Company M) provided overhead fire. The battalion also had M-10 Tank Destroyers with 3" guns in support.

This was the first major action for many of the troops, and they were understandably tense. They advanced only about sixty yards before meeting strong enemy resistance in well dug in positions covering all approaches with intense machine gun cross fire and heavy mortar concentrations. The enemy made very heavy use of hand grenades for about thirty minutes, and were answered in kind.

A soldier from Company K later wrote: *"As the attack progressed, the going became much tougher and our casualties kept mounting. Orders were issued to commit the third platoon. The M-10 was now in action providing overhead cover. In spite of the fact the tank (sic) was drawing heavy mortar and machine gun fire, two of our men volunteered to climb on the tank to assist Captain Crosby, who was wounded about the head by enemy mortar shrapnel while manning a .50 caliber machine gun. Disregarding his painful injuries and streams of blood that impaired his vision, Captain Crosby courageously manned the weapon until the mission was successfully completed. In fierce and determined ground fighting, some of our men overran and disposed of several machine gun nests with bayonets and hand grenades. Others were carrying out the wounded just far enough back to provide shelter so they could be given first aid.*

"Every time a man fell, eager hands took up their weapons to carry the fight to the enemy. Finally, seeing that the position became untenable, the advancing platoon leaders ordered a withdrawal. L Company, up until now in reserve, was immediately committed to cover our orderly withdrawal and to allow K Company time to reorganize and establish a perimeter.

"This accomplished, L Company slowly drifted into the K Company perimeter for the night. While this was taking place, the heavy machine gun section from M Company gave strong support with devastating overhead fire. A spot check was made on casualties, food and ammunition. At this time, it was disclosed that Lieutenant Talbott (1LT Eugene L. Talbott), our heroic and courageous second platoon leader, was killed. Other losses in this battle were three officers, six noncommissioned officers and eighteen riflemen wounded.

"Shortly after the company had been consolidated into three platoons, the order was given to assault under the same plan, with

a few tactical modifications. This time, our attack was hampered by torrential rains, making our advance more difficult and much slower. Nevertheless, our courageous men were not to be denied. K Company gained a foothold on the hill, but scorching enemy mortar, 40mm and heavy machine gun fire forced us to withdraw only after we had expended the major part of our ammunition. We suffered an additional seven casualties in this second assault.

"It was decided to dig in for the night, after an order to attack the next morning had been given. Early the next morning, we were given the estimate and change of plan for the attack. Changes noted were that both the M-4 and M-10 tanks (M-4 Sherman tanks and M-10 tank destroyers) *were to be used; the M-4 supporting the company attack, the M-10 on the left flank firing on caves and 20mm positions. In addition, heavier regimental and divisional artillery would be laid on the objective just prior to the attack.*

"The company jumped off in a spirited attack, vowing to take the hill today. During the night, the enemy had reinforced their positions, making every foot of ground gained more bitterly contested than the day before. Every available man and weapon was employed to gain the stubborn objective. Great courage and fighting skill were displayed by everyone in the company. At the end of this memorable day, our unit had secured its objective. Counted enemy dead were sixty-seven against our losses of five killed and thirty-one wounded. Captured enemy equipment included: thirty-two rifles, six heavy machine guns, two 37mm anti-tank guns, numerous pistols and quantities of ammunition."

This important hill was later dubbed "Grenade Hill." The appellation came naturally, for as one participant described the action early in the battle: "...for about thirty minutes the sky was literally blackened with enemy hand grenades." Interestingly, one section of machine gunners of Company M joined the assaulting ranks when their fires were masked (they could no longer fire without hitting their own troops). They were the first soldiers on the objective, and were awarded the Bronze Star.

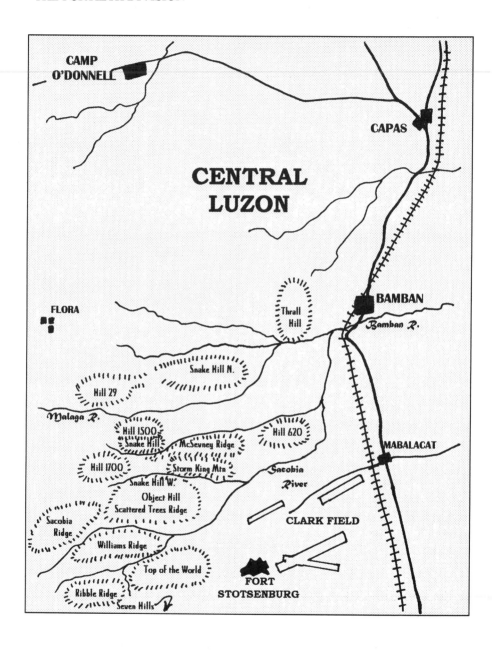

CHAPTER SEVEN

SECURING CENTRAL LUZON

By late January, soldiers of the division were looking and acting like seasoned veterans. They had successfully fought through many of the caves, tunnels and spider holes in the mountains of Luzon while suppressing enemy sniper fire. Nonetheless, they had yet to face Storm King Mountain, one of their tougher challenges thus far in the campaign.

The 160th Infantry was given the mission of taking Storm King Mountain, just northeast of Fort Stotsenburg and Clark Field. Their densely wooded objective was occupied by the highly regarded Japanese 2nd Glider-borne Infantry. Most of the enemy's caves and tunnels were mutually supporting, and were further protected by fire from a series of gun positions dug-in on high ground above and to the flanks. The many personnel and weapons positions were extremely well constructed and camouflaged as described in the previously mentioned War Department Intelligence Bulletin later published in May 1945.

On January 28th, the 160th launched their attack from Hill 620, halfway up the long, razor-back Murray Ridge leading from Stratta Hill to Storm King Mountain. While they immediately faced opposition, the most violent response against the division was delayed for a day. During the late afternoon of the 29th, Japanese soldiers of the *Okaamota Butai* five times charged the division's lines and five times were repulsed with a known 53 Japanese killed in the hour's action. These banzai counterattacks were the first of many launched against the division during the course of the Stotsenburg-Bamban campaign in futile piecemeal actions that merely dissipated their forces.

During the first several days in February, two battalions from the 160th Infantry advanced up Storm King Mountain, with soldiers hauling individual artillery pieces behind them as they fought their way up the mountain. The caves and tunnels could only be reduced by continuous direct artillery fire, white phosphorus smoke, demolitions, flame throwers, and field expedients devised on the spot. Support was provided by M-8 armored cars, M-10 tank destroyers, and 105mm and 155mm artillery. However, in the final analysis, it was the infantry that completed the job. In just one example, three separate demolitions, twenty hand grenades, a large volume of fire from automatic weapons, and finally a full case of TNT, were required to rout the Japanese from one compartmented cave.

The 160th finally took most of the mountain, except for enemy troops isolated on one extremely rugged promontory. That promontory was eventually named McSevney Point in memory of Major John D. McSevney, the battalion commander that was killed in action while reconnoitering the hill prior to the attack. Major McSevney had just returned from emergency leave, and chatted a minute with Major General Brush behind an embankment near a destroyed bridge. They no more than separated, each to return to his duties, when a knee (light) mortar round exploded right next to McSevney. He died of massive head wounds.

The only suitable avenue of approach to the promontory was from the east along a narrow neck of ground connecting the main mass of Storm King Mountain and this last out-jutting promontory overlooking the reverse slope of the mountain. The sides of the ridges were all but unscalable, especially when the defenders rolled grenades down on attackers. The slopes of this ridge were completely covered with heavy timber, canebrake, and undergrowth. This promontory's only approach was over 300 yards long and 75 yards or less wide. This single approach was defended by a 70mm field piece, three heavy 90mm mortars, 10 knee mortars, 10 heavy and 17 light machine guns and 150 concealed rifle pits protected against artillery fire.

The positions had been well prepared, some being formed by digging the earth from under the roots of large trees. All had been covered with logs and earth, and concealed by fresh and growing bamboo. Being almost impossible to locate until fire was delivered, their destruction was costly.

The 3-160th on February 6th launched an attack against the fiercely defended ridge. As the infantrymen struggled forward against determined resistance, communications platoons had great difficulty maintaining wire laid between various command posts. Part of the problem was to be expected - - it is always tough to keep wire communications to rifle companies that are constantly on the move in rugged terrain. More dangerous, however, were the Japanese patrols that infiltrated friendly lines at night cutting phone lines. One wire section team repairing lines on McSevney Ridge encountered a Japanese patrol, and killed four of them before the others ran off.

The Japanese held out for ten days of bitter fighting. The comparatively small area was secured only after bitter fighting at close quarters. The enemy had inflicted more casualties on the division here than had the entire reinforced *Kamoto Butai* in its defense of the lower Stratta, Stout and Ruckle Hills and Hill 620. In spite of that, all of Storm King Mountain was cleaned out and secured by February 6th.

Some of the artillery were ordered to displace (move) to Fort Stotsenburg on that same day. They moved in very carefully, as the Japanese had left behind many mines and booby traps. The bomb disposal unit in the Clark Field-Fort Stotsenburg area removed about 550 bombs, some as large as 500 pounds, that had been buried in holes with their fuzes up.

The artillerymen also occupied a couple of the very deep tunnels in the Clark Field-Fort Stotsenburg area that had been abandoned by the Japanese. The large entrances were eight by nine feet in size, and about thirty feet apart. They were about 100 yards deep, with a connecting tunnel about thirty yards from the back that joined the two main tunnels. The tunnels were well braced, supplied with electricity, and had beds, which the troops immediately put to good use. Side compartments included first aid stations and other facilities. The entrances were protected by ditches, making them tough nuts to crack. Many other tunnels were covered to seal the enemy inside rather then expend lives in rooting them out.

On the Clark Field plains a battery of Japanese 120mm dual-purpose guns had been captured in perfect firing condition, along with a great deal of ammunition. Division artillerymen manned the guns, and test fired them to ascertain their characteristics and develop range charts. Over 1200 rounds were subsequently fired by those guns against long range targets in support of division objectives.

Patrols probing the wooded draws and slopes at the base of Scattered Trees Ridge and Snake Hill West, the next defensive position to be attacked, had suffered casualties from intense machine gun and rifle fire. It was apparent the enemy had based his defenses on the assumption the Americans would advance along the valleys. It was therefore decided to attack along the steep bare ridge line.

American intelligence officers provided translations of captured documents and maps that showed details of the cavernous defense system. Defense using these mutually supporting and self-sufficient fortifications was entrusted to the *Takaya Butai*, composed of elements of the 2nd Glider-borne Infantry with attached naval units. The Japanese headquarters of the *Takaya Butai* was found on a captured map to be on Objective Hill, 1500 yards southwest of Snake Hill West. From the beginning of the action, it was apparent that the enemy had placed some of his best troops in this sector. They turned out to be well equipped, well fed, and imbued with the Bushido doctrine of suicidal defense.

A forward regimental combined command and observation post was installed by the 160th on Storm King Mountain, providing excellent observation to the front. Individual 155mm guns from the

222nd Field Artillery Battalion, and later a single 90mm gun, were towed up the mountain and emplaced to provide direct fire on suitable targets. The combination provided the regimental commander with an unusually rapid means of bringing accurate direct fire to bear on any enemy which could be detected.

On the evening of February 10th, there were various attempts by the enemy to penetrate unit perimeters. The 2nd and 3rd Battalions of the 185th RCT continued towards their objectives with the 2nd Battalion reaching Snake Hill 23 in the morning. After arriving at the top of this hill it was necessary to drive out the Japanese that were dug in on the reverse slope. To assist the assault there was supporting artillery fire and some fine sharpshooting by M-7 105mm howitzers shooting directly at enemy positions. At the end of the day, 2-185th was mopping up on Snake Hill 23 and counted 55 enemy dead. The 3rd Battalion continued its attack on Hill 1000 and captured it on the 12th, after meeting strong resistance.

On February 11th, 1-160th jumped off to attack Scattered Trees Ridge, and 2-160th opened up on Snake Hill West. Both battalions encountered heavy, short range fire from emplaced weapons in this assault on a very complex portion of the remarkable defense system established by the Japanese in the Bamban-Stotsenburg area. As the troops advanced, thrusting demolitions in successive tunnels and caves, they were under fire from automatic weapons of several sizes.

By dark on February 12th, 160th troops had fought to the top of both Scattered Trees Hill and Snake Hill West. But the task of routing the remaining enemy resistance from strongholds in the hillsides was far from completed.

The 185th was attacking towards Hill 1500 by February 12th. The combat engineers had to build roads so that the Cannon Company and tank destroyers could provide direct support. The artillery fired strong artillery preparations and the air corps bombed Hill 1500 prior to units crossing the line of departure on February 15th. The infantrymen were closely supported by tanks, tank destroyers, and M-7 self-propelled artillery. Two companies advanced under fire to the summit, while one company slowly made its way up around the northwest slope. By the end of the day the troops had attacked over the crest of the hill. On the west slope of the hill, six Japanese, recognizing the futility of their situation, committed suicide by holding grenades to their chests.

Numerous caves and dug-in positions remained on the west and northwest slopes to be wiped out before the hill would be free of resistance. Mopping up on Hill 1500 continued for several days as pockets of stubborn resistance were blasted out of caves. The caves that were not within the M-7's range were destroyed through 2-185th's use of gas drums. The drums were lowered from above the cave openings and electrically detonated instead of the more costly tactic of frontal assault. Securing Hill 1500 gave the battalion a view of Objective Hill as mopping up with artillery, explosive charges, gas drums and flame throwers continued for a week.

The 160th Infantry was then given the mission of taking Objective Hill. Objective Hill was a commanding hill in the Zambales Mountains honeycombed with caves and gun positions. In addition, the hill was covered by enemy fire from adjacent hills on both flanks.

The 2-160th was the battalion given the mission of taking Objective Hill, and sent Companies F and H into the attack on February 14th. They were quickly pinned down by fire from the objective and flank hills, and found themselves unable to move. For the next two days they could only be supplied ammunition and water by drops from small cub aircraft.

Company I of 3-160th was next given the mission. Leaders made their reconnaissance, and saw how difficult the terrain was, and how well fortified the entire area was. They knew they had a daunting task. Nonetheless, they made their first attempt late in the afternoon.

The company advanced approximately 1,000 yards, when they encountered very heavy machine gun and knee mortar fire. They pressed forward until reaching a ridge that paralleled their front, approximately 300 yards short of and below the topographical crest of their objective. Here they were stopped by intense fire from the rear, both flanks, and the front.

The remaining distance had very little vegetation, and required a very steep climb. They would be exposed if they continued, so it was decided to wait until the sun went down before continuing with the assault. The men hunkered down, using what little cover they could find, and waited for it to get dark.

The next assault was made at about 3:00 a.m. the morning of the 15th. The men had carried only one canteen of water, and minimal rations. The draws they moved through were so dark they were required to hold hands and walk single file. The last 50 yards could only be climbed single file regardless of visibility. One platoon reached the top of Objective Hill and was inside the Japanese positions by 4:00 a.m., where they were confronted with one position after another.

Initially the platoon had the advantage of surprise, and made good headway against the well fortified and camouflaged Japanese positions. It got much tougher as the element of surprise was lost. The fighting became up close and personal, after which the enemy retreated into a bamboo draw about thirty yards down the reverse slope.

The plan called for the balance of Company I to quickly follow in reinforcing and resupplying the assault elements. These supporting troops reached the base of the hill at about 6:00 a.m. There, two Japanese who had infiltrated through the column were spotted and killed as they attempted to drop hand grenades among the troops. As dawn began to break, the troops were hurrying up the hill single file. Everyone wanted to be on the objective before there was enough light for enemy machine gunners on adjacent ridges to spot them.

As dawn began to break, the troops scrambled to improve their defensive posture. The ground was rocky, including areas of solid rock, so the troops could not dig in as the enemy's fire began to build up. If an attacker wanted a hole, he had to kill an enemy soldier to get one. The hand-to-hand combat from spider hole to spider hole was bloody as men used their bayonets, rifle butts and grenades. One soldier threw a grenade into a spider hole twice, only to have the grenade quickly fly back each time. The third time, he crawled up to the hole, dropped in the grenade, and beat the Japanese on the head until just before the grenade detonated.

The hill was finally taken, and the wounded were pulled back into a position of relative safety. No holes were available to put the wounded in, so they were comparatively exposed. By this time, almost no one had any water left, and the wounded were suffering from intense thirst. The unwounded gave up what water they had to ease the suffering.

The unit consolidated their position and redistributed the remaining ammunition. Crew served weapons were placed carefully with fields of fire to assist in repelling the counterattack all were sure was coming. As dawn broke, the unit was subjected to heavy fire from the front and flanks, beating back a counterattack that came from the left front.

Every attempt by carrying parties to resupply them failed to get through that day and the following night because of enemy action. Regardless of how hard they tried, they were unable to get past a draw about 800 yards to the rear of Objective Hill.

That evening knee-mortar rounds began to hit the hill. Several landed near the wounded, but they grimly remained silent in spite of their exposure. There were a series of attacks through the night, some frontal, as well as the usual attempted infiltrations. All were stopped, sometimes using final protective fires of the machine guns.

The second day brought more suffering. There still was no food and water, and the heat grew to be unbearable. Lips cracked and tongues became swollen. It was extremely dangerous to leave protected positions, as the enemy had sniper and machine gun positions only 500 yards away. There also were some Japanese still on the hill.

By noon the wounded were pleading for water. Their wounds were beginning to fester and in many cases, infection had set in. The unit's last aid man had been killed the night before during one of the infiltration attacks, so the wounded were not receiving much needed medical attention. In addition, there was no more plasma or morphine.

Attempts to supply by air drops were frustrated because of the narrowness of the hard rocky hilltop, the steep cliffs on three sides, and the nearness of the enemy on the fourth side. When one drop finally landed near enough for a recovery effort, three volunteers ran through a gauntlet of machine gun fire to retrieve the supplies. When they reached the packages of badly needed water, they found the packages had been broken by the fall and the contents smashed. As a result, only one box was recovered, and it consisted of machine gun ammunition and four canteens of water.

The unit held the hill against repeated enemy attacks, in spite of having no food and almost no water for over thirty-six hours. There was a final coordinated attack by the enemy that was beaten back in spite of dwindling ammunition supplies. It was obvious that the defeat of this last effort broke the back of the resistance. Very little activity by the enemy was noted thereafter.

Company A of the regiment was finally able to reach the survivors at 1:30 a.m. on February 18th. Most of the litter bearers evacuating the wounded were Company I soldiers. The wounded had to be tied to the litters, and lowered by rope. The terrain was so difficult that eight to ten men were required for each litter.

Thirty-nine of the ninety-six men in Company I who had attacked Objective Hill were killed or wounded. There were 187 enemy dead left on the field of battle. Observers were struck by the fact that the survivors, though obviously tired and haggard, returned with high morale and esprit de corps. Even the wounded typified the spirit, concerned about their unwounded but weakened comrades, who were carrying them down the hill after fighting hard for two days with no sleep, food or water. The four-day battle ended organized resistance in that area, opening the way for a long swing southwest to Sacobia Ridge.

Throughout this action the 185th Infantry from positions on Hill 1500 placed M-7 105mm and M-10 3" direct fire on caves along the reverse slope of Snake Hill West and on enemy entrenchments on the reverse slopes of Objective Hill. Toward the end of the operation, on February 27th, four large caves estimated at 50-man capacity were taken under artillery and mortar fire and destroyed with an estimated 100 Japanese killed and an ammunition dump blown up.

The losses suffered by the *Takayi Butai* destroyed their combat effectiveness. Intelligence sifted through information from prisoners, civilian reports, and captured documents, estimated that the Japanese (at least the naval personnel) were withdrawing southwest toward Sacobia Ridge. Only isolated pockets of resistance remained on the reverse slopes of Snake Hill West and in the draw between the two hills then in the rear of the division's lines. To the end of the division's occupation of the zone, however, scattered enemy resistance continued in isolated areas despite repeated artillery and air strikes.

An attack on Sacobia Ridge became the next mission for the 160th. However, before this could be undertaken the Japanese defenses further south in the area west of Top of the World had to be reduced and the forces routed from their hill positions. The Battle of Seven Hills, then drawing to a close, effected this and cleared the area south of the Sacobia River.

In the meantime, the 108th Infantry completed mopping up the Thrall Hill area. On February 2nd, the 108th relieved the 129th Infantry of the 37th Division on the division left flank, being relieved in turn by 3-185th.

From the 108th's positions on Top of the World, seven hills immediately confronted the infantrymen as mopping up around Top of the World drew to a close. Arbitrarily numbered one to seven, these hills comprised the series of strong points that protected the right flank of the Japanese defense, strong points which one by one were eventually destroyed. Hills 1, 2 and 3, 1100 to 1300 feet in elevation, were to the front. To the left, at a distance of 1500 yards, and at a slightly lower elevation, stood Hill 4. On the right, 1500 yards northeast of Top of the World, stood Hill 5. Further south, Hill 6, 1000 feet high, formed the enemy's extreme right flank anchor. A thousand yards west from Hill 6, Hill 7 rose 1300 feet from the rock precipitous bank of the Sacobia River's south fork.

To the entrenchments throughout the seven hills the battered *Eguchi Butai* had withdrawn after its loss of Top of the World. Composed in the main of airfield battalions, the *Eguchi Butai* had the mission of halting the division's advance west of Stotsenburg. They also were given the mission of launching infiltrations into the Clark Field-Stotsenburg area. They had every knoll and knob of ground liberally studded with light and heavy machine guns and 20mm and 25mm weapons taken from the destroyed aircraft on Clark Field. Furthermore, the area, as captured documents indicated, contained a large central supply depot, the defense of which was of critical importance to an enemy hopelessly isolated from any resupply sources. This then was the general picture on the enemy's right (south) flank on the morning of February 9th, when the 108th left positions on Top of the World, overran Hills 1, 2 and 4, and advanced toward Hills 3 and 6.

In the drive to swing back the enemy's right flank, the 3rd Battalion attacked Hill 6, and the 2nd Battalion Hill 3, with the 1st Battalion in reserve. They ran into intense opposition and for the first 24 hours 1-108th was under repeated counterattacks supported by mortar and automatic weapons fire. By the end of the day 2-108th had secured Hill 3 and was moving south into the valley floor to assist in the development of strongly defended Hill 6 the next day. Two enemy tanks were encountered on this move. One was destroyed by machine gun and bazooka fire. This marked the first tank action in the area since the 129th Infantry destroyed three out of nine tanks encountered on Clark Field in the early stages of the operation.

On the morning of February 10th, a Japanese counterattack against Hill 4 was repulsed by division troops and the massed fires of division artillery. By the end of the day, despite the adverse terrain, Hill 3 was free of enemy, Hill 4 remained secure, and Hill 6 was under heavy fire from the 108th's encircling troops. As an indication of the intensity of the 24-hour action:

304 enemy dead were counted during the 24-hour period;

8 twin 20mm guns were destroyed;

5 single 20mm guns were destroyed;

3 120mm dual purpose naval guns were destroyed;

1 medium tank was destroyed.

After an unremitting three-day struggle across rugged, almost impassable terrain and intense fire from strongly emplaced Japanese weapons, Hill 6 fell to the 108th late the afternoon of February 12th. However, isolated cave and tunnel positions remained intact.

The next step was the reduction of Hill 7, 1000 yards to the west, the last strong point on the enemy's right flank A short, stubby knob on a broad, gently rising base, Hill 7 became the focal point for the enemy's fanatical last-ditch stand. The Intelligence and Reconnaissance Platoon of the 108th, patrolling around the enemy's right flank, had failed to find a route suitable for movement of a battalion to a point from which an attack could be launched against the flank or rear. The attack therefore had to be made frontally by crossing an open flat leading to the base of the hill.

Two battalions struck. Japanese machine guns and mortars lay down deadly final protective fires. Throughout the 13th, 14th and 15th, the 108th struggled for possession of this hill. Having once gained the crest, supplies could not be replenished because of the exposure of carrying parties to intense enemy fire. Repeated counterattacks finally exhausted the supply of small arms ammunition within the perimeter, and the troops were forced to withdraw for the night.

On the 16th, the advance was resumed and by late afternoon the attack succeeded. The 3rd Battalion secured the hill and the 1st Battalion, 300 yards to the south, was still advancing. In the next two days, troops of the 108th continued 2000 yards west, wiping out the diminishing resistance on the division's left flank and firmly establishing control over the extensive supply area along the south fork of the Sacobia River.

During these battles by the 108th the progress was too slow for General Krueger, who had watched the impasse develop at the base of the hills where there was no cover or concealment for our troops. Observers were convinced that General Krueger was again visualizing timetables in his head, expectations that he had probably shared with General MacArthur. General Brush wanted to bring more artillery and air power to bear to reduce projected casualties among the 108th troops. General Krueger wouldn't stand for it, and over General Brush's objections relieved the 108th's highly regarded commander, Colonel Marvin C. Bradley, on the spot. Colonel Maurice D. Stratta was brought in from the outside to replace Colonel Bradley, but progress under his leadership was just as painfully slow.

The huge supply installation that had previously been spotted and bombed from the air fell into the division's hands after the enemy's rout. Beginning at some point 1500 yards southwest of Top of the World and extending west for over 3000 yards, this supply area apparently had been designed to serve the entire Fort Stotsenburg area.

Captain Munyon decided it would be a good time to reconnoiter the area where he and Major Williams had spotted all the Japanese and their extensive supplies. When he and his driver got there, they found a long, beautiful, black, seven passenger Cadillac. It was spotless, highly polished, and had white seat covers. His driver put a couple of gallons of fuel in it, and it started right up. Munyon took the Cadillac for his own, and drove it around the division headquarters, which made the division commander more than a little uncomfortable.

There were an uncounted number of supply caves sealed during the process of eliminating enemy resistance, which made it impossible to determine how much materiel had been lost by the enemy. The following partial list of captured items serves to give some idea of the type and extent of the dumps:

- 210 vehicles (military and civilian) including tracked personnel carriers and bulldozers;
- 167 machine guns, light and heavy;
- 63 20mm guns (German make);
- 51 13mm guns (German make);
- 2 75mm guns;

There also were uncounted quantities of radios, telephone equipment, tires, transmitters, generators, wire, tools, miscellaneous equipment, and food. In addition, two 150mm self-propelled guns were found, one completely destroyed and the other burned. These guns had delivered fire upon our troops in Top of the World and Snake Hill West areas, and at the time were believed to be Japanese medium tanks mounting 70mm guns and employed as artillery. The capture of these guns was the first indication that weapons of this type were in use by the Japanese Army.

Interesting because they gave a clue regarding the desperate straits the enemy was in, Japanese planes were sighted on three occasions making air drops over enemy positions to the division's front. On both February 9th and 13th, two planes circled positions west of Top of the World and were observed to drop several bundles by parachute. They were later found to contain booby traps.

Four days later, on the 19th, two more planes circled the same area, dropping three groups of parachutes northeast of Snake Hill

West. A note found later in the vicinity of the parachutes was addressed to a Vice Admiral Kondo, and informed him that a drop was being made for him to include whiskey and cigarettes from Singapore.

The purpose of these air drops may never be known, outside of course, of the understandable supply of whiskey and cigarettes for the Admiral's sinking spirits. The enemy could hardly have expected these few bundles to alleviate his supply situation which, aggravated by the loss of his main supply dump, had become critical.

On the 19th of February, leaving one battalion to hold the division left flank, the 108th Infantry was moved from the Stotsenburg area to the north in the vicinity of Hill 29, on the right of the 185th Infantry.

The division now had three regiments in line, and was confronted by a concentrated area of resistance bedded in rock and stretching 6000 yards from mountain top to mountain top. The north flank was based on Hills 1700 and 29. to the south, where the two forks of the Sacobia River cut their jagged way through rocky ground, the rugged and harsh terrain of Sacobia Ridge formed the southern anchor.

Life for combat soldiers was no better than in other wars. Most lived in foxholes, with the foxholes often waterlogged with mud at the bottom. However, the Japanese soldier was a master at night infiltration. Just one example will illustrate the stress and danger the soldiers were exposed to. One young artillery sergeant who had just turned twenty-one was laying in his foxhole when a Japanese soldier peered down at him while holding a rifle and said "hello Joe." The young sergeant shot him, almost as a reflex action, and couldn't understand why the Japanese soldier didn't shoot first. It was a memory that haunted him for many years after the war.

On February 21st, the 40th Division was transferred to XI Corps, commanded by Major General Charles P. (Chink) Hall. On February 23rd, a coordinated attack by the three regiments was launched against the remaining enemy positions. On the right, the

108th Infantry advanced along the hill mass leading southwest toward Hill 29. Intense mortar and machine gun fire was encountered approximately 1200 yards northwest of the hill, where an enemy force was able to deliver direct fire from caves and flanking fire from positions cleverly concealed by cogon grass and brush in a small draw on the regiment's right. A Napalm air strike the following morning destroyed enemy positions in the draw, and the advance continued. The following day saw the 108th troops in control of Hill 29 and the high ground to the north and west, and an attack underway on a hill 2000 yards to the southwest, where the Japanese also occupied caves and dug-in positions. By February 26th this latter hill was in the division's possession and mopping up operations were being conducted to rout the remaining Japanese from their strongholds.

Thus, in three days the 108th had rolled back the enemy left flank. The number of extensive positions found abandoned with ammunition and weapons left in place gave evidence that the enemy had intended to make a determined stand in and about Hill 29. Prevented from doing so by the weight of the division's ground attack and heavy pounding by artillery and air, the enemy was forced to withdraw behind Hills 1700 and 1400. The Japanese possession of those two hills was being hotly contested by the 185th.

Hill 1700, rocky and barren, was connected by a low saddle with Hill 1500, 1000 yards to the northeast. Three steep, converging knife-edged ridges offered the only approaches to its peak. Japanese entrenched in deep caves midway up the precipitous sides and atop the pinpoint peak of the hill commanded all three approaches. Two thousand yards northwest of Hill 1700, Hill 1400, sloping upwards at the southwestern end, dominates the Malago and Marimla Rivers and the lower areas behind Hill 1700. Under cover of the thickly wooded river beds were several hundred enemy troops.

Hill 1500 was secured by the 185th troops on February 15th, leaving in that sector only Hills 1400 and 1700 in Japanese hands. In coordination with the 108th and 160th Infantry, the 185th, led by its 2nd and 3rd Battalions, launched its attack. B-24's pounded enemy rear areas while P-51 Mustangs and P-38 Lightnings conducted air strikes against Hills 1400 and 1700. Progress against Hill 1700 was extremely slow because of the withering crossfire the enemy was able to direct at our troops scaling the precipitous approaches.

To outflank the enemy and clear the area to the north, from which direction a second attack against Hill 1700 could be mounted, the 3rd Battalion was given the mission of circling wide and advancing southwest onto Hill 1400. On February 23rd, at 7:05 p.m., 3rd Battalion launched its attack following a preparation fired by the division artillery. The objective was secured by the end of the day.

This quick victory placed the 3rd Battalion on the right flank of Hill 1700 and in an excellent position to support an attack on that hill. As infantrymen eliminated enemy holdouts in their extensive trench system, the engineer platoon attached to the regiment began work on a road up Hill 1400 that night and through the next day. This permitted tracked vehicles to work their way up the mountain and place direct fire into caves on the reverse slope of Hill 1700.

Meanwhile, the 2nd Battalion reached a shelf-like position on the northeast slope of Hill 1700 and dug in for the night. The day's action had cost the enemy 140 dead. On February 24th the 2nd Battalion reverted to regimental reserve and the 1st Battalion assumed the mission of attacking and securing Hill 1700.

At 9:15 the morning of February 25th, 1st Battalion jumped off in the attack on Hill 1700 and the adjacent Hill 1750 following a devastating concentration of division artillery, tank destroyers, tanks, M-7's, mortars and machine guns. The tremendous hail of explosives completely enveloped Hill 1700 with dust, making it unnecessary to use smoke. Taking advantage of the concealment

149

afforded by the dust and the shock of the explosions, Company C fought its way to the top of Hill 1750 under close overhead fire support from Company D. Elements of Company B fought their way up the southwest approach, and at 10:20 a.m. planted the American flag on top of Hill 1700. Twenty minutes later Hill 1700 was secured and mopping up of isolated pockets of resistance was in progress. That night the Japanese made frequent but unsuccessful attacks in a feeble attempt to win the hill back. A total of 343 Japanese were killed in the battles for Hills 1400, 1700 and 1750.

Rugged mountains around Clark Field on Luzon. Note the hundreds of caves and rugged terrain. (Source: Robert W. Munyon)

The Japanese had been driven from their mutually supporting defensive positions, and had no further prepared positions to fall back on. Their supplies had long since been captured or destroyed.

The enemy had no place to go except the precipitous, rain forest-covered slopes of the Zambales Mountains, where he would be forced to forage for himself or die.

The mopping up continued, with die hard enemy soldiers being rooted out of caves. Company E, mopping up on the southeast nose of Hill 1700, flushed out and killed forty Japanese from just one deep cave.

Losses by the 185th were minimal in capturing Hills 1400, 1700, and 1750, while providing the division positions that dominated the entire central division zone and made enemy use of nearby hills untenable. Movement along the Marimla, Cauayan and Malago Rivers was denied to the enemy, and areas to the southwest in front of the 160th Infantry were within range of 185th Infantry observation and fires.

The enemy made one last attempt to loosen the division's hold on their former left flank when, in the early hours of the 28th, they attempted a night attack against the 3-185th perimeter on the southwest end of Hill 1400. An estimated seventy-five Japanese advanced on the perimeter and began to dig in. Caught in position by illuminating flares, they were fired on at short range by heavy machine gun and mortar fire. The next morning forty-seven dead were counted.

On the morning of February 24th, the 2nd and 3rd Battalions of the 160th Infantry attacked Sacobia Ridge, adjacent to the Sacobia River which flows by the north edge of Clark Field. The attack was made with 2-160th approaching from the south side and the 3-160th coming down from the north.

Almost impassable terrain impeded the advance. Deep gullies and ravines had to be crossed under heavy enemy fire, and the steep, sheer cliffs bordering the Sacobia River made direct advance impossible and deployment slow and costly. The ordeal of one company, Company E, 160th Infantry, serves as an example of the travails faced by the troops.

Company E moved at 2:00 a.m. on February 24th in order to reach the line of departure by "H" Hour. While moving along a draw on the north side of the ridge, they saw a column of Japanese moving parallel with them towards the line of departure. When the unit crossed the line of departure at dawn, Japanese opened fire on the unit from all directions. The Japanese then set fire to the tall kunai grass, and followed behind the flames while closing in on the attackers. The attackers had suddenly become defenders, and withdrew under the cover of heavy machine guns from Company M. One man was killed and two wounded in the brief action.

As the attack was renewed, three enemy counterattacks launched against 3-160th troops were repulsed with several friendly casualties. Enemy action continued throughout the night, keeping the troops under constant mortar and machine gun fire. Carrying parties attempting to reach troops from the northeast were pelted with mortar fire, and the enemy repeatedly launched night infiltration attacks.

Heavy artillery concentrations the following day preceded the 160th's renewed attack which was launched in the face of machine gun and mortar fire. Twelve hundred yards were gained in the day's action. The 160th troops then occupied positions on Williams Ridge, overlooking Ribble Ridge, named in memory of Major James A. Williams and Major Frank Ribble. Both were shot down while making a reconnaissance of that area in an artillery cub plane. In succeeding days, mopping up continued and by the 27th, Sacobia Ridge was secured.

Since the beginning of the Luzon campaign other divisional units had been busily engaged ensuring the uninterrupted advance of the regiments. The 115th Engineer Battalion, having performed a remarkable job of bridge building and road repairing from Lingayen to Bamban, assumed additional and even more difficult duties during operations at Bamban. Early in the operation, work was begun on clearing the extensive minefields in the Clark Field area. Following closely behind the advancing troops, engineer demolition crews also sealed or destroyed the caves and pillboxes overrun by the infantry to destroy any small groups hiding therein and to prevent reoccupancy by the enemy. Virtually a never-ending job, over 600 caves were closed up to the time of the division relief.

Roads capable of handling the heavy traffic of tanks, artillery pieces and supply trucks were constructed close behind each regiment as it advanced over terrain where only foot paths had previously existed. Bulldozers, often subjected to enemy small arms fire, pushed the roads up steep rocky grades, along knife-edge ridges and through densely vegetated areas as far forward as the front lines. Despite the ruggedness of the terrain, the regiments were rarely without a means of bringing their heavy supporting weapons and supplies forward.

Medical personnel performed outstanding service in the difficult and dangerous work of carrying wounded from forward areas down the precipitous slopes to collecting points. Frequently under fire, numerous individual acts of heroism on the part of the litter bearers were recorded.

The reconnaissance troop continually patrolled the Capas-O'Donnell-Tiaong road, as well as roads on the division left flank. Several small contacts were made during the period, and an entrenched enemy outpost of approximately 100 was routed by fire from foothills south of O'Donnell.

By March 1st, after 53 days of continuous fighting and 37 days after entering Bamban, the enemy had been driven into the mountains. From 10,000 to 17,000 yards west of his first line of defense, enemy organized resistance had ceased to exist, and huge quantities of supplies had been destroyed or captured. In addition, illness was making greater and greater inroads upon his dwindling strength; 6087 Japanese had been counted dead, and additional hundreds were known to have been killed by air and artillery fire. What forces the enemy could muster from the battered remnants of the *Takayama*, *Takaya* and *Eguchi Butais*, would serve only as isolated small groups in scattered positions in the Zambales Mountains.

To the east, friendly aircraft were safely operating from Clark Field and Fort Stotsenburg was secure. Traffic on the National Highway to Manila was free from enemy fire. Only the distant mopping up of withdrawing groups of stragglers remained of the Stotsenburg-Bamban operation.

Relief of the 40th Division in the Stotsenburg-Bamban area by the 43rd Division was started February 28th, and became effective March 2nd. The division moved to the San Fabian-San Jacinto-Manaoag area, near Lingayen Gulf, for a brief rest. The division on March 2nd was transferred from Krueger's Sixth Army to Lieutenant General Robert L. Eichelberger's Eighth Army.

This ended a very unfortunate and generally strained relationship. General Krueger had tried to get Major General Oscar Griswold of the XIV Corps to relieve General Brush while the 40th Division was fighting on Luzon. General Griswold met with General Brush, and was told that neither General Krueger nor any of his staff had been to the front lines to see the division fighting. General Griswold then told General Krueger that he could relieve Griswold if he chose, but he (Griswold) wouldn't recommend General Brush's relief. General Krueger then transferred the 40th Division to Major General Chink Hall's XI Corps, and tried to get General Hall to relieve Brush. General Hall also refused. This rather sordid episode included a letter of commendation from General Krueger to General Brush for his inspired leadership on Luzon. As General Brush described the letter, "it dripped honey from every pore." As mentioned previously, General Krueger's ultimate solution was to transfer the 40th Division out of his army.

Later it was revealed that General Krueger thought he was giving General Eichelberger his worst division. General Eichelberger saw it very differently, and was pleased to receive the 40th. He and General Brush enjoyed a warm association in addition to their professional relationship.

General Eichelberger was highly regarded by senior leadership of the division, and those feelings were reciprocated. General Eichelberger, when Superintendant of West Point, used to have his cadets train with local National Guard units. General Eichelberger, considered one of the Army's intellectuals, was a direct competitor with General Krueger. In fact, there was considerable bad blood between the two of them, as there had been between the division's leadership and General Krueger.

During one of General Eichelberger's visits to division headquarters, he spotted the shiny black Cadillac that Captain Munyon had appropriated some time before. When the general asked who the Cadillac belonged to, Munyon admitted he was the culprit. It was apparent to Munyon that Eichelberger would like it, so he gave Eichelberger the Cadillac, which was promptly shipped off to his headquarters.

The division was proud of their first real combat. They had killed or captured a total of 6,145 Japanese troops on Luzon. After the bloody fighting for several weeks, the division was disappointed they were not selected to take Manila. Many soldiers were convinced that "the brass" didn't want a National Guard regiment to take Manila, and sent in the Army's 5th Cavalry. Actually, a regiment of another National Guard division, the 37th, played a significant role in clearing Manila.

After the division was placed under command of General Eichelberger's Eighth Army, the division received word they were to be used in regaining control of Panay and Negros. When elements of the division closed into the San Fabian-San Jacinto-Manaoag area, in Pangasinan Province, preparations for the operation began. Naval units under command of Rear Admiral Arthur D. "Rip" Strubel arrived in Lingayen Gulf to coordinate planning for the landings.

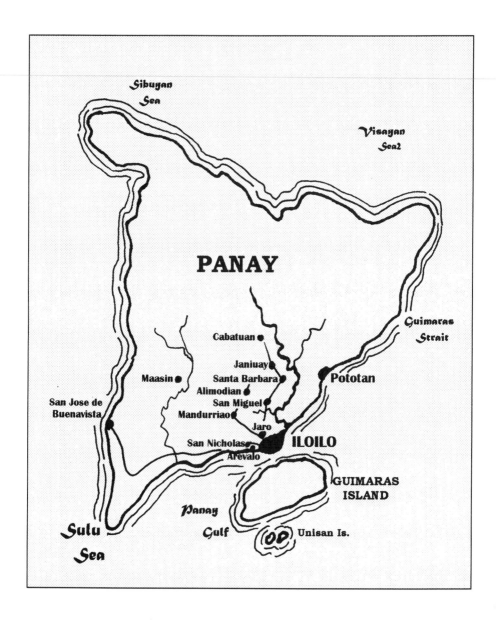

CHAPTER EIGHT

PANAY, LEYTE, MINDANAO AND SMALLER ISLANDS

The Japanese stranded on the various Philippine Islands had been left to their fate. It was apparent to senior Japanese commanders that their empire had lost control of both the air and sea, and they could no longer count on resupply or reinforcement. They had stockpiled munitions, but were woefully short of artillery ammunition. Transport of all kinds had been decimated by American aircraft and submarines, and communications were continually disrupted.

Lieutenant General Sasaku Susuki, commanding the Japanese XXXV Army, originally had his headquarters on Leyte, but intended to make his last stand on the big island of Mindanao. Plans to redeploy forces failed due to lack of shipping. Even movements using small native craft were usually intercepted by allied aircraft or PT boats. General Susuki managed to move to Cebu, but lost his life in April when he attempted to move on to Mindanao.

The defense of Panay, Negros and neighboring islands was vested in the Japanese 102nd Division under the command of Lieutenant General Sarehira Fukuei. The division was organized in 1944, expanded from an independent mixed brigade by adding troops, many of whom were under trained and second rate. What strength the division had was already diluted by having to send reinforcements to Leyte, reinforcements which in most cases were never seen again. To compound the problems, General Fukuei was hospitalized, so command was delegated to the two brigade headquarters, the 77th and 78th.

The strength on Panay, primarily the 170th Independent Infantry Battalion (IIB) and a company each from the 171st and 354th IIB's, totalled about 2,775. Of that total, only about 1,500 were combat troops, and there were 400 civilians.

Lieutenant Colonel Ryoichi Totsuka, commander of the 170th IIB, was the senior commander, with most of his forces concentrated around Iloilo. The approximate enemy dispositions:

Iloilo City and vicinity (Panay)	2,000
Guimaras Island	250
Tigbauan	50
Tiring Airfield	225
Inampulugan Island	25
Tagabanhan Island	25
San Jose de Buenavista	200
	2,775

The Japanese garrisons were actually rather compressed in the areas listed above. If they strayed far, they ran into the guerrillas, who tended to ignore normal rules of warfare, as atrocities on both sides were commonplace.

The major elements of the Japanese forces had been engaged in the campaigns of Luzon and Leyte. However, the existence of enemy strong points athwart the main sea lanes of the archipelago could not be ignored. It was determined that the occupation of Panay and Negros was necessary for a successful conclusion of the Philippines campaign. Panay had the fine harbor in the Philippine's second largest city of Iloilo, which was adjacent to the protected shipping lanes of Guimaras Strait. It was therefore decided to make Panay the next objective, with subsequent landings to be made on Guimaras and Negros Islands.

Through the efforts of the guerrilla organization on Panay - - the 6th Military District, with approximately 1,500 Filipino officers and 21,000 enlisted men under the command of Colonel Marcario L.

Peralta, Jr. - - the enemy situation on the island was relatively well known to our forces prior to landing. Peralta was only about thirty years old, but well educated and a tough-minded soldier. The guerrillas on Panay controlled the countryside, while the Japanese remained primarily in town or village enclaves.

Although Panay was originally intended to be used as a major supply base by the Japanese forces, Panay had evolved to serve principally as a hospital and rehabilitation base for the enemy troops. Because of our air and naval blockade, the enemy had for some time been dependent upon submarines for supply, and for his subsistence upon whatever products could be secured from local sources.

The plan of operation called for the main effort of the division to be made against Iloilo, with a secondary attack by one battalion in the direction of Jaro to block any movement from the city in that direction. The action was to be primarily conducted by the 185th RCT. The 40th Reconnaissance Troop was to move north and in the direction of Santa Barbara airfield to interpose themselves between the Iloilo garrison and the mountains to which they might attempt to withdraw, and to detect and delay the consolidation or movement of any enemy forces along the roads. Combat aircraft were directed to strafe all serviceable barges in the harbor to prevent evacuation by water.

The beach selected as most suitable for landing operations was a stretch about 11½ miles long between Tigbauan and Iloilo. The beach, which consisted of loose and shifty non-coral sand with patches of gravel, did however look like it would be difficult for motor movement across or along the beach.

The mission of the 185th was to:

1. Secure the DBHL and advance rapidly to the East and Northeast to seize the Iloilo area out to Phase Line O-1.

159

2. Upon completion of the occupation of the Iloilo area, and the destruction of hostile forces therein, on division order the 185th RCT was to initiate operations to destroy remaining enemy forces within the area bounded by Objective Line O-2.

3. Be prepared on division order to initiate overland or amphibious operations to destroy all remaining enemy forces on Panay Island.

The 2nd Battalion, 160th Infantry, was to remain in reserve initially and defend the beachhead. In addition, amphibious patrols of the 160th were to be prepared to land by rubber boat on the northwest and southeast coasts of Guimaras Island on S plus 1, to determine enemy strength and activity there and locate suitable landing beaches for the battalion in the event a landing became necessary. The 160th Infantry (less the 2nd Battalion) was to move from Luzon on the turnaround shipping, arriving in time to participate in the Panay operation on S plus 10 days.

American commanders had been increasingly relying on guerrilla reports in planning assault landings. In spite of many heroic accomplishments by guerrilla forces, their contributions were erratic enough for commanders to be very cautious in using information from the guerrillas. One example was a report by guerrilla forces that they had checked Samal Island and it was unoccupied by Japanese. When the Army Commander then sent American forces there, they were quickly pinned down by heavy enemy fire. Questionable reports had been received from the guerrilla forces on Luzon and Mindanao, as well as from Panay.

General Eichelberger had met earlier with Colonel Peralta, and tended to distrust some of his reports. As a result of those concerns and experience with the guerrillas on other islands, General Eichelberger asked General Brush to meet him at the Mangaldan air strip on March 13th. There he discussed the Panay operation, and specifically admonished General Brush to ensure that tactical decisions were not affected by the guerrillas. He also emphasized the need for speedy and aggressive action, and stressed the importance of maintaining constant contact with enemy forces.

The 1st and 3rd Battalion Landing Teams of the 185th, which were the assault elements, were embarked March 12, 1945 on LST's. The plan was for the 3-185th to land on the west (left) side, on the beach designated Blue Beach; while the 1-185th was to hit the Red Beach to the east (right). The 2-185th (Regimental Reserve) and the 2-160th (Division Reserve) were loaded on Landing Craft, Infantry (LCI's). The assault waves were to be landed in LVT-4's.

Loading was completed on March 14th, and the transport convoy consisting of nine LST's and four LCI's departed on that day and the next. The convoy went by way of Mindoro, picking up elements of the 542nd Engineer Boat and Shore Regiment (primarily LCM's), which they towed on towards Panay. There was little of the excitement, including kamikazes, experienced during the previous movement to Luzon. The uneventful passage, other than a heavy storm at sea, was completed on schedule March 18th.

In the meantime, taking advantage of the airfields which had been built in the relatively secure northern end of the island by the guerrillas, artillery cub planes were transported in C-47's to Panay two days before the invasion. When assembled, the planes were test flown and held in readiness to provide aerial observation over the target area prior to and during the landing.

There were two key bridges just west of the village of Tigbauan. The landing was planned near the bridge farthest west. The plans therefore called for naval gunfire to destroy the bridge between the landing areas and Tigbauan in order to delay any Japanese reinforcements from the village. The destroyers commenced firing about 6:47 a.m. on March 18th. The destroyer U.S.S. Thatcher started firing at the wrong bridge, but quickly caught the mistake.

The command group was aboard the U. S. Coast Guard Cutter Ingham. When Rear Admiral Strubel, commanding the Victor I Attack Group, saw the Thatcher was firing at the wrong bridge, he ordered an immediate cease fire. When the firing stopped, a group of about fifteen or twenty Filipino guerrillas emerged from cover near the Tigbauan Bridge where the navy guns had been impacting. They stood on a sand spit, and began waving to attract attention. General Brush and Admiral Strubel saw that they looked legitimate, although it was difficult to tell at that distance. Not sure what the situation was, General Brush's aide, Captain Bob Munyon, volunteered to go find out.

Admiral Strubel ordered an LCVP brought alongside, as landing craft with the assault troops continued to circle. Lieutenant Colonel John K. Wright, commanding the 115th Combat Engineer Battalion, volunteered to go along. At 8:42 a.m. the two of them jumped aboard the LCVP, the machine guns on the craft were uncovered, and they headed for shore. The craft got to within about 35 yards of shore, but hit a sand bar. The two of them waded ashore, where the young leader of the guerrillas met them. Speaking excellent English, the guerrilla leader told them that the Japanese were hurriedly loading up to get out of Tigbauan, but their route was blocked by guerrillas.

Leaving the rest of the guerrillas on the sand spit, the three of them then crawled over to the all-weather road that paralleled the beach. From there they peered through and around the heavy underbrush looking down into the town square, only three or four hundred yards away. There they saw a typical village center, complete with a fountain and a circular drive around the square. More important, they saw Japanese running everywhere, loading materiel on water buffalo carts, obviously preparing to get away into the hills.

The two officers then took the Filipino officer back to the ship with them. He gave the admiral and General Brush a detailed report, and noted that the approximately thirty-five Japanese at Tigbauan were confined to the area of the church. In addition, about twenty Japanese had been reported by guerrillas the previous day to be dug in on a hill called Cordova Tigbauan. As a result, the naval bombardment was cancelled, and both bridges were left intact. The problem the LCVP had when it hit the sand bar was confirmed by a hydrographic test conducted by the Red Beach Beachmaster. He recommended that all landings be moved west to Blue Beach, just west of the Sibalon River. When it was clear that recommendation was feasible, Admiral Strubel directed all craft to land on Blue Beach.

From that point on it was anti-climatic. In direct contrast to the Luzon landing, all was quiet, broken only by the steady hum and vibration of powerful engines, and the lapping of white-caps against ship hulls. The first waves hit the beach at 9:15 a.m. on the 18th, with the 3-185th on the left and the 1-185th on the right. Some of the troops were met by guerrillas, all lined up in clean khakis, complete with decorations. Only a few rounds of scattered rifle fire were received from the handful of enemy who had been left behind by the withdrawing garrison. Seven of these Japanese were killed and two who were wounded and left behind were captured. Identifications thus secured confirmed the presence of elements of the 2nd Company, 170th Independent Infantry Battalion.

Both battalions quickly cleared the beaches and called for the 2-185th to land. That battalion did so at 10:15 a.m., quickly moving to an assembly area ready to jump off in the direction of Iloilo some seven miles to the east.

Immediately following the initial landing, one platoon had secured the important concrete bridge over the Sibalon River and the barrio of Tigbauan. There was only scattered resistance, as the invasion appeared to be a surprise based on the number of mined facilities overrun before they could be exploded. By the close of the first day, 1-185th Infantry, advanced ten miles to Arevalo, 5000 yards west of Iloilo, and the other two battalions were in position at Oton and San Nicholas.

Shortly after noon, a cub aircraft dropped a message from Colonel Peralta. He stated that his guerrillas could contain the Japanese in Iloilo if provided more ammunition and a radio. At 12:40 p.m.,

General Brush and Captain Munyon went ashore in the admiral's gig. They returned at 5:10 p.m., and an hour later went ashore with a full load of personnel.

Most of the Japanese garrison at Tigbauan had withdrawn to the north. Elements of 2-160th Infantry, using guerrilla guides, made several contacts with this group as it continued its retreat into the hills, while the 40th Reconnaissance troop moved in two columns, one north toward Alimodian and the second toward San Miguel and Santa Barbara. A small group of enemy near Cordova, who withdrew when fired upon, was the only contact made.

On the nineteenth, on the southwestern outskirts of Molo, the 1-185th met their first resistance in the form of rifle fire. As they closed with the enemy, they came under intense machine gun fire from numerous stone buildings. Supporting medium tanks were called for and provided direct fire to blast the enemy from behind the thick walls. The Japanese responded with mortars as they mounted a tenacious but unsuccessful defense. The town of Molo was quickly secured and approximately 500 civilians, temporarily imprisoned in the church, were released.

On the same day, the 3-185th attacked and secured Mandurrio Airfield against only token resistance. By noon, elements of the battalion had reached Carpenter Bridge, spanning the Iloilo River north of Molo. The bridge had been prepared for demolition through extensive use of electrically controlled aerial bombs, but the small Japanese guard detachment was taken by surprise and the pillbox from which the mines were controlled was captured intact. The enemy entrenched in pillboxes and foxholes just south of the bridge fought until late in the evening with sporadic rifle, machine gun and knee mortar fire.

Capture of the bridge facilitated lateral coordination, as the 1st and 3rd Battalions were separated by the Iloilo River. At Jaro, north of Iloilo City, a patrol received light mortar and small arms fire, and 300 yards southeast of the barrio the enemy destroyed the small bridge over the Tigon River, which had been mined in much the same way as the Carpenter Bridge.

As it grew dark on March 19th, 22 enemy had been counted dead, 15 by divisional troops, and 7 by guerrilla forces. Three of the enemy had been captured. The division had suffered 6 KIA and 23 WIA.

Soldiers of the 185th Infantry relax on the road near Molo as a tank passes them. (Source: National Archives)

Elements of the 40th Reconnaissance Troop driving north to Maasin and northwest to Pototan and Janiuay had not found any enemy troops. Other elements were attacking enemy targets near Santa Barbara airfield, where guerrilla leaders reported their forces had surrounded an estimated 125 Japanese.

The suburbs of Iloilo had many Spanish-style homes, often surrounded by thick eight foot tall adobe walls. This made each home a veritable fort. The tactic that evolved was to have tanks shoot an antitank round point blank to penetrate the walls, after which a high explosive shell would be fired, or grenades thrown through. There was great concern that fighting to take Iloilo would be extremely costly as the troops fought from house to house.

The evening of March 19th found the enemy around Iloilo under attack by divisional troops in a pincers from the direction of Molo and Mandurriao. The western outskirts of Jaro had been reached, and guerrilla forces were in defensive positions along a road straddling the Iloilo-Pavia road just north of Jaro. The focus was on defeating the enemy while minimizing damage to the city, and at the same time preventing his escape up to the western high ground.

That night, large fires were observed burning in Iloilo and Jaro. In the dark of the early morning hours virtually the entire enemy garrison of Iloilo began an orderly but hasty withdrawal northward from the city. Burning their vehicles along the road to delay pursuit, the Japanese attacked the guerrilla line in strength with a heavy concentration of mortar, machine gun and rifle fire. The Filipino forces, unable to offer sustained resistance, were forced to give way. It was later estimated that 1000 Japanese, accompanied by approximately 200 Japanese and Filipino civilians, participated in the evacuation.

A warning order was dispatched to the 2-185th, who moved into assembly areas behind the 1-185th and prepared to attack Iloilo the morning of the 20th on the right of 1-185th. Supporting field artillery moved into positions at Arevalo and commenced their registration fires on Iloilo.

The roar of tank engines announced the attack in the morning, as all three battalions moved forward. Notification was radioed to regimental headquarters at Arevalo that the line of departure was crossed at 8:17 a.m.

Troops of the 3-185th raced towards the Northern outskirts of Jaro, with armored vehicles in the lead. That battalion reached Jaro with only minor contacts, sending patrols out in all directions seeking the retreating enemy.

The 1-185th again ran into stiff resistance from the Japanese still around Molo. The supporting tanks established a base of fire with high explosive shells while the infantry maneuvered, eliminating the resistance by shortly after noon. They were then given the approval, along with the 2-185th on their right flank, to attack Iloilo.

The race for Iloilo began, with troops from both battalions mounted on the decks of tanks. By 1:35 p.m. on March 20th the news was flashed that Iloilo was secure, overflowing with our troops. Unfortunately, the city had been 80% destroyed by the Japanese. The towns of Jaro and La Paz were also occupied by friendly troops.

Despite the acute food shortage, caused by the Jap-imposed restrictions of movement to and from the city, American liberating forces were warmly welcomed by the civilians with gifts of eggs, fruit, and candies made from the local comotes and coconuts. Unfortunately, law and order broke down, and civilians started looting everywhere in the city. People were seen running through the streets of the city with everything from food and bolts of cloth to sewing machines. The 2-185th was given the mission of bringing order to Iloilo. Looting was stopped, including warehouses along the docks, and guards were posted.

Increasing evidence obtained from prisoners of war and captured documents indicated that until the very last minute, the Japanese commander in Iloilo had intended to remain and defend the city. The final decision to abandon Iloilo City came as a distinct about-face, a last and desperate attempt to avoid possible annihilation at the hands of the American forces. The suddenness and power of the division's attack had created a strong element of panic. Fraught with indecision, and pressed for time, the enemy failed to execute the defensive measures they had worked so hard to prepare. Bridges prepared for demolition were not destroyed; roadblocks were left undefended; mines in position to offer considerable delay to our mechanized elements were detonated long before our tanks and armored cars approached; and demolitions

167

that remained were poorly installed and easily detected. The Iloilo City power plant had been extensively mined but suffered only minor damage from the division's artillery fire. The port of Iloilo, one of the best in the area, was still repairable. The 115th Engineers opened the harbor for American shipping 48 hours after the city's capture.

The chaos in the enemy command was strikingly demonstrated just before midnight on the 20th when, obviously unaware of the Japanese retreat, a 75-foot Japanese motor launch came confidently chugging up the Iloilo River from the sea. The 2-185th sent troops to investigate, as the boat berthed at the dock near the Customs House. Fire was exchanged, and a Sherman tank added to the firepower with one of its machine guns. Two of the Japanese, debarking to tie up the boat, were captured and the remaining five of the crew of seven attempted to escape. One of the five was killed, and the other four were subsequently captured. One of the captured soldiers stated they had just returned from Guimaras Island, and had no clue that our troops were in Iloilo.

In the meantime, the main body of Japanese troops succeeded in passing through the guerrilla lines, and hurried north along the road to Pavia. Elements of the 40th Reconnaissance Troop were directed to proceed toward Pavia from the north to intercept the force. Contact was made with the enemy on the northern outskirts of the barrio, and a fire fight ensued. As the enemy units were attempting to elude our forces by taking to the Tigon River valley, combat aircraft strafed and bombed the area.

Meanwhile, the 1-185th was ordered to regroup and move north through La Paz and Jaro to reestablish physical contact with 3-185th. Armored spearheads of 3-185th veered north and northeast from Jaro, rolling through Panda and on to Pavia. Small arms fire was received as the unit charged into Pavia, only momentarily slowing the drive as determined troops closed and destroyed the enemy. The troops kept running into groups of enemy stragglers and rear elements of the enemy column. Dispersed, disorganized and forced to leave behind all supplies other than those which could be hand-carried, the Japanese forces quickly degenerated into small groups, avoiding contact with our troops whenever possible in their attempt to gain refuge in the mountains northwest of Cabatuan. At least 100 enemy were known to have been killed in the Pavia action and in scattered contacts along the evacuation routes.

Combat patrols of the 1-185th reached Zarraga on March 21st, seven miles east of Santa Barbara, and Pototan, eleven miles east of Santa Barbara, without enemy contact. North of San Miguel, fifteen of the enemy were killed, while still more fled north. During the two preceding days, elements of the 40th Reconnaissance Troop had been in contact with the Japanese in the Santa Barbara area, leveling barracks, destroying supply and ammunition dumps and maintaining harassing fire upon the Japanese garrison. As a result of the combined action of the 40th Reconnaissance Troop and the guerrilla forces, 54 Japanese had been counted killed. By the morning of the 22nd of March, Santa Barbara Airfield was secure and the routed Japanese survivors had joined the groups of stragglers headed northwest. On the same day, northwest of Cabatuan a combat patrol from 2-160th Infantry, which had moved the day before to the barrio with the mission of intercepting any enemy forces attempting to reach high ground from the east, contacted an unestimated number of enemy in the vicinity of Jimanban.

Elements of the division had made excellent progress on Panay. The Japanese were incapable of mounting significant attacks, and both Santa Barbara and Mundurriao Airfields had been converted into first class strips for use by American aircraft. In accordance with the original plan, efforts were started to clear the enemy from neighboring islands. An amphibious patrol from the 2-160th, early on the 22nd of March landed by rubber boat on Guimaras Island, off the southeast coast of Panay. At Buenavista, on the west coast of the island, guerrillas reported they had recently wiped out the small garrison of approximately 20 Japanese. In this barrio the bodies of 28 civilians, slaughtered by the Japanese, were found, at least seven of them having been tied together and bayoneted. The only enemy remaining on the island were small groups which had long since taken to the hills. The guerrillas were confident they could handle the remnants.

Company G, 2-185th was given the mission of destroying the mine control station on tiny Inampulugan Island between Panay and Negros. On March 22nd a small combat patrol proceeded in LCM's to the island, and were met by scattered rifle fire. The small garrison of 24 enlisted men and one officer of the Japanese Naval Guard Force then fled into the central hill area, abandoning the mine control station. The unit moved inland as far as Hill 457 without reestablishing contact, so returned to the Japanese installation. They destroyed the installation, radio equipment, some electric generators, and a remote control sea mine field, which turned out to be one of the most elaborate systems discovered up to that time in the Pacific. Several new items of equipment were brought back for technical study. The unit returned to Iloilo at noon on the 23rd.

Meanwhile, elsewhere on the island of Panay, isolated contacts were continuing with small groups of stragglers in the general Alimodian-Cabatuan-Pototan area (north of Iloilo). About 3000 yards southwest of Pavia, Warrant Officer Lee Cree and three ordnance sergeants from Service Company 185th were in a jeep approaching Baluarte on March 24th. Excited villagers flagged them down, and told them there were "many Japs" in a nearby draw. Warrant Officer Cree investigated and found twenty-one Japanese preparing their lunch. He quickly deployed his three man task force and took the enemy under fire with an M-1 rifle, two carbines and a sub-machine gun. The surprised Japanese put up a feeble resistance, throwing hand grenades which exploded harmlessly. In a few minutes it was very quiet. All of the enemy were dead.

By March 25th, the Panay campaign came to an end as both the 1-185th and 2-185th finished sweeping the outlying areas. The

160th continued mopping up the sizeable Japanese remnants. Those remnants had been slowly making their way to the high ground west of Cabatuan, avoiding contact with our forces when possible. From numerous barrios in the path of these stragglers, civilians reported Japanese foraging parties murdering entire families after stealing their food. One American officer investigating these reports in the northern outskirts of San Miguel found one man and fourteen women and children, all Filipinos, who had been tied together by the Japanese and then bayoneted in the stomach or stabbed in the neck.

After the Jimanban contacts, where our infantry and cannon company fire in scattered engagements had annihilated close to 200 of the enemy, few contacts were made in the lowland of the Iloilo Plain. Later, elements of the 160th Infantry began establishing contacts with hastily organized enemy positions in the Mount Tigbauan area, in the mountains northwest of Leon, and in the northern Sibalon River valley. Mechanized reconnaissance by the 40th Reconnaissance Troop had confirmed the report that the island's northern coastal regions were free of enemy, and only in San Jose, Antique Province, did an enemy unit exist that still maintained its tactical and organizational integrity.

Throughout April and May, 2-160th made repeated contacts with enemy groups in the Cabatuan area. On the 7th of May, intense machine gun and rifle fire was received from an estimated 150 to 200 Japanese in well dug-in positions in the mountains in the vicinity of Bucari, twelve miles northwest of Cabatuan. In addition, one of the division's supply trains moving north in the Sibalon River Valley 4000 yards northwest of Leon, was attacked by approximately fifteen Japanese. On the 13th of May, eighteen B-24's bombed enemy positions in this area, destroying the fortifications and dispersing the enemy forces. Subsequent to this air strike, no major contacts were made with Japanese troops and the elements of 2-160th withdrew to the Iloilo Plain for garrison and training activities. From this point on, patrols were used to investigate reports of Japanese foraging parties and to destroy those groups which attempted to descend into the lower plain.

Prisoners and captured documents disclosed that the enemy's original intention had been to establish a second line of defense in the Cabatuan area, but the rapidity of the division's drive had frustrated that aim. The 1st Company of the 170th IIB, stationed at Cabatuan at the time of our landing, had never been contacted by our troops. It was believed following the dispersal of the enemy forces in Iloilo, that company had withdrawn into the northwestern mountains.

Many Japanese married Filipinos during their occupation of Panay. The Japanese took their families with them when they pulled back into the hills. Gruesome evidence of the hopeless situation into which the enemy had been forced after his evacuation of Iloilo was furnished by the account given by two Filipino women, who with four Japanese babies were the only survivors of the mass suicide and murder of 62 Japanese civilians in the area south of Jimanban. A group of Japanese soldiers, their flight evidently slowed by the civilians whom they had forced or persuaded to evacuate with them from the city, were overtaken by divisional troops. Driven to a final stand, they stabbed and bayoneted the women and children prior to their own destruction by our fire. The bodies, along with the few severely wounded survivors, were found by a patrol from 2-160th Infantry.

In La Paz, northern suburb of Iloilo, Japanese prisoners were captured who testified further of the desperate measures taken by the Japanese during their evacuation. In the La Paz hospital, on the night of the withdrawal, about fifty bedridden military patients were given an injection of a drug to render them unconscious. The hospital was then set afire. Only a few of the patients were able to escape cremation by crawling out of the burning building before the drug injection took effect.

The guerrilla forces played a key role during the division's operations on Panay, and for a considerable time afterwards. In spite of previous warnings about their reliability, they provided timely and accurate intelligence, and shouldered much of the fighting themselves. Our air strikes had rendered the airfield at San Jose inoperative, and the guerrilla harassment of the enemy had contributed to their ineffectiveness. On April 9th, elements of the 63rd Infantry (Guerrilla Forces) attacked, and by the end of the next day had secured both the town and the airfield. A total of 118 Japanese had been killed, with the remainder fleeing into the mountains to the northwest.

*Generals Eichelberger and Brush leave Colonel Peralta's
Headquarters with Colonel Peralta shortly after decorating him
with the Distinguished Service Cross (Source: Robert W. Munyon)*

As a consequence of the significant contributions made by the guerrillas, it was recommended that Colonel Peralta be decorated. This was not a routine proposal, because Colonel Peralta had jailed several of his political rivals. At least one was a brother of a member of Philippine President Sergio Osmena's cabinet. General

MacArthur wanted to get the brother out, so approved award of the Distinguished Service Cross, but only if Peralta cooperated. Otherwise, Peralta was to be jailed. In General Eichelberger's words later, "There had been some question whether we would arrest him or decorate him, but it is evident he decided to be a good Indian."

General Eichelberger then personally pinned Colonel Peralta with the Distinguished Service Cross during a ceremony at 4:00 p.m. on March 20th 1945, with General Brush reading the citation. A guerrilla band provided music for the ceremony. They played four musical ruffles instead of three, a rather subtle thank you to General Eichelberger.

On March 8, 1945, the 108th RCT, including the 164th Field Artillery Battalion; Company C, 115th Engineers; and Company C, 115th Medical Battalion sailed from Lingayen, Luzon to Ormoc, Leyte. There the 108th RCT relieved the 164th Infantry of the Americal Division on March 23rd. The 108th RCT was placed under the 8th Army Area Command and was given the mission of working with the guerrillas in destroying enemy forces still operating in the northwestern part of Leyte.

Before embarking from Luzon, 1,038 officers and enlisted men from the 108th had been transferred to the 160th Infantry and 185th Infantry, bringing those units to strength. On its arrival at Ormoc, the 108th and other units of the Regimental Combat Team were brought up to strength with the addition of 67 officers and 1,860 enlisted men.

From April 10th to May 1st the First and Third Battalions conducted an offensive in the Villaba-Abijao-Bugabuga area killing 1,007 Japanese while losing 15 men killed in action. On April 7, 1945, the Masbate Task Force, commanded by Lieutenant Colonel George Wood, landed at Masbate town on the island of Masbate, north of Leyte. The task force consisted of the 108th's Second Battalion, Antitank Platoon, and Cannon Company; platoons from

Company C, 115th Engineers and Company C, 115th Medics, plus other attached units.

Masbate is a small L-shaped island with over two hundred miles of coastline. The island was sparsely populated, and had almost no improved roads. The Japanese there, estimated at about four hundred, were primarily ill-equipped survivors of Japanese ships sunk in the Sibuyan and Visayan Seas. The ships had been sunk during the abortive attempts to reinforce Leyte in late 1944.

For three weeks the Masbate Task Force covered Masbate's hills destroying the enemy until there were not enough Japanese left to be considered a threat, and their elimination was turned over to Filipino guerrillas. The task force returned to Leyte on May 4, 1945. They had killed about 120 and captured fifteen, at a cost of five men killed and ten wounded.

Estimates of enemy strength on the big island of Mindanao ran from 34,000 to 42,000. Clearly there was a considerable enemy presence there, and it was decided to land in mid-April using the 24th Infantry Division. Before the campaign was ended, the 31st Infantry Division had joined the 24th along with elements of other divisions, including the 40th Infantry Division. Sizeable guerrilla forces were also involved.

The 31st Infantry Division was having a tough time with logistical support on Mindanao, as the further they advanced from Illana Bay towards the Davao Gulf and to the north, the more difficulty they had with resupply. It was decided to put the 108th RCT ashore at Macajalar Bay in Northern Mindanao on May 10, 1945 as part of X Corps both to speed up the conquest of Mindanao and to open up a new route of supply for the 31st Division. The problem was a particular challenge, because the region was poorly mapped, and it was known that what were shown as roads often turned out to be mere trails that were all but impenetrable for vehicles.

Without a rest after successfully terminating its operations on Leyte and Masbate, the 108th RCT was assembled and combat loaded at Ormoc on May 8th. At 8:30 a.m. on May 10th, 1945, the First Battalion made an assault landing, which was surprisingly unopposed, at Bugo on Macajalar Bay on northern Mindanao. The rest of the RCT was ashore by noon and the advance down the Sayre Highway, the main tactical highway on Mindanao, was begun.

Many defensive positions were found along the highway, but none were occupied. The Japanese were reported withdrawing, so U. S. Air Force aircraft were dispatched to bomb and strafe the column.

The Del Monte airdromes were secured by the Third Battalion on the morning of May 12th. Again many well-organized unoc-cupied defensive positions were found along the highway, and large quantities of enemy mortar ammunition, aerial bombs, and disabled trucks and engineering equipment were captured.

On the 13th, First and Third Battalion patrols ran into heavy fire at the entrance to Mangima Canyon and the First Battalion com-mand post received 31 rounds of 90mm mortar fire. This was the first determined resistance encountered by the 108th on Mindanao, and developed into one of the more difficult operations in the Philippines.

After an air strike on the morning of the 15th, the Second and Third Battalions launched an attack with the Third Battalion running into heavy mortar, artillery, and rifle fire, in addition to a wired-in mine field. The enemy occupied advantageous positions, expertly camouflaged, and covered his mine fields with fire.

The attack was continued the next day by the First Battalion, and the Mangima River was crossed against stiff resistance supported by fire from tanks. As the attack pressed forward, the 108th's covering fire drove the enemy into their caves, allowing the assault platoons to move up to the entrances and destroy many Japanese soldiers and positions, using bazookas, grenades, and rifles.

It was imperative that an early junction of the 108th and the 31st Infantry Division be expedited to open adequate supply lines to American forces operating in Central Mindanao. On Q-plus 7, May 17th, while the First Battalion was still engaged in the bitter fight for Mangima Canyon, the Second Battalion, bypassing the resistance, was once more advancing on the Sayre Highway. The Third Battalion had been withdrawn from the canyon and ordered to follow the Second Battalion. Japanese prisoners reported that all Japanese troops were withdrawing to Malaybalay.

Upon completion of mopping up operations in Mangima Canyon, the First Battalion joined in the advance. Artillery had displaced from Del Monte to the rim of the canyon after an effective bombardment on Maluko had severely damaged the enemy and influenced his evacuation and abandonment of the town.

At Maluko the bridge across the Calaman River had been destroyed, as well as numerous smaller bridges along the route of advance. It was impossible to keep supply lines open and to displace artillery because of the rapid advance, which continued with the help of supplies dropped from the air.

At 2:30 p.m. on May 24th, leading elements of the 1-108th contacted leading elements of the First Battalion, 155th Infantry, 2,000 yards south of Impalutao. Recognizing the significance of this meeting, Lt. Gen. R. L. Eichelberger, Commanding General of the Eighth Army, sent the following commendation:

"My wholehearted commendation goes to every member of the 108th Regimental Combat Team for the courage, determination, and speed displayed in their successful junction with the 31st Infantry Division at Impalutao, Bukidnon, Mindanao. This rapid thrust over extremely difficult terrain and against enemy resistance has succeeded in dividing the Japanese forces on Mindanao. It will materially assist in the ultimate, complete destruction of the Japanese forces. It is with a feeling of utmost pride that I congratulate each officer and man of your command for the completion of a job well done."

However, this junction did not end operations of the 108th on Mindanao. The regiment was ordered to proceed to Malaybalay, arriving there at 10:30 a.m. on May 26th, where they reverted to 31st Division control. The 865th Engineer Aviation Battalion, with the 108th Antitank Company attached for security, was ordered to continue construction of bridges along the Sayre Highway to Malaybalay, assisted by Company C, 115th Engineer Battalion.

On May 30th, operations began by separate battalions. The 1-108th was attached to the 124th Infantry and began shuttling to Managok. Contact was not made until June 7th when a patrol from Company A reached the 124th Infantry position west of Maglamin. Activity of this battalion until June 15th consisted of securing the lines of communications, supply, and evacuation for forces operating in the vicinity of Maglamin.

The initial assignment of the 2-108th was to relieve elements of the 155th Infantry guarding lines of communications along the Sayre Highway and vital installations in the Malaybalay area. Company G (reinforced) moved to Alnib to seek out and destroy the enemy in an independent action. A patrol from that company was ambushed on June 11th in the vicinity of Kratoan by group of approximately 40 Japanese who faked surrender. Fifteen Japanese were killed in the ensuing fire fight; Company G's casualties were one killed and five wounded.

By June 6th, the 2-108th had been relieved of security missions in the Malaybalay area and moved into an assembly area 3,500 yards west of Managok. Their orders were to relieve the First Battalion, 124th Infantry, on the Managok-Maglamin trail. This relief was effected June 8th and the advance continued against heavy machine gun and sniper fire. Due to the extreme difficulty of supply along the trail, the advance had to be halted to allow rations to be brought up. Supply by air drops began on June 13th. The enemy was found to be in a desperate condition for food, but scattered groups still fought bitterly.

On June 5th the 3-108th participated in a parade, reviewed by General of the Armies Douglas MacArthur, celebrating the opening of the Sayre Highway. The 3-108th was attached to the 124th Infantry the next day. During the ensuing six days the battalion fought its way through Silae to Cabanglasan. Patrolling was carried out to the east, south, and west, and on June 15th contact was made between the Second and Third Battalions.

The 164th Field Artillery Battalion reached Malaybalay on June 3rd and went into an assembly area. From positions at Managok, they provided supporting fires until June 14th, when all friendly forces were out of range. In the Mindanao campaign, the 164th Field Artillery Battalion fired thousands of rounds in 50 concentrations.

Two were killed and eight wounded on June 10th when 20 rounds of enemy knee mortar fire dropped on the 115th Engineer Dump and Third Battalion field train at the Malaybalay air strip. The work of Company C, 115th Engineer Battalion in constructing bridges and improving the heavily used Sayre Highway was considered particularly outstanding.

Expert medical aid and hazardous evacuation were performed by Company C, 115th Medical Battalion. Casualties for the RCT were 43 killed or died, and 148 wounded. Two hundred eighty-six Japanese were killed, 19 captured. In addition, guerrilla forces killed 151 of the enemy and took three prisoners.

As a result of the operations of the 108th RCT on this island, the Bugo-Del Monte area was secured for use by friendly forces, organized defense of a large part of the island was destroyed, and the vital Sayre Highway was opened as the primary route of supply to forces operating inland.

The 108th RCT was relieved on June 15th and retraced its steps back over the Sayre Highway to Bugo where it sailed for Panay to rejoin the 40th Division on June 20th. In July, as the division consolidated, the 108th assumed positions in the Oton area.

Soon after its arrival on Panay, the 108th RCT received another commendation, this time from Major General F. C. Sibert, Commanding General of the X Corps. It read:

"I wish to express my sincere gratitude to the 108th Regimental Combat Team for its contribution to the Victor Five Operation.

"The manner in which it accomplished all assigned missions, under the most trying conditions, was notable and reflects great credit on the proficiency and experience of your command.

"The Commanding General, Eighth Army, felicitated the X Corps upon the success of the operation. That success was due in no small measure to the cooperation and effect of your personnel."

*Guerrillas participate in a victory parade in Iloilo, Panay, P.I.
They were disarmed shortly after this photo, as Americans were
increasingly concerned by the influence wielded by the
communists.
(Photo: Captain Robert W. Munyon)*

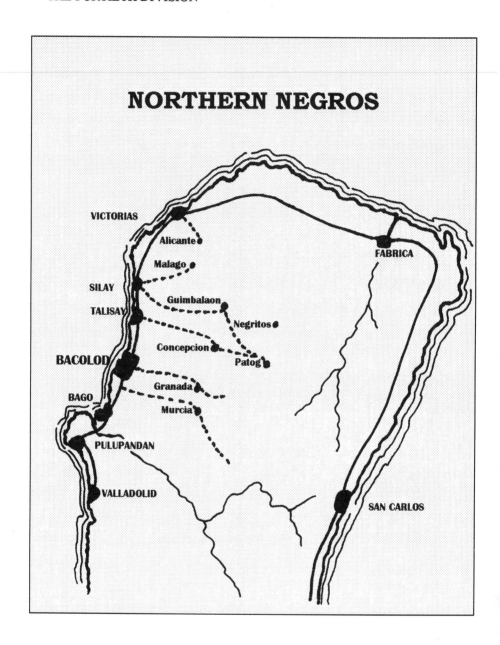

NORTHERN NEGROS

CHAPTER NINE

THE NEGROS CAMPAIGN

The operations order for the attack on Negros was disseminated to all the troops on March 28, 1945. At this time the guerrillas estimated that there were approximately 11,000 Japanese in the northern Negritos area. Fourth largest of the Philippine Islands, Negros had been an important enemy air staging base during the Leyte operation. The island was also important for its many sugar centrals which the Japanese were using for the production of fuel alcohol, and for the sawmill at Fabrica on the north coast, the largest hardwood mill in the world. By now, however, American air attacks had rendered all of the island's numerous airfields unserviceable, and the major fuel plants inoperative.

Cut off from outside sources by our seizure of adjacent islands, the Japanese forces were extremely short of supplies, particularly food. Sufficient weapons and ammunition to effect a limited offensive or a stubborn defense, however, were on hand. Also available to the enemy, as had been utilized on Luzon, were machine guns formerly mounted on numerous wrecked planes dotting the island airfields. The food problem had been partially alleviated by commandeering all available civilian stocks.

Y-Day was set for March 29th, H-Hour for 8:00 a.m. The landing was to be made by the 185th RCT in LVT's, followed by the 160th RCT (less 2-160th and Cannon Company). After seizing and securing the beachhead, the troops were to push rapidly northward to secure the city of Bacolod, capitol of Occidental Negros, and the towns of Talisay and Silay, with their adjacent airfields. The 503rd Parachute Combat Team, then on Mindoro, was to be prepared to make an air landing at a time and place to be designated by the Division Commander, at which time the 503rd would come under division control.

Elements of the 40th Reconnaissance Troop were to land shortly after H-Hour and push reconnaissance immediately along the roads north and east to Cancilayan, Murcia and Concepcion to locate any enemy forces or enemy movement on that flank, with a secondary mission of intercepting and delaying the evacuation of enemy forces toward the mountains. At the same time, one platoon of the troop was to perform similar missions in the Maao Sugar Central-La Carlota-San Enrique-Valladolid area to the south and east of the beachhead.

Prior to the landing at Pulupandan, the guerrillas had reported that the enemy had established their first line of defense at Granada, their second line at Lantawan, approximately due east of Guibaln, and their third line of defense at Guimbalaon. The Japanese had been reported to be digging caves at Guimbalaon for several months.

The division was greatly concerned about the wide and swift Bago River, across which our forces would have to move to reach their objective. The Bago bridge was a five span, steel and concrete structure over 600 feet long which spanned a deep chasm near the mouth of the river. If the bridge was destroyed, which seemed inevitable, our advance to the north would be seriously delayed and the shock of our attack mitigated. If the crossing was to be seized intact, the bridge guard and control operators would have to be completely surprised and quickly overcome. A plan to land a reinforced platoon under cover of darkness three hours prior to the assault landing to secure the crossing was therefore adopted, with the mission assigned to Company F, 2-185th.

Company F appointed First Lieutenant Aaron A. Hanson to lead the attack on the key bridge over the Bago River. His reinforced platoon of 64 enlisted men included three heavy weapons squads, a demolition squad, and a radio team. They disembarked at 5:30 a.m. from two LCM's at Pulupandan as scheduled, without being detected by the enemy, and quickly headed inland towards the bridge.

Several miles inland, the platoon was met by an excited guerrilla, who informed them that a group of nine Japanese were driving three carabao carts towards the bridge. Lieutenant Hanson speeded up their pace on a course parallel to the trail in order to reach the bridge before the detachment of Japanese did. When they got to the bridge, he carefully deployed the men so they could take both the bridge guards and approaching enemy detachment under fire at the same time. Had the platoon opened fire before reaching the objective, the bridge guards would have been forewarned, the element of surprise lost, and the mission a probable failure.

When signalled, the men opened fire killing several of the Japanese and scattering the rest. Members of the platoon then rushed the bridge which was known to be mined and ready for demolition. While several soldiers rushed across the bridge others poured a hail of fire into a small building which was believed to contain the detonating switch. Leading the charge was Private First Class Theodore C. Vinther who seemed to lead a charmed life in that swarm of bullets. Suddenly he collapsed mortally wounded, the first division soldier to die on Negros. Private Vinther was awarded the Bronze Star posthumously for his heroism. While all the firing was going on, several demolitions experts from the 115th Engineers were working feverishly to disarm the large aerial bombs which were wired for electrical detonation. A few minutes after 7:00 a.m. the bridge was in our possession, and the troops quickly prepared for counterattacks.

Troops looked inside the small bullet-scarred shack at the other end of the bridge, and found a Japanese soldier riddled with bullets. His hand was stretched out just short of the detonating switch. The engineers found twenty electrically controlled aerial bombs, ranging in size from ten 110-pounders to two of 1000 pounds each, lashed to the bridge trusses or buried at the abutments.

At 8:00 a.m. an estimated sixty Japanese attacked the platoon with mortars and machine guns but were repulsed by soldiers from a combination of preexisting and newly dug emplacements. Capturing the bridge intact and successfully defending it against recapture and destruction saved at least two days for the division, and undoubtedly reduced friendly casualties.

The main body of the assault force, having departed Panay on the 28th, began moving out of Iloilo Straits at 3:00 a.m. on March 29th, headed for Occidental Negros. They landed at Pulupandan under a protective smoke screen.

The 1-185th landed to the north, and with its troops still in LVT-4's, forded the Bago River and seized the town of Bago with only minor opposition. In Bago they were joined by a company of light tanks which had crossed the recently secured bridge, and were attached for further operations. The battalion moved out as the spearhead of the rapid attack towards Bacolod, the provincial capitol about twenty miles away, using the LVT-4's to transport the infantry.

They met only slight resistance at the many bridges which often were mined and protected by a few delaying enemy riflemen. In every case, the enemy was driven back before they could destroy the bridge they were defending. The first serious enemy resistance was not met until the Magsungay River, 1500 yards south of Bacolod. There intense small arms and some 90mm mortar fire was received before the enemy was routed from pillboxes and the crossing secured. Later it was determined that the Japanese Brigade Headquarters at Bacolod didn't know that Americans had landed on Negros until our advance elements had reached that bridge.

Within six and one half hours after landing, leading elements reached Bacolod Airfield and the southern outskirts of the capitol of Occidental Negros. As shadows began to lengthen on Y-Day, the troops reached the Lupit River bridge, at the southern outskirts of Bacolod, and key to the capture of the city. Here there was the most serious fire fight of the day, as Company C and the balance of the combined arms team secured the bridge after dark. The 1-185th organized its perimeter to protect that key feature for the night.

The 2-185th, which had landed earlier, reinforced the platoon defending the Bago River bridge and further deployed to secure the DBHL. They were relieved by the 3-185th about 1:00 p.m., and hurried up the road after the 1-185th.

That night the enemy attempted the first of a series of infiltration attacks on the principal bridges under divisional control. The Bago bridge guard was fired on by a small party in an unsuccessful attempt to recapture or destroy the crossing. Sporadic attempts that first night by the Japanese to recapture the Lupit River bridge were also successfully repulsed. Similar attacks made by small demolition parties continued during the first few weeks at various points on friendly lines of communication, but were repulsed with most of the enemy involved killed.

Colonel Frank Bowen, Eighth Army's dynamic and innovative G-3, had accompanied General Brush during the assault on Negros. He flew back to Army Headquarters after dinner that night to report to General Eichelberger. He gave a vivid account of the division's impressive first-day success.

The 1-185th moved into the attack again the morning of the 30th, supported by a company of medium tanks, but ran into stiff resistance just 750 yards north of the Lupit River Bridge. One of the supporting tanks was hit by a pole charge carried by a fanatical Japanese soldier. The tank wasn't damaged, but the Jap was blown into a nearby building, where his gory remains hung from the rafters. The troops fought through the resistance, and nearby delaying actions, entering the center of Bacolod by 10:15 a.m. They found that the principal business district of the city had been torched and several ammunition dumps destroyed by the Japanese as they withdrew under the cover of darkness. The Japanese left a delaying force to make capture of the city as costly as possible, but the city was quickly captured about seventy-five percent intact. One interesting aspect of the entry into Bacolod was the unusually cool reception given the soldiers by the Spanish civilians in that city.

Bacolod was completely secured by noon after eliminating the snipers that had been left behind, with seventy-five enemy dead counted. Forward elements continued advancing north beyond the town, and by the end of the day had reached within 500 yards of Talisay without further contact.

Shortly after the troops had landed, guerrillas informed them that to the south, between Valladolid and La Carlota, scattered groups of Japanese were attempting to reach the hills to the northeast by traveling cross-country through the swamps. Various estimates of the total enemy moving to the northeast ranged from 200 to 500. What had been anticipated was now evident. The main enemy force did not intend to defend the coastal area, but rather was accelerating the movement of supplies and personnel to the hills surrounding Negritos. Negritos was a small village almost directly east of Talisay, and almost half way across the island. In the meantime, the 160th Infantry had landed to assist in securing northern Negros.

The 40th Reconnaissance Troop was operating independently, in true cavalry fashion, running their own campaign separately from other elements of the division. No contacts were developed along the roads in the San Enrique-La Carlota-Pontevedra sector. On March 30th, other elements of the troop, operating in the Alimodian area northwest of the Maao Sugar Central, intercepted approximately 125 Japanese concealed in a bamboo thicket. Deploying armored cars on three sides of the thicket, the troop opened fire. A heavy fire fight ensued, until with air support the troop all but annihilated the enemy force. One hundred fourteen enemy dead were counted, and five Filipino collaborators were captured.

The following day, a platoon from the 40th Recon reached Murcia and found it recently evacuated, while approximately 6000 yards east of Bacolod the Intelligence and Reconnaissance Platoon of the 185th Infantry observed an estimated 100 enemy moving east along the road toward Granada. The group was believed to be the tail end of a larger force moving to Concepcion. A platoon from the 40th Recon, moving down the same road the following day, met resistance from entrenched enemy at Concepcion. Contact was maintained until the end of the day, when the decision was reached to send one battalion of the 160th Infantry to that area the following morning. During the night the enemy withdrew farther east, and only small contacts were made by the battalion.

Another report of a sharp engagement in progress was received. The 40th Reconnaissance Troop was fighting an estimated 100 Japanese in a wooded area 2500 yards northeast of the Maao Sugar Central.

The advance by the 185th RCT continued to the north on March 31st without serious incident. As March turned to April, the columnar advance of the 185th RCT was halted when the troops reached Talisay. Machine gun and mortar fire up to 90mm forced the 1-185th to dig in for the night, while the 2-185th deployed to open terrain on the right flank to assist in the general advance.

General Eichelberger was delighted with the speed of the division's advance. He was convinced that the speed of the advance saved many Filipino lives as well as much of their infrastructure, including bridges and towns. He sent General MacArthur a message to that effect.

On April 1st, General MacArthur announced the capture of Bacolod. He noted that the advance had been so swift that bridges across the Magsungay and Lupit Rivers had been saved even though they had been prepared for demolition. The advance so surprised the Japanese that three of their fighter planes on the Bacolod airstrip were seized before they could leave the ground. General Eichelberger had lunch with General Brush that day, followed by a ceremony where he presented General Brush with the Silver Star.

It was reported that a Japanese patrol had been sighted approximately one mile east of Bacolod and just south of the Bacolod airstrip. The estimate of the patrol's size varied from four to fifteen. A patrol of nineteen men from the Anti-tank platoon, 3-160th Infantry was sent to investigate on April 2nd.

The enemy patrol was spotted in a thicket of bamboo and mano trees near a small stream. When the friendly troops flushed them out of their hiding place, they found themselves faced with a heavily armed force of forty Japanese. The battle raged for thirty minutes before the Americans pulled back as their ammunition was nearly exhausted. They radioed for help while attending to their ten casualties.

Their call for support quickly brought help from the 81mm Mortar Platoon of Company M. The platoon sergeant, a Technical Sergeant Willson, placed his mortars about 600 yards behind the stream. He then moved to the near bank of the stream where the engaged patrol pointed out the Japanese positions about fifty to seventy-five yards across the stream. Willson then called for area fires. The response was immediate, with the Japanese heard screaming and yelling as the rounds began to land.

After the mortars had saturated all of the thicket hiding the enemy, the patrol moved across the stream and took the area without further losses. Twenty-three enemy bodies were counted compared to a loss of two American dead and eight wounded in the Antitank Platoon. They found that the Japanese had been engaged in a mission of sabotage behind American lines.

On April 1st and 2nd, 1-185th with both Company C, 716th Tank Battalion and the regimental cannon company attached, forced several bridgeheads across steep-banked rivers and secured the town of Talisay by dusk on April 2nd. The bridge at Talisay had been blown, forcing a wide envelopment across flat open terrain. As the troops advanced on Talisay Airport, many wood, earth and concrete pillboxes were found by troops, apparently abandoned by the Japanese. Initial reports said only sixty of the enemy had been left behind as a delaying force.

The 185th was moving as rapidly as possible to overtake the retreating Japanese. The 1-185th Infantry, moving north and north-east from the Bacolod-Talisay area, on April 3rd captured the town of Silay after only minor resistance. The Silay Airfield area to the east, and the Imbang River bridge, were both quickly secured, re-ducing the enemy's evacuation routes to those farther north. Three of those routes were most notable. The first and most important was the road leading generally from northeast of Silay along the south bank of the Malago River to Negritos, then southeast to the Patog area. The Japanese had expended considerable labor on the mountain terminus of this road, extending and improving it to support their operations. The second route was southeast from Victorias and north of the Malago Valley. The third, used by troops evacuating from the Fabrica and northeast coast areas, ran south from Manapla through the barrios of Santa Isabela and San Isidro. Both these latter routes also led into the Negritos area.

New roads were observed running from the Concepcion area to Hill 3155, 12,000 yards east of Concepcion, suggesting that high point might prove to be the keystone in the enemy's left flank positions, with his right flank anchored on the high ground north of Negritos.

The 1st Battalion of the 185th, after securing Silay, was given the mission of securing lines of communication in the vicinity of Silay and continuing to recon northward with strong armored patrols. At the same time, 2-185th with armored support swung to the east.

Japanese in reinforced platoon size elements were observed in defensive positions at Concepcion. An estimated 100 Japanese at Guimbalaon directed mortar, machine gun and rifle fire at elements of the 40th Reconnaissance Troop in that area on April 3rd.

Contact late on April 4th between the 40th Reconnaissance Troop and about 150 of the enemy east of Atipulan resulted in 114 dead Japanese. Armored combat patrols from the 185th reached Talisay on April 5th and received machine gun, rifle and mortar fire from the north bank of the Minuluang River. Pillboxes and trench systems at Granada were found abandoned.

Civilians near the Saravia, Malago, and Alicante Airfields reported the Japanese withdrew from those areas April 3rd towards mountains to the east. Guerrillas also reported that about 2000 Japanese passed through Victorias about the same time in the direction of Patog (Southeast of Negritos), and that Victorias was now clear of the enemy. Prisoners captured on April 4th in the vicinity of Silay offered the information that the enemy was withdrawing in the direction of Maeda and Hukyuro. However, some Japanese reoccupied Concepcion during the night of April 2-3rd, but were forced to withdraw by division troops the next day.

The enemy had been transporting huge quantities of supplies inland from the coastal towns to the Negritos-Patog defensive area for months prior to the invasion by division troops. When the threat of the division's landing became a reality, every effort was made to hasten the uncompleted task. Trucks, carrying parties and carabao carts were feverishly moving along roads from Guimbalaon to Patog. Day and night concentrations of fighters and dive bombers couldn't help spotting these targets, and attacked the columns from March 31st until Guimbalaon was taken. Daily they destroyed trucks, installations and dumps, and inflicted uncounted personnel casualties, forcing the enemy to limit his movements to the hours of darkness. As the 185th Infantry fought forward, evidence of air power's effectiveness was everywhere. Supporting aircraft had caught Japanese trucks in the open, and burned out hulks dotted the area. Aerial bombs were found neatly stacked under their grassy camouflage, along with burnt helmets, shoes and other equipment that littered the area.

The barrio of Guimbalaon was known to be the rendezvous and supply point for the fleeing troops, and became the next objective of the 185th Infantry. There were indications that the enemy had originally made plans for an initial stand along the line Guimbalaon-Concepcion, but by April 1st it became apparent that the enemy was forced to alter plans due to the unexpected swiftness of the division's advance.

On April 3rd a platoon of the 40th Reconnaissance Troop, moving up from the Granada area to reconnoiter the eastern portion of the Silay-Guimbalaon road, made only minor contacts until it approached within 500 yards of Guimbalaon. There fire was encountered from enemy entrenched around the supply point. The platoon deployed and attempted to approach the barrio, first from the west and then by the south. Both times, it was repulsed by heavy rifle, 20mm and 37mm fire. Dense undergrowth in the wooded area prohibited complete observation, but at least 100 of the enemy were estimated to be in the immediate vicinity of the barrio, and several gun positions were definitely located. During the action, the troop directed supporting aircraft against the enemy with good results.

Elements of 2-185th followed up the next day and secured the area after a brief fire fight. Harassed by air and artillery fire in their attempts at evacuation, and pursued by ground troops advancing from the west, the enemy was forced to leave behind considerable quantities of undamaged supplies and equipment. Principal items captured in the dumps were vehicles, engineer, medical and signal supplies, some arms, ammunition and vital stocks of food.

East of San Fernando and 3,500 yards north of Concepcion, an estimated 60-100 Japanese occupied positions and directed small arms fire at a foot patrol from the Intelligence and Reconnaissance Platoon of the 160th Infantry. The infantry then reached a point in the Murcia-Patog trail in the Manapla area without contact.

The division had made surprising progress. In less than a week, all primary objectives on the west coast were secured. The division controlled the most important section of the west coast, Silay to Pulupandan, and the area south of Pulupandan was in the hands of the guerrillas. Inland, guerrillas were in control of the plains area south of Murcia. The only enemy remaining in these occupied areas were small groups of stragglers attempting to reach the main force. Although portions of the capital city, Bacolod, had been burned, its principal utilities had been saved and were being put into operation by service troops. The towns of Talisay and Silay had been secured with a minimum of damage to civilian life and property. Known enemy casualties for the first six days were 382 killed and eight captured.

The 40th Reconnaissance Troop initiated recon east toward Guimbalaon, and then towards the north coast. Following a route through Saravia and the airfields of Alicante and Malago, they found the area completely evacuated by the enemy. Fording the Malago River near the destroyed bridge, the troop moved on to Fabrica through Manapla, finding several bridges mined but only one destroyed. Guerrillas and civilians stated the enemy had been hurriedly moving southwest for the past week or more, skirting the Mount Silay foothills to rendezvous with Bacolod forces in the Patog area. The troop reached the American-owned Insular Lumber Company just west of Fabrica on the 6th of April. A platoon of armored cars quickly captured this, the largest hardwood sawmill in the world. There was no opposition, but the Japanese had destroyed eighty percent of Fabrica by fire.

The cavalrymen found elaborate two story mahogany homes, formerly housing the Americans who managed the mill, deserted. Only the planing mill was untouched. Prior to the war, the mill had produced between 200,000 and 250,000 board feet of hardwood every day, running two 8-hour shifts. The Japanese, in three years, only produced 19,000,000 feet, less than ninety days' normal production. They also tried to build patrol boats on the Himoga-An River in Fabrica. Only two were completed, each about sixty feet long, and were then used for transportation between the islands.

The south end of the Sumag River bridge and the road in that vicinity was mined. Two 100 lb. bombs buried nose up but unfuzed were found at the Magsungay River Bridge. Worse, the bridge over the Himugaan River was destroyed and there was no ford, so the 40th Reconnaissance Troop was unable to continue westward until the attached engineers could construct a ferry crossing. Meanwhile, the troop contacted one of the mill superintendents and made a hasty survey of the sawmill area. Although most of the mill had been burned, much machinery and cut lumber were found undamaged. Engineers set to work to salvage as much of the equipment and materials as possible and place the mill in operating condition.

Moving its command post to the sawmill area, the troop continued patrols to the west and provided security for the engineer detachment working at the mill. Reports were frequently received from guerrillas and civilians that some Japanese were still evacuating toward the mountains, but no contacts were made. These same sources also stated that occasional groups of enemy stragglers from Cebu were landing on Negros and on the small islands just off the northeast and east coasts.

On April 8th, the Japanese used artillery fire on the division's forward elements for the first time in the Negros Island campaign. Guerrillas reported that scattered groups of the enemy were wearing women's clothing in an effort to escape from our forces.

Organized Japanese defensive positions were being encountered April 8th and 9th in the areas north and east of Napilas. These were believed to be outposts of the organized defense system known to exist in the Negritos-Patog area. A large amount of heavy mortar fire joined the artillery fire used by the enemy. The tempo picked up as elements of the division came up against the defensive lines where the Japanese were determined to hold.

The division commander originally intended to air land the 503rd Parachute Combat Team at Alicante Airfield at the northern tip of Negros with the mission of seizing the airfields and clearing the enemy from northwest Negros. However, when reconnaissance patrols confirmed that the enemy had already abandoned that area, the plan was changed. The regiment, less one battalion, moved by sea transport and landed at Pandan Point on April 8th. The division was now near normal strength for the first time since the 108th RCT was detached for service on Leyte.

40th Division troops on Negros with tank support on April 1, 1945
(Source: National Archives)

The three regiments lined up, north to south, in preparation for a general attack to the east on April 9th. The 503rd PCT was on the left astride the Silay-Manzananares road adjacent to the 185th RCT. The 160th RCT was on the right. All jumped off in the morning, and in places ran into heavy rifle, machine gun and mortar fire, especially in the 185th sector. Divisional artillery and mortars added their power to the offense, and slow progress was made. That first night, there were four distinct infiltration attacks against just one company, Company F of the 2-185th. Some of the attempts along the line were sizeable, involving mortars as well as small arms and grenades. Many Japanese were killed (six in HHC

3-160th's area alone), including a captain in the 185th sector, and many more were wounded during these abortive attacks.

No place was really safe. The 143rd Field Artillery in support of the 160th was set up on the east bank of the Matabang River. Sniper fire from Japanese across the river caused some casualties to the artillerymen. The troops then put out five men with automatic weapons to protect troops when they bathed, although they had orders to stay close to the near bank. Native kids quickly joined them in the river, with women doing laundry for the soldiers on the bank. The troops paid them with what little candy, food or cigarettes they had, as the natives had no use for money. The men were bathing buck naked, while the women worked, to the considerable embarrassment of the men. It didn't seem to bother the women. The carabao were driven into the water, where they lay down in the deep part, keeping cool with nothing exposed but their noses.

There was cautious but continual progress over the next several days, with considerable help from air strikes and artillery. The night of April 9th and early the next morning, there were clashes with several large enemy groups. Around Hill 3155, Japanese placed mortar and machine gun fire on advancing troops of the 160th.

Civilians told the 40th Reconnaissance Troop on the northeast coast of Negros that Japanese using sailboats from Cebu were landing on the beach in that area, as well as nearby islands, in an effort to reinforce their forces. The 40th Recon tried unsuccessfully for several days to confirm the reports.

Throughout the week following capture of Guimbalaon, enemy action remained essentially delaying and harassing. The number of night infiltration attempts and diversionary raids "to confuse the enemy as to the location of the main defenses" increased. Demolition squads again made several feeble and unsuccessful attacks on installations in rear areas, notably bridges.

The enemy's antiaircraft guns, principally 20mm and 40mm, were somewhat more successful. Firing short bursts as our planes swooped low overhead, they shot down one B-24, one F4U, and damaged two other planes. Before the operation came to a close, a total of seven planes were lost over the Patog area, and several additional damaged.

As the battle moved farther east, resistance became stronger. The first organized defense line, in the vicinity of San Juan, fell April 11th, just one week after the capture of Guimbalaon. This "line" consisted of mutually supporting pillboxes and trenches, but many of these were found to be unoccupied. Night attacks continued but were growing more costly to the enemy. In just two days, April 11th-12th, the 185th killed sixty-one of the attackers.

The 40th Reconnaissance Troop had been held up in their westward drive waiting for the bridge over the Himugaan River to be repaired. On April 12th, the necessary materials arrived, and the engineers established a ferry across the river. The troop immediately extended its reconnaissance on around the coast, finding some bridges destroyed, but crossing the streams by various expedients. San Carlos, on the east coast, was reached on the 13th, and the Escalante area to the north was thoroughly searched but no contact was made.

Over the next several days, the division troops overran several supply points. Most of the equipment was of little use to the enemy at that stage of the fight, such as vehicles, generators and tools. However, there was some food and medical supplies, both badly needed by Japanese soldiers. By April 12th, after fighting in the Philippines for three months, the 40th Division had accounted for a total of 7,501 Japanese killed.

The night of April 13th, the Japanese struck back with a vicious night attack in an effort to destroy supporting weapons which were creating havoc in enemy positions. Locations from the 185th's front lines to as far down as Company B of the 115th Engineers were attacked by several hundred Japanese. In the 1-185th area, where 155mm howitzers were being used in a direct fire role, the attacks continued sporadically until 4:00 a.m.. However, the guns were undamaged, and 44 Japanese dead were counted the next morning. About thirty enemy had attacked the 185th Regimental Command Post area. Patrols were sent out the next morning and found seven Japanese dead and indications that many wounded had been carried away. Headquarters and the Mine Platoon of the Antitank Company suffered six casualties, none serious, in the three hour battle.

Aggressive patrolling continued from the 13th to the 17th, supported by air strikes, artillery and mortar concentrations on enemy held positions in the vicinity of the Lantawan Plateau. It was during this time that heavy mortars from the 80th Chemical Mortar Battalion were attached and started providing close support that was to prove a nightmare to defiladed Japanese.

Now that the enemy had withdrawn into the higher foothills, the familiar pattern of the Bamban operation on Luzon became evident. Narrow roads along knife-like ridges - - so easy to defend and so hard to take, became the order of the day. Japanese dug into caves on the reverse slopes with tunnels through the thorny lantana bushes to their forward positions. These well concealed positions were the source of many bullets, but live Japanese were rarely seen.

On April 14th, the 185th RCT took the high ground at San Juan and stood at the gateway of the long narrow corridor reaching to Lantawan. Before launching an attack against this formidable defense area, a two-day preparatory bombardment was conducted. Not only was there heavy artillery support, but the air force provided much support, and lost an aircraft to enemy antiaircraft fire. The third day brought torrential rains which forced the postponement of the attack until the following morning, the 17th.

The attack was preceded by a 16-plane air strike at 7:30 a.m., with the attack jumping off at 8:55 a.m. Company A, 1-185th led the attack, and almost immediately ran into heavy enemy fire. The enemy positions were of the same type and arrangement as those found in the 503rd area, and their defenders used the same tactics. From numerous well constructed bunkers, pillboxes, trenches and foxholes came fire of calibers ranging from small arms to three-inch guns. The attack was brought to a stop when the troops hit the second of a series of three tank traps.

The tank trap was a particularly strongly defended position encountered 4000 yards west of San Juan. The trap, dug to a depth of eighteen feet at a point where the road narrowed to a bare ten feet with sheer cliffs on either side, was covered by enemy fire. The area was blanketed by mines. Self-propelled weapons could not be brought forward to support the infantry until the high ground beyond was secured to permit bulldozers to fill the trap. One of the tanks covering the work around the tank trap was hit by a three inch shell but the only damage was a thrown track. The three inch gun was then knocked out.

Repeated attacks were launched against the hostile positions. Each time the attackers were subjected to heavy mortar concentrations and artillery fire. As it started to get late, Companies A and B dug in around the tank traps for the night. Troops could hear activity outside of the perimeter that night, but had learned a long time before that it wasn't healthy to go outside of defensive perimeters during the hours of darkness. In the morning, they found the trap mined and booby-trapped again by the Japanese. Brigadier General Bob Shoe, the Assistant Division Commander, was wounded by a Japanese machine gun when he went forward to see if he could help. Struck four times, he was sent to the hospital on Leyte, where he eventually recovered.

In the meantime, the 3-185th had swung around to the left flank and was coming along a ridge in an effort to join the 1-185th on the Lantawan Plateau. They were slowed by heavy resistance from machine gun and sniper fire. The following day, a 1-185th tank-infantry team crossed over the trap that had been filled in by bulldozers. They advanced a thousand yards and knocked out five enemy positions along the edge of the plateau. After two days of bitter fighting, the area was finally cleared, bulldozers repaired the road, and tanks rumbled forward.

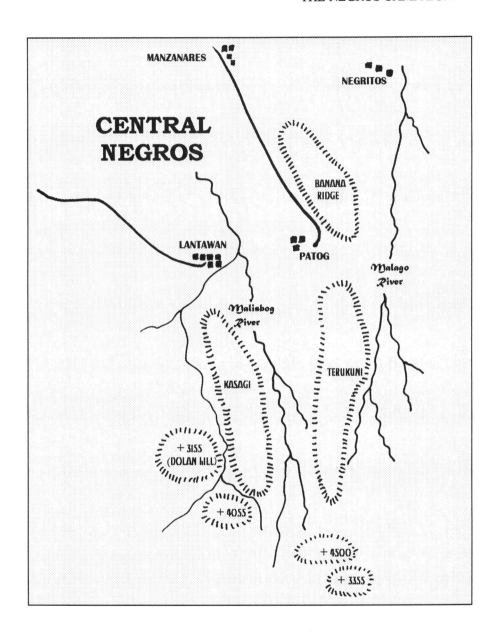

Moving onto the wide, flat Lantawan Plateau, surrounded by growth covered ridges and jungle-filled draws, the 1-185th deployed under heavy mortar and artillery fire. The 3-185th on the left, pushing across deep ravines, reached the north edge of the plateau on the same day. On April 24th, the battalions joined and supported by tanks fought to the eastern edge of the plateau, where they began cleaning out caves, spider holes and pillboxes along the fringes of the deep Malisbog draw. In the 1-185th sector, patrols probed forward and into the deep draws on both sides of the plateau. Japanese were flushed from the wooded draws and the almost inaccessible caves overlooking the draws. Large quantities of equipment were found, including abandoned radios and office supplies, plus rice. Every once in a while troops would spot hastily dug, shallow enemy graves. On April 28th, the 1st and 3rd Battalions met on the high ground to consolidate their gains.

In the meantime, X Corps opened its command post on the island of Mindanao effective March 18th. The 40th Division was moved to the operational control of X Corps after having been under the direct operational control of Eighth Army since March 2nd.

The 160th Infantry had entered combat on Negros a little later than the 185th. On Y-Day, the 160th, minus the 2nd Battalion and Cannon Company, which remained on Panay, constituted the Division Reserve afloat. On Y-plus-1, the 160th landed and took over the beachhead area. On Y-plus-2, one battalion moved down the Talisay-Concepcion road to engage the Japanese force which reconnaissance had contacted the day before. Patrols preceding the battalion reconnoitered east from Granada to Concepcion, where civilians had reported several hundred of the enemy dug in along the road. Only minor contacts were made, as the enemy continued to withdraw. Combat elements moving forward the following day, however, found Concepcion reoccupied by the enemy during the night. After a brief fire fight the barrio was finally secured on the same day the 185th occupied Guimbalaon. Moving approximately two miles farther east, the 160th encountered only moderate resistance.

The next regimental objective was the prominent terrain feature, Hill 3155, later named Dolan Hill in tribute to First Lieutenant John W. Dolan, the first officer to be killed in the attack. This hill commanded the approaches to the Patog area from the west and was indicated as the left flank of the enemy's defensive line. During the approach it was believed that elements of Colonel Yamaguchi's 172nd Independent Infantry Battalion, and probably elements of the 102nd Division Transport Regiment, the 32nd Airfield Company, and the 61st Anchorage Unit were among the defending forces. However, nearly all the 172nd Independent Infantry Battalion (less the Third Company, destroyed at Alimodian by the 40th Reconnaissance Troop) and elements of the 355th Independent Infantry Battalion were actually engaged before Dolan Hill was finally taken. In this sector, too, the enemy fought a delaying action from prepared and temporary positions on the flat open terrain west of the hill, his resistance stiffening as the battle neared the mountains. The Japanese were particularly active at night, using harassing fire freely against friendly perimeters in addition to frequent night infiltration attacks and diversionary raids.

As the advance elements drew within range, enemy positions on the forward slopes of Hill 3155 opened up with heavy fire which they maintained on a sporadic basis for the next several weeks. Mortar and 20mm automatic fire was particularly heavy.

Patrols were sent out to reconnoiter to the south. They reported minor contacts and located enemy defensive positions near the base of Hill 4055, just southeast of Hill 3155. One company was sent to the area to develop the situation on that flank. Separated from the battalion by deep ravines, the unit received supplies by air drops from cub planes. It was during one such drop that Major Francis E. Tredget, the regimental supply officer, lost his life when the plane was shot down by enemy fire.

The 3-160th was working across draws on the northern slopes of Hill 3155 in an effort to support and establish contact with the 185th Infantry which was approaching Lantawan just west of Patog. The 3-160th met determined resistance from well entrenched enemy at several points. Impeded in their movement by the deeply cut, thickly vegetated draws, three days were spent in reducing the hostile positions and mopping up bypassed areas.

On April 17th, after two days of artillery and air preparation and one day of bad weather, 1-160th attacked up the northwest slopes of Hill 3155. Initial advances were slow even though opposition was light the first day. Troops had to climb the steep slopes by grasping branches and roots. They eliminated each enemy position they passed, and by late the second day, were within 100 yards of the crest. There the battle grew even more intense.

The battalion established a perimeter on the steep mountainside, and dug in for the night. They didn't have to wait long. The enemy launched strong counterattacks from their strongly entrenched positions above the infantry. They accompanied withering small arms fire with blocks of dynamite, pole charges and grenades tossed down the mountain. The friendly forces in support were unable to bring direct-fire weapons to bear, and the enemy was too close to call in artillery support. A dangerous impasse resulted, so the 1-160th was withdrawn.

At 3:00 p.m., two wiremen in a jeep from the 143rd Field Artillery were injured at the base of Hill 3155 by an improvised Japanese grenade. The grenade consisted of several one pound blocks of dynamite with metal fragments wrapped in cloth and tied around the end of a short bamboo pole. It was thrown a considerable distance, and hit the side of the jeep. Both Corporal John J. Berrett and T5 Reuben Strobel were injured, but they returned fire. They managed to return to the safety of their own lines, but Berrett died several days later in the hospital at Bacolod.

There were repeated artillery and air strike places on Hill 3155, followed by attempts to reach the crest. The enemy was well dug in, and very little progress was made, as casualties mounted on both sides. Finally, on April 21st, a small knoll near the crest was reached and held. The extent of the enemy fortifications was becoming increasingly apparent. Personnel caves on the reverse slope of the hill were connected by a network of communications trenches to pillboxes and dugouts well hidden on the narrow ridge. High on the crest of Hill 4055 to the rear of these positions, machine guns were later found sited to cover the forward positions on Hill 3155.

Heavy rains hampered operations from April 22nd through 24th, reducing visibility to near zero. The 160th on the right flank and the 503rd on the left continued to receive heavy enemy fire. Caves were spotted on the reverse slope of Hill 3155 from which the Japanese were reinforcing the positions on the summit. There were dugouts, trenches, spider holes, and bunkers everywhere, and only small gains were registered.

The last few days of April saw some costly combat. Toughest was in the Hill 3155-4055 sector of the 160th. There they suffered fire from adjacent enemy-held ridge lines. A "Bouncing Betty" anti-personnel mine installed by friendly troops in front of 1-160th killed seven of the enemy. Several others were killed by small arms fire. A security patrol killed a Japanese soldier armed with a Filipino knife and six aerial bombs without fins to use as hand grenades. He was wearing an American jungle sweater, American Herringbone Twill (HBT) trousers, and had U.S. currency in his pockets.

The 3-160th met stiff resistance in a draw near Hill 3155, killing 60 Japanese and an estimated 15 more. Captured documents indicated that the ridge 1,000 yards northeast of Lantawan from which 3-160th had been receiving heavy fire was being defended by elements of the *Nose Butai*, Japanese 355th Independent Infantry Battalion.

The 2-185th Infantry was attached to the 160th RCT from April 26th through the 29th. The 160th employed that battalion on the regiment's right in an attempt to reach the crests of Dolan Hill and

Hill 4055 from that flank. The advance under enemy fire, however, was slow due to the virtually impassable terrain, and the battalion was finally returned to the 185th at Lantawan where it could be more effectively employed.

For several days the situation remained unchanged on Hill 3155. Sandbags were stacked in front of friendly forward positions for protection against snipers and machine guns. Any movement forward of these positions met with heavy fire from automatic weapons and mortars. Attempts were made to flank the enemy pocket, but the sheer sides of the rocky ridge precluded such moves. A trench dug forward from 1-160th positions to a point where the enemy could be observed was partially successful, but observers were subjected to heavy small arms fire.

Captured documents showed that the command post of the Japanese 77th Infantry Brigade was in a large draw east of Hill 3155. Both Lieutenant General Kono and Colonel Yamaguchi were reported to be in that location.

The exhausting task of supplying the assault units became more complicated. Hundreds of native carriers were employed in carrying ammunition and rations up the precipitous slopes to free up all available infantrymen for the actual fighting. Engineers began bulldozing a winding road up the mountain to replace the "trail of a thousand steps" which the troops had blazed for the carriers.

Weather was another impediment. Heavy rains were common, and although mornings were frequently clear, low lying clouds almost invariably settled over the high ground during the afternoon, cutting visibility to a few feet.

Finally the decision was made to withdraw the troops from the hill for four days while all available air and artillery was concentrated on the enemy positions. P-38's, F4U's and A-20's dropped 250 and 1000 pound bombs and strafed the hilltop in over a hundred sorties. Massed fires of the division artillery were laid in successive concentrations on the area, with intermittent shelling both day and night so the enemy couldn't rest.

The 3-160th Infantry relieved the 1-160th Infantry at Hill 3155 on May 12th. At 5:00 a.m. the battalion jumped off with Company I as the assault company. The company advanced up the hill along a steep narrow trail which required the unit to move in a single column. Protected by heavy artillery fire, they advanced with little or no opposition.

The unit found that the four days of preparations fired at the hill had a devastating effect, both on vegetation and human flesh. The once dense vegetation was completely cleared. Not a leaf remained on the bare tree stumps. When the company reached the enemy positions, they discovered forty-one enemy pillboxes blasted apart, and counted over two hundred enemy dead. The rest of the Japanese had deserted these positions for more favorable emplacements at the top of Hill 3155. The men paused only a few minutes at this position, and then continued their climb through a narrow saddle known as the "Bottleneck." The leading platoon advanced to a spot very near the crest when they encountered heavy enemy machine gun and rifle fire coming from the Japanese above them.

First Lieutenant Stanley W. Ostman's Company I quickly secured the entire hill except for about 200 yards of the northeast ridge. They then hunkered down, took a hard look at the ridge, and made a quick estimate of the situation. Their assessment was that the enemy had a reinforced company on the ridge, dug into caves, pillboxes, spider holes and covered trenches. There was just one trail leading to the objective, and it was well covered by automatic weapons and mortars.

The ridge occupied by the enemy was roughly Vee-shaped, with the apex of the Vee pointed towards the attacking force, and a sheer drop of two to three hundred feet on either side. The ridge at the apex of the Vee was from twelve to fifteen yards wide, and widened out from there to approximately forty yards. Companies E and L were on the opposite side of the enemy from Company I.

The first enemy pillbox was at the crest of a knoll on the ridge, and this position covered the only approach with automatic fire.

The pillbox itself was protected by ten infantrymen in spider holes. By crawling and climbing along the edge of the ridge in front of the pillbox, it was possible to get underneath the automatic weapons and protecting sniper fire. Any such tactics were however, subject to explosive charges and aerial anti-personnel bombs being dropped down on top of attackers. Because of the proximity of friendly troops, it was impossible to place effective mortar or artillery fire on the enemy positions.

It was not for lack of trying. The mortar platoon felt this target was the most difficult mission they had during World War II. The enemy enclave was only 200 yards wide, with friendly troops on each side. Due to the terrain, the mortars had to set up 2200 yards away. Rainy weather made it almost impossible to keep mortar base plates from burying themselves in the ground, making it extremely difficult to keep the mortars properly positioned.

The attack for morning of May 23rd was planned for Company I, 3-160th Infantry from south to north, and Company L, 3-160th from north to south. The enemy positions had been narrowed to 150 yards wide, so a single 105mm howitzer was used for precision artillery adjustment before a battery was used for preparatory fires. The mortar platoon's four guns fired about 1500 rounds that morning, including 500 rounds in a short twenty minute period.

That morning Company I's Staff Sergeant John C. Sjogren led his squad in the final assault on the enemy positions. He knew there had been repeated unsuccessful frontal attacks, so he decided to attack by going down and to the left of the enemy positions. The terrain was so steep that often the men had to pull themselves up by grabbing vines and saplings that grew along the route of advance. The troops reached the enemy positions after climbing through a hail of grenades rolled down on them by the enemy.

In order to attack the initial pillbox, the snipers who were covering the pillbox on the crest of the hill had to be eliminated. There was no cover, so Sjogren was forced to expose himself to the aimed fire of the snipers as he led his squad in the attack. He used all of the grenades he had and those of his squad, then called for four more boxes of grenades. When these arrived, he started a barrage of grenades with the intention of keeping the enemy down in their holes. This gave the remainder of the squad a chance to take up exposed positions and obtain fire superiority. During this phase of the attack, his assistant squad leader on the left flank of the squad was hit and mortally wounded by an enemy sniper. In spite of the heavy aimed fire from snipers on the enemy right flank as well as dynamite charges, Sergeant Sjogren crossed the exposed twenty yards of open terrain to his next in command. He then removed the wounded man to a defiladed position and administered first aid.

Returning to the attack, with grenades and his M1 rifle, he succeeded in eliminating the remaining enemy riflemen who were covering the only avenue of approach to the pillbox. In this second attack on the protecting snipers, Sergeant Sjogren killed a total of eight Japanese soldiers in the spider holes, clearing the way for an attack on the pillbox

After instructing his men to concentrate their fire on the firing slit of the pillbox, Sjogren crawled up to within two or three yards of the pillbox and started throwing grenades in through the slit. The first several were immediately thrown back out by the enemy. Sergeant Sjogren was wounded by one of these grenades but, disregarding his own wounds, he continued throwing grenades into the pillbox. By throwing them in faster than they could throw them back out, he killed the three Japanese inside.

After eliminating the first pillbox, Sergeant Sjogren jumped up and yelled for his squad to advance and cover him. He then started to reduce the remaining enemy positions. The systematic reduction of these positions made it possible, for the first time, for the attacking troops to advance beyond the knoll and complete the destruction of the remaining positions.

Before each succeeding pillbox it was necessary to eliminate protecting snipers in spider holes and trenches. As he approached the third pillbox, he passed an apparently dead Japanese soldier in a spider hole. The second scout, following behind and covering Sjogren, came upon the apparently dead Japanese soldier and noted that he was still breathing. He called to Staff Sergeant Sjogren that there was a prisoner they should take. Sjogren immediately returned to take the prisoner and was only three feet from the spider hole when the Japanese soldier suddenly came to life. He fired point blank at Sjogren with his rifle. He somehow missed, and was immediately killed by the second scout. All of this time bullets from weapons in the remaining pillboxes and from dug in Japanese were flying by and kicking up dust and rock fragments. Sjogren proceeded to wipe out the third pillbox as he had the first two, using grenades after crawling into position.

Staff Sergeant Sjogren then crawled up on another pillbox from which a light machine gun was firing. He grabbed the muzzle of the gun, dragged it from its emplaced position, and passed it to the rear where it was taken by another member of his squad. He then threw grenades into the slit until all activity inside the pillbox ceased.

As Sjogren advanced towards the Japanese, enemy rifle and automatic weapons fire reached another crescendo. He jumped into a trench in an attempt to obtain cover from the intense fires, but saw a Japanese soldier at one end of the trench. He rushed and closed with the soldier in the hope of securing a prisoner. In the resulting hand to hand fight, Sjogren had to kill him.

Sergeant Sjogren continued to crawl forward from trench to trench, killing Japanese soldiers as he progressed. As he reached pillboxes, he eliminated them with hand grenades. In the process, Sjogren personally destroyed nine enemy pillboxes and killed a total of forty-three Japanese.

The enemy counterattacked in an attempt to retake the hill by using pole charges and dynamite. The soldiers of Company I held on in spite of the heavy concussions, and drove the enemy back with a barrage of grenades. Staff Sergeant Sjogren's elimination of the first key pillbox, and his incredible valor demonstrated to so many of his comrades, inspired the rest of the unit as they success-fully completed the mission.

The score in this one operation included a total of forty-two enemy pillboxes and numerous spider holes, trenches and covered trenches cleared. Fifteen machine guns were captured or destroyed. One hundred and eleven enemy dead were officially counted. It was impossible to count the many enemy dead in blown up and caved in pillboxes. A total of 297 enemy dead were left strewn on Dolan Hill before the Japanese gave up in their attempts to hold and retake the hill.

During the next few days several enemy stragglers were killed, but the battle for Dolan Hill, the core of the enemy defense on Negros, was over. Sjogren was recommended for and later award-ed the Medal of Honor.

In the meantime, the 503rd had been facing tough clashes in fighting along the road to what came to be called "Banana Ridge." The road over which the 503rd Parachute Infantry Regiment fought its primary campaign after being attached to the division for the fight on Negros, wound its way up to and followed the crest of a long, narrow steep-sided ridge. As the advance progressed the road was found to be extensively mined. Fortunately, the inexpert installation made detection simple and they were easily removed. Enemy defensive positions along the crest, consisting of pillboxes connected to the personnel caves deep in the adjacent ravines, were difficult to destroy until the road had been widened and improved to permit tanks to move forward. Tank traps, constructed by cutting about a ten-foot section of the road to a depth of eight feet were encountered at several points. Roofed with saplings and covered with a layer of earth to give the appearance of a continuous road, they were immediately discovered when crossed by foot patrols. They presented no problem other than the inconvenience of moving material forward to bridge the narrow gap. The rugged terrain on either side of the road, with its precipitous slopes, enemy-infested, jungle-filled draws, and numerous fingerlike, divergent ridges, was combed by patrols as the advance progressed.

The 503rd's advance against tough defenses in that rugged and highly defensible terrain could only be made at considerable cost. Nevertheless, the regiment succeeded in inflicting considerably more casualties than it suffered, and took a heavy toll of enemy arms and equipment. During the period April 17th to May 1st inclusive, 307 enemy dead were counted.

The 1-503rd, which had been held at Mindoro in Army reserve, landed on Negros and rejoined the regiment on April 24th. By May 2nd, the main force of the 503rd had pushed eastward to a point approximately 3500 yards southeast of Manzanares and onto Banana Ridge, perpendicular to the axis of the advance, and the last remaining high ground west of the deep gorge cut by the Malago River. As the enemy's main positions were approached and his major supply points threatened, his resistance got much stiffer.

In early May, the infantrymen of the 185th RCT had their own challenges in the area adjacent to the 503rd. Their objective was the high and wooded Virgne Ridge, named in memory of 1st Lieutenant Sidney E. Virgne. Virgne had been killed during the preparatory patrolling prior to the attack, and the ridge was named in his honor. Virgne Ridge commanded both the Lantawan plain and the Patog area. Separating Virgne Ridge from the division's forward positions, the forbidding Malisbog draw, deep and dense with vegetation, concealed an unknown number of Japanese. Firing artillery point-blank from the brink of the gorge and pounding rear areas by successive air strikes, two days were again spent in softening up enemy positions.

On May 1st, the attack on Virgne Ridge began. Shortly after daylight, shells poured into the ridge from all supporting weapons. In a sight never to be forgotten, lined up on the ridge held by the 185th were batteries of heavy machine guns, a company of medium tanks, quadruple 50's of the 470th Automatic Weapons Battalion, Cannon Company's M-7's, a couple of 90mm guns and the mortars of 1st and 3rd Battalions along with the 4.2's of the Chemical Mortar Battalion. The climax to this stupendous barrage came with two volleys of the entire artillery of the division.

Under cover of this fire, Companies B and C jumped off at 8:30 a.m. Twenty minutes later they were at the bottom of the draw and starting to advance up the slopes against scattered resistance. By noon, Company B was on the ridge and consolidating while Company C was advancing to join them. The bulldozers of Company B, 115th Engineers immediately started to extend the supply road across the draw and up to the ridge.

During the period of the entire attack fifty of the enemy were counted dead. Now the 185th Regiment was in possession of the key terrain feature of the Patog area and was preparing to push the enemy further into the inhospitable mountains.

During the period of May 2nd through the 5th, all three battalions of the 185th consolidated their positions and sent out numerous daily patrols. On the 2nd, these patrols accounted for 39 of the enemy during their mopping up and reconnaissance operations. One platoon of Company B advanced to a small knoll three hundred yards beyond the forward elements of 1-185th and dug in to hold it. The 3rd of May alone added another 52 enemy dead during vigorous patrolling along Virgne Ridge spur and the draws around the high ground. There were 38 more Japanese killed over the next two days. Patrolling disclosed numerous caves honeycombing the precipitous sides of all the draws, and from several of these caves cornered Japanese were flushed and killed. During this period, daily air strikes and artillery support continued to rake the enemy's rear area.

All this activity, however, was no deterrent to the repeatedly attempted night infiltrations of the suicidal enemy. Wires were cut, booby traps sprung, knee mortar shells dropped into friendly perimeters and rifles and machine guns fired sporadically throughout the night. Even the 185th Regimental Headquarters perimeter was not immune, for on the night of the 2nd, just before 2000, an attack started with the earth-shaking crump-crump-crump of three mortar shells. The protective machine guns on the perimeter opened up and sprayed the area but to no avail. A few minutes later the sharper detonations of 2½ pound aerial bombs (used like hand grenades) mixed with the chattering of small arms. Seven headquarters troopers were wounded during this action.

General Brush told General Eichelberger that he felt that the Japanese were beginning to weaken. He partially based that view on the increasing number of banzai attacks, with the Japanese soldiers often stimulated with sake or some type of dope. These attacks were often a prelude to defeat, and rarely succeeded against veteran troops armed with automatic weapons. While much hard fighting was to follow, commanders were increasingly speculating about how much longer the war was going to last.

In the meantime, numerous minor contacts but no serious threat had developed on the left flank of the 503rd PCT. On the right, contact was maintained with the 185th Infantry. Plans were then laid for a coordinated attack on Patog by the 503rd PCT and the 185th RCT. The scheme called for the 503rd PCT to move south on Banana Ridge into the Patog area. At the same time, the 185th RCT, then at Lantawan, would advance on Patog from the east.

Artillery preparations were fired on May 4th and 5th. Heavy rains hindered air strikes and delayed construction of the supply roads needed to bring forward heavy equipment. Nonetheless, the coordinated attack started.

The 185th RCT assisted the 503rd PCT, including the 503rd's final drive on Banana Ridge. They then continued to slug their way deeper into the Patog area despite the various frustrations, especially mud. The 2-185th, on the right flank, with the mission of exploiting the treacherous Malisbog River Draw, was by the very nature of the confining terrain, limited to patrol action. Two known trails existed in its sector - one in the draw itself, the other on the high ridge of the east bank of the river. Both were easily defended.

It was apparent that the Japanese, with the exception of the forces in the Malisbog draw area, were falling back to new positions. The 185th began to reorient their attacks to the southeast. Again, the Malisbog was the key, for it was the evacuation route for the Patog area. Dogged resistance against the advance of the 2-185th marked that phase of the campaign.

On May 10th, 3-185th took up the drive to the southeast to the juncture of the Malago and Malisbog Rivers. Still the Japanese were determined to hold the southeast Patog area, for once that was lost, nothing remained but steep mountains and heavy rain forest. The 3rd Battalion began to probe its way along the few trails leading to the junction, but the enemy fought hard at every turn.

Despite the tenacity displayed by the enemy, captured documents and prisoner reports showed he was weakening as his food supplies were rapidly dwindling, his casualties were heavy, and he was running short of ammunition. It was apparent that he only fired a weapon when certain of his target.

According to intelligence estimates, all that remained of his original defensive line was a small pocket on the north end of Dolan Hill and the Hill 4055 entrenchments. The enemy's division headquarters had been discovered and shelled by artillery and finally overrun by infantry. It was believed that the seizure of Hill 4055 would render his forces impotent and end the Negros operation.

By May 11th, the 185th Infantry was pushing south from Patog. The 3-503rd was meeting stubborn resistance along a line running west from the Malago and several hundred yards south of Patog astride the ridge which the Japanese had named Terukuni. The 2nd and 3rd Battalions of the 185th were engaged in cleaning out the deep ravine of the Malisbog on the right of the 503rd, while 1-185th advanced up a ridge running south from Lantawan. This slope, actually the northern part of Hill 4055's mass, the Japanese had named Kasagi Ridge.

From the crest of Dolan Hill the 160th was in position to observe the advance of the 185th on Kasagi, and assist using their organic weapons. Elements of the 185th advanced 500 yards the first day and 400 on the second. The ground had been well prepared by the enemy, with particular attention to sniper positions. Automatic weapons were numerous, and many heavy machine guns were encountered. Terukuni Ridge just to the east was also strongly fortified in the same manner. Its heavy rain forest was spotted with snipers both on the ground and in the trees, and on at least one occasion a machine gun was encountered mounted on a platform built in a tree. Also in this area were the enemy's last known 20mm guns.

Both Terukuni and Kasagi were bombarded by artillery, mortars and aircraft as the 185th moved forward. Gains were still in hundreds rather than thousands of yards. Enemy positions were cleverly concealed, and the enemy was careful not to give them away unnecessarily. Patrols carried the burden of the operation, locating defense points and in most cases destroying them on the spot.

The final phase of the campaign for Negros was at hand. To achieve a complete and utter defeat of the enemy, three objectives, and these were within immediate reach, had to be gained: the junction of the Malago and Malisbog Rivers on the left flank, the forks of the Malisbog in the center, and the high hill mass, designated as Hill 4055, on the right. To accomplish this, the 185th Regimental Commander assigned to 3-185th the mission of gaining the river junction, gave a joint assignment of attaining the forks of the Malisbog to the 2nd and 3rd Battalions, and committed 1-185th against the strong enemy on Hill 4055.

The 185th was poised for the finishing blow. On the morning of the 15th, after two days of constant artillery, mortar and air bombardment, the attack began. Company C moved up Ridge "D" but was halted by heavy fire and a counterattack from the rear. But the ground gained was held, and there was now a salient into the enemy's line in the 1-185th's sector.

Only Hill 4055 remained as a significant barrier to destroying the potency of the Japanese as a fighting force on Negros. Captured documents and prisoner of war statements indicated that an Independent Infantry Battalion was ensconced on Hill 4055, while several hundred survivors of an Air Depot Regiment were defending in the southeast Patog area.

During the last week of May, the 185th continued to exert strong pressure with the help of endless bombardments. Yard by yard the infantrymen advanced, and held against repeated counterattacks. The battle for Hill 4055 was particularly bloody, but by the end of the month the pinnacle of the mountain was in the hands of 1-185th.

The occupation of Dolan Hill lent security to the 185th's right flank on Kasagi Ridge, but the problem of hunting down each separate enemy position continued there and on Terukuni. Gradually the enemy withdrew from both Terukuni and Kasagi. Rear guards maintained the stubborn resistance while hospitals, food stocks and other supplies were evacuated. Until May 29th, heavy fire was received from enemy on Kasagi, just below the crest of Hill 4055. That night, the enemy evacuated, and patrols and advance elements which reached the top of the hill the next day did so with only minor contact. On May 31st, the positions in the Malisbog area, described above, were strongly defended. On June 1st, they were found abandoned. Numerous prisoners of war reported that the enemy was making their withdrawal to the south and east toward Mount Mandalagan and Sulphur Springs.

The disastrous defeats suffered by the enemy in the Patog area and on Dolan Hill had rendered the enemy force impotent. Less than 2000 effective combat troops remained and they, suffering from fatigue and hunger, and exposed to sickness and disease, were incapable of any offensive action. Small arms ammunition was limited and food stocks were sufficient for not more than two months. Morale was extremely low and mutual disrespect between officers and enlisted men was rampant. To attack was impossible, to continue the defense in the forward areas meant annihilation, and to remain long in the mountains meant starvation. The only possible hope of survival was to disengage and seek sources of food in the cultivated areas along the coastal plain or in the valleys to the south and east.

As was later determined, General Kono, the Japanese commander, ordered a withdrawal to Yamamoto Valley near Mount Mandalagan. The force was divided into four main groups. The first of these, including the division headquarters, was to bivouac in Yamamoto Valley; the second would forage north along the Himugaan River to the Fabrica area; the third in the direction of San Carlos; and the fourth along the upper reaches of the Bago River. Rear guards consisting largely of personnel who were physically incapable of movement were left in position to delay pursuit forces.

Routes to these areas passed southeast of Hill 4055 and over Hill 3355 and Hill 4500, known to the Japanese as Tenshin Mountain. Sulphur Springs, near Hill 3355, became a temporary resupply point. The plan was learned from various sources almost as soon as it was contemplated, and moves were made to counter the enemy strategy. Immediately following the capture of Patog the 503rd Parachute Infantry had been moved to the Division right flank near Murcia and was given the mission of cutting the withdrawal route by securing Hills 3355 and 4500.

Moving quickly through the wide draw which led to Hill 3355 from the west, the regiment encountered generally moderate resistance from small organized enemy groups in the area. A stiffer defense was met, however, when the top of Hill 3355 itself was reached. The main attack was up the northwest slope over a ridge running southeast from Hill 4055. Along this ridge ran one of the enemy's main evacuation routes. A secondary attack was also made on the southwest slope of Hill 3355.

Both assaults met strong resistance. The enemy still had a number of automatic weapons and sufficient ammunition in this area to contest the severance of his routes of withdrawal. All advances against the hill met with fire from prepared positions. Patrols searching in the direction of Hill 4055 encountered strong opposition both on and off the trail. In the draw along which the approach had been made both stragglers and small organized groups continued to be encountered and destroyed. However, the enemy's plan did not contemplate defending Hill 3355 to the bitter end, and when friendly advance elements reached the top of the hill on May 27th they found the area evacuated.

Documents and prisoners indicated that Hill 4500, just to the north, had been an assembly area for the retreating enemy. Forces were immediately dispatched to clear that area and destroy such installations or supplies as might be found. Resistance was sporadic and whenever withdrawing enemy troops could be contacted a brisk fire fight generally ensued, but the enemy's desire to avoid our troops as much as possible and to complete his evacuation as planned was obvious.

The action resulted in the capture of many supplies which the Japanese could ill afford to spare. Prisoners, who now began surrendering in increasing numbers, regularly reported extreme shortages of food, arms and ammunition. They confirmed reports that their field hospital, which had been forced to move time and again, was totally without medical supplies. Abandoning all hope for their sick and wounded, and unwilling to "waste" food on the dying, patients were put on half rations. When the hospital was moved, patients who were not able to stand the long trek over the mountains were deserted and left to their fate. Their only hope of relief were the hand grenades they had been given with which to destroy themselves.

By June 1st, division patrols were operating east of Hill 4500 as well as beyond 3355. Few contacts were made. A reconnaissance patrol up the Bago River toward Mount Mandalagan made no contact, but guerrillas in the area reported frequent contacts with small foraging parties.

It was obvious by now that the Japanese on Negros were thoroughly beaten. Every terrain feature which in their original plans they had contemplated defending had been overrun and the survivors scattered.

From the beginning of the campaign in the hills, regular drops of surrender leaflets had been made on all enemy areas. Following the capture of Dolan Hill, the G-2 Language Section, with the voluntary help of a prisoner, delivered via public address system appeals for the enemy to surrender. Broadcasts were also conducted in the Patog and Hill 3355 areas. Results were not immediate, but propaganda coupled with the enemy's calamitous situation eventually brought daily surrenders of groups averaging from five to ten men.

In their statements these prisoners universally confirmed reports regarding the enemy's shortage of supplies and loss of personnel and acknowledged the hopelessness not only of their own situation but that of the Japanese nation as well. At the close of May, 4000 enemy dead had been counted and 4,600 more estimated killed, with 90 prisoners captured or surrendered.

Only minor patrol clashes occurred during the first days of June. The 503rd Parachute Combat Team, augmented by the 7th Military District, took over the former sectors of the 160th and 185th Infantry Regiments. The division disengaged, leaving the enemy remnants to be eliminated, primarily by the guerrillas.

CHAPTER TEN

FIGHTING STOPS, OCCUPATION BEGINS

On the July 1, 1945, responsibility for all of Negros, and operational control of the 7th Military District and certain non-divisional Army units passed to the Commanding Officer, 503rd Parachute Combat Team. Word was received that day that the Eighth Army was to release the 40th, 41st, 81st and Americal Divisions, as well as the 503rd Parachute Combat Team to train in preparation for the invasion of Japan.

What this meant to General Brush was that he was to again serve under General Krueger. General Krueger had not only relieved one of Brush's regimental commanders without (in Brush's view) any justification, he had also directed his Corps commander, General Griswold, to relieve Brush. General Griswold refused to relieve Brush, as had General Chink Hall of XI Corps when Krueger transferred the division to his other corps. The division was quickly vindicated when people in senior headquarters began to refer to the 40th Division as the "Rattlesnake Division" following the Panay and Negros campaigns. The division earned this appellation because they had a reputation for striking swiftly and without warning.

General Brush was devastated when he heard he was again going to have to serve under General Krueger, and told General Eichelberger he intended to retire as soon as the war ended. Even though General Brush had lost a lot of weight and was in poor health, General Eichelberger urged him to hold off before making a decision. In General Eichelberger's words: "Rapp's service after taking Panay and Negros is on a very high curve and I have recommended him for the DSM (Distinguished Service Medal) so he need not worry about the future."

As the 40th Division elements and certain attached units were relieved, they were moved to Iloilo, Panay, where the division was being concentrated. After six months of continuous combat, broken only by fifteen days in which the division was busily engaged in preparation for the Visayan campaign, the division started a well-earned period of rest and recreation.

Also in July, the 108th RCT returned from Mindanao and rejoined the division on Panay. The division consolidated its forces with the 108th Infantry in the Oton area, the 160th and 185th Infantry Regiments in the Santa Barbara area, and the division artillery in the Tigbauan area. The Division Commander, Major General Rapp Brush, who had led the division throughout its Philippine Island campaigns, returned to the United States on temporary duty and subsequently retired; Brigadier General Donald J. Myers was then assigned to the division and assumed command effective July 22, 1945.

The division's role in the Philippines campaign was finished. All major islands in the Philippines were once again in American hands, and battered remnants were all that remained of the once proud Imperial Japanese Army.

Captured Japanese staff studies were analyzed, and revealed just how surprised the Japanese were by the 40th Division. The Japanese were having communications problems, and their headquarters didn't even know the division was ashore until troops were at a point south of Bacolod. In the words of the Japanese staff officers, "The American ability to organize and deliver hard driving assaults and their alertness in meeting our night raids was astonishing." They were particularly impressed with the division's mortars, considering them to be the division's most effective weapon.

The 40th Division was scheduled to play an important part in the forthcoming invasion of Japan. Under the aegis of 6th Army, the division was to make a preliminary landing against several islands off Southern Kyushu four days in advance of the main effort of Operation OLYMPIC on November 1st. These amphibious landings were intended to secure the principal islands of the Koshiki-Retto Group. The 40th Division would establish radar and early warning stations on the islands while providing security in the area. The main effort by nine sea-landed and two airborne divisions was to be directed against Southern Kyushu by the 6th Army. The 40th Division would then be available to reinforce the main effort if needed. The overall mission of the invading force was to secure half of Southern Kyushu, establishing bases and airfields for the culminating attack and invasion of Honshu in February of 1946.

In two carefully guarded planning buildings, the staff of the 40th Division held continuous planning conferences, and worked out in detail the complex problems presented by this amphibious mission. Plans were discussed down to the battalion commander level early in July of 1945. Careful coordination with the Navy was established and elaborate plans laid for supplying troops fighting on barren, volcanic islands in a cold and wet climate, yet without local water supplies. Shortly before V-J day, tentative Field Order No. 19 was completed and prepared for submission to Sixth Army Headquarters.

In addition to planning for Operation OLYMPIC, the division was, from July 1st until the Japanese surrender on August 16th, concerned with the relief and return to Panay of supporting service units still concluding missions on Negros, the reception and screening of replacements, the reequipping of the division, and, finally a detailed program of combat refresher training. Troops attended division schools on the M-7 Self-propelled Howitzer, combined tank-infantry tactics, chemical warfare, operation of the Weasel supply vehicle, graves registration, and signal training. Of outstanding importance to troops destined for a campaign of island warfare were the amphibious training school at Subic Bay, Luzon and the amphibious training exercises on Panay and Negros. The schooling was conducted by General Headquarters, United States

Army Forces, Pacific, and the division sent selected officers to attend. In the amphibious problems conducted by the Division, using ships of TRANSRON 47, troops made actual landings on the southwestern coast of Negros, near the little town of Himamay-Lan, 25 kilometers south of Valladolid and at White Beach, Tigbauan, Panay. Only one RCT at a time could undergo the amphibious training, so the others were subjected to intense combat training punctuated by field exercises.

As planning for the invasion progressed, senior leadership of the Army was becoming increasingly concerned about Japanese preparations to repel an invasion of their home islands. The number of enemy divisions defending Kyushu quickly doubled over earlier estimates to a total of about 600,000 men. In the meantime, obsolete and training aircraft were being converted for use as Kamikazes, while piloted torpedoes and flying bombs were being built as well as suicide boats. Atomic bombs were then dropped on Hiroshima and Nagasaki.

On August 16th, Japanese Imperial Headquarters announced the cessation of all hostilities and although an estimated twelve days were needed for the orders to reach all outlying Japanese outposts, the war was officially ended. In order to disseminate the surrender news to about 1,700 Japanese soldiers on Panay, liaison planes dropped information pamphlets throughout the island. The pamphlets stipulated that surrender panels were to be displayed by all units, and that a preliminary surrender meeting was scheduled for August 27th. A surrender party of no more than twenty-five Japanese was directed to report on that day to American officers at the dam above Maasin. On August 28th, a day late, an American reconnaissance plane observed the surrender party near the dam. The meeting was then conducted, and in the ensuing conference, plans were made to receive the formal surrender of all Japanese forces on Panay. The Japanese were then to be evacuated from the Mt. Singit and Bucari areas. On September 1st, Lieutenant Colonel Ryoichi Tozuke, Commander of all Imperial Japanese Forces on

Panay, along with his staff surrendered their arms and samurai swords to the Commanding Officer, 160th Infantry. On the following day, the formal surrender ceremony was held and by midnight on September 2nd, over 1,100 Japanese soldiers and civilians camp followers, including women and children, had been confined in the Santa Barbara Prisoner-of-War Compound. Within a few days approximately 1,750 Japanese were made prisoners of war.

The division was credited with 6,145 Japanese killed or captured on Luzon, and with killing or capturing 4,732 Japanese on Panay and Negros. Casualties suffered by the 40th Division during World War II included 715 killed in action, plus five missing. The killed in action included one lieutenant colonel, five majors, four captains, 33 lieutenants, and 87 sergeants. The missing included two lieutenants, one sergeant, and two privates.

When the surrender of Japan was announced on August 16th, the planning for OLYMPIC ceased and a training program was developed to prepare troops of the division for occupation duty in Korea. Personnel records were screened and volunteers sought who had experience that would be useful in helping Korean government offices and services at all levels return to normal. These soldiers were formed into Military Government teams.

Information on the "hermit kingdom" was very limited, but personnel were briefed on their Military Government responsibilities, and on customs, habits and history of the Korean people. There was considerable emphasis on the need to display military courtesy and discipline, while manifesting a "kindly but firm" attitude to both the conquered Japanese and the liberated Koreans. The few divisional soldiers of Korean ancestry were immediately put to work helping their fellow soldiers learn as much as they could about Korea. It was explained to the troops that the American forces intended to impose no set government upon Korea but expected the Koreans to determine their own political destiny.

Lieutenant General John R. Hodge, the Commanding General of XXIV Corps, was appointed as Commanding General, United

States Army forces in Korea. He was told he would "act for CINCAFPAC in reception of surrender of senior Japanese Commanders and all Japanese ground, sea, air and auxiliary forces in Korea south of 38 degrees North Latitude."

On August 20th, Brigadier General Myers assembled a large planning staff from division headquarters on Panay and departed for Okinawa. On the 22nd, the division was notified that it had been transferred as of August 15th from control of Sixth Army to the XXIV Corps. During the meeting on Okinawa, plans for the occupation of South Korea were discussed in detail.

The division commander and his staff returned to Panay on August 24th. They were followed on the 28th by a liaison officer who was carrying XXIV Corps Field Order No. 55, dated August 28th. The field order directed the 7th Division to land at Inchon on (tentatively) September 7th, and occupy the Kyongsang area in the north. The 40th Division was to then to occupy Pusan and Southeastern Korea. Finally, Southwestern Korea's Kunsan-Chongju's area was to be occupied.

The division consolidated its personnel and equipment at Iloilo as it prepared for movement to Korea during late August and early September. The movement was to be made in shipping under the control of the 7th Amphibious Force, landing at Inchon or "as directed." The plan called for the 40th Division to land at Inchon, move inland to relieve the 7th Division of responsibility for the area south and east, and establish headquarters at the Port of Pusan. The division was directed to be prepared for possible resumption of hostilities. Therefore the ships were combat loaded so the troops could disembark prepared for the worst.

The first ship departed Iloilo on September 7th with the advance party of the division and elements of the 532nd Engineer Boat and Shore Regiment. The next, slow convoy primarily carried the 160th Infantry Regiment. They left on September 13th accompanied, as all convoys were, by a token escort, whose primary function was to protect the convoy from the floating mines found so often in the Yellow Sea area. The final convoy was a fast convoy that departed September 22nd. Two LST's carrying heavy replacement equipment followed.

There were strong storms at sea which not only delayed the passage, but made unloading difficult. This was complicated by changing guidance on where the division was to disembark. The division's advance party landed at Inchon on September 15th. Finally, XXIV Corps on September 20th reported that the Port of Pusan was prepared to receive the division. However, the first convoy arrived at Inchon. They quickly departed for Pusan, where the rest of the division landed, via rail because reconnaissance parties reported the roads were "fair to impassable."

Moving the division around in Korea was a daunting challenge. As logisticians began planning the dispersal of the division to various parts of Korea, they found there were only about 300 flat cars in all of Korea. The standard for movement of a U.S. Infantry Division at the time was 347 cars. Facing a shortage of rolling stock, complicated by competing requirements of other commands, the division found itself shuttling rail cars and equipment up and down the length of Korea.

Advance elements of the division were establishing bivouac areas by early October. The Regimental Headquarters with 1st and 3rd Battalions of the 185th began to establish a permanent bivouac site at Taegu. At the same time they dispatched reconnaissance patrols throughout their zones of responsibility. By October 7th, the 108th had occupied Ulsan, Andong, Yongdok, Kyongju and other main towns in its zone. Division Artillery opened their command post at Chinhae Naval Base by October 8th and started reconnaissance.

The 2-108th had remained at Inchon to function as the division shore party. XXIV Corps directed the division be prepared to extend control into Cholla-Namdo Province until arrival of the 6th Division. That battalion was therefore moved to Cholla-Namdo Province as the occupation force.

Typical of the government responsibilities assumed by tactical commanders was the administration of Chinju. There a lieutenant colonel became Military Governor of Chinju Gun (County), a lieutenant became mayor of Chinju city, and a captain became the Chief of Police. These tactical troop commanders received, inventoried, and guarded Japanese installations and supplies while at the same time they organized, coordinated and supervised the administration of municipal and county government.

Many of the division's small detachments scattered over much of Korea found themselves challenged in maintaining peace and order. Frequently civil governments were overrun by the People's Republic Party who refused to accept the officials initially sanctioned or established by the area commanders. In Yongsan, within the 108th's Zone of Responsibility, thirty members of the party expelled all high officials of the city based on the charge they were pro-Japanese and traitors to Korea. In Hadong, the People's Republic Party occupied all public offices and flatly refused to recognize the Military Government as a legitimate instrument for governing Korea. Party members threatened to seize all Japanese property for redistribution to Koreans, and promised civil war if they were thwarted by American troops. When division troops had been dispatched to the city and order was restored, Counter Intelligence Corps investigation revealed that the party's claim to the support of a popular majority in the city was unfounded. In fact they found that the citizens of Hadong were terrified by the excesses committed by party members. On October 31st, the People's Republic Party at Hyopchon seized the government, burned the courthouse and all municipal records, forced the city treasurer to open the safe, and extorted donations and enrollment in the party on threat of burning and looting their homes. Party members then embarked on a campaign of urging the people, by posters and public demonstrations, to kill all pro-American officials and to agitate against the occupation forces so as to prevent the proper functioning of Military Government. In Chinju, American troops imprisoned five men implicated in burning the courthouse. On January 5th, however, members of the Korean Revolutionary Alliance Association released these prisoners by threatening the local police chief.

Many of these demonstrations of antagonism to the American occupation forces were inspired by communist agitators. In a letter dated October 9th, censored and translated by Civil Censorship Detachment, the Japanese writer stated:

"If the United States Military Government gives up political power to Koreans the administration of Korea will be communist. The idea of communism is deeply rooted in the Korean people."

It was difficult to determine the extent to which communism was "deeply rooted in the Korean people." However, the People's Republic Party was the most aggressive party in Korea, had numerous affiliated youth organizations, farmer's associations and labor groups, and rallied together the radical and discontented elements of the Southern Provinces. In a meeting of all youth organizations in Kyong-Sang-Namdo Province in which support to the People's Republic was pledged, it was stated that "because Military Government officials are traitors against the Korean race, we must have friendly relations with Soviet Russia as that government is the representative of the farmers and laborers."

The relationship became more obvious on December 28th, when a premature press release announced in fragmentary form the conclusions reached by Russia and America at the Moscow Conference pertaining to the political and economic future of Korea. Immediately following the announcement, all political parties joined in demonstrations, though with few disorders, against what was termed the proposed "trusteeship" of Korea. Military Government employees and civil officials went on strike, markets closed and every large city was the scene of parades. Banners were carried with such messages as "Opposition to Trust Rule in Korea," while it should be noted that some strikes were engineered rather than expressions of genuine opposition. Repatriation shipping was halted in expectation of a railroad strike. Typical of the brightly colored posters which adorned conspicuous walls and poles is that which was posted in Pusan:

> To our allied country!!!
> Give to Korean liberty or give to we death.
> We at any risk support Anti-Trust Government.
> Give we Atom Bomb or give we Free!!

In Changnyong, two interpreters for tactical troops quit their jobs because they feared attacks directed against their families if they refused to oppose trusteeship and continued in Military Government employ. The pastor of the Holiness Church In Taegu was threatened by men who insisted that because he was pro-American, he must also be anti-communist, and opposed to the welfare and independence of Korea. This assumed opposition between the two ideologies was frequently encountered as justification for defiance of Military Government, particularly from the People's Republic Party.

Agitation against the plan gradually diminished throughout the Division Zone of Responsibility following the wide dissemination of a speech delivered on December 21st by the Commanding General, XXIV Corps. In this speech, Lieutenant General Hodge explained in some detail the ramifications of the Moscow Communique and pointed with clarity at the benefits which Korea would enjoy under a temporary trusteeship. As a result, on January 2nd the crisis had passed and shipping was resumed, and by January 7th all workers had returned to their jobs without further threat of strikes.

On January 2nd the Communist Party announced its support of the "Trusteeship" and was shortly followed by the People's Republic Party headquarters in Seoul. Unfortunately, communications were poor, so many branches of the People's Republic Party in

South Korea continued to protest the plan long after the party headquarters had announced its support. On January 15, 1946, the Nationalist and Democratic Parties were united in opposition to trusteeship, although they continued to urge cooperation with Military Government. On the other hand, the Communist and People's Republic Parties were united in favor of the plan, while they continued to exert riotous pressure on those officials who supported Military Government.

While these political issues created problems for the Military Government teams and divisional troops, there were missions that had to be accomplished. The greatest concern surrounded the hundreds of thousands of Japanese that remained in Korea when the war ended in August of 1945.

Thousands of Japanese civilians in Korea anticipated rigid allied control of repatriation to their homeland. Shortly after the surrender was announced, many fled to Japan with all their possessions. It was suspected that they were leaving with plundered goods, so it was recognized that occupation troops would have to quickly gain control of the situation and clamp down.

In XXIV Corps Field Order No. 56, dated September 21st, the division was directed to *"maintain control of Japanese civilians and Japanese Armed Forces moving through the Ports of PUSAN and CHINHAE for Japan* (and) *to move repatriated Koreans from PUSAN to native provinces."* These duties were given to the division in addition to its duties of occupation, the establishment of Military Government, and the supervision of disarmament within the 40th Division's Zone of Responsibility.

The specific task of processing and loading Japanese civilian and military personnel aboard ships from Pier No. 1 in PUSAN was assigned to the 160th Infantry Regiment. The 160th knew they faced some challenges in addition to the limited language skills of their troops and the shortage of qualified translators. They had to move people through the port quickly to prevent bottlenecks.

However, they also had to prevent looted Korean wealth from being transported to Japan.

The Port of Pusan was under control of the Japanese when the advance party of the 160th arrived. The Commander of the Japanese Garrison was directed on September 21st to evacuate Pusan except for specified liaison, medical and supply detachments. Most of the 160th had arrived by September 26th, prepared bivouac areas, and initiated relief of the Japanese guards at local installations.

The division developed a Standing Operating Procedure (SOP) for processing outgoing Japanese troops and incoming Koreans, based on the SOP used on Panay Island. The 160th Infantry implemented the SOP using a composite battalion consisting of Companies E, F, K and L. The battalion was divided into three eight-hour shifts, with each shift split into inspection teams. The rest of the regiment performed guard and police duty in the regiment's Zone of Responsibility.

A series of meetings were conducted with the Commanding Officers of the Japanese Garrison in Pusan. Information was gathered on the location and size of Japanese Military Forces so planning could begin for their return to Japan. A transportation officer then began scheduling movement within the area so that Japanese arrived at the port in numbers appropriate to the flow of refugee ships through the port.

These meetings were conducted in the dining room of the Railway Hotel on a daily basis starting September 23rd. Routine attendees included the Pusan Shipping Master, a railroad executive, representatives of local Japanese relief societies, and ranking members of the Japanese garrison. An American officer from the 180th Language Detachment acted as interpreter as policies were established. At least 4000 Japanese troops and civilians were to be evacuated through Pier No. 1 each day, with all troops and civilians to remain in their areas until called. The call was to be placed four days in advance through Japanese military communications agencies. A "pool" of 5,000 people was to be retained in the port area to accommodate unplanned exigencies. This system remained in place until October 18th. From that point a Military Government liaison officer attended the meetings, and calls for troops and civilians were routed through Military Government Headquarters in Seoul.

All moves were complicated by language barriers and the fact that inexperienced Korean workers were replacing the Japanese infrastructure in their country. A typical pencilled note explaining the failure to meet a schedule might read: "engine is little no good now is improving and then shortly will depart." The "little" might refer to anything from a misplaced nut to an exploded boiler. The "shortly" could mean one hour or one day.

The first refugee ships, the Konei Maru and Koan Maru, left Korea on September 26th. They had brought 7,031 Koreans from Japan, and left for the southern island of Kyushu with 3,675 Japanese troops and 5,341 civilians. The Japanese military ensured there was exacting adherence to schedules published by the Transportation Officer, and by the end of the first week 23,843 soldiers and 17,413 civilians had been evacuated.

Sanitation was of concern to American medical personnel. Japanese troops, with the assistance of the Pusan Fire Department pumps and hoses, had cleared out all of the filth and hosed down the area of Pier No. 1. They then sprayed DDT furnished by the Americans into every nook and cranny of the pier and adjacent warehouses. Medical personnel also insisted that all repatriated Japanese be immunized to prevent the transmission to Japan of communicable and lice-borne diseases endemic to Korea. As a further service, all repatriates after October 1st were also vaccinated for typhoid and small-pox.

The various sanitation and medical programs were supervised by the Division Surgeon. On October 20th, a delousing program was initiated, and all repatriates were dusted with DDT by hand and motor sprayers. People too sick or ailing to board the ships were temporarily treated in two civilian and one military hospital. When a sizeable group of these repatriates had accumulated, they were evacuated to Japan accompanied by Japanese medical personnel and medicines.

All Japanese troops having been cleared from the 40th Division's Zone of Responsibility by October 5th, evacuation of Japanese troops in other American zones started. Civilian movements had been curtailed after the first week to expedite the demobilization of Japanese troops. This permitted 55,632 military personnel to be evacuated between October 5th and 18th. By that time almost all Japanese soldiers stationed in South Korea had been evacuated. Exceptions included the Pusan Liaison Detachment, scattered guard posts in several cities, and soldiers awaiting to accompany their families. Finally, there were over 12,000 *Kempei Tai* (Japanese Secret Police) and Allied Prisoner-of-War Camp Guards being investigated by the American Counter Intelligence Corps in Taiden for possible connection with war crimes and atrocities.

There were 7,328 troops evacuated between October 19th and 25th, primarily soldiers accompanying their families. The release of many *Kempei Tai* after investigation resulted in 10,771 soldiers being evacuated from November 2nd to 8th. The total of Japanese troops shipped exceeded 100,000 by that date, and permitted the transition again to almost exclusively civilian movements. There were 164,344 civilians evacuated between October 18th and November 15th. In spite of the large volume of evacuees, it was not anticipated that the job would be finished, for repatriation of both Japanese and Korean civilians, until January 1946.

Pier No. 1 in Pusan had a total flow of 589,628 Japanese military and civilians, and Korean civilians. Handling the 291,977 incoming Koreans was relatively simple. They arrived at Pusan in everything from small launches carrying 50-75 passengers to 5000-passenger steamers. They were met by Korean Refugee Societies that provided them train schedules, sold them tickets, and informed them of possible accommodations and sources of food and clothing.

There were concerns about the unequal value of Japanese and Korean currency. The 160th Infantry set up exchange booths. One exchanged limited amounts of Korean yen for Japanese yen, while serving as the collection agency for Y300,949,105 of excess Korean currency confiscated in routine searches or voluntarily surrendered by repatriates. This excess currency was deposited in a special account in the Bank of Chosen. The other booth accommodated incoming Koreans, exchanging Y39,313,000 of Japanese for Korean yen between October 21st and November 15th alone.

Based on experience gained during the initial processing, a revised Operations Memorandum (see Appendix 8) was published by the division. The Operations Memorandum clearly laid out the rules, serving as a consolidation of directives that had been coming out from CINCAFPAC.

The most important task by far was to prevent Japanese repatriates from taking contraband out of Korea. The Japanese soldiers marched onto Pier No. 1 and opened their packs for methodical searches by the teams of thirty to fifty American soldiers. The inspectors collected contraband goods, dumping them into Jeep trailers, and then transporting them to nearby warehouses. As each group completed this inspection, it was moved to a holding area on the pier, while a new group took its place. The processing teams were prepared to evacuate Japanese soldiers from Pier No. 1 at the rate of five hundred per hour twenty-four hours a day. A docked American destroyer used its searchlights at night to provide illumination for the process.

The inspection of civilians, particularly women, was rather perfunctory during the first five days of the process. The American troops were rather reluctant to pick through the comparatively meager possessions the repatriates were permitted to carry with them. Then the G-2 reported that large amounts of contraband were being carried out of Korea by Japanese civilians. Information from other sources added to the concern. One Japanese advised his friends: "when you go to Japan have a woman carry your money as the United States soldiers are not strict in the search of women, otherwise you are only permitted 1000 yen." Another writer advised his friend "...all surplus is confiscated...sew your money inside your pants or prepare other safe means." Still another counseled "hide your money in your cigarette pack or in your soap." It was obvious that soldiers were using civilians to carry out their excess currency and contraband.

The inspections were immediately tightened up and civilians were searched with the same strict adherence to regulations as were the soldiers. The problems in searching women were solved when Korean women were brought to handle that. Immediately the inspectors started confiscating large amounts of contraband. Many of the repatriates, when informed of currency restrictions, converted their money into clothing and articles valuable in Japan. One civilian converted his savings into seventy kimonos of high quality hand-stitched silk.

Searchers found excess currency hidden in thermos bottles, or baby blankets, or sewed into the lining of apparel. One sergeant was surprised when a venerable old man's walking stick fell apart and spilled 80,000 yen on the pier. From the guarded doors of the women's inspection chamber came valuable silks and excess kimonos, and many thousands of yen which had been sewn into undergarments or concealed about their bodies.

The defeated Japanese, both military and civilian, had always felt superior to the Koreans. This, coupled with impacts of the defeat of their nation, led to scattered incidents of sabotage. They didn't want to leave anything of value in Korea, and often destroyed machinery and equipment. One example was the large Gunzi Clothing Factory in Taegu, which was torched the night of September 30th. Three Japanese civilians later admitted their role in the arson, as well as sabotaging the water system so there would be inadequate water pressure that hampered efforts to control the blaze. In addition, public utilities such as water, electrical, and communications systems were often sabotaged as the Japanese left.

A fire in a private home in Pusan was blamed on the former Japanese landlord who was quoted as saying "No one, much less the United States Government, will live in my house." Some Japanese soldiers left hand grenades in chimney flues. On October 15th, one such booby trap exploded, without causing significant damage.

Counter Intelligence Corps investigation revealed that the *Kempei Tai* had many members unaccounted for, but few acts of violence or sabotage were ascribed to former members of that organization. However, two interpreters employed by Military Government units were identified as either working for or members of *Kempei Tai*.

A few Japanese plotted revenge by advocating future wars. In one letter the censorship detachment translated "We should not fail to note the reasons for defeat in this war. We must be victorious in the next war which is certain between America and Japan." In another, the writer proclaimed his commitment to scientific research so he could "get revenge in the next war." Another on November 5th suggested the Japanese retain control of firms in Korea, stating "On the surface Koreans will manage this company, but secretly, Japanese will occupy the key positions in the firm."

There were also problems at sea. A group of pirates attacked the refugee ship Taiko Maru in October. The ship was stopped and plundered en route to Pusan, and arrived at Pier No. 1 with three corpses aboard. Survivors reported that eleven other passengers had been thrown overboard by the pirates.

There were also problems with smugglers. Field Order No. 21, dated October 4th, directed area commanders to "apprehend Japanese civilians and/or military personnel attempting to depart Korea from points other than Pier No. 1, Pusan." The disciplined Japanese military personnel did not attempt to leave, but many civilians continued to attempt to leave Korea on smuggler's ships, and often succeeded.

Two monitored telephone calls from Pusan to Seoul on October 8th confirmed the existence of active smuggling. Letters translated by the Civil Censorship Detachment also provided much intelligence about the illicit industry. One typical letter written on October 7th read "Mr. Kallone, who was discharged from the military service, had left Pusan for Japan by secret passage on a ship of about sixty tons." Another writer advised a friend in Japan to arrange for the sale of valuable silk because "I will arrive and return by secret ship when I leave here. Many secret ships leave Pusan every day." A Seoul businessman informed a partner in Japan that "I intend to send many cargoes by secret ship from Moppo harbor..." Other letters mentioned Mokpo, Chinhae, Masan and scores of other coastal cities as ports of exit for secret ships. On October 15th, a particularly revealing letter was translated by censors that illustrated the careful organizing that contributed to the initial success of the smuggling trade:

"There are many secret ship companies in PUSAN. The prices are posted on bulletin boards and are usually about 150 yen per person. In going by secret ship you also avoid inspection by the military police and Korea women. The Nippon Sewakai Relief Society will tell you what companies to go to for secret passage. Three ships are sailing, on one the 16th, one on the 17th, and one on the 18th."

Pusan was not only one of the largest ports in Korea, but was the major port closest to Japan. Pusan was obviously a hotbed for the new smuggling trade, so the 40th Division started crackdown efforts. The division published Memorandum No. 9, dated October 20th, directing that "all sea-going craft except fishing vessels leaving Pusan Harbor must be inspected by U.S. Customs Officials at Pier No. 1. All privately owned craft will leave port via the North Entrance." During the following week, however, Counter Intelligence Corps investigation and Military Police raids on ships loading at small docks and jetties other than Pier No. 1, revealed that most illegal shipping went through the South Channel, evading the necessity of passing Pier No. 1. It was then required that custom certificates be issued to all craft operating on legitimate business and two harbor boats, manned by Army troops, were established to stop all craft leaving the harbor and inspect them for possession of proper papers.

The rules continued to be circumvented, and it was found that many Japanese were pooling quantities of baggage, the accumulated wealth of 35 years in Korea. They entrusted it to shipping masters under the watchful eyes of two or three refugees. The rest of the refugees went through proper channels on Pier No. 1, and upon arriving in Japan, met the smuggler's ship with their illicit baggage.

As Counter Intelligence Corps investigation and Military Police raids provided more information on methods used to circumvent the rules, the division tightened up enforcement even further. A crew member on a ship in Masan was shot by U.S. Army guards on October 13th when the ship failed to halt for a patrol inspection. Patrol activities in Pusan's South Channel were increased when it was discovered that ships were slipping out after midnight. The division requested, and the commander of LST Flotilla 15 then ordered, the U.S.S. Cofer and LST 54, docked at Pier No. 1 to make searchlight sweeps every fifteen minutes during the hours of darkness. This was started "in order to abolish the practice of transferring contraband goods from Japanese junks onto Japanese merchant vessels loading evacuees." Finally, on October 31st, a patrol system was established in cooperation with the Navy that extended along the entire coast of South Korea. The Navy ships were ordered to sink all craft not properly certificated and to confiscate all contraband goods.

Many smugglers were apprehended and tried in Provost Courts. One particularly successful raid, executed by a Navy officer with Army patrol personnel, was conducted after midnight in the harbor. During this raid, twelve men were seized, three ships were impounded with tons of valuable contraband silk, and two shipping companies were implicated. Eleven of the men were found guilty, and sentenced up to five years in a penitentiary and a 75,000 yen fine. The Nippon Jim Sewakai, an organized relief society officially sanctioned by the United States Military Government, was also implicated.

The crackdown had a significant impact. Although the smuggling was never completely stopped, the incidence was diminished to the point that the Navy relieved their ships from patrol duty in mid-November. It simply was no longer worth the considerable effort.

Japanese acts of sabotage and circumventing of rules were a serious problem, especially early in the occupation. However, the Koreans themselves were also proving a challenge to soldiers of the 40th. Even before the occupying troops arrived, many Koreans took advantage of the confused interim after the Japanese surrender to exact vengeance against the Japanese. In order to curb increasing robberies and incidents of brutality throughout South Korea, many communities organized Peace Preservation Societies or *Chian Tai*. Occupation troops soon learned, however, that these supposed law enforcement agencies were actually involved in much of the large-scale terrorism directed against the Japanese and their property. Typical of such acts was the beating and robbing of the Taegu Police Force who had been in office under the Japanese. The *Chian Tai* organizations were forced to disband and by early October they had turned over to occupation troops many weapons and considerable ammunition after announcing their official dissolution.

Terminating *Chian Tai* police powers did not stop depredations committed against the Japanese by the Koreans. Many Koreans were aware that the occupation troops were spread rather thin and were handicapped by language difficulties that made apprehension of offenders difficult. Trains carrying Japanese civilians to Pusan were frequently boarded by small groups of armed Korean bandits who robbed the passengers and then disappeared. On October 28th, the Farmer's Committee at Kokei Station set up a road block to stop all vehicles transporting Japanese refugees, and demanded

500-1000 yen toll per vehicle. Three men were arrested by U.S. troops and tried in Provost Court, but only 24,400 yen was recovered.

Several secret organizations arose which, like the *Chian Tai*, had to be rigorously suppressed. The Iron Blood Party, which terrorized passengers going through Jakuboku Station, had the avowed intention of frightening Japanese civilians into immediately leaving for Japan. Typical of several extortion rackets perpetrated by lawless Koreans against their one time oppressors was the case of a Japanese civilian who sold his home preparatory to leaving for Japan. On September 30th a Korean buyer gave the Japanese civilian a 5,000 yen deposit on his home. Two days later the Korean returned with several accomplices, purporting to be from the Independence Army (an unidentified organization). They assaulted the seller, retrieved the deposit money and, after forcing him to sign a bill of sale, evicted him.

Several acts aimed specifically at Japanese were committed by Korean civilian ex-convicts the Japanese released from prison following the surrender. A Japanese sea captain's home was looted by such ex-convicts on October 8th. His family was beaten and slashed with sabers, and his money and jewelry stolen. In January, several serious disturbances in Ipsil-Li that involved the destruction of several homes and beating of the mayor, vice mayor and labor secretary of the city were blamed on seven Koreans recently returned from Okinawa. They had been selected by city officials during the Japanese regime to serve as labor troops. Upon their release they sought vengeance against these officials who they felt were pro-Japanese traitors to Korea.

In a formal letter on October 2nd to the Corps Commander, General Hodge, the Commanding General of Japanese forces in Korea, General Tashimaru Sugai, protested the terrorism. He expressed concern about enforced seizure of homes, of parties ostensibly formed to preserve peace seizing Japanese baggage, and of the press inflaming the Koreans to increase their anti-Japanese demonstrations.

Unfortunately, crimes against Japanese didn't fully cease until the repatriation was completed. Japanese homes were invaded by Korean youths who took money and property. As businesses were taken over by Koreans, prices went up and Japanese were concerned about starving to death before they were evacuated to Japan.

Division troops were not only challenged to stop these depredations against Japanese people and property, but had to contend with general lawlessness.

They were constantly faced with incidents of general looting and burglary, usually involving warehouses or isolated boxcars containing valuable foodstuffs, contraband silks, and other material. Looting necessitated the consolidation of these supplies under U.S. troops for security. During the initial weeks of the occupation, looting of supplies became so widespread that on October 5th, in Daily Bulletin No. 85, "shoot to kill" orders were published which authorized guards to open fire on any looters failing to halt when challenged. All guards were instructed in the Korean word for "halt." On December 5th, however, the Division Commander issued a directive intended to curb the enthusiasm of green troops who were killing Koreans near warehouses, sometimes only on suspicion. The key sentence in the directive read: "Because instances in which the shooting of civilians is necessary to the proper performance of military duties are very few, Military Police and guards will resort to shooting only (a) in self-defense, (b) when necessary to overcome active resistance."

Both the occupiers and the occupied took some time to get used to working with peoples of greatly differing cultures. The oriental culture was alien to most of the division's soldiers, but some of the Japanese were just as mystified by the American soldier. The division temporarily retained some Japanese troops in Pusan as a labor battalion. Letters written by one of that battalion's officers on

November 19th reflect the attitude most frequently encountered by American troops:

> "In spite of our working as common laborers, almost as though prisoners, we can spend our time comparatively pleasantly. The reason for this is to be found in the nature of the Americans and so we have to think much of the Americans...
>
> "But I also find them a mystery to us. They are very generous to us, especially individually. They are neither arrogant, rude, oppressive, nor cruel to us--the defeated. They are, on the contrary, rather kind to us...If the situation were reversed, and we were the victorious, and employed them, as they do us, we would never be able to be so kind as they are. It is this very fact which mystifies us.
>
> "The reason that our soldiers can work so wholeheartedly is due to the nature of the American Army and the Americans. Why is their attitude so moderate? It is a mystery I cannot solve."

American troops were not exempt from unlawful acts. Exigencies of the occupation subjected many troops to great temptations, which occasionally led to criminal activities. In order to curb such depredations as intimidating shopkeepers or appropriating watches and other small valuables from refugees, regulations governing military courtesy and discipline were rigorously enforced.

The policy of rigidly enforcing regulations regarding troop conduct appeared to be successful. Proof was again found in letters censored by the Civil Censorship Detachment. One in November said the "Soviet Army's treatment of Japanese women in North Korea cannot be described. I shaved my head and dressed myself to look like a priest and escaped by foot...I do not worry about my life here as the city is in good order and the Americans are gentlemen."

In addition to handling the repatriation of both Japanese and Koreans, the 40th Division was directed to locate, protect and dispose of large quantities of captured enemy supplies. During the first weeks of the occupation, units in each of the division's Zones of Responsibility sent out numerous patrols and located many warehouses, supply dumps, and caves.

Japanese materiel was disposed of in four ways: (1) by destruction--either by burial, by fire or by dumping at sea, (2) by transferring to the Korean Commodity Company, or the Materials Control Commission under auspices of the United States Military Government, (3) by issue to American troops as souvenirs or, (4) by sale to American troops by the Materials Control Commission. All weapons of souvenir interest were held for issue to troops. Japanese sabers which were valuable were tagged for placement in museums. Items such as cameras, watches and other personal possessions that were obviously not loot were retained by the Japanese as legitimate property items

The 40th Division in Operation Memorandum No. 16, announced on October 30th its intention to intensify its program for disposing of enemy equipment. The 115th Engineer (Combat) Battalion, which had its companies distributed among the Regimental Combat Teams for the purpose of constructing or repairing vital roads and bridges, was recalled to Pusan to play a key role in disposing of enemy materiel. The memorandum made it clear that the division wanted to dispose of the enemy materiel by December 1st.

Some useless equipment was destroyed in caves by the simple expedient of sealing the cave entrances by demolition. But the bulk of heavy explosives within the Division Zone of Responsibility were carefully loaded in box cars and shipped to Pusan. There, the 115th Engineer Combat Battalion coordinated the operations of an ocean-going tug, four flat-bottom and five shell-backed barges, thirty U.S. Army trucks, and in addition to American soldiers, an average of 200 Japanese labor troops a day. Explosives were carried far out to sea and dumped in areas authorized by the Port Director.

The division got involved in disposing of a very broad spectrum of enemy materiel. Either destroyed or transferred to the Korean Commodity Company or Materials Controls Commission: 87,055 blankets, 180,000 pairs of socks, 9,360,041 pounds of beans, 5,656,146 pounds of dried fish--a Japanese delicacy which, with 176,395 pounds of dried seaweed, left most American soldiers unimpressed--17,029 artillery shells, and 4,468 tons of dynamite.

In addition to inanimate supplies of war, many horses had been left behind by the Japanese. A radio message from XXIV Corps on October 6th directed that Japanese hostlers be retained to supervise the care of the animals, many of which were dying of starvation and disease. Area commanders then placed them up for public auction and in Taegu alone, 640 of these animals were sold. Months later, the same horses, formerly ridden by Japanese officers, were pulling "honey wagons" for the Korean merchandisers of night-soil.

During the first two months of the occupation, division troops disposed of eighteen cannons, 1391 sabers, 948 pistols, 16,000 rifles and 20,000 bayonets. Tons of supplies and equipment were destroyed. One regiment (the 185th) under division order destroyed at the Taegu airfield:

6 - Twin engine Medium Bombers
22 - Dive Bombers
16 - Attack Planes or Scout Bombers
13 - Fighters
4 - Observation Planes

In addition, 1500 tons of foodstuffs were turned over to the Korean Commodity Company. Thirteen twin-engined transports and eleven single-engined biplane trainers were turned over to the military government in Taegu.

The various activities required of the troops were not risk-free. Four serious accidental explosions occurred in spite of elaborate precautions. On October 15th, a ship's hawser struck a steel plate on a pier in Chinhae, causing a spark which fired loose black powder. That detonated 1,200 pounds of TNT, flattening houses, killing three Koreans, and severely burning about 150 others that were treated in the 21st Portable Surgical Hospital. In Pusan, a brisk wind blew sparks from a small fire in the Army Support Command warehouse area which detonated almost 30,000 pounds of Japanese explosives loaded on a munitions barge. The explosion scattered fire and point-detonated ammunition over a large area, igniting quantities of food and woolen garments. The minor injury to five soldiers was less disastrous than the hardship borne by all troops in the 40th Division as a result of curtailed rations and inadequate woolen clothing. On November 12th, a freak explosion killed three Korean pillagers and destroyed three warehouses in Pusan. In order to secure powder for fashioning depth bombs to kill fish, the three adventurous Koreans attempted to remove, with hammer and chisel, the fuze of a large mine which had probably been dropped by a B-29 in early 1945. The mine exploded.

Early in the occupation, public officials in disfavor were forcibly removed or fled of their own accord. Division soldiers had to take forceful action. Military Government Teams did not begin to arrive in most of Korea until November. In the meantime, area commanders were responsible for curbing terrorism, so many military commanders replaced Japanese and Korean officials who were in disfavor.

Some of the transition occurred routinely as trained personnel became available. Other transitions were urgently required because of the lack of experience among many tactical troops in governmental operations. One example of that need was the telegram dispatched October 10th by the 40th Division Artillery:

"The situation in MASAN indicates emphatic desirability of immediate occupation by Military Government personnel. This is a seaport city of 50,000, complex political and economic structure. Army troop personnel do not possess necessary technical and professional qualifications for effective direction of this city."

On November 24th, the Commanding General of XXIV Corps directed that Military Government Field Agencies "take over the affairs of government as rapidly as possible to where the territorial commanders act as guardians of the peace, advisors and occupational heads of areas." As peace and order settled over the country, and an increasing number of qualified Military Government personnel became available, there was a gradual transfer of responsibilities from tactical troops to Military Government Agencies. On December 21st XXIV Corps announced that on January 14, 1946 the full responsibility for all government affairs would pass to United States Military Government and directed that until that date territorial commanders were "to place upon Military Government Field Agencies those responsibilities which are shortly to fall to them, and by close supervision to teach those agencies to walk alone..."

Gradually Japanese civilians and military personnel were removed from the Zone of Responsibility and replaced with qualified Koreans or American soldiers, and local governments became stabilized. As time passed, the transition to trained Military Government officers was completed. By December 19th, the division was able to report to the Commanding General of XXIV Corps that they had processed 394,089 outbound Japanese as well as 482,193 inbound Koreans, for a total of 876,282.

Christmas 1945 was celebrated in as close to an "at-home" atmosphere as possible. A particularly impressive effort involved construction of a huge cross, complete with a Christmas star on top, high on the hills above Pusan. The cross was faced with stainless steel, and was illuminated at night by an antiaircraft searchlight three quarters of a mile away. It was spectacular, and could even be seen by ships at sea.

There was considerable personnel turnover in the division, which started shortly after the Japanese surrender. The total strength of the division on August 18, 1945 was 741 officers, 32 warrant officers, and 13,064 enlisted men. Over the next month, 1,166 enlisted men left the division, offset by 550 enlisted replacements. A significant contributor to soldier morale was the policy adopted by the division to furnish a war trophy to all men readjusted home on points. From weapons confiscated throughout the division zone a large stockpile of souvenirs was built up which included sabers, rifles, binoculars, pistols and flags. They were issued to troops based on their length of service with the division.

The 40th Division troop list on December 15th consisted of the following organic units: Hq & Hq Co, 40th Division; 108th Infantry Regiment; 160th Infantry Regiment; 185th Infantry Regiment; Hq & Hq Battery, 40th Division Artillery; 143rd Field Artillery Battalion; 164th Field Artillery Battalion; 213th Field Artillery Battalion; 222nd Field Artillery Battalion; 115th Engineer Combat Battalion; 115th Medical Battalion; 740th Ordnance (LM) Company; 40th Signal Company; 40th Military Police Platoon; 40th Mechanized Reconnaissance Troop; 40th Counter Intelligence Corps Detachment; and the 180th Language Detachment. Attached units included: 749th Field Artillery Battalion, 20th Portable Surgical Hospital, 21st Portable Surgical Hospital, 175th Malaria Control Unit, 216th Malaria Survey Unit.

By January, all of the original members of the division had left unless they signed waivers. By January 15th, the strength of the division fell to 314 officers, 4 warrant officers, and 6,594 enlisted men.

The 40th Infantry Division was scheduled to play only a temporary role in the occupation of Korea. Zones of Responsibility were in a constant state of flux, as the division gradually began to withdraw almost immediately after the situation stabilized. The division began to turn over areas to the 6th Infantry Division in October of 1945. On November 12th, XXIV Corps announced that the 40th Infantry Division was to be inactivated in the United States. The division was to embark from Korea in three groups, one each in January, February, and early March.

The return home did not materialize as planned. The impetus to speed things up ended up with almost all of the troops returning home in January and February. A token force of less than 50 officers and enlisted men was to have custody of the division records, colors and guidons and represent the division. In Field Order No. 22, Headquarters 40th Infantry Division, final orders were issued regarding relief of the 40th Division by the 6th Division and indicated that between 10 January and 15 February the 108th Infantry would concentrate at Kyongju (Kwangju), 185th Infantry at Taegu, the 160th Infantry and Division Headquarters at Pusan, and the Division Artillery at Chinhae.

The 40th Infantry Division was to enter the United States through a California port in order to quicken the interests of citizens of that state. However, so many troops had already been returned that the issue became rather academic. The token detachment that assembled in the Railway Hotel in Pusan with Brigadier General Myers consisted of only thirty-four officers and twelve enlisted men. They had responsibility for movement and security of all division records, as well as formal deactivation of the division.

The trip home was an ordeal in itself. The detachment was shipped home on the S.S. Marine Devil, but on the way two cases of oriental small-pox were discovered. That caused the immediate quarantine of the ship when it arrived in San Francisco Bay. General Myers had flown back in advance of the detachment, and pressed for their early release after they arrived in San Francisco. He obtained assistance from the U.S. Public Health Service, and the quarantine was lifted after four days in port.

The final inactivation of the division took place at Camp Stoneman, inland from San Francisco. The Federal duty of the division ended officially on April 7, 1946. The Camp Stoneman paper, the "Stoneman Salvo," provided the division's epitaph:

"REMNANTS OF 40TH DIVISION HOME
"Forty six members of the once mighty 40th ("Sunburst") Division, the first division ever staged at Camp Stoneman, SFPE, during the early days of the war, returned here last Thursday for deactivation. The 40th, composed principally of California National Guards, was staged here in August and September, 1942. From here they went on to glory in Pacific campaigns.

THE FORTIETH DIVISION

"Veterans of action on New Britain, doughboys of the 40th Infantry Division struck the Japs on Luzon in the Philippines on S-Day, and were first to reach Clark Field. In 53 continuous days of combat, the 40th Infantry Division killed 6,145 Japs and then went on to kill 5000 more on Panay and Negros before participating in the Mindanao campaign.

"They went into Korea after V-J Day and there processed more than a million repatriates in addition to other occupation duties. High point men of the 40th have been discharged during the months since the end of the war, with only the small remnant of 46 members returning here last week."

CHAPTER ELEVEN

BETWEEN TOURS IN KOREA

There was no California National Guard immediately following the Second World War. In early 1946, the State Guard of 5,512 soldiers (of whom, fifty-four were on active duty) was being disbanded. Former California Guardsmen volunteered their time to get the state's National Guard reorganized.

In forming the post war National Guard, two divisions were assigned to California, the 40th and 52nd Infantry Divisions. The state immediately appealed to the National Guard Bureau that the 52nd instead be designated the 49th because of California's obvious forty-niner heritage. Nonetheless, General Order Number 7 dated August 15, 1946 created both the 40th and the 52nd Infantry Divisions effective one minute after midnight on that date.

The 159th, 184th, and part of the 185th Regiment were assigned to the 52nd Infantry Division headquartered in Alameda near San Francisco. No sooner was the new 52nd Infantry Division organized than National Guard Bureau advised that California's renumbering request had been granted. General Order Number 56 dated October 31, 1947 redesignated the 52nd as the 49th effective August 5, 1946.

The 2nd and 3rd Battalions, 185th Infantry formed the nucleus of the 223rd and 224th Infantry Regiments which, with the 160th, formed the reborn 40th Infantry Division. The division was reorganized effective August 15, 1946 with Brigadier General Harcourt Hervey commanding, and federally recognized in Los Angeles the following October 14th. Temporary armories began to spring up all over Southern California.

The organization of the division after World War II was an entirely different experience than that following World War I. Where the previous reorganization had been bottom-up, the opposite was now true. The Office of the Adjutant General was federally recognized on August 13th. The division headquarters of both the 40th and 49th were recognized on October 14th, with the regimental and division artillery headquarters next, followed by the battalions, and so on. California was fortunate in having a large pool of battle-hardened veterans to assist in reorganizing the peacetime National Guard. For example, Colonel Homer Eaton, a Corps G-3 in World War II, left his assignment as G-5 (Plans) in the state headquarters to help organize the 160th Infantry.

Governor Earl Warren returned the colors to eighteen major units of the California National Guard in a colorful ceremony in Sacramento on November 11, 1946. General Hervey then presented the Governor with the division's prized trophy, the "Togo Eagle." The trophy, "liberated" from the former Japanese naval base in Chinhae, Korea, honored Admiral Togo's victory over the Russian fleet at Tsushima Strait in 1904. The trophy was to be permanently displayed at Camp San Luis Obispo to commemorate the victories of California troops over the troops of the Imperial Japanese Army.

Major General Daniel H. Hudelson took command of the division on December 2, 1947. Hudelson, an executive of a petroleum company in Los Angeles, started his military career with the 160th Infantry Regiment in January 1925. He was assistant Operations Officer (G-3) of the division by the time it was called for World War II. In 1942 he took command of the U.S. Commando Training Detachment in Scotland. Later he served as a battalion commander and commanded Combat Command "R" during the 14th Armored Division's World War II battles in the Rhineland and Central Europe. During that war he was awarded the Silver Star, the Bronze Star, and several foreign decorations.

A recruiting campaign was started. When the division started the recruiting campaign, it was twenty-third among the twenty-seven National Guard Divisions in strength. To reach fighting strength, General Hudelson put his full time soldiers, called "Unit Caretakers" in those days, to work. He made it clear to the division's Unit Caretakers that either they bring in thirty new recruits, or they would find themselves out of work. The Unit Caretakers spent a sizeable portion of each work day out recruiting. They hit the drive-ins (fast food restaurants) and the beaches, any place they could talk to young men. When they recruited one, they would have him bring in his buddies. Every Unit Caretaker was successful, and when the recruiting campaign was finished, the division was third in strength. The strength of the division was one of the reasons the division was selected to fight in Korea a few years later.

The 40th Division conducted its first summer field training encampments since World War II during the first two weeks of August, 1948. Along with the 112th AAA Brigade, the division trained in basic military subjects at Camp San Luis Obispo, Hunter Liggett Military Reservation, and Camp Cooke (now Vandenburg AFB). Reinstitution of the traditional Governor's Day occurred the middle Saturday, with a parade by all elements of the division plus a flyover by the division's aircraft.

The division trained at the same three sites during the middle two weeks of July 1949. There were short field maneuvers in addition to routine military subjects. The troops at Camp San Luis Obispo paraded for Lieutenant General Mark Clark, Commanding General of Sixth Army, and Lieutenant Governor Goodwin J. Knight.

The National Guard could not have survived without volunteerism in those days. Budgets were extremely tight, and there was only one full time soldier per unit. Members of the unit would come in evenings and weekends to help with administration and in the supply room. Training between the wars was somewhat constrained by prohibitions against use of live ammunition in what was called "battle-indoctrination" training. In 1948, General Mark Clark, by then Chief of Army Ground Forces, specifically banned the use of live ammunition in training exercises. As there was an abundance of ammunition left over from World War II, the motivation clearly was safety. The use of live ammunition during training exercises was not resumed until July 17, 1950, after troops were committed to combat in Korea.

To encourage recruiting and demonstrate their economic impact on the community, several units paid their troops with distinctive money. Unit payrolls for the quarter generally totalled somewhere between $3-4,000. When Corona paid its Guardsmen in silver dollars, and Hemet paid in two dollar bills, the impact was immediately obvious to all of the merchants in those towns.

Before the 40th Division had an opportunity to depart for annual field training the summer of 1950, they were alerted for Federal induction. When it was announced that the 40th was to be mobilized for Korea, the number of drills were increased to three a week. Some officers and enlisted men went on active duty in the division to update records and prepare for the mobilization. Ordnance soldiers were sent to the Long Beach Field Maintenance Shop to help get the division's equipment ready.

Induction Order Number 7, Headquarters Sixth Army, dated August 10, 1950, inducted the division into Federal service, to be effective one minute after midnight on September 1, 1950. All 110 units of the division reported to their armories in forty-six communities on September 1, 1950. Division strength at that time was 694 officers, 117 warrant officers and 8,650 enlisted men. About a third of them were veterans.

Brigadier General Homer O. Eaton, Jr., the Assistant Division Commander, took a large advance party to Camp Cooke on the first day of Federal service to prepare for the rest of the division. The balance of the division started their move on September 5th, with all units closed in by September 15th. The short division history, *Fortieth in Review,* published by the division in Japan in 1952 after the division arrived there, provided a soldier's colorful perspective of the trip:

"Twenty-three MPs left the Armory at midnight. An open truck carried them, tired and huddled together in the cold night, along the convoy route to Camp Cooke. Here and there along the two hundred miles, on the lonely road or in the middle of an empty town, the MPs were dropped off, silently, singly.

"They were the living guideposts, marking the way for the convoy, an advance detail of about five hundred men, that was starting for Camp Cooke at three o'clock of this morning, the first day of September.

"The convoy left Exposition Park on schedule. As the procession poked through Los Angeles, the streets seemed unreal, unused, an old movie set with no backs to the houses. The trucks rolled heavily along Highway 101.

"The convoy passed the Los Angeles city limits. The trucks took their assigned intervals, strung out like hikers on a road march. They passed through dark towns. The lights flicked on in many kitchens. The day turned slowly blue from chilly dawn.

"Between Santa Monica and Santa Barbara the convoy followed the ocean. Through the morning mist, the ocean looked cool and desirable. According to the regulations governing the movement of troops, the headlights of the trucks, like weak unnecessary eyes, stayed on in the new daylight.

"People parked in drive ins or walking down quiet streets or working in their green gardens grinned pleasantly and waved 'Hello.' Young men still in sports shirts and slacks yelled good natured abuse.

"The sun climbed fast. The first day, someone said, would be a hot one. Every thirty minutes, the convoy passed one of the twenty-three MPs. Anxious to appear military, he would wave the convoy along with stiff and unfamiliar motion and then watch

wistfully as the last truck grew smaller and disappeared, finally, around a bend in the highway.

"The convoy drove up and around the winding, soon familiar road, that led into Santa Maria and then through that placid, asleep-in-the-sun community and, at last after eleven hours, with one stop for coffee, the trucks moved through the Camp Cooke gate, past a straight and shining Sixth Army MP.

"The convoy, crawling now at twenty miles an hour, moved past the yellow cluster of Post Headquarters buildings, housing the few hundred personnel the Army kept at Camp Cooke for housekeeping purposes, and onto the camp's main street, California Boulevard.

"The area that was to contain the Division started, roughly, with the field house. It was a big, high ceilinged gymnasium. Most of the windows were broken but the floor was fine for basketball and the stage was adequate for the shows that were to come.

"High over the field house a dozen buzzards flew. They swung in somnolent, predatory circles , their black, powerful wings moving sluggishly, the buzzards evil and out of place in the blue, untroubled sky.

"The comedian in each truck made the crack about this proving the place really was for the birds and the second comic said: 'Just some of our master sergeants.' Soldier humor, an observer could safely say, hadn't changed much since World War II.

"And this was the way it was at Camp Cooke, on that hot, first day, as the men, explorers in ODs, rode down California Boulevard, with the taste of dust in their mouths, past the barracks that soon would hold almost twenty thousand men.

"It was bleak and dirty and going to pieces; a great sprawling, forgotten-about desert. There was a wind that blew always, stirring the dust. The many weathers and the eternal wind had almost wrecked the buildings. They were peeling their paint, rotting, splitting, hanging off at the hinges."

Camp Cooke had been built in 1941 as an Armored Training Center. The 5th, 6th, 11th, 13th and 20th Armored Divisions had trained there, as well as the 86th and 97th Infantry Divisions. In October of 1944, it become home to a German prisoner of war camp. The 96,000 acres were placed in caretaker status in the fall of 1946 until it was reactivated on August 4, 1950. Better than some Army posts, no worse than most, even when very busy and with combat so imminent, it was never a place you'd want to call home.

One soldier said it looked like a Hitchcock movie when the division arrived in 1950; a dark, cold, foggy ghost town, with weeds everywhere. The barracks and other buildings needed repairs and lacked lights and heat. It was clear that nature had come back to claim its own. The sidewalks were overgrown with weeds, and for a post next to the Pacific Ocean, not surprisingly there was sand everywhere.

The men went to work with a will. They quickly set to cleaning up the mess accumulated over four years. Men with experience in the building trades supervised as the plumbing and electrical systems were repaired. Shelving was constructed or repaired, and paint was applied.

The first two months were spent in housekeeping, administration, and preparation of a twenty-six week training program as the division waited for fillers to arrive. Part of the workload was driven by the incompatibility of National Guard and Active Army forms. Personnel sections worked long hours to get the proper forms filled out. They were also handicapped by the number of underage Guardsmen whose parents called the division to get them released, generating another round of administration.

Many units were handicapped with shortages of just about everything. One infantry battalion was typical, having expended their stocks of paper and other office supplies shortly after being activated. The battalion didn't even have enough paper to publish its training program. The solution to the problem was definitely not

257

typical. A soldier in the operations section of the battalion described what happened next:

"To our surprise and joy, we discovered that the office supplies for the 40th Division Headquarters had been mislaid in our battalion headquarters supply room. We took up the floor in our battalion headquarters building and hid the division headquarter's office supplies from the division staff who were looking for it. Our Operations Officer purchased his own mimeograph machine and was able to publish training and other directives in quantities unmatched by any other element of the division."

National Guardsmen were given refresher training as they prepared to instruct thousands of recruits. Physical training was emphasized, along with training in weapons and infantry tactics. Company grade officers were required to take a two week "killer course" in completing the transition from civilian to soldier. All of the refresher training was completed in October, preparatory to commencing the recruit training on November 6, 1950.

The division had reported with under 10,000 soldiers, so was about half strength. Told they would receive about 10,000 fillers by the end of October, to bring the division over strength, intensive planning was initiated to prepare for the huge influx. However, only a comparative trickle actually showed up at first.

The first fillers arrived on October 7th, with 2,266 received by the end of the month. The number of fillers had grown to 9,780 by the end of the year, with a total of 14,273 having joined prior to March 1, 1951. Some were recently discharged soldiers, but most were drafted civilians.

In the meantime, the division commander instituted "speed marches" to get the men in shape. They started with short marches of four miles or so at a comparatively relaxed pace, and then picked up speed as the men got in shape. Eventually they were making forced marches of over twenty miles, carrying their weapons and gear. The division standard, which all units were required to pass, was fifteen miles in three hours with full field packs. All units passed the test, although there were instances where soldiers were carrying their buddies across the finish line. All troops were required to make a twenty-five mile hike before completing their basic training.

There was not enough space at Cooke, so elements of the division would continually have to be sent elsewhere to train. For instance, units made heavy use of Hunter Liggett Military Reservation eighty miles up the coast. The artillery couldn't shoot at Cooke, so all they could do was go through gun drills with dummy rounds. At HLMR they could shoot, but it took about a four hour convoy each way.

Night training at Camp Cooke, January 1951
(Source: National Archives)

The division had been handicapped several ways in preparing for combat. First was the failure of the Department of the Army to send fillers in the numbers and schedule that had been promised. Then the situation was complicated by repeated levies for fully trained soldiers to ship over as replacements in Korea. In January, 1951, the division was levied over six hundred soldiers. This was extremely frustrating to the division. Not only were some of the most experienced soldiers stripped out of the division, but morale and esprit de corps of the units suffered.

The division was also handicapped by a severe shortage of equipment. In spite of the United States having just demobilized a huge army only four years before, the Army and its National Guard were short much of their authorized equipment. The division felt it was short changed, and much of the equipment it received was in marginal condition. The active Army, however, was suffering the same problems, although to a lesser degree.

Commanders were also frustrated by the proximity to Southern California, and the scramble for weekend passes. As a consequence, it was difficult getting anything done on weekends. Nonetheless, the first eleven weeks of basic training were followed by the thirteen week unit training phase which started on January 22, 1951. Rumors were spreading around the division that the Fortieth was destined for Europe. The rumors grew with the telling, and the troops began to make big plans for their "European adventure." The rumors and that phase of training ended with a jolt. The division was in the midst of a 28-week training cycle when the signals suddenly changed.

MacArthur sent his last combat division (The 3rd Infantry Division) from Japan, leaving the islands defenseless. He wanted the four National Guard divisions that had been called up sent to Japan. On February 25th, the Joint Chiefs of Staff notified MacArthur that two National Guard divisions would be sent to Japan in April. The word leaked in Washington, but became official on the 28th when the division was officially notified that they were going to Japan.

General Hudelson had been convinced, right up until the official notification, that the division was destined for Europe. On February 24, 1951, the division received alert orders for deployment to Japan. There they were to continue to train while providing added security for that strategic area.

All training ceased March 3rd as the division prepared for the move. Units of the division then faced the frustration of finding lumber for packing crates, and in the turn-in of what is called Post, Camp and Station supplies and equipment. Those supplies ranged from sheets, blankets and mattress covers to brooms and mops. One company commander had a novel solution to the problem. In his words:

"I found to my concern that the company was very short on sheets, pillow covers (sic) and mattress covers. I was informed I would likely have to pay for these shortages. At the time I couldn't afford such costs, and I was rather desperate.

"At the next company formation I reminded the company members of the division commander's earlier admonition to look at the man on your right and left, that we would soon be engaged in fighting communists on the field of battle, and that some would not be coming back. It was my suggestion that now would be a good time to visit home and that I would give a day's leave for each extra sheet or mattress cover turned in and a half day's leave for every pillow case. Interest in going home was outstanding, and the sheets began to pile up. Soldiers returning from the hospital came back with sheets wound around their waists under their uniforms.

"Not only was (my unit) able to turn in all bedding previously issued, but we were able to fill the regimental shortage and use the extra sheets in packing fragile equipment for shipment to Japan. I was never able to determine where all of the extra bedding came from, and really didn't want to know, but I was deeply impressed by the ability of Guardsmen to find whatever supplies and materials were needed for this and later operations."

The division was having a tough time estimating the requirement and obtaining the necessary packing and crating material. Division engineers fabricated over 3000 special boxes for typewriters, spare parts and other items without standard boxes. Eventually all the problems were solved, but the deployment bogged down when the division arrived at the port. The Army port inspection team arrived almost two weeks late. The division put together an ad hoc port liaison team to coordinate inspectors, port staff and divisional units. This group helped speed up the division's load out for Japan.

General Eaton again was the advance detachment commander, and flew out for Japan with nine officers on March 28th. When sizeable advance elements of the division landed in Yokohama, Japan on April 10, 1951, they were the first troops of a National Guard Division to arrive overseas since World War II. The 40th Division was closely followed by the 45th of Oklahoma, another National Guard Division with an impressive World War II heritage.

The main body of the division moved out by rail on March 28th, detraining at Oakland Army Base. They were given coffee and doughnuts served by the Red Cross before taking the ferry across the bay to San Francisco. The troops sailed out from San Francisco on March 29th and 30th, 1951. The 45th Division left the port at New Orleans about the same time.

The division commander and his staff set up headquarters on the convoy's flagship, the U.S.S. J. W. Butner. Lieutenant Colonel Donald N. Moore, 160th Infantry Regiment, was appointed as Commanding Officer of Army troops on the ship. On the Butner, the Division Commander and his staff continued planning until arriving in the port code-named "Evil" (Yokohama) on April 11, 1951. As the ships approached Yokohama, word flashed through the ranks that General MacArthur had been relieved of his Far Eastern Command, and replaced by Lieutenant General Matthew B. Ridgway. There was considerable speculation regarding the reason for the relief, and what the significance might be. All troops were landed over the next three days from the Butner, the General Nelson M. Walker, the General M. C. Meigs, and other troopships. Many landed to the sound of an army band on the pier playing "California, Here I Come.".

The Communists had spread rumors that Guardsmen were criminals, so many of the Japanese watched the troops move in with considerable apprehension. This dissipated however, as the troops quickly made friends with any Japanese willing to return a smile. Some of the troops studied the Japanese language. Others went to Tokyo and Fujiyama sightseeing. Most of the troops in the division found the Japanese fascinating.

Any concerns harbored by the Japanese quickly melted when the troops got involved with orphans and orphanages. The troops gave generously to support local Catholic and Protestant orphanages. They also "adopted" waifs suffering from malnutrition who seemed to have fallen through the cracks in a country still struggling back from a war-torn economy.

The Fortieth and Forty-Fifth Divisions were immediately assigned to the General Headquarters Reserve Corps, later redesignated the XVI Corps. The Fortieth was moved into various locations on Honshu, the largest of the islands, while the Forty-Fifth moved on to defend Hokkaido, Japan's most northern island. The mission of the Fortieth Division was to defend Northern Honshu while conducting additional training.

The new United Nations Supreme Commander, Lieutenant General Matthew B. Ridgway, made 40th Division elements in Sendai the destination for his first inspection of combat troops in Japan. On Thursday, April 19th he told the troops of the 223rd Infantry Regiment they were "under the imminent threat of war" and urged them to "use every minute of the time you've got (to train) because you don't know, and I don't know, when the chips will be down."

Elements of the Fortieth Division were scattered over an area approximately a hundred miles wide and five hundred miles long, with troops from Mount Fuji and Tokyo in the south up to Hachinohe on the northern tip of Honshu. They were scattered in order to provide a defensive presence, but often were at some distance from good training areas.

Organizations of the division were located at:

> Camp Schimmelpfennig, near Sendai: Division head-
> quarters, headquarters troops, and the 223rd
> Infantry Regiment less one battalion.
> Camp Younghans, near Yamagata: Headquarters of the
> division artillery, 625th and 981st Field
> Artillery battalions, and 1st Battalion, 223rd.
> Camp Haugen, near Mitsu-ichikawa: 160th Infantry
> Regiment and the 143rd Field Artillery
> Battalion.
> Camp Zama, near Yokohama: 224th Infantry Regiment and
> the 980th Field Artillery Battalion. The
> 224th moved to Camp McNair on the
> slopes of Mt. Fuji near Yoshida in July,
> 1951.
> Camp McGill, near Yokohama: The 140th Tank Battalion
> Camp Matsushima, near Shiogama: The 578th Engineer
> Battalion
> Camp Whittington, a former Japanese air base near
> Yokohama: The 140th AAA AW Battalion

Unit training was resumed on April 30th. In addition to their normal training schedules, General Hudelson made it clear he expected the arduous marching regimen to continue in Japan. The troops were told he expected no less than twenty hours of speed marching per week, to be conducted during other than normal training hours, usually at night. One march was to be five miles and completed in no more than fifty minutes. All other marches were to completed at a pace of five miles per hour.

The intensive training was often conducted in several inches of snow, especially in the northernmost locations. Others fought wind and rain, and even some dust. The division had reorganized into regimental combat teams after arriving in Japan, and unit training was initiated. The training was much more interesting for the soldiers, in spite of the weather. They had more of their equipment, they did not have the distractions of home, and unit training was much more interesting than individual training.

The division was again impacted, however, by levies for experienced soldiers. The levies started again as soon as the division arrived in Japan, until General Hudelson put his foot down. Concerned that the personnel levies were adversely impacting on the readiness of the division, as well as morale and esprit, General Hudelson rather profanely made it clear he wasn't going to permit any more levies. He was fortunate that Congress was making its voice heard just about this time, and no more replacements were sent off to Regular army units. Unfortunately, the division had already lost thousands of men since being mobilized.

In the meantime, real missions in Japan were impacting on training programs. Engineers from the 578th Engineer Battalion threw their formal training plans into the waste basket. They didn't have time for the formal training schedule, but quickly found themselves with missions similar to many they would face later in Korea. They accompanied scouts and reconnaissance troops as they surveyed bridges all over their part of Japan. The purpose was two-fold. One was to shore up bridges as necessary so the division's heavy equipment could get around. The other purpose was to survey bridges for demolition if required during a Russian invasion.

On May 31, 1951, a mortar shell fell short of the target, killing one and wounding seven from Company G, 223rd Infantry during maneuvers near Camp Younghans. The training during this period was very intensive. Amphibious exercises were conducted in June and July, with units coming ashore on Chigasaki Beach, near Yokohama.

The imposition of many thousands of troops on a war ravaged economy did much to jump-start many small businesses in Japan. However, there was a significant shortage of electrical power, mainly due to the shortage of rainfall. In Sendai, for instance, power was turned off intermittently during the dark hours. This resulted in a nightly cycle of thirty minutes on - thirty minutes off - which required soldiers to have candles or flashlights when they were away from portable electrical generators.

While the division was still at Camp Cooke, General Hudelson created a special unit to train malcontents and problem soldiers. The unit designated for this purpose was Company F of the 160th Infantry Regiment. The company commander was Captain Walter Pierce, and the platoon leaders were carefully selected. All were former Los Angeles Police Department officers, and the first sergeant was General Hudelson's son.

Many soldiers knew about this special unit, but all pretended it was no different than any other. The discipline in the unit was extraordinarily stringent. In fact, no one could even go to the Post Exchange without permission of the first sergeant. Most importantly, the unit evolved into an effective outfit in a surprisingly short time. Its "special purpose" ceased when the unit later shipped out of Japan for combat.

A rear detachment had been left at Camp Cooke to train late arriving fillers. This was necessary because the Army required all men to have fourteen weeks of training before they were sent overseas. The division tried to get an exception to that policy, but the request was denied. The rear detachment consisted of sixty officers and warrant officers, and 448 enlisted men, all under the command of Lieutenant Colonel Horace Bradbury, the executive officer of the 160th Infantry. This contingent rejoined the division after they landed in Yokohama on August 4, 1951.

The Army decided to organize a ranger company in some of the divisions, and in early 1951, the 11th Ranger Company was created from and for the 40th Division. Volunteers were called for, carefully screened, and sent off for airborne training. Interestingly, the test scores turned out to be higher than required for entrance into Officer Candidate School. After airborne training, the unit was sent to Fort Carson for three weeks of mountain training, followed by ranger training. In July the unit arrived in Japan and joined the division. The unit was deactivated September 13, 1951, simultaneous with the 10th Ranger Company of the 45th Division. It would be many years before the Army had ranger units again.

Too many division soldiers lacked uniforms and boots. Many had only one pair of boots, often in poor shape. Others had no boots at all. Some wrote home asking folks to buy them fatigues and send them over because their two uniforms that had been issued were getting worn out from the rugged training. One battalion commander heading into the field during the rainy season said he had fifteen men with no boots, and 75 with one pair of boots, generally in poor shape.

This made the news in the Los Angeles Examiner in addition to other media. The Examiner's Julian Hartt was with the division, providing daily news dispatches. Later the division commander confirmed that the troops were inadequately clothed. Senators William F. Knowland and Richard M. Nixon then raised the issue in Washington. The problem was exacerbated by the fact that the division was only authorized to requisition once a month from the Japan Logistical Command.

The pressure made things flow better, and the soldiers started to get their clothing much faster. Governor Earl Warren had heard of the problem, and flew out of Travis Air Force Base in August to visit the troops in Sendai.

Mixed signals were being sent to soldiers as well as the folks at home. Some were initiated by the misperception of those families that thought National Guardsmen were for home defense, not foreign service. Some legislators, such as San Diego's Congressman C. D. McKinnon, introduced bills to get the troops returned home. A headline in the Los Angeles Herald Express of July 19th read "40th Div. May Be Ordered to Korea Soon." A headline in September read "Cal. 40th Division Won't Be Sent to Korea."

The division completed its twenty-six week training cycle under supervision of the XVI Corps staff. The division started air

267

transportability training in September, with the 160th flying out of Atsugi Naval Air Station, the 223rd out of Matsushima Air Base, and the 224th out of Misawa Air Base. About half the division had completed this training, including orientation flights in C-119 Flying Boxcars, when the division was alerted for shipment to Korea.

The first edition of the *Sunburst*, the division's new weekly newspaper, was published November 1, 1951. The first several issues devoted some space to the home front and sports, but most of the coverage included human interest stories and training items.

The winter around Sendai was much colder than most of the Fortieth's troops were used to. Many of them invested in Japanese clay pots, used by the Japanese to heat their homes. The Japanese sold these pots to the troops for 200 yen, which included charcoal. They turned out to be ideal for pup tents, as long as they were ventilated, and were also used for cooking.

By this time, the Japanese on Honshu had gotten used to Americans everywhere, either on training missions or sightseeing while on pass. They had found the Sunbursters friendly and out-going, and returned that warmth in kind. Even in tiny villages that rarely saw Americans, the troops were gratified by the friendliness of the people.

Many celebrities visited the division over the years. One memorable visit was by Heavyweight Boxing Champion Joe Louis. He joined the Headquarters Company of the division on November 22nd for Thanksgiving dinner. A traditional dinner, it included turkey with corn bread dressing, candied yams and mince meat pie, in addition to many other items. Joe also boxed a sparring match with Sergeant Lindy Brooks of Los Angeles, the division's heavy-weight champion.

A classified letter had been received from General Matthew B. Ridgway, Commander in Chief of the Far East Command, on November 16, 1951 advising the division they were destined for Korea. On 22 December, units of the division were alerted for duty in Korea, where they were to relieve the 24th US Division. Brigadier General Eaton left on December 26, 1951 from Matsushima Air Base with an advance detachment consisting of 54 officers and 106 enlisted men. A second detachment followed a few days later.

While in Japan, the troops had seen several examples of what fire could do to towns and villages constructed of wood. The Japanese fire fighters rarely tried to save a structure, considering themselves fortunate if they kept fire from spreading to adjacent structures. Outside of the cities, their fire fighting equipment often was hand pulled pumps on small trailers, pulling water out of the ditches that ran through every village and spraying water out of what appeared to be a garden hose. On April 30th, a kitchen and mess hall were destroyed at Camp Schimmelpfenning, with two people injured while battling the blaze. On December 27, a fire started in a boiler room raced through seven barracks at Camp Zama's south camp shortly after 2:00 a.m. No one was injured, but all personal gear and uniforms were lost in the fire, and had to be replaced. Damage to structures and equipment was estimated at $3,000,000.

The division was well trained as its combat tour approached, in fact, many felt it was over-trained. Two Marine veterans of World War II, noncommissioned officers in Company F, 223rd Infantry, agreed they were "trained a lot more" than they ever were in the Marines. The troops felt they were ready for anything, but even though forewarned, didn't expect the weather in Korea to be as terribly cold as it turned out to be.

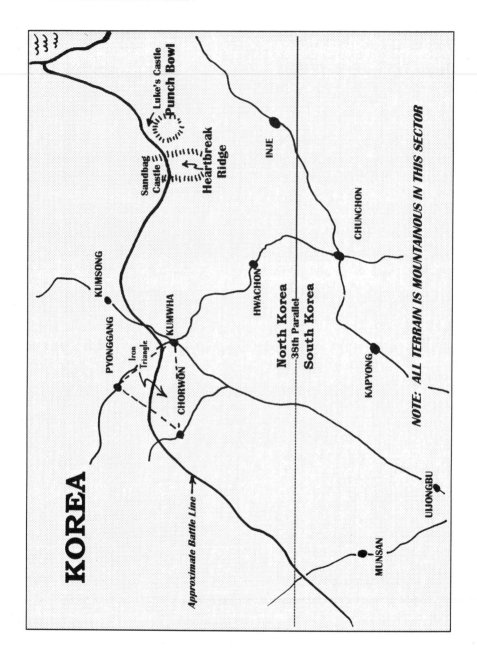

CHAPTER TWELVE

KOREA, THE FRONT LINES

The first echelon shipped to Korea was the 160th Regimental Combat Team (including their 143rd Field Artillery Battalion) accompanied by the Headquarters of the Division Artillery, the 625th Field Artillery Battalion, and Battery A of the 140th AAA AW Battalion. They departed from Yokohama January 7, 1952 aboard Navy transports.

When the troops were transported to Korea, they were told how cold it would be. Many of them went down into the hot troop holds, and struggled into long johns, olive drab (wool) shirt, two pairs of fatigue pants, field jackets, and gloves with liners. They then put on their field packs and waited. When they got outside, the temperature hovered around 5 degrees below zero. They could see that there was little left of Inchon. They loaded their gear into railroad boxcars, and climbed into little Korean rickety and battered third class coach cars. They crossed the Han River to Chunchon. There they were put into 2½ ton trucks, sometimes without tops, for the rest of the move. It was incredibly cold, with icy wind cutting through flimsy field jackets. Those that could quickly broke out their extra blankets or used their sleeping bags to keep warm. Later on they were given fur-lined parkas and "sno pak" overshoes plus fur lined gloves with trigger fingers. By that time they were already half frozen.

As advertised, the troops found the sub-zero weather bitterly cold. Many soldiers would recall this period in Korea as the coldest time of their lives. Artillerymen had to be careful. When they swabbed the bore of their howitzers, water would drip and freeze, which formed a miniature ice rink below the breech. That made it extremely slippery and dangerous when servicing the weapon. The artillerymen always had to have their gloves on. If they accidentally put a bare hand against the frozen metal, they could lose a layer of skin. Troops without hot water or open fires found they could defrost their C-rations enough to eat by putting them under their armpits.

When the troops arrived in Korea, they were immediately put into the front line. As troops passed the war-weary veterans returning from the front lines, anxiety and apprehension were heightened. The veterans of the Twenty-Fourth Division looked physically tired and emotionally beat. As they pulled off the line into reserve, many of them whispered to 40th soldiers as they passed, wishing them luck and a safe trip home next year.

The relief plan called for the Fortieth to leave its equipment in Japan, and take over the Twenty-Fourth Division's equipment in Korea. The Twenty-Fourth would fall back on the Fortieth Division's equipment left in Japan. This was a complicated move, but the most frustrating aspect was the condition of the equipment the division took over in Korea. Battle-weary and worn, much of the equipment was in extremely poor shape. The advance detachment of the division was shocked at the condition of the equipment. For example, the S4 of the 160th found that the 19th Infantry Regiment had thrown weapons and equipment in tents with no accountability of any kind. It was apparent that maintenance had been just about nonexistent on all weapons and vehicles. This was not something that had been allowed to happen only after the 24th Division found they were to leave Korea, as it was apparent that the condition had existed for many months. The morale and esprit de corps of the troops being relieved was about as low as the condition of their equipment, so some of the 40th Division troops had to wonder what they were getting into.

Eventually, some equipment rebuilt by depots in Japan arrived to help the situation. However, the great majority of the equipment had to be laboriously repaired by organic ordnance and maintenance elements of the division.

Many of the division's soldiers were returning to Korea. A poor country when they left in 1946, they found the countryside much worse due to the ravages of war. The foreign smells were unforgettable. The smell of human excrement was mixed with the pungent odors of kimchi, the spicy dish made from pickled cabbage, peppers and garlic that is unique to Korea. Huge kimchi jugs were everywhere, sometimes on balconies, and sometimes buried in the ground. Trees had been stripped by artillery, or by villagers for fuel. There was very little scrub brush left for concealment. The war had hit before Koreans had an opportunity to recover from decades of occupation by the Japanese, and most of the peasants were extremely poor. The many widows and orphans made a lousy situation worse, a situation that troops tried to help, each in his own way. But first they had a war to fight.

The division officially launched its first action on January 13, 1952, when Sergeant First Class Gary Ducat of Santa Monica pulled the lanyard on a 105mm howitzer of Battery B, 143rd Field Artillery Battalion. The battery was chosen by lot from the 143rd, the first field artillery battalion in position. The lanyard was yanked at about 10:00 a.m., with a great many officials and reporters observing.

The 160th started relieving units of the 19th Infantry of the 24th US Infantry Division on January 13th, and assumed responsibility for the zone on January 19th. Patrols were immediately sent out. Company A, 160th Infantry sent out the first patrol, ten men led by Sergeant First Class Loren J. Knepp. A designated sniper in the patrol, Private First Class Pete Romus, developed a leg cramp when they were about 800 yards into enemy territory. He sat down to massage the cramp as the rest of the patrol went on. He then noted that an enemy patrol of about fifteen men was circling around to ambush their patrol in the rear. Romus yelled at his comrades, but they were too far away to hear him. He carefully aimed and fired at the first man in the enemy patrol when the Chinese soldier reached the crest of the hill. The enemy soldier was hit, and then fell down the hill. Private Romus continued to fire, as his comrades, warned by the firing, quickly returned to assist him. When the short, intense fight ended, at least two Chinese had been killed and several wounded. Sergeant Knepp was wounded in the leg by a burst from a "burp" gun, for which he was treated by the patrol's aidman, Corporal David M. Oliveria of Hayward, California. Knepp then ordered Oliveria to withdraw. Oliveria refused, carrying the 200-pound sergeant about 125 yards to friendly lines. The assistant patrol leader, Sergeant Robert O'Connor, covered them by fire as they withdrew through heavy enemy small arms fire. Oliveria was later awarded the division's first Bronze Star by the Eighth Army Commander, General James A. Van Fleet.

The division suffered its first combat death on January 20th. On that day, Sergeant First Class Kenneth Kaiser, Jr. of Los Angeles was killed by a mortar shell that fell into the 160th's positions near Kumsong. It was one of the first mortar shells that landed after 1-160th Infantry took over the area. The shell hit just as Kaiser, his platoon's section leader (assistant platoon sergeant), was going into the command post bunker. Sergeant Kaiser was only 18-years-old when he was killed, having joined the National Guard when he was sixteen. It was very common before and after World War II for men to lie about their age and join the National Guard when they were underage.

The division's second echelon left Yokohama on January 18th, and consisted of the Division Headquarters, the 223rd Infantry Regiment, and the 980th and 981st Field Artillery Battalions. When this echelon with the Division Headquarters landed at Inchon on January 22nd, the division was attached to IX Corps of Eighth U.S. Army. The division commander and his staff flew across from Haneda Air Base near Tokyo on January 19th. The 223rd completed relief of the 24th US Division's 21st Infantry on January 28th. On that day, the Commanding General of the 40th Division assumed sector responsibility (Kumsong-Chwapae-Ri in the central front) from the 24th US Division, effective at 7:55 a.m. on January 28, 1952. When the 40th assumed responsibility for the sector, the 24th's 6th Tank Battalion and 5th Regimental Combat Team were attached to the 40th Division. The division was now deployed with the 223rd Infantry on the left, the 5th RCT in the center, and the 160th Infantry on the right. The 224th Infantry and the division's 140th Tank battalion were en route from Japan as the month ended, having departed Yokohama on January 30th.

PFC Melvin W. Knott of Cody, Wyoming (left)covers Martin Aserud of Portland, North Dakota as he prepares to fire at communist positions during a firefight in the Kumwha Valley. Both were from Company E, 160th Infantry (Source: National Archives)

A tank-led, two platoon raid by the 5th US RCT resulted in the destruction of eight enemy bunkers, highlighting the combat activity for the period. Small scale patrol clashes characterized the combat activity, with numerous combat and reconnaissance patrols being dispatched by division units.

The Army publicly revealed the presence of the Fortieth in Korea on February 3rd. On that date, the 224th Infantry Regiment with the 140th Tank Battalion landed at Inchon and began their movement to the division sector. The 140th quickly began its relief of the 6th Tank Battalion, which was immediately released from attachment to the division. The 224th relieved the 5th US RCT in the center sector on February 10th, with the 5th then relieved from attachment.

The division's command post was initially located at Korisil, approximately seven miles southeast of Kumsong. The division rear was initially located at Ascom City near Seoul, but shortly moved to the vicinity of Chunchon.

The division's sector was on the east central front and occupied 9,300 meters of the Main Line of Resistance (MLR). The 160th was on the east, the 224th in the center, and the 223rd in the west. The sector was a bulging salient that reached well into Chinese and North Korean positions. The 3rd ROK Division was on the division's east, and the 2nd ROK Division was to the west.

Patrols were sent out every night. One patrol that headed out in the freezing weather consisted of a reinforced platoon from Company K, 223rd Infantry Regiment. They were spotted by the Chinese as dawn broke, and started taking heavy fire from four Chinese bunkers. The platoon retaliated with their 57mm recoilless rifle, followed by grenades. They killed several of the Chinese, with no losses to themselves. There were close calls, including helmets dented by burp gun bullets.

The "face" of the division had changed by this time. Earlier levies on the division had siphoned off many trained National Guardsmen. They were primarily replaced with draftees, plus a few Regular Army enlistees, and a few transfers from other National Guard divisions. These troops were quickly becoming combat veterans. Many found that they could smell the Chinese, who evidently consumed lots of garlic.

An aggravation to commanders throughout the division was the exceptional interest shown by Corps and higher staffs about minor details of routine daily operations. It was not uncommon to get a call from Corps wanting to know why a recon patrol the previous day had a BAR assigned to it, or why there were a certain number of men assigned to a combat patrol. The impression was that some staff officers in higher headquarters didn't have enough of their own work to do.

The division pursued an aggressive program of company-size raids, and tank and artillery attacks on prepared positions. The control of the artillery was centralized, with all four battalions responsive to the division artillery fire direction center. The division artillery was commanded by West Pointer Brigadier General Horace Harding, with his tall executive officer, Colonel Charles O. Ott, Jr. serving as ramrod of the outfit.

The division was directed to participate in Operation "CLAM-UP" from February 10th to 15th. This was an operation across the front, ordered by Eighth Army Headquarters. It was also called Operation "SNARE" by some of the allied units. It was designed to lure Chinese patrols into ambush through cessation of friendly fire and patrolling, together with a simulation of withdrawal. It was hoped that a great many previously-hard-to-get prisoners would be snared by the ruse. The operation required a great deal of ammunition and other supplies to be stockpiled in advance, which was difficult due to the great number of unserviceable vehicles received from the 24th Infantry Division.

Operation CLAM-UP started at 6:00 p.m. on February 10th. All unnecessary daytime movements and activities were suspended. Friendly troops remained in concealed positions on the MLR and in strong points. Necessary activity was postponed until after dark. Initially, the desired reaction was forthcoming. Freedom from division artillery and infantry weapons fire brought numbers of enemy troops out into the open and patrols were sent out by the enemy to find out what the situation might be. In spite of the new boldness of the enemy, friendly troops were unable to capture any POW's without danger of compromising the plan. Soon it was apparent that enemy higher headquarters had become aware of the United Nations strategy because the enemy became more cautious and used the time to improve their defensive positions and to move closer to UN lines, encroaching on what was previously considered no man's land.

Operation CLAM-UP was brought to a crashing close at 2:00 p.m. on the 15th by a coordinated display of firepower designed to inflict maximum shock and casualties upon the enemy. The operation was declared a success, with many valuable lessons learned. The truth was that the most valuable lesson learned was that such an operation could and did work more to the enemy's advantage than ours.

After Operation CLAM-UP, it was necessary to take steps to clear the enemy from the new positions which they occupied during that period. The plan included aggressive patrolling and company sized raiding attacks by elements of each regiment. However, only one of the planned raids was carried out.

The United Nations enjoyed air superiority, so weapons of the 140th Antiaircraft Artillery Battalion were primarily used in a ground support role. The quad 50's mounted in half tracks put out a deadly amount of firepower, and could quickly have a decisive effect in a fire fight. They played a key role in the one "raid" conducted by the 224th Infantry on February 18th.

The 224th's commander was Colonel Jim ("Walking Jim") Richardson. Colonel Richardson was a very personable, highly competent commander who was well regarded by all of his troops. He had emphasized to all of his units the importance of never leaving a comrade in need.

He had an opportunity to personally demonstrate this when the 224th was chosen to make a limited predawn attack or raid, on

February 18th. He met with Lieutenant Colonel Emmett A. ("The Red Fox") Rink, commander of 3rd Battalion of the 224th. Captain John Wilt's Company L from Orange County was given the lead in attacking the well-entrenched Chinese positions on a ridge line that pointed right into the 224th's lines. Company L was supported by other elements of the 3-224th, including Captain Norman H. Young's Company M, the Heavy Weapons Company. Others in support included the 224th Tank Company, division artillery, and the division's quad-50's of the 140th AAA Battalion. Colonel Richardson knew the mission was extremely hazardous, and decided to accompany Company L in the assault. He actually placed himself at the lead with one of the platoons, accompanied by his radio operator.

The company attacked with the support of twenty-two tanks and three quad 50's, just as dawn broke. The troops moved out with two platoons abreast, and a third in reserve, as the armor in support poured 90mm shells and .50 calibre bullets into the bunkers and suspected enemy positions in front of the troops. The Communists responded initially with mortar and artillery fires, and then with grenades as the troops closed for close-in fighting.

The Chinese Communists on adjacent ridges tried to support their comrades with automatic weapons fire. Much of it was suppressed by heavy fires from the Fortieth Division artillery. Almost immediately, a radio reported that First Lieutenant James Ingelsby of Santa Ana had been killed. He wasn't supposed to be involved in the attack, and was due to take command of the company shortly after the attack. He chose to be with his soldiers during the attack. When he was hit by mortar fragments and fell, Master Sergeant William Cathcart, Company L's First Sergeant, rushed over to help rally the survivors of Ingelsby's platoon.

Soldiers from both sides fell in the violent clash. Several soldiers from the Fortieth died on that ridge line. One was Colonel Richardson's radio operator, who was mortally wounded during the assault. Colonel Richardson, who had a minor wound himself, carried his radio operator down the hill while under enemy fire, placing him on a tank deck for evacuation to the rear. Colonel Richardson was covered with blood, some his own, but mostly that of his radio operator, as he went up and down the hill to help pull the casualties off.

When Colonel Richardson decided to disengage, the mortars laid down a curtain of fire to cover the withdrawal. The enemy took heavy casualties during the total of about four hours they were under fire. Losses included 27 KIA, 46 estimated KIA, and 65 estimated WIA. The 224th lost 4 KIA, 2 MIA, and 30 WIA.

The 3rd Battalion, 223rd Infantry conducted a company-sized raid to clear enemy bunkers and entrenchments along "The Boot" from map coordinates CT790508 to CT800520. The operation was going well until the unit tried to disengage. They called for assistance from the regiment's supporting 625th Field Artillery Battalion, which fired white phosphorus into the objective area to protect and screen the withdrawal.

The operations during February surfaced definite information about the enemy and provided some valuable experience. It also pointed out some of the training deficiencies in the division, such as insufficient combined arms training, a result of training area limitations in Japan and the wide dispersion of units necessitated by the dual role of training and defense of Northern Honshu.

Another significant combat action involved a two-phased operation in the Kumsong area on February 29th, employing armor supported by artillery. The first phase was carried out by two companies of the 140th Tank Battalion near Kumsong, and resulted in the destruction of six bunkers, and damaging of thirty-two more. There were an estimated 24 enemy KIA and 47 WIA. One of the 140th's tanks was damaged by a mine, but all tanks returned safely without any friendly casualties.

The second phase was conducted by the Tank Company of the 224th Infantry Regiment, kicking off at noon on the same day. The unit attacked bunkers on the reverse slopes of Hill 378 and vicinity until recalled at 2:30 p.m. That action resulted in ten enemy bunkers destroyed, with 8 enemy counted KIA, 12 estimated KIA, and 10 estimated WIA. Three of the 224th's tanks were so badly damaged by mines that they had to be stripped and destroyed in place because it would be too costly to recover them. Friendly casualties were three slightly wounded.

A lengthy episode that sullied the reputation of the division started in January, and really started bubbling up during February. As mentioned previously, some Guardsmen and their families believed that the division would not be sent outside of the United States. Centered in San Bernardino, wives of Guardsmen were writing to protest the fact that the 40th and 45th Divisions were being sent into combat while so many other divisions were not. One former recruiter from San Bernardino, even said he had been told to tell prospective recruits they would not be sent overseas. The great majority of Guardsmen, however, told reporters they did not question their role in Korea. Nonetheless, the seeds of dissent had been sown.

The complaints began to surface shortly after it was revealed that the Fortieth was in combat, and grew after the division suffered its first casualties. Soldiers sent strong letters of protest to their families, pointing out that they were being called the "cry-baby division," because of complaints from their wives and mothers.

A dozen soldiers of the 224th wrote to the editor of the San Bernardino Sun-Telegram. They said "we view the (letter writing) campaign as emotional, unpatriotic, futile and unwise...We do not intend to return because of a successful protesting campaign on the home front. We intend to return because of a successful military campaign on the battle front."

After the letters from Korea, the great majority of those few family members who had been protesting shut up. However, the damage had been done, and many brave soldiers died for a division that had difficulty shaking the "cry-baby" label.

When the snows began to melt, the troops had to be especially wary. Old mortar shells, both friendly and enemy, were uncovered everywhere. The remains of many bodies also began to be exposed. Some were enemy, but many were Koreans who had been killed by the Chinese the previous year. It was a humbling experience.

There was an unfortunate incident on March 2, 1952. Marine Corsairs strafed and bombed the division rear, killing several troops of the division's postal section. A Marine colonel later came to division headquarters to apologize, but was not well received.

An active defense was maintained during the month of March. Most of the contacts with the 12th CCF Army Corps were initiated by aggressive 40th Infantry Division patrols. The defensive line of the division, running generally from map coordinates CT775493 to CT910987 was improved. The program of aggressive patrolling was continued to maintain contact while inflicting maximum casualties and denying the enemy the opportunity of permanently entrenching himself south of Line BILL, a line parallel to and 1000-3000 yards in front of the MLR. Organic tanks were used effectively, in both day and night operations, conducting direct fire missions against enemy positions.

The enemy's lack of tanks and antitank weapons other than mines encouraged the division to make widespread use of tanks to destroy enemy bunkers. Tactics evolved wherein tanks were used at night in the same role so that the enemy had difficulty repairing bunkers during the hours of darkness as he had in the past. There was some equipment damage due to mines, but the results were considered excellent, and very few friendly casualties were sustained.

The enemy initiated eight engagements during March in a vain effort to capture United Nations prisoners. They were almost successful, however, during the early morning hours on March 18th. Three members of an enemy patrol infiltrated a friendly ambush position, and addressed a BAR man on the flank using English while attempting to take him prisoner. The soldier was able to free himself, and the two forces clashed later that morning in a brief fire fight.

During the period March 21st through 30th, the division was relieved by elements of the ROK Capitol and 6th Divisions. Sector responsibility was assumed by the ROK forces on March 30th. The division immediately began a movement to relieve the 2nd ROK Division. The 160th Infantry Regiment completed the relief of the 32nd ROK Regiment, and the 223rd Infantry Regiment had relieved the 31st ROK Regiment as the month ended. Now the division found itself with the 7th U.S. Division on its left (west) flank, and the 6th ROK Division on its right. The three Regimental Combat Teams maintained the same relative positions as they had before, with the 223rd on the left, the 224th in the center, and the 160th on the right.

A rotation system had been established throughout Korea, and the 40th Replacement Company had structures constructed to house 750 incoming and 750 outgoing personnel simultaneously. The first large group to be rotated, 389 enlisted men, departed Chunchon en route to the port city of Inchon on March 23, 1952. The tempo of returning National Guard personnel was accelerated and the final major group left the division area on June 8, arriving in Seattle and San Francisco during the first week of July 1952.

On March 30, 1952, the division's command post was moved from Korisil to Chaegung-dong in the Kumwha Valley. The division rear was moved from Ascom City near Seoul to the Chunchon area.

On April 1st, the division completed the relief of the 2nd ROK Division and assumed control of the Kumhwa-Kumsong sector, with the MLR running from CT665409 to CT7766493. The division was deployed with the 223rd Infantry Regiment on the left, the 160th Infantry Regiment on the right, and the 224th Infantry Regiment and 140th Tank Battalion in division reserve.

The boundary between the Fortieth and the 2nd US Division changed on April 3rd, so the 224th Infantry Regiment was moved into the line on the left of the 223rd. Battle lines remained unchanged as the division constructed and improved positions in the new area, and conducted patrols and numerous tank operations against enemy positions. The experiments with tank operations the previous months were highly successful, so the division continued to send tanks forward of the MLR to engage enemy installations and positions with direct fire. The only damage to the tanks was mine damage to tracks which could be easily repaired. For the first time, the enemy was seen to use antitank weapons, including recoilless rifles and rocket launchers.

The division sustained several company-size probes by the enemy during April. It was decided to seize the ground west of a 223rd Infantry outpost between CT695434 and CT693436. Coordinated planning was conducted between the 223rd and 224th Infantry Regiments for a reinforced company-size operation on April 16th. On that day Company C, 224th attacked west through the 223rd outpost position and occupied the ground without enemy opposition.

Considerable effort during the month of April was devoted to a IX Corps exercise dubbed "Exercise MUSHROOM." This was a training exercise in defense against atomic attack.

One attack on Company M, 223rd Infantry at 3:30 a.m. on April 13th was particularly well planned and executed. An enemy force approached friendly positions from the rear, and with well-timed point blank burp gun fire killed the sentries at both ends of the platoon position. The enemy quickly moved to individual personnel bunkers, simultaneously attacking six by hurling a grenade inside with immediate burp gun fire when the grenade exploded. The enemy rapidly withdrew and was well away before the surprised friendly units brought effective fire to bear. The Chinese had killed ten and wounded one, and probably suffered no casualties themselves.

There was a marked increase in enemy probes and enemy-initiated fire fights, all at night. This was especially true towards the end of the month. One particularly violent attack was made by an estimated company on Company A, 223rd Infantry Regiment on April 28th. After a brief fire fight the enemy withdrew, leaving eight enemy killed with an estimated 25 wounded. Company A suffered two killed and three wounded.

Since moving into the Kumhwa-Kumsong sector in April, troops felt a two or three-fold increase in incoming mortar and artillery fire. They were very conscious of the fact that the enemy looked right down their throats from Hill 1062 in the vicinity of CT648458. By May, an intensified program of bunker building and improvement was under way to increase the defensive capabilities of the division and to decrease friendly casualties. Commanders were also concerned about improving the siting and drainage of fortifications with the rainy season just around the corner.

Other than indirect fire from the enemy, there was very little enemy contact. It was decided to send out sizeable elements against enemy installations. There was concern that the enemy might be establishing installations south of Line BILL. The Division G2 coordinated tactical terrain studies of known and suspected enemy positions, and four were selected. Orders were given for large patrols to seize their objective, kill or capture enemy personnel encountered, and then destroy the enemy fortifications. Four company-size night patrol actions were conducted in May, and all four were successful.

On May 19th, IX US Corps revised the division's left boundary to the rear of the MLR and relieved the division of responsibility for the vital Kumhwa Valley. The 7th US Division assumed responsibility for the valley.

The tactic of having tank units advance forward of the MLR and bust bunkers with direct fire was repeated in May. There were ten such attacks, but it was becoming apparent the enemy was reacting differently. They no longer were rebuilding the bunkers under cover of darkness. Unfortunately, one tank suffered a direct hit from an 82mm mortar, and was destroyed by fire. Luckily, there were no casualties among any of the tank crews.

A couple of T-6 "Mosquito" aircraft from the U.S.A.F. base at Chunchon appeared over the Fortieth Division's lines early in the afternoon of May 27th. Dispatched on a reconnaissance mission across the IX Corps front, a Tactical Air Control Party (TACP) requested one of the aircraft make a low level reconnaissance of three possible gun and mortar positions. The aircraft turned south, and passed over the target at approximately 600 feet. Both the pilot and observer heard 20mm fire, followed quickly by flames in the cockpit.

The American pilot died in the crash of the aircraft. The observer, First Lieutenant W.P.R. ("Peter") Tolputt of Norfolk, England, had his moustache singed before he could bail out only 400 feet above the ground. Tolputt, on detached duty from the 14th Field Regiment Royal Artillery (1st British Commonwealth Division), hit the ground on the sloping side of a hill with considerable impact. His red and white parachute did not have time to fully deploy, so he ended up with a twisted knee. He looked around, trying to orient himself, and saw that he appeared to be surrounded on at least three sides by enemy-held hills. He used his URC-4 radio to contact the other T-6, piloted by Captain John Payer (who retired as a Colonel in Tennessee). Payer told Peter not to move, Peter later finding out he was only about 75 yards from the Chinese, and 1000 yards from the Americans. About that time, continuous enemy small arms and automatic fire started hitting in the vicinity. Artillery fire shortly began to fall all around Peter, and when he asked the Mosquito pilot whether it was enemy or friendly, the pilot told him it was both.

Four F-51 Mustangs and two F80 jets arrived on the scene. The Mosquito fired marking rockets, and the fighter aircraft engaged enemy targets with their .50 calibre machine guns. The Mosquito brought the air and artillery strikes closer and closer to Lieutenant Tolputt to protect him from the Chinese.

The troops of Company E, 224th observed all this to their right front. First Lieutenant Arthur L. Belknap, the company commander, radioed to see if anyone was going to rescue the "pilot." When it was obvious no one else was going to, he called for volunteers. He quickly assembled a combat patrol with ten sergeants (four of whom were platoon sergeants), three corporals, and a private first class medic. His assistant patrol leader was Second Lieutenant Edward C. ("Shy") Meyer, Belknap's First Platoon Leader. Meyer had been assigned to Company E just five days before, along with Second Lieutenant Donald E. Rosenblum. Shy Meyer eventually rose to four star general and Chief of Staff of the Army, while Don Rosenblum ended up as a Lieutenant General and commander of First Army.

The Chinese, as determined from an intercepted radio transmission, were trying to capture Tolputt alive. The race was on to see who could get to Tolputt first. The patrol quickly moved out, threading their way through mine fields to reach Tolputt. One of Company E's mortars knocked out a Chinese machine gun while covering the patrol's advance. At least three enemy patrols were trying to reach Tolputt at the same time as Belknap's patrol, but with the air and artillery fires delaying the enemy, the friendly patrol won the race. As they approached, Tolputt radioed the Mosquito, "Here comes a bloody lot of American sergeants!"

Tolputt the next day said "I later discovered that the abundance of high rank was due to the fact that this was an all-volunteer patrol. I was so delighted to see them that I shook hands with the nearest sergeant...Two members of the patrol shouted that they saw enemy troops and (started) firing their weapons. We departed in such haste that I neglected to bring my chute or URC-4 out with me...We reached friendlies after a walk of approximately one thousand meters, some of which I covered on the litter born by the medics and some assisted by members of the patrol helping me in pairs as I had twisted my knee on landing and suffered a head wound in the aircraft."

Soldiers assisting British aerial observer Peter Tolputt, May 1952
(Source: Colonel Arthur L. Belknap

The patrol from Company E killed several Chinese as they covered their buddies who were assisting Tolputt back to friendly lines. As Tolputt wrote several years later, "The patrol lumbered with me, when returning to friendlies, in fact had a spirited fire fight nearly the whole way back, and in particular, Corporal Jack Appleby, who was in the unenviable position of 'Tail End Charlie,' himself accounted for at least 3 Chinese trying to catch up and surround us." Members of the patrol were awarded the Silver Star following the action. It had been an exciting end to a comparatively quiet period on the front lines.

Major General Hudelson turned command over to Brigadier General Joseph P. Cleland at 9:00 a.m. on June 2, 1952. On the same day, Colonel Gordon B. Rogers arrived to replace Brigadier General Homer O. Eaton, the Assistant Division Commander. Colonel Rogers had been wounded twice on Buna during World

War II as General Eichelberger's G-2, and had extensive experience in the Pacific Theater.

General Hudelson departed via air the same day, arriving in Los Angeles on June 8th. By June 6th, all Guardsmen had been released except those who signed an extension. During the first phase of Korean combat for the division, while still under command of National Guard officers, the following statistics were recorded:

Casualties:

Killed in action	66
Wounded in action	327
Missing in action	6
Total casualties	399

Awards:

Awards:	
Silver Star	10
Soldier's Medal	1
Bronze Star	86
Air Medal	28
Commendation Ribbon w/Pendant	67
Purple Heart	277
Combat Infantry Badge	10,188
Combat Medical Badge	661
Total awards	11,318

General Cleland had an almost immediate impact on the division. The division had slipped somewhat in combat efficiency as many of the veteran Guardsmen had been shipped home and replaced with draftees and other replacements. General Cleland immediately shaped the division up again, having had considerable experience, primarily in airborne units. A comparatively small man, he was in exceptional physical shape for a man of his age. He could do a standing back flip, so had earned the nickname "Jumping Joe"

Cleland. Almost his first order of the day was that everyone in the division would run two miles in the morning before calisthenics and morning chow. He personally led the officers in the division headquarters, some of whom were advancing in age and not as fit as they should have been. They quickly shaped up.

General Cleland had a personal habit, whenever time allowed, of having his driver stop at the bottom of hills. Korea is a very hilly country, so this happened quite often. General Cleland would then jog up the mountain, where he would be picked up by his jeep driver. General Cleland was a very competent commander who quickly gained the respect of the division. The division perceptively improved when he assumed command.

Shortly after General Cleland assumed command of the division, a couple of significant and controversial changes were directed to be made in the division's patch and nickname. The division's patch was converted from a blue and gold square with one corner up, to a multi-colored diamond sewn on laterally. The patch was made in the far east and issued at no cost to all of the troops.

The division's nickname was changed from "Sunburst" to "Ball of Fire." The change served to immediately signal a shift in command style and philosophy. The patch design meant nothing to the replacements and draftees who joined the division. On the other hand, it was seen as an affront by many veterans of the division who had seen thousands of their comrades lost as casualties in two wars while they were wearing the traditional (and Department of the Army-approved) patch. Many derisively called the new patch the "Flaming Asshole."

Someone from Corps saw the unauthorized patch, and the issue went all the way up to Eighth Army. General Cleland was admonished, and the traditional patch returned.

Major General Hudelson criticized conduct of the war shortly after he returned to California, stating the war was becoming more political than military. He wrote a series of articles for the Hearst newspapers, headlined "We Are Not Fighting to Win in Korea." He pointed out that the troops stopped at the truce line, not because they were stopped by the enemy, but because they had been ordered to. He felt that served no purpose except to give the enemy time to build up their forces opposite ours, and strongly said so. General Hudelson was *persona non grata* from that point on. He received a letter of reprimand from Lieutenant General Joseph M. Swing, Commanding General of Sixth Army, for his remarks about the fighting in Korea.

The division, under cover of darkness in early June, occupied the former OPLR in strength. There was no enemy contact, and the division remained deployed with the 224th on the left, the 223rd in the center, and the 160th on the right.

The division took some pride in patrolling more aggressively, and deeper, than other divisions. Patrol plans were rather elaborate, routinely involving dozens of patrols each night. Patrolling activity in June was no exception, and included several company-sized night raiding operations with the primary mission of seizing prisoners. Bunker busting operations continued, employing both tanks and towed 90mm guns along MLR positions. Two tank operations were conducted by units of the 140th Tank Battalion in support of company-sized attacks by 6th ROK Division units against enemy outposts. Three tanks were lost in the second of these two engagements.

The mission of June 14th to take prisoners was a particularly bloody effort. Patrol Number 21 called for Company F, 223rd Infantry to attack Hill 449 near Minari-gol to obtain a prisoner. The Battalion Intelligence Officer, who wanted a prisoner for interrogation, estimated that there were only about a dozen enemy on the hill.

The unit officers planned the attack, with the start time to occur just before dawn. Volunteers were called for, with a total of ninety officers and men responding. The men were briefed and coordination accomplished, when just four hours prior to the attack, a new plan was received from the battalion S-3. The revised plan was not as complete, and took the unit over another route that required them to traverse over a hill before assaulting the objective.

The unit moved to the line of departure to attack with three platoons abreast. The platoon on the left was lead by First Lieutenant Richard C. Wagner. As his platoon was guided to the line of departure through another company, the guides became disoriented, and dawn was breaking before the platoon moved out. They were slightly behind the platoons on their right as they moved up the hill with little or no cover.

Lieutenant Wagner's platoon no sooner got started when the word came that the company commander, Captain Curtis Weeks, was wounded (losing one eye, with another bullet through his shoulder and neck) and Wagner was to take command. In Wagner's words, "Studying the terrain, I decided to take my platoon up the two hills, keeping (close to the ridge line) to use as cover from enemy fire. Running forward we scrambled over one hill and up the second to (an enemy) bunker. The fifties passing overhead from our company perimeter were giving us excellent support. We advanced to within twenty feet of the bunker. The fifties could not have been more than four feet over our heads.

"The bunker was made of large logs and had no port for any large weapons. I saw a slit between the two lowest logs from which the North Koreans could observe the total area on either side of the ridge that ran from the base of the hill up to the bunker."

Lieutenant Wagner directed his radioman to fire the green smoke signal to lift the supporting fires so they could assault the bunker. When the green smoke popped, three riflemen raced towards the left end of the bunker. Wagner's narrative continues, "just before they reached the bunker I fired three carbine rounds through the slit to pin down anyone inside. Immediately after that a stick grenade with a metal ball shaped top was thrown to the left of me, landing on a rocky ledge on level with my head, exploding a foot from my helmet." Wagner was badly wounded, but not knocked unconscious. He passed command to the platoon leader on his right, and then tumbled down the hill where the medics eventually got him evacuated to a mobile hospital in the rear.

The enemy opposition was much more intense than intelligence estimates had anticipated. Rather than about a dozen enemy, there were at least three times that. There were several automatic weapons on the hill, as well as supporting enemy small arms, artillery and mortars from adjacent hills. Corporal Clifton T. Speicher's squad was pinned down by heavy fires, and Speicher was wounded. He leapt up and charged the bunker directly in front of his squad, but was hit again as he approached the enemy position. Speicher was heavily wounded, with penetrating wounds to his stomach and hip. In spite of his wounds, he continued on, and killed the three North Koreans in the bunker, two with his rifle and one with his bayonet. The machine gun silenced, his men continued with the mission while Speicher worked his way to the foot of the hill where he died. In addition to two killed and two missing, seventy-five of the original Fox Company volunteers were wounded.

Sergeant David B. Bleak, from the Medical Company, was accompanying the Reconnaissance Section of Second Battalion's Headquarters Company in a supporting mission. That platoon crossed the line of departure early, bypassing the hill to be attacked by Company F, and established a position in the rear and at the base. As they climbed the hill, they suffered very heavy casualties at a rate similar to those suffered by the Fox Company volunteers. Sergeant Bleak ministered to the wounded as he worked his way up the hill. As he neared the military crest of the hill, he was fired on from a trench as he tried to reach some wounded. He raced to the trench, killing two of the enemy with his bare hands, and another with his trench knife. Jumping out of the trench, he saw a grenade fall near a fellow soldier. He quickly moved to place himself to shield the soldier from the blast. A few minutes later, he was struck by a bullet in the lower left leg, while treating the wounded. Though suffering a perforating wound himself, he picked up a casualty and started down the hill. On the way down he was attacked by two enemy soldiers with fixed bayonets. He put the casualty down, and grabbed the two North Koreans, smacking their heads together. He picked up his helpless patient, and carried him down the hill to safety.

The combat chronicle for the day reported fifteen of the enemy counted as KIA, and twenty estimated WIA. Company F got their prisoner of war, but at heavy cost.

Both Bleak and Speicher were later awarded the Medal of Honor, Speicher posthumously. Several factors contributed to this being an extraordinarily bloody affair, with comparatively few men escaping unscathed. Not only was the position heavily defended, with last minute changes contributing to misunderstandings and confusion, but the planned artillery barrage to keep the enemy pinned down never came. As Lieutenant Wagner noted, "The mortar companies fired a record number of shells. I wasn't there at the end, but I was told they saved all our butts."

The enemy prisoner of war was interrogated. He turned out to be a mortar squad leader from the 133rd Regiment, 45th Division, 15th CCF Army Corps. The prisoner provided the location of gun positions opposite the 223rd Infantry, and stated the Chinese were at full strength when they moved into the positions across from the 223rd.

The division artillery was kept busy, and well forward. The 105mm howitzer batteries would often move up right behind the mortars of infantry heavy weapons companies, and then lob shells over the hill by reducing the propellant to only charge one or two. When the infantry regiments were pulled into reserve, the artillery would support ROK regiments, some of which had little or no artillery of their own.

The relief of the division by the 2nd ROK Division was accomplished from June 26th to 28th. On June 30th, the division (less the division artillery and tank battalion) moved into Field Training Center (FTC) #5 to begin a period of training and rehabilitation in conjunction with assuming the mission of IX US

Corps reserve. The division artillery and tank battalion were placed under IX US Corps control to support the 2nd ROK Division.

Units that were not on the front line often had Korean "house boys" assigned on the basis of as many as one per staff section and one per squad tent. Korea hadn't even recovered from the Japanese occupation when the war broke out, so there were many Koreans without a means of support. In a mutually advantageous accommodation, house boys helped the troops with many housekeeping chores, for which they were provided food, shelter, and sometimes pay. This was considered such good "duty" by the Koreans, that units had to occasionally have a face-to-face identification check to control the number of bogus house boys.

The Korean police could be brutal to their own people, so when the division returned underage or bogus house boys to their communities, a sergeant would often be sent with them to ensure they got all the way home with whatever clothes, blankets, or other items the troops had given them. Otherwise they would be stopped, the Korean police would take the items for themselves, and send the former house boys on with only their underwear.

The summer of 1952 was unforgettable for many of the soldiers, especially when compared with the freezing winters. It was very hot, and the soldiers complained about rats which they claimed were as big as small dogs, and poisonous snakes. However, the snakes did have one redeeming virtue, when the troops noted that they helped by eating the young rats.

Korean soldiers, or "KATUSA's," were assimilated into each of the regiments in great numbers. Americans got to quickly know the soldiers with names like Kim, Chung and Lee, and the language barriers were gradually stripped away.

On July 1st, 3-223rd Infantry Regiment was dispatched to the Sangdong Mine Area to perform a security mission. There they provided security for the mines, the US IX Corps Forward Command Post, and a radio station. Most of the 224th Infantry Regiment was attached to the 2nd Logistical Command on July

2nd, and left for Pusan to provide security for POW enclosures on Koje-do. The 3-224th, reinforced by two tank platoons, was given the same mission at Cheju-do.

A soldier from Company M, 224th described the duty on Cheju-do as "terrible." It was hot and humid, and the troops were not given any time off. They finished building the POW enclosures and stringing of barbed wire. The Special Orders for prisoner guards made it clear troops were not to permit abuse, beating, ridicule or maltreatment of prisoners. They spelled out the rules in great detail, including instructions on who was to handle discipline, how often work details were to get rest breaks, and other mundane details. Three of the twenty-two paragraphs also made it clear when deadly force was to be applied:

"16. If a Prisoner of War attempts to escape, the prisoner guard will call "Jon Ju." (This is the Chinese term for "Halt") If the Prisoner of War fails to halt the call will be repeated once. If the Prisoner of War still fails to halt the prisoner guard will shoot to kill the escaping Prisoner of War.

"17. Any incident where Prisoners of War are observed attacking or threatening to attack UN personnel by throwing any objects such as rocks, metal pieces, boards, etc., which could injure, maim or kill such UN personnel, the Prisoner(s) of War will be shot at that moment in order to protect the UN personnel concerned.

"18. In any incident where Prisoners of War are observed hitting, striking, kicking, biting or in any other way observed doing injury or maiming or threatening to maim UN personnel, such Prisoner(s) of War will be shot at that moment in order to protect UN personnel concerned."

Back on the mainland, General Cleland was promoted to Major General effective July 6th. A week later most of the division moved from FTC #5 to a new training area near Kapyong (sometimes spelled "Gapyong") after nearly six months of continuous combat. The division completed the move by July 20th, resuming training and security missions.

General Cleland temporarily was assigned command of the IX US Corps on July 31st, while Brigadier General Gordon B. Rogers assumed command of the Fortieth.

The division's move to Kapyong brought them to a formerly picturesque area just a few miles south of the 38th Parallel. For several months, residents of the city had suffered under the rule of the North Koreans. They were freed by the first United Nations push to the north, but had to escape south when friendly forces were again pushed back. Thousands of Kapyong residents died of starvation, disease, or the bitter cold as they trekked to the south. The city was repeatedly fought over, and was all but completely destroyed.

Soldiers of the division were struck by the plight of Kapyong's children, who hadn't had a school building for two years. Village elders were teaching the children using old boxes for desks and otherwise making do as best they could. The soldiers were determined to do something about it.

Building a new school became a division project, one of many under the Armed Forces Assistance to Korea (AFAK) program. Almost $14,000 was collected within a week. During just one payday, soldiers contributed over $17,000. The division's 578th Engineer Battalion quickly produced plans for a ten classroom high school, and the Koreans donated an eight acre site. A joint Korean-40th Division committee had agreed that the school would be built of native stone, and materials would be purchased in Korea to help the war-torn economy. Other men of the division came by to assist the engineers in the work, although most of the work was done by the Koreans, and the school was ready for use by October 18, 1952. The school was dedicated on that date to the "future leaders of the Republic of Korea by the officers and men of the 40th Infantry Division, United States Army."

The school was named for Sergeant First Class Kenneth Kaiser, the young Angeleno from Company B, 160th Infantry who was the first member of the division to be killed in action. Kaiser had joined Company B, 160th Infantry in Los Angeles when only sixteen. A good soldier, he had learned fast from the senior sergeants in the company, most of whom were veterans of World War II. He was second in command of his platoon, and only eighteen-years-old when he was killed by mortar fragments on January 20, 1952 just three days after his unit arrived in Korea.

A monument was constructed near the entrance to the school. It has a plaque with Major General Cleland's face on one side, and Sergeant Kaiser's on the other. There is also a plaque with the division crest at the top which tells the story of the school.

The school was the first coeducational school in Korea, with three hundred children as its first occupants (although it quickly grew to an enrollment of almost 2,000). There was one short-lived threat to the school. The Korean National Police were impressed with the school, the only large building in the region that was undamaged, and were determined to make it their local headquarters. The division commander immediately made it clear that his troops could tear it down even faster than they put it up, and it had been built for children, not police officers. The police quickly backed off.

While the division was located in and around Kapyong, there were military missions to be accomplished. Elements of the division remained detached in support of the 2nd ROK Division and the 2nd Logistical Command.

The 160th and 223rd Infantry Regiments kept training in the Kapyong area while most of the 40th Division had an additional mission as reserve for the IX U.S. Corps. Extensive plans and preparations were made to prepare the division for instant employment as a counterattacking or blocking force should that be required. The two regiments rehabilitated and improved reserve defensive positions on the division's portion of Line KANSAS, a defensive line selected by General Van Fleet. That defensive line followed the twisting curves of the Imjin River from the west coast, and then generally paralleled to the north of the 38th Parallel.

On August 9th, Major General Cleland returned to command of the division. The 160th and 223rd Infantry Regiments participated in battalion-size combat firing exercises. The 224th Infantry Regiment was relieved from its security mission at Cheju-do on September 23rd, and rejoined the division. The division continued to rehabilitate defensive positions on Line KANSAS while performing various training and security missions.

The First Battalion of the Turkish Brigade was assigned to the division in October, 1952. The division was ordered on October 16th to relieve the 25th US Division in the Paeam - Ihyon-Ni sector. On October 21st, the division artillery and the 140th Tank Battalion were returned to division control. By the next day, the 224th Infantry Regiment had relieved the 25th Division's 27th Infantry Regiment, and the 160th Infantry Regiment had relieved the 14th Infantry Regiment. The Commanding General of the Fortieth Infantry Division assumed sector responsibility on October 22nd.

The division then passed to control of the X US Corps. The 5th Regimental Combat Team was attached, with the 160th Infantry deployed on the left, the 224th in the center, and the 5th on the right. The 223rd arrived a day later, and was placed in division reserve. On October 31st, the 5th RCT moved to division reserve positions after being relieved by the 223rd.

Infantrymen of Company A, 223rd Infantry assault bunker positions. February 20, 1953 (Source: National Archives)

CHAPTER THIRTEEN

THE FIGHT TO THE END

During most of the month of October 1952, the division continued in defensive positions, maintaining enemy contact by aggressive patrol activity. Combat was highlighted by a series of enemy attacks which ranged from reinforced platoon up to almost battalion size.

The heaviest combat during the month of October occurred early the morning of the 26th. On that date an estimated understrength battalion, supported by heavy artillery and mortar fire, attacked Companies F and G, 160th Infantry on Heartbreak Ridge. A one hour and twenty minute fire fight ensued, with the enemy advancing to within 35 yards of friendly positions. They were then forced to withdraw with an estimated twenty KIA and forty WIA. Heavy casualties had been inflicted on the enemy during the various attacks, and the MLR was firmly in friendly hands at the end of the month.

The division, with its command post firmly entrenched at Tokkol-li in the center of the X US Corps sector along Line MINNESOTA, continued to have the 160th Infantry on the left, the 224th in the center, the 223rd on the right, and the 5th RCT in reserve. There were numerous small unit actions and night patrols during the month. Tanks continued to play a key role through heavy direct-fire destruction of enemy installations.

The fighting on Heartbreak Ridge had evolved into trench warfare, with extensive fortifications and bunkers. The soldiers fought from the forward slope, which was always manned to some degree. They slept and had such positions as administrative bunkers on the reverse slope. Artillery and mortar fires had stripped the foliage from the few trees that remained. Each night patrols would be sent out by both sides to probe for weaknesses, gather information, or capture prisoners.

The tedium of front line duty was broken up by entertainment from "Peking Sally," who broadcast daily over loudspeakers from "Station WWW." The soldiers never knew what those initials meant, but enjoyed the broadcasts from a woman who spoke excellent English. She played music the soldiers enjoyed, gave out baseball scores, and talked about wives at home. She talked to "you GI's," often by name. The troops were convinced that much of her information came from the Korean Service Corps (KSC) workers, sometime called "chogies," who carried chow and supplies to the units each day. She would end her broadcasts saying such things as, "Good evening all you GI's, and all of you on ambush patrols."

As October changed to November, enemy activity grew. There seemed to be increased enemy patrol activity, and enemy artillery and mortar fire on Hill 851 grew in intensity each night. Intelligence information pointed to 2-160th Infantry's positions as the target for attack. On the afternoon of November 3rd, enemy artillery and mortar fire interdicted the entire battle position of the 160th Infantry.

The 2-160th Infantry's portion of the line included Hill 851, and had an unusual mix of companies. Lieutenant Colonel Robert H. Pell had deployed four companies on line, from west to east his Companies E and F, plus the attached Companies C and A. In reinforcing positions to the south were his Company G and attached Company B.

As it grew dark on November 3rd, a patrol left Company C heading into "no-man's land." They ran into an enemy patrol, and killed a North Korean soldier. The body was hauled back to American lines and searched. A pair of wire cutters were found in his clothes, so the unit was immediately brought to 100% alert. Five minutes later, at 9:07 p.m., "all hell broke loose."

Many mortar rounds hit Hill 851, and some artillery, totalling approximately 4,500 before the night was through. As bugles blew all up and down the line, soldiers of a reinforced battalion of the North Korean People's Army 14th Regiment hit E, F and C Companies.

Company C, commanded by Captain Willard J. "Wild Bill" Hardy, was particularly hard hit. His third platoon, some troops of which had been transferred as replacements from Ohio's 37th Division, defended Castle Rock with a ridge finger in front of them that stretched for about 500 yards towards the enemy. Their first soldier to open fire was an automatic rifleman with a BAR. Friendly searchlights, about two miles behind the front lines, swept back and forth reflecting off the clouds to illuminate the battlefield. The North Koreans looked like ants as they covered the forward slope of hills in front of Company C. They threw sticks or their bodies over the barbed wire, so their comrades could quickly rush the 160th positions. The next few minutes were described by many as a "turkey shoot," as enemy soldiers came within rifle and machine gun range while well illuminated by the searchlights. The 143rd's forward observer in the platoon area called in artillery, some of which was purposely called into the third platoon's area.

The fighting quickly was close and personal. A black machine gunner from Detroit yelled over and over at the North Koreans, "yi lhee wah (EE-lee-wah)" meaning "come here." He was having trouble being heard over the din of combat, but finally they heard him and started in his direction. When they did, he opened fire. He killed a great many before they overran him. The two tanks in the platoon area were fully engaged, and soon had North Koreans crawling all over them. Some were shot off by infantrymen, but others were removed when the tankers brought machine gun fire to bear on each other.

The fighting slacked off in front of all companies except C and E, both of which had lost several bunkers to the enemy. At 10:49 p.m., Company C requested additional fires in front of their positions. A minute later the artillery forward observer with Company E reported the enemy had broken through into their positions. At 10:56 p.m., Company C reported that the enemy seemed to be withdrawing. This turned around a few minutes later when Companies C and E were again hit.

Captain Hardy, normally armed with a pistol, had picked up a carbine and was using that. He seemed to be everywhere, always followed by his company wireman, moving through intense enemy fire to direct the fire of his platoons. In spite of their efforts, the enemy deeply penetrated the unit's positions, including the command post, and the enemy gained the company's high ground. It was after midnight when Captain Hardy charged up the hill against the enemy, firing his carbine and throwing hand grenades, until an enemy grenade blew his helmet off and knocked him back down the hill.

Dazed and bleeding, he stumbled into a platoon position, obtaining another helmet and carbine. He quickly put together a small assault team, and charged back up the fire swept slope, the small group succeeding in driving the enemy back, as the company reestablished a defensive perimeter. He also retook the company command post, with a carbine in one hand and swinging an entrenching tool in the other.

Company C restored the MLR, and a little while later Company E reported the same. Litter jeeps were requested for the many casualties. It was clear that the enemy had given up after almost four hours of trying to get through.

The North Koreans were repulsed without committing any of the regiment's reserve companies. In the morning, the troops moved over the battlefield to survey the damage. They found the machine gunner from Detroit dead with a bullet through his head, but many enemy dead stacked in front of him. They found another machine gunner sitting with his machine gun in his lap, holding it with one hand on the pistol grip and another on the barrel. He was alive, but not moving or responding, sitting there with the classic

"1000-yard stare." They pulled the machine gun out of his hands, but some of the skin from his left hand stayed on the barrel. The gun barrel had obviously been very hot when he was fighting.

The North Korean dead and wounded were everywhere. They were wearing quilted uniforms, similar to mover's blankets in the United States, and tan in color. They didn't wear underwear underneath, which surprised our troops. They were carrying rice, indicating they intended to stay when they captured Hill 851. Some had mortars strapped to their legs. Their attack had seemed fanatical, in fact, some were convinced the North Koreans were high on something when they attacked.

The enemy paid a high price, with 137 KIA's, 266 additional estimated KIA's, 3 WIA's, 523 estimated wounded, plus 7 captured. Enemy materiel captured included automatic rifles and machine guns, ammunition, documents and rations. The documents indicated the enemy had intended to seize, hold and reinforce Hill 851, and continue the attack to seize Hill 930. The 160th Regiment had suffered also, with 73 casualties, including 19 dead.

On November 4th, "Peking Sally" said the 160th had been hit with two battalions the previous night, and would be hit by two regiments that night. Nothing happened. In the aftermath, Company C dubbed themselves "Chop-em-up Charlie."

Captain Hardy, a native of Ringwood, New Jersey, was highly respected by his men. A veteran of the Normandy invasion, commissioned after reaching Staff Sergeant as an enlisted man, he had earned two Purple Hearts before he received his third in Korea, along with the Distinguished Service Cross for the action described above.

The division suffered 287 battle casualties during November. The winter was very cold, and some units had to remove their batteries each night and take them into the bunkers to keep them from freezing. Many of the troops had little oil stoves for heat, but it was so cold that they had to thin the cold oil with gasoline to make it liquid. They had to be careful, because too much gas could cause an explosion. One explosion killed three Koreans attached to an artillery battery.

The terrain was so steep that vehicles could not resupply troops on the MLR. As a consequence, the engineers designed and constructed spectacular lifelines for infantrymen perched on otherwise inaccessible Korean mountain peaks. These aerial tramways were used to haul water, rations, ammunition, clothing and weapons to the MLR. Just as important, those trams were used to quickly evacuate casualties. A tram operator's school was conducted in November 1952 to train one officer and ten enlisted men from each lettered company supported by a tram.

The division retained its defense mission along a static front and limited its operations to aggressive patrol activity, improvement of defensive positions, and the continued training of the reserve regiment. Patrolling changed, with a trend toward fewer but larger and better organized patrols. Fire support for these patrol missions was earlier and closer. Ambush patrols, as well as combat and reconnaissance patrols, were fully utilized. Construction and repair of defensive positions progressed in spite of winter weather, with first priority on the MLR given to barbed wire, trenches, and bunkers.

An interesting order in the midst of all this was issued in Division Daily Bulletin Number 117, dated December 13, 1952. The third paragraph referred to guidance from X Corps regarding relief of drivers for inefficiency. Those who were caught speeding, driving recklessly, or under the influence of alcohol, were to be immediately reassigned to an infantry or heavy weapons company unless they already belonged to such an organization.

Christmas in the 160th Regiment's sector was memorable for many reasons. One was the few trees that were left had been festooned with Christmas decorations. The other involved two soldiers from Company A who had been captured by the North Koreans. On Christmas they turned one loose. He came across the line in red long johns with a cotton beard and carrying a sack full of cigarettes and Chinese candy. Battle casualties for December totalled 163.

As December turned to January of 1953, Corporal Eldon Wattles of Merced, California watched an enemy sniper come out of his hide hole each morning on the hill opposite his Company E, 224th positions. The sniper would do a few exercises before breakfast at the same time each morning, and then the sniper would disappear for the day. The mortar section was notified. The next morning the sniper came out of the hole, but didn't even have time to start before the mortars got him. "We had to get him," laughed Wattles, "We didn't want our first sergeant to get any ideas."

On January 8th the 5th RCT relieved the 223rd Infantry Regiment, which then moved to division reserve. There were an increasing number of patrol engagements and enemy probes of the MLR during the month. The largest of these occurred the early morning of January 28th, when Company G, 5th RCT was hit by an estimated 100 enemy along the MLR in the Punch Bowl area. The enemy penetrated the MLR to a depth of 20 yards before being ejected.

One routine patrol ended with a not-so-routine rescue. A 223rd Infantry Regiment patrol was well out in front of friendly lines when the patrol leader was cut down by enemy machine gun fire only thirty or forty yards in front of them. PFC Charles Holloway of Niagara Falls, New York ran forward to assist while screaming for a medic. When he tried to stop the flow of blood, he saw the wounds were too numerous and the patrol leader would have to be immediately evacuated. Taking hold of his parka hood, he started dragging him down the hill.

The enemy opened fire, with bullets tracing the route of withdrawal down a snow-covered finger. In a draw at the bottom, he paused to see if he could do anything further about the wounds, but was concerned at the way blood was flowing. Holloway then started the grueling 800 yards across "no-man's-land," but was again fired on by the enemy when they spotted them. Holloway tried to carry his wounded leader on his back, but he was too heavy. They struggled across a frozen creek, and eventually fell into a hole where he tried to regain his breath. When he started again, his hands were frozen and raw, and his patrol leader was unconscious. He struggled, usually at a crawl, dragging his man to the barbed wire at the foot of a hill held by Company F, 223rd Infantry. He couldn't get up the hill as he kept sliding back. Half way to the crest he yelled for help. Immediately three soldiers raced down the slope and carried the wounded patrol leader the rest of the way.

Both he and Holloway were rushed to the aid station. When the doctors finished with them, Holloway was assured his patrol leader would live. Holloway was told, however, that he was going to have to lose four fingers from one hand, and two from the other. Exhausted, but thankful he had been successful in saving his leader, Holloway broke into tears.

The division suffered 191 casualties in the month of January. This was also the month that saw the division's last of the original contingent of National Guardsmen leave. That was Captain Donald B. George of the 140th AAA AW Battalion, who left on January 28, 1953.

The relief of the division by the 45th US Division began on January 28th when the 224th Infantry Regiment was relieved by the 180th Infantry Regiment. On January 30th, the 160th Infantry Regiment was relieved by the 279th Infantry Regiment, and the Commanding General of the 45th Division assumed sector responsibility. On January 31st, the relief was completed when the 223rd was relieved by the 179th Infantry Regiment. Division artillery remained in position, and along with the 140th Tank Battalion, passed to control of the 45th.

To economize on equipment, transportation and supplies while conserving manpower during the intense cold, all possible equipment and facilities of the 40th Division were left in place. The property records were adjusted with the 45th Division after the relief. The security and secrecy measures that were taken to prevent knowledge by the enemy were successful, evidenced by the lack of enemy patrol activity, mortar and artillery fire during the relief. The Army Commander commended the division after the relief had taken place, and stated the division had "established a precedent which undoubtedly will be followed in the future."

As the month ended, the division was in X Corps reserve, with its command post at Nambakchon. The 160th was located in the vicinity of Hwachon, the 223rd at Kowanton, and the 224th at Inje.

The only reorganization of organic elements while in Korea was effective the first of February. On that date, the 740th Ordnance Maintenance Company was reorganized and redesignated the 740th Ordnance Battalion.

The Fortieth Division artillery, under X US Corps control, relieved the 45th US Division artillery in direct support of the 12th ROK Division on February 3rd. The 140th Tank Battalion relieved the 245th Tank Battalion along the MLR in the same sector on February 11th, joining the division's artillery in direct support of the 12th ROK Division.

In the meantime, the first edition of the division's new four-page weekly, *The Fire Ball,"* was distributed on February 6th after being printed in Seoul. During a short ceremony Colonel Thomas W. Dunn, the Division Artillery Commander, pulled the lanyard on a 981st Battalion howitzer. The 600,000th round fired by the division's artillery was sent on its way.

The division inaugurated a training program on February 9th, stressing weapons, small unit tactics, and physical fitness training. Plans were drawn up and construction started on a semi-permanent division training center. The 160th Infantry Regiment sent a task force to the Sangdong Mine area on February 17th to assume security duties there.

The 224th Infantry Regiment was attached to the 45th US Division on March 17th. The regiment displaced to Wondang-ni in the 45th's sector, where it moved into reserve positions for that division. Tactical units conducted training exercises at platoon and company level. The most extensive training operation conducted during the period was TRAINER ONE, the purpose of which was to test the ability of the 160th Infantry Regiment and part of the division headquarters to move from X US Corps to execute the IX US Corps Attack Plan, HOOKER ONE, in the Chorwon sector. The operations started on March 21st, involving a move of about 135 miles. In the meantime, the division was designated Eighth US Army reserve from March 6th through the 28th, 1953.

The 224th, still under control of the 45th US Division, moved into the line on April 14th. On that day it relieved the 5th RCT. Major General Ridgley Gaither assumed command of the division from General Cleland on April 17th. At a banquet, officers welcomed General Gaither and said goodbye to General Cleland. They presented General Cleland an engraved Chinese burp gun while the division band played "For He's a Jolly Good Fellow." There was a colorful goodbye ceremony held at the airstrip the next day. Tanks from the 223rd Infantry Regiment fired a thirteen gun salute, General Cleland said goodbye to the officers and men, and he boarded his plane to the strains of "Auld Lang Syne."

General Gaither's record included a combat jump with the 17th Airborne Division in World War II. Following World War II he had several assignments including assistant division commander of the 82nd Airborne Division, and commander of the 11th Airborne Division at Fort Campbell, Kentucky.

On April 19th, the 160th Infantry Regiment was placed under operational control of the 45th US Division. The 160th replaced the 279th Infantry Regiment in the 45th's reserve positions. The 223rd Infantry Regiment initiated the Fortieth's relief of the 20th ROK Division when it relieved the 61st ROK Regiment in line on April 26th. On April 27th, the 224th Infantry Regiment and the 40th Division Artillery with the 625th and 980th Field Artillery Battalions returned to division control, and the 40th Division Commander assumed sector responsibility. The 160th passed from

45th Division control to X Corps control at that time, and occupied reserve positions.

The 140th Tank Battalion continued its support of the 12th ROK Division with two tank companies during the entire month. As April ended, the division was emplaced along the MLR (Line MINNESOTA) in the Punch Bowl, or Ihyon-ni-Kalbakkumi sector. The division was deployed with the 224th Infantry Regiment on the left, and the 223rd on the right. The 143rd and 981st Field Artillery Battalions continued to support the 12th ROK Division under X US Corps control, along with two companies of the 140th Tank Battalion. The 160th was in X US Corps reserve. The division had a total of 35 battle casualties in April.

The 981st Field Artillery Battalion returned to division control on May 7th. The 143rd remained in support of the 12th ROK Division, along with two companies of the 140th Tank Battalion. The division engaged in numerous small-scale patrol clashes with the enemy in actions typical of that period in the Punch Bowl area. The 160th Infantry Regiment on May 27th was relieved from X US Corps Reserve, and sent to Koje-do under Korean Communications Zone (KCOMZ) control to guard prisoners of war.

This last mission was not without incident. There is always some tension between the guards and those guarded. There was the infamous incident of May 7, 1952 when Brigadier General Francis T. Dodd had been seized and then held by the prisoners in POW Enclosure #1 for seventy-eight hours. He was released on May 10th, and later was reduced to the rank of colonel. When control had been restored, Operation BREAKUP resettled the prisoners in stockades that held between 500 and 1000 prisoners. This resettlement was completed by June 19, 1952. However, this was a year later. The greatest problem for division troops was not expected. The greatest tension experienced by our troops involved their supposed allies, the South Korean ROKs.

South Korean President Syngman Rhee was strongly opposed to forced repatriation of any North Korean prisoners who claimed to be anti-Communist. The negotiators in Panmunjom finally reached an accord calling for such prisoners to be placed with a neutral Custodial Commission. President Rhee ordered his troops to free any prisoners on Koje-do who claimed to be anti-Communist. About 25,000 were set free on June 18th when South Korean guards threw the gates open in a move some felt was an attempt to sabotage the peace talks. Less than 10,000 others refused to be repatriated.

The 160th found themselves in the middle of this tense situation. The experience of the Company C, 160th Infantry serves to illustrate the stress involved. They were quartered in Quonset huts on the island, with their quarters surrounded by barbed wire. Their mission was to guard POW Enclosure #13, which supposedly held high ranking officers. They wore no badge of rank, so the guards couldn't tell for sure.

The ROKs unceremoniously took over the mission when their President ordered the prisoners turned loose. Nerves were really on edge with all those prisoners running loose around the island. Many of the American troops did not know where all of this was going to lead, and suspected the worst. One of many incidents that followed is described by a squad leader in Charlie Company:

"We almost went to war with the ROKs! Lieutenant Stone (First Lieutenant John Stone, the Company Commander) called a squad leader's meeting at the rear edge of our barbed wire company area. We met as scheduled and crossed the barbed wire, then going outside of our area. We hadn't gone five yards before an entire ROK platoon commanded by a ROK captain popped up out of concealment. It was Lieutenant Stone's intention to dig in a defensive position and we were going out to determine where the positions would be. If we were going to die, we were going to die fighting, not just standing there and waiting."

The ROK Captain asked "Stoney" where he was going. When Lieutenant Stone told him the group was out for a leisurely walk, the ROK captain strongly suggested the Americans get back behind the wire. Lieutenant Stone responded that he would after they finished their walk. Every ROK soldier then moved two paces towards the Americans, and the ROK captain said "I strongly suggest you go back now!" Lieutenant Stone said "We will--in a few minutes." Eventually Lieutenant Stone turned around and led his troops back to their area.

"We were under constant observation by the ROKs, and they held the high ground. The only place they couldn't see was inside the Quonset huts. We set up machine guns (two per hut) facing each door (one at each end). They were manned by crews twenty-four hours per day. Charlie (Company) was pissed. It turned into a stand off with no hostile action by either party."

Extensive small-scale patrol activity, both ambush and reconnaissance patrols, continued along the MLR through June. A total of ninety-four patrols were dispatched by the division during the month. The heaviest combat of the month occurred on June 2nd. On that night there was an exceptionally heavy concentration of artillery and mortar fire. This was followed by about forty or fifty enemy that attacked elements of the 223rd Infantry Regiment in the vicinity of DT2341. After 30 minutes of hand-to-hand combat, the enemy was repulsed. Enemy casualties totalled 17 KIA, 5 estimated WIA, and one POW.

The 140th Tank Battalion had continued in support of the 12th ROK Division on the 40th Division's right since February. June found two companies of the tank battalion positioned on four vitally strategic hills in the vicinity of Nojonp-Yong. On the first of the month there were heavy preparatory fires followed by a large attack on one of the hills near "Luke's (Luke the Gook's) Castle."

The enemy pushed the ROK infantrymen off the hills, leaving a tank platoon of Company B surrounded by North Koreans. The tanks were quickly covered by North Korean infantrymen crawling all over the tanks looking for a weak spot, but the tanks used their coaxial (mounted in the turrets beside the main gun) machine guns to shoot them off of each other. The tanks held their ground in an action that made national news. That night, another platoon of tanks fought their way forward under covering fires of two tank companies of the battalion to reinforce the beleaguered platoon. Another platoon joined those two the next morning.

The North Koreans tried to drive the tanks off the hill all day the 2nd, but the tankers refused to budge. On the morning of the 3rd, a tank-supported counterattack was launched which reestablished 12th ROK Division control of the crest and most of the hill. There were heavy attacks against the ROK's up and down the line, but the Koreans continued to hold with the aid of the tankers.

These same tankers of the 140th were to play a key role in July, when the North Koreans again attacked the 12th ROK Division the night of July 16th. Attacking in battalion strength, they were driven back with the help of strong flanking fires from the tankers. Two nights later the enemy tried it again in regimental strength, but were again driven back. In every case the determined and resolute defense of the tanks played a key role in stopping the enemy.

Like the artillery, the tankers were rarely given an opportunity for rest during the Korean War. During the war, in addition to supporting normal combat missions of the division when the division was on line, the tankers were in direct support of five different ROK Army Divisions at various times.

The division continued to occupy positions in the Punch Bowl sector until July 10th, when the division was relieved by the 20th ROK Division. On July 11th, the division relieved the 45th US Division in the Heartbreak Ridge-Sandbag Castle sector, which extended from Paem to a point west of Ihyon-ni. The 160th continued to guard prisoners on Koje-do until July 20th. On that date the 160th disembarked at Sokcho-ri and moved to the vicinity of Inje, where it passed to operational control of X US Corps as Corps reserve. The 143rd Field Artillery Battalion remained under X US Corps control in support of the 12th ROK Division, while the rest of the 40th Division Artillery continued in support of the 40th Infantry Division.

While in the Punch Bowl sector, the division was deployed with the 223rd Infantry Regiment on the right and the 224th on the left. When the division moved to the Heartbreak Ridge-Sandbag Castle area, the 223rd was emplaced on Heartbreak Ridge to the left, while the 224th was in the Sandbag Castle sector to the right.

Tanks of the 224th Infantry in the area of Sandbag Castle. July, 1953 (Source: National Archives)

In July of 1953, Company F, 223rd Infantry was directed to send a combat patrol out in front of the Punch Bowl to inflict casualties on the Chinese, and capture prisoners if possible. Second Lieutenant Richard S. Agnew was designated to lead the patrol, and the next day scheduled a daylight aerial reconnaissance.

A couple of things were obvious as Agnew and the pilot flew in the L-19 observation aircraft over Chinese lines. One was the ruggedness of the terrain. The valley north of the rim of the Punch Bowl was marked by precipitous ridges and valleys, with rocks and boulders everywhere. The terrain would be extremely difficult to traverse at night. The other was the presence and aggressiveness of the enemy. Lieutenant Agnew wanted the pilot to fly lower so he could get a good look at terrain the patrol would have to cross. As ground fire built up, the pilot refused to go any lower. When they landed after the foray, they counted over twenty bullet holes in the aircraft.

Lieutenant Agnew organized and briefed his patrol of a dozen or so infantrymen, with Corporal Gilbert G. Collier as his assistant patrol leader and point man. Observation post #322, just north of the Punch Bowl, overlooked a very steep slope leading down into the valley. The patrol left OP #322 on July 19th, after it was completely dark. Corporal Collier was leading, slowly picking his way through the tough terrain, immediately followed by Lieutenant Agnew. It was a couple of hours later when Corporal Collier suddenly lost his footing, and started to fall off the cliff. Lieutenant Agnew reached out to grab Collier and pull him back, but instead fell down the steep 60-foot cliff after him.

Another member of the patrol climbed down to them. He found the lieutenant immobilized with a badly sprained ankle, and Collier with a painful back injury, though still mobile. Lieutenant Agnew told Collier to take the patrol back before dawn broke, but Collier refused to leave his lieutenant. The other soldiers left extra grenades, .45 calibre ammunition for Collier's sub-machine gun, and .30 calibre carbine ammunition for Agnew's weapon. The main body of the patrol then returned to friendly lines without further incident.

Lieutenant Agnew and Corporal Collier could hear Chinese patrols out looking for them. As quietly as possible, they laboriously crawled up and over the steep ridge into the next valley until they reached a small creek. The two concealed themselves in some brush and then took turns keeping watch as the Chinese continued searching for them.

The next day, Agnew took off his boot and soaked his injured ankle in the creek. That night they both felt better, and decided to make an effort to return to friendly lines. Agnew's ankle was so badly swollen that he couldn't lace his boot back on, but they started back as soon as it got dark.

They were suddenly ambushed around midnight by a Chinese patrol throwing hand grenades and firing small arms. Collier moved to the left flank, yelling and shooting, as Lieutenant Agnew threw four or five hand grenades to their right. Agnew was hit by a Chinese grenade that threw him in the air and wounded him in the head, arms and leg. He felt the blood on his face as he fought the loss of consciousness. Agnew had lost his trench knife in an earlier fight, so when he was then assaulted by a Chinese soldier, he killed the soldier with the soldier's own knife.

Lieutenant Agnew said, "As the cobwebs cleared, I didn't know where Collier was. I finally found him, surrounded by several Chinese he had killed, but badly wounded with the loss of a leg. I then heard Chinese voices, and was convinced we'd had it. I pulled the pins on two grenades, and lay on my stomach with the two grenades under me. That way I could take a few with me when they rolled me over. The Chinese came up and kicked me once or twice...I don't know, because I passed out."

A patrol from Company F, complete with litter bearers, was searching for their missing comrades after dark. They finally found them, turned Agnew over, and quickly threw the grenades out of harm's way. Both were immediately evacuated through medical channels. Corporal Collier died a couple of days later, though not without asking each day about Lieutenant Agnew's health. Lieutenant Agnew spent a few hours at the battalion aid station, followed by about a week being administered to by a MASH unit. He then returned to duty. Corporal Collier received the Medal of Honor posthumously, while Lieutenant Agnew was awarded the Distinguished Service Cross. Many months later, American forces named one of their key observation posts near Panmunjom in the DMZ after Collier. The post is still used, and named after Collier, as this book is written.

The last significant combat action occurred on July 27th, just prior to the armistice going into effect. The enemy shelled friendly positions for four hours with 4700 rounds of mortar and artillery. There were few casualties and only slight damage. Division artillery responded with approximately 11,000 rounds of artillery and mortar fire. The cease fire went into effect that day, and the division prepared to withdraw to the Post Armistice Main Battle Position.

Troops of the 223rd Infantry are the last to leave Heartbreak Ridge following signing of the peace agreement. July 29, 1953 (Source: National Archives)

The division continued to maintain its special relationship to Kapyong. After the Kenneth Kaiser High School was finished, the division sought other needed projects for "their" town. In 1953, the engineers provided a progress report on construction projects in Kapyong. A church had been completed, using $4500 contributed by men of the division at Protestant church services. The engineers also built a dispensary, and helped build a grade school. While most of the work on the grade school was accomplished by the Koreans, the engineers fabricated and put up the rafters. They later also helped stock the classrooms.

On January 24, 1954 the division learned that its colors (flags) and eligible members would return to California. Planning started for a proper send-off.

In the meantime, the 578th Engineer Battalion completed construction of what was named "Sunburst Village" (or Tandongil-ri in Korean), in the farmlands of the Chorwon Valley. They dug wells for their model township, and among other buildings, constructed what became the city hall, courthouse, welfare office, middle and high schools, a county office, and the post office. A foot-and-a-half long key, engraved with the division patch and presented on May 15, 1954, is still on display in the city hall.

The division's engineers had performed many missions during their deployment to Korea, from the mundane to the extraordinary. Routine engineer work included installing and removing mines, maintaining roads, bridges and culverts, and bunker building. The engineers operated four water purification units, each capable of supplying 40,000 gallons of water per day. The engineers furnished nails, lumber, barbed wire, sniper scopes, sandbags, paint, and thousands of other engineer items daily.

Not so routine, the engineers also worked to keep the troops warm during the freezing winters. They fabricated 46 charcoal kilns, and produced an average of 6000 pounds of charcoal daily to warm front line bunkers. The division engineers also operated a sawmill, furnishing lumber for the many construction projects, as well as building the spectacular tramways for resupply in steep terrain.

The Final Review of the 40th Infantry Division in Korea was conducted at the Division Review Field on May 8, 1954. The setting was unusual, as a series of seven tableaux had been created as a back drop.

The tableaux for the final review represented:
> The Punch Bowl, and was sponsored by the 578th Engineer Battalion
> Heartbreak Ridge, sponsored by 223rd Infantry Regiment
> Sandbag Castle, sponsored by the 224th Infantry Regiment
> Kumwha (Papa-San), sponsored by the Division Artillery
> Chorwon, sponsored by the 160th Infantry Regiment
> Eighth Army Patch, sponsored by the 578th Engineer Battalion
> The Rose Bowl (in California), sponsored by the 578th Engineer Battalion

In addition to the tableaux plus the normal formation of major commands, a group called "The California Contingent" was formed at the end of the parade field. The California Contingent, consisting of approximately 1200 officers and men, were those scheduled to return the colors, standards and records to California. The commander of the group was Colonel Louis V. Hightower.

There were many distinguished guests who participated in this final ceremony. While waiting for them to arrive at 2:00 p.m., there were two exhibitions. One was by a Scout Dog Platoon, and the other was an exhibition drill by a platoon of the Provisional Honor Guard Company. The distinguished guests arrived to Ruffles and Flourishes, followed by a 21 gun salute. Speakers included President Syngman Rhee, who awarded the division the Republic of Korea Presidential Unit Citation. General Maxwell D. Taylor, Commanding General of Eighth Army, also spoke to the troops, lauding their combat record.

After the reviewing party trooped the line, there was a color ceremony in which the United Nations and Republic of Korea Army colors were turned over to honor guards. The Division Colors were turned over to Colonel Hightower, and the division passed in review for the final time in Korea. The division's colors paraded with battle streamers for the Second Korean Winter; Korea, Summer-Fall 1952; Third Korean Winter; and Korea Summer-Fall

1953, in addition to the Republic of Korea Presidential Unit Citation. It was a fitting goodbye ceremony for the division.

In Korea, the division had:

342	Days of combat
376	Men killed in combat
1457	Wounded in action (and actually hospitalized)
3	Medals of Honor awarded
9	Distinguished Service Crosses awarded
246	Silver Stars awarded
675	Bronze Stars for valor awarded
1783	Bronze Stars for merit awarded
3110	Commendation Ribbons awarded

A silver punch bowl played a key role in many ceremonies after the war. Major General Ridgley Gaither had contracted with a Tokyo silversmith to craft a special punch bowl modeled on the "Punch Bowl," where the division had fought, and suffered, so many casualties. The natural bowl was formed several thousand yards in diameter, with a sandy floor, and a rim of sharp mountains with decomposed granite on all sides. The two main roads bisecting the floor of the bowl were named "Hollywood" and "Vine" by the division.

The artisan was given a relief map, and told what was desired. He then crafted a replica of the "Punch Bowl," which was delivered with a ladle to the division several months later in a handsome, leather-tooled box.

The first ceremony involving the punch bowl in the continental United States occurred in June of 1954. Camp Stoneman was hosting the returning soldiers for demobilization processing. A reception and buffet, honoring the officers of the 40th U.S. and 40th National Guard Divisions, was conducted in the Officers' Club at Friday, June 18th. Brigadier General William J. Bradley presented, on behalf of his 40th U.S. Division officers, the silver punch bowl. Major General Homer O. Eaton Jr., commander of the 40th N.G. Division, accepted the punch bowl. Dancing followed in the club which had been decorated for the occasion.

The division's battle flags were officially returned to the United States in impressive ceremonies the next day. Hosted in the City of San Francisco, 1,156 returning officers and men marched up Market Street behind their Commanding General, General Bradley. They followed behind the Sixth Army Band and honor guard in chrome plated helmets, and parade marshal Major General William F. Dean. General Dean was a former California Guardsman who earned the Medal of Honor in Korea as Commanding General of the 24th Infantry Division before being captured by the North Koreans. Token elements representing the Navy, Marines, and Air Force followed.

In the grandstand were Governor Goodwin J. Knight; General Matthew B. Ridgway, Chief of Staff of the Army; and several other dignitaries, as well as General Eaton. Actor Walter Pidgeon narrated events for the public. The troops marched up Market to the sound of applause from the crowds lining the street, but the crowd burst into cheers when the troops rounded the Civic Center Plaza.

The troops formed in the plaza for the ceremony, and then the dignitaries took their positions. General Bradley passed the colors to the Sixth U.S. Army Commander, Lieutenant General W. G. Wyman saying, "These are the colors of the Fortieth Infantry Division...hold them high and guard them well." General Wyman passed them to the Governor while saying "Preserve it...cherish it...guard it!" The Governor replied simply, "We shall." He in turn passed them to General Eaton, who then gave them to his aide-de-camp, Captain James F. Battin, II.

That solemn ceremony marked the end of the 40th "Sunburst" Division, and the short period when there were two 40th Divisions. The flag passed to the 40th "Grizzly" Division.

This ceremony not only marked the end of the 40th Division's combat campaign in Korea, but marked the end of an extraordinary period in which two 40th Divisions existed.

In the spring of 1952, the division had been told while in Korea, that it would be reorganized as a "cadre organization" in California with 50% officers and 25% enlisted men. The division had 421 National Guard of the United States officers due to be released by August 31, 1952, plus 2990 enlisted men with enlistments to complete in the California National Guard. They were to form the nucleus of the new 40th Infantry Division in California.

The division had 62 armories for 111 units when it was called to service in 1950. In March of 1952 there were still 24 state-owned and 12 leased armories for a total of 36. It was felt it would be comparatively easy to hire Unit Caretakers (Property Custodians) because their starting pay had just been raised to $260 per month.

The new 40th National Guard division was organized and federally recognized with headquarters in Los Angeles on September 2, 1952. Brigadier General (later Major General) Homer O. Eaton, Jr. was named division commander. General Eaton had been executive officer of the 160th Infantry during most of its Pacific campaigning in World War II. He later was intelligence officer (G-2) of XIV Corps. He won the Silver Star for gallantry during the crossing of the Passig River at Manila, and the Bronze Star during the Luzon campaign.

While combat continued with the 40th U. S. Division in Korea, the reorganization of the 40th National Guard Division continued and strength grew in California   A unique and unparalleled relationship developed between the two divisions.

National Guardsmen who had rotated back kept in touch with old comrades as well as new soldiers who had replaced them in Korea. They were very much interested in the Kapyong project, which many of them had helped start. Even those who weren't remembered vividly the plight of Korea's children.

In Kapyong, the division had only partially solved a larger problem. Korea had been so badly devastated that the citizens of Kapyong were barely surviving. The division had given the citizens a beautiful high school, but the nearby grammar school only had a makeshift building of four mud-walled rooms and thatched roof, supplemented by four damaged squad tents. Fifteen teachers were trying to teach 1,160 students with less than a dozen textbooks and only a handful of pencils.

The division had provided a modern facility for the older children, and had even equipped a first aid room in the school with medical supplies. They also provided the school with a school bus, actually a converted and overhauled enemy truck. Financial contributions continued to be solicited from the soldiers to assist. However, it was obvious to all that much more needed to be done. The 40th U. S. Division became busily engaged in assisting the Armed Forces Aid to Korea program which aimed at helping the South Koreans rebuild their war-torn country.

The 40th National Guard Division's Adjutant General, Lieutenant Colonel William B. Henderson, took a particular interest. He proposed that the stateside division adopt the Kapyong School project as one of its own, and the division commander quickly agreed. Major General Eaton told Major General Gaither in Korea that "your stateside counterpart would take the greatest pride in assisting your projects." General Eaton proposed that the stateside division collect clothing, books, sports equipment and other items needed by the school. General Gaither quickly accepted the offer, and the division mounted a huge collection effort.

The division's 43 armories became collecting points where people brought clothing, canned food, pencils, erasers, paper, school books and other supplies. Such personalities as popular Los Angeles disc jockey Johnny Grant, who had a long history of supporting the 40th, got behind the effort. He also helped arrange for the involvement of other entertainers, such as Penny Singleton and Roscoe Ates. Additional publicity was provided by two half-hour television shows on the popular series "Before Your Eyes" that were devoted exclusively to the project.

The drive came to an end in early April, 1954. This jointly-produced and record-breaking contribution assured that the 40th Division would long be remembered for its role in Korea. More than 200 tons of needed school materials and clothing had been turned in to the armories. Schoolbooks alone required over 1,500 large crates for the more than 70,000 texts. In addition to the schoolbooks and clothing, over 10,000 cans of food and a great deal of athletic gear was collected. The Pacific Far East Lines was a big help, and their freighter Indian Bear departed Long Beach Harbor on April 24th for Pusan, Korea. Arrangements had been made with officers of Armed Forces Assistance for Korea to deliver the goods from Pusan to city fathers in Kapyong for needed distribution. That coordination was needed because the 40th United States Division was preparing to leave Korea.

No estimate was ever made of the cash value of the shipment. Men of the 40th Division had contributed over $200,000 to various charitable projects while they were in Korea. Support for the Kapyong School continued for many years after the war. General Cleland's widow made at least one trip after the war. Various division commanders visited the school, as recently as 1988, and occasionally delivered additional cash contributions from soldiers of the division. The school is in a beautiful and prosperous resort area, and the school's athletic teams are renowned, especially for bicycle racing.

The division is proud of its combat record in Korea. Soldiers of the 40th are just as gratified by their contributions to the civilians of Korea, most especially the children.

Division soldiers of Task Force Grizzly in an observation post on the border with Mexico looking for drug smugglers. 1988 (Photo: The author's collection)

326

CHAPTER FOURTEEN

POST KOREA TO PRESENT

The first summer encampment following their combat tour in Korea was conducted the following August 16-30, 1953 at Hunter Liggett Military Reservation. There were 1,940 troops in attendance.

At a staff meeting on July 1, 1954, Major General Eaton announced to the staff that the division was to be reorganized and redesignated as the 40th Armored Division. The Fortieth conducted its first summer encampment as an armored division again at HLMR, and again during the last two weeks of August. The division's strength had more than doubled since the previous year, with 4,658 troops attending.

The 1955 encampment was conducted August 13-27th at Camp Roberts. As an armored division, they had received four new self-propelled 155mm howitzers and five dual 40mm AA guns. For the first time that most of the soldiers could remember, they were housed under roofs at Camp Roberts rather than the canvas they were used to at HLMR, Camp San Luis Obispo, Yosemite and Del Monte. There were a total of 5,483 troops in attendance.

The Reserve Forces Act of 1955 was enacted by Congress to improve readiness of the Reserve Components. The legislation had a tremendous impact on the National Guard. Troops without prior service were to attend basic and advanced individual training before joining the ranks, and would have a shorter overall term of enlistment. The program was to be voluntary, but not enough troops were volunteering. The program was then made mandatory, and by 1958, all men joining the National Guard went through basic training, performing about six months active duty.

The division was called for civilian emergencies twice in one week in January, 1956. On Sunday, January 22nd, a two-car high speed Santa Fe passenger train had just left Los Angeles' Union Station bound for San Diego when it was derailed. Initial reports were sketchy, but it was clear there was great loss of life.

The 40th Signal Company had been conducting range practice at the Irvine Range in Orange County. They had just returned to their armory on Hope Street to clean and store weapons and equipment. At 6:05 p.m. they got the word about the train wreck, and were on the scene within twenty-five minutes to aid the police.

When the Guardsmen arrived, they found authorities struggling with a grisly scene involving mangled bodies scattered along two hundred yards of track. The toll was 30 people killed and over 130 others injured. The police used the troops to form a cordon around the traumatic scene. The troops found themselves keeping the morbidly curious away, as well as some looters who were trying to take personal belongings. They used their trucks to help move some of the bodies to the morgue. Guardsmen remained on duty until 11:30 p.m. that night.

That disaster was quickly followed by a freak eight inch downpour of rain the night of January 24th, which quickly flooded low-lying areas in Los Angeles County. On Wednesday, January 25th, calls for assistance commenced pouring into division headquarters, as the rain continued.

The situation in Torrance is typical of what was happening all over the area. Torrance's Civil Defense Director called the first sergeant of Torrance's Company E, 132nd Armored Engineer Battalion. When the first sergeant heard how serious the problem was, he phoned his company commander at his civilian job. The two of them then accompanied the director to look at the situation. An hour later they had two heavy trucks with winches working on a volunteer basis to pull debris from the Dominguez flood channel. Weary troops went home for rest just before midnight.

Early Thursday morning, it was obvious the situation was not under control, so Torrance's city manager formally requested assistance. Company E was formed up at the armory shortly after 7:00 a.m. Trucks were sent out, sometimes through water up to six feet deep, to clear culverts and flood channels, evacuate stranded families, and guard evacuated areas from looters. Things were under control by Friday, and the troops were released.

The 132nd Engineers used two companies to assist the communities of Manhattan Beach and Torrance. The battalion had a total of about ninety officers and men on duty.

Other units were also involved. Drivers from the 980th Field Artillery Battalion took eight trucks to assist Civil Defense authorities. They transported materials and first aid supplies through mud in the vicinity of Sierra Madre, and evacuated civilian personnel. Some of Arcadia's artillerymen from the 215th Armored Field Artillery Battalion were also used to evacuate storm-stranded civilians. Guardsmen from the 111th Reconnaissance Battalion of Inglewood used heavy vehicles to transport nurses and other key personnel.

In 1956, the 40th Armored Division conducted its summer field training camp at Camp Roberts August 11-25th. By then the strength of the division had risen to 7,053. The strength of the division was growing rapidly, and it was decided to split the division into two training sites for 1957. Most of the division trained at Camp Roberts August 11-25th. However, Combat Command C, the 133rd and 139th Tank Battalions, and the 217th Anti-Aircraft Artillery (AAA) Battalion trained at Camp Irwin in the desert of San Bernardino County August 10-24th, 1957.

When the division was reorganized following the Korean War, there had been a great shortage of officers, especially junior officers. The state OCS program, called the California Military Academy, was organized in 1950, graduating their first class in 1951. By 1957 the program had grown significantly, with candidate companies in Sacramento, Fresno, Alameda, Ontario, and San Diego. Second lieutenants were also being produced by Army special OCS courses, infantry out of Fort Benning, Georgia, and artillery out of Fort Sill, Oklahoma.

The fifties saw a renewal of interest in weapons marksmanship. Most regiments had shooting teams, and composite teams from California participated in the National Matches at Camp Perry, Ohio. Teams fired at regional matches at Fort Ord, California, and in Hawaii. In 1958, the division was split into three increments for annual field training. Most of the division trained at Camp Roberts August 10-24th. The 140th Tank Battalion trained at Camp Irwin July 5-19th, while the 134th Tank Battalion trained at Camp Irwin August 9-23rd, 1958.

The troops at Camp Roberts were able to take advantage of a tank trail that ran through several large ranches, connecting with HLMR. Hunter Liggett did not have the large cantonment area with barracks found at Camp Roberts, but had huge maneuver and impact areas for tank gunnery and artillery firing. Troops in 1958 participated in weapons competitions. They also had many sports competitions to choose from, including boxing, swimming, basketball, softball, volleyball, bowling, and a two mile cross country run. The annual parade was conducted at Camp Roberts on Saturday, August 16th.

In 1959, the division directed that henceforth, all troops were to be qualified on their individual weapons during the training year rather than at Annual Training. This would permit the troops to concentrate on crew-served weapons and unit rather than individual training at Annual Training.

The division underwent a reorganization in what was called ROCAD (Reorganization of the Current Armored Division) effective July 1st, 1959. The maneuver elements of the division then consisted of the 2-160th Infantry, 2-185th Armor, and 5-185th Armor Battalions in Combat Command A, the 1-160th Infantry, 1-185th Armor, and 4-185th Armor Battalions in Combat Command B; and the 3-185th Reconnaissance Squadron with the 3-160th Infantry and 4-160th Infantry Battalions in Combat Command C.

Most of the 40th Armored Division trained at Camp Roberts and HLMR on August 15-29, 1959. Combat Command A trained at Camp Irwin August 16-30th, and Combat Command B trained at Camp Irwin July 11-25th.

Brigadier General Charles O. Ott Jr. assumed command of the division on July 3rd, 1960, and was promoted to Major General on August 15th of that year. General Ott was an artilleryman who had been an honor graduate from Stanford University ROTC late in 1941, and whose early service included a stint with one of the last horse-drawn artillery outfits at Fort Ord in 1942. His World War II combat started with the Normandy beachhead through service in France, Belgium. Germany and Czechoslovakia, where he ended the war as an Artillery Group Executive Officer.

When the 40th Division was reconstituted following the war, he organized the 981st Field Artillery in Santa Barbara. During the Korean War, he was promoted to Colonel and served as the Division Artillery Executive Officer. He had been promoted to brigadier general on September 1, 1952, at the extraordinarily young age of 31, serving as the Division Artillery Commander and then Assistant Division Commander.

The division was split into four increments for its Annual Training in 1960. Most of the 40th Armored Division was at Camp Roberts (and Hunter Liggett) July 30th through August 13th. Combat Command A trained at Camp Irwin July 9th through the 23rd, Combat Command B at Camp Irwin July 23rd through August 6th, and Combat Command C at Camp Irwin August 6-20th.

In 1961, Camp Irwin was redesignated Fort Irwin, acknowledging the importance of this 1,200 square mile post, which was the Desert Training Center for many armored troops in World War II, and which later became the National Training Center. Troops training at Fort Irwin that year included Combat Command B from July 22 through August 5th, and various elements of the division from August 19th through September 2nd. Most of the division trained at the Camp Roberts-HLMR complex. The bulk of the division was reviewed at Camp Roberts by California's Governor Edmund G. (Pat) Brown on Saturday, August 26th.

Major General Ott had a different approach with his General's Mess. He would traditionally invite six outstanding company commanders to join him at the mess, and would elicit their input. For the table he had a small flag fabricated with the division patch flanked by captain's bars and armor brass, and inscribed "Company Commander's Table" and the Latin inscription for "Cavalrymen of the night."

In 1962 the Army moved to reduce the number of divisions. The Army Reserve was tabbed to lose four, and the National Guard lost the 34th, 35th, 43rd, and 51st, which were to be converted to brigades. More resources would then be diverted to some of the remaining divisions to improve their readiness. The plan stalled under Congressional opposition. Annual training for 1962 would be primarily at Camp Roberts-HLMR, with Combat Commands A and C training at Fort Irwin.

In 1963 the division converted to the ROAD (Reorganization Objectives Army Divisions) configuration prior to the summer 1963 Annual Active Duty for Training (ANACDUTRA). The reorganization was designed to use "building blocks" of infantry, mechanized and armor battalions for use in specific geographical areas or tactical roles, attached to Headquarters, 1st, 2nd and 3rd Brigades. The "combat command" designation was dropped. The division's aviation company expanded to the 140th Aviation Battalion, an aviation maintenance company was added to the 40th Maintenance Battalion, a sky (aircraft) cavalry troop was added to the 1-111th Reconnaissance Squadron, and the 5-144th Missile Artillery Battalion with Honest John rockets was organized.

Annual Active Duty Training (ANACDUTRA) for the 40th Armored Division base and First Brigade was conducted at Camp Roberts, with the Division Artillery at HLMR. The Second and

Third Brigades, along with 1st Reconnaissance Squadron, 18th Cavalry, conducted their ANACDUTRA at Fort Irwin.

In 1964, California's Adjutant General's Office published guidance on civil disturbance training requiring orientation and refresher training on crowd control and riot prevention. This training was actually started in the division the previous year by General Ott, and was to prove valuable during the next year.

Exercise DESERT STRIKE, the first large scale armor exercise conducted since World War II, was conducted May 17th through 30th. The exercise involved about 100,000 soldiers from III and XVIII Corps, and the 1st and 2nd Armored Divisions, the 5th Mechanized Division, and the 101st Airborne Division. The Air Force was also a major player.

The exercise was designed to test communications and air-ground cooperation, and the use of nuclear weapons. The maneuver area involved about 13,000,000 desert acres bounded by Fort Irwin and Kingman, Arizona in the north, and Blythe and Twenty-Nine Palms in the south. Unlike many exercises which are carefully scripted, Desert Strike was a free play exercise and had no phase lines or set patterns.

The Second Brigade of the 40th Armored Division, commanded by Colonel Alvin E. Howell, with a strength of 3,407 officers and men, participated in Annual Field Training (AFT) status. They acted as the aggressor. The Regular Army was a little unhappy with the Guardsmen, who used "Indian tactics" to capture sentries and tank crews outside of their vehicles, cutting down their armor strength considerably.

In 1964, AFT 1964 was conducted with most of the 40th Armored Division at Camp Roberts and HLMR. The 1st Brigade was at Fort Irwin, as was the 2nd Brigade who pulled their AFT earlier while participating in Desert Strike.

The City of Los Angeles burst into flames August 11th, 1965, following what started as a rather routine traffic stop early that evening on Avalon Boulevard near 116th Place. The California

Highway Patrol stopped 21-year-old Marquette Frye and his older brother Ronald in their mother's 1955 Buick one block from their home. What should have been a routine arrest of Marquette for driving under the influence of alcohol rapidly grew out of control.

Lieutenant Colonel Donald D. McClanahan was Fire Marshal for the City of Pasadena when the riots broke out. He immediately went to division headquarters on Hope Street in Los Angeles. Assigned as the G-5 of the division, he was made the acting G-3. He climbed to the roof and could see fires being set and spreading out of control. He then proposed to the senior staff officer present that the division stop the brigade that was then on the road heading north for annual training at Camp Roberts.

Chief of Police William H. Parker's office reported the situation was under control the morning of August 13th, but they expected things to get worse by that evening. The National Guard was alerted then to be ready by 7:00 p.m. Chief Parker complained that he asked for the National Guard at 11:00 a.m. and couldn't understand why the Lieutenant Governor had not acted.

The division had to wait for an official request for assistance from the civilian authorities to come through the Governor's office, and that took unconscionably long to occur. The Governor was in Greece, with Lieutenant Governor Glenn Anderson then acting as Governor. Lieutenant Governor Anderson appeared rather indecisive, so there was a considerable delay before any requests for assistance came down. There was considerable speculation that the division was allowed to continue on to Camp Roberts so the situation would get worse, and this would be of great assistance in the election of Ronald Reagan as California's new governor.

There was sniper fire everywhere when the Guardsmen were finally called. The National Guard was ordered into the city five hours after Los Angeles Police Chief William H. Parker made the request. Lieutenant Governor Glenn M. Anderson signed the order in his Los Angeles office at 5:15 p.m. on August 13th.

Later, when McClanahan was serving in the Pentagon, he had the opportunity to relate the foregoing to then Congressman Anderson. The Congressman agreed in retrospect that he should have acted sooner.

When the division was given the call, they acted quickly. First employed on August 13th, they spread over the city, working closely with the Los Angeles Police Department. Colonel Irving J. Taylor, commander of the second brigade and a police officer in civilian life, coordinated the effort from the Police Department field command post. By the fourth day, 63 police, 17 firemen, and two Guardsmen had been injured. Two of at least three people killed by Guardsmen were Negroes who drove through barricades. One was a female, riddled with at least twenty rounds of machine gun fire.

Troops were used to aid law enforcement personnel reestablish law and order in curfew areas; providing armed security for fire stations and fire fighting crews at scenes of fires. They helped public utility crews restore utilities in the riot areas, various agency personnel distribute food stuffs in riot area, manned roadblocks in curfew areas, and provided security for jails housing arrested rioters and courts trying offenders. In Long Beach, firemen were chased out of the riot area and prevented from putting out the fires. Division soldiers then began riding "shotgun," and the trouble stopped.

Several Guardsmen were injured during the riots. One was seriously injured when a car ran a roadblock and into a line of Guardsmen. He was Sergeant Wayne Stewart, 21, of Company A 4-160th Infantry, who had his leg broken. The driver was killed and his accomplice captured. Those injured during the riots totalled 73 Los Angeles police, 5 other police, 37 firemen, 4 military, and 693 citizens. A total of 34 people were killed.

During the riots of 1965, 13,393 troops of the 40th and 49th Divisions were employed until they were released on August 24th. A total of 65,858 man days were expended.

AFT 1965 was conducted with the entire division at Camp Roberts-HLMR with the exception of most of the 132nd Engineer Battalion, which trained at Camp San Luis Obispo.

In September of 1965, the Selected Reserve Force was organized under the direction of the Department of the Army. The intention was to designate certain units for a special category that would reduce to a minimum the time required to mobilize, complete training and deploy anywhere in the world. Administrative and logistical actions were to be accomplished permitting those Selected Reserve Force (the acronym "SRF" was pronounced "surf") units to be mobilized and report to mobilization stations after a seven day alert.

The SRF training objective was to complete a battalion level Army Training Test by the end of field training 1966. To accomplish their new mission, units were authorized 6 additional training assemblies per quarter in addition to the 48 authorized per training year, making a total of 72 training periods.

The 40th Armored Division supplied 2,225 men to that newly created SRF component, called "super ready force" by many of the troops. Part of a three division, three brigade basic force, augmented by other units, the 40th Armored Division units designated for the Selected Reserve Force included the 4-160th Infantry Battalion, the 29th Aviation Company, Troop E, 111th Cavalry, and the 1st Squadron, 18th Cavalry. The twelve units of the 40th Armored Division were designated to become SRF units on November 1st, 1965, and to be part of the 29th Infantry Brigade (Separate)(SRF) Hawaii National Guard. Many equipment shortages, especially signal equipment, were filled by April of 1966. Completing physical examinations and producing identification cards for all soldiers turned out to be the most difficult administrative requirement.

In 1966, there was concern there might be a repetition of riots in the Watts area in the month of March. Five hundred troops were placed on standby. Troops from the 1-160th Infantry, 3-160th Infantry, and the 4-160th Infantry Battalions, as well as the 1-18th

Cavalry Squadron were called on March 15th, and released one day later.

In 1966, most of the 40th Armored Division conducted AFT at Camp Roberts from August 13th to 27th. The Division Artillery was at Twenty-Nine Palms, and the 1st Brigade at Fort Irwin, on the same dates. The 2nd Brigade was at Fort Irwin on June 18th through July 2nd.

By 1967, the division consisted of 106 company-sized units in 55 communities, from Atascadero in the North to San Diego in the South, to El Centro and Barstow inland. In that year, the Division base and 1st Brigade were at Camp Roberts, the Division Artillery at Twenty Nine Palms, and the 3rd Brigade at Fort Irwin, all during the middle two weeks of August. The 2nd Brigade trained during their AFT at Fort Irwin in July. During the middle weekend at Camp Roberts, the division conducted a review on the morning of August 19th, with Lieutenant Governor Robert H. Finch acting as the Reviewing Officer. The training at Camp Roberts included riot control, using three lieutenants who were also Los Angeles Police Officers wearing their police uniforms. They were provided a police car by Los Angeles Police Department Chief Tom Redden to help in playing their role.

There was considerable concern about the low numbers of blacks in the National Guard nationwide, a subject that was being actively discussed in Congress and the Pentagon. Part of this was driven by the riots of 1965-67 around the nation, and accusations that the National Guard used too much force. Major General Ott, as commander of the 40th Armored Division at the time, testified before a House Armed Services subcommittee on the subject. There was a proposal to add 5% over strength to units if they would fill the slots with blacks. Major General Ott was opposed to that.

General Ott, in his testimony of August 25, 1967, favored a deliberate approach to increasing the number of Negroes. He acknowledged that the Guard had only 1.97% Negroes, but opposed "such 'rush moves' as a Pentagon directive that would permit the New Jersey Guard to rise 5% if they could enlist 700 blacks to fill those slots." He did say however, that he thought the Guard should have more Negroes.

He also talked about riot control training that had started in the division in 1963, pointing out that much of the standard riot training dealt with handling and dispersing large mobs, but that did not apply to Watts and other big city disorders. Regarding the National Guards' ability to fight riots, General Ott stated the Army's lesson plans were not realistic with such doctrine as using fire hoses to disperse mobs. He noted that all hose and fire hydrants were in use during the rioting in Watts as fire departments fought major fires.

General Ott also said the training placed too much emphasis on dispersing mobs, in spite of sniping and looters being the major problem. He said the best training was "sound individual basic training for the soldier." His experience-based testimony matched the lessons learned during the Los Angeles riots in 1992, twenty five years later.

The division's flag with its battle streamers was again furled in 1968. This occurred as the result of a study initiated by Secretary of Defense Robert McNamara, after which he directed that many divisions be eliminated. The 40th Armored Division was reorganized and redesignated as the 40th Armored Brigade on January 29, 1968. In addition, the 40th and 49th Infantry Brigades were organized using elements of the division.

General Ott's tenure as commander had spanned almost eight years. He had rotated key assignments in the division every two or three years to maximize opportunities and capabilities. The division's strength, and the status of training and maintenance, were well above accepted norms in spite of routine limitations in time and resources available.

The Vietnam War was primarily fought by the U. S. Army from 1964 to 1972. In spite of the Army's need to grow significantly to fight that war, very few National Guard and Reserve units were mobilized. A couple of former 40th Division units were activated for Vietnam service. The 40th Aviation Company was activated to augment the rapid expansion of aviation assets during the war. In addition, the 1-18th Cavalry Squadron, commanded by Lieutenant Colonel Robert F. Brainard, was also activated.

The Cavalry Squadron was activated on May 13, 1968, and sent to Fort Lewis, Washington. To the consternation of the Army, the 1-18th was organized differently than they expected. The Guardsmen were just as frustrated. One of the attractions to service in the National Guard is the commitment that troops will serve in combat with their buddies, often buddies who enlisted at the same time. Unfortunately, the Army used the 1-18th Cavalry troopers as replacement fillers in other units. Many of the troopers protested this treatment, to no avail. What was left of the unit was released from Federal service on December 12, 1969.

The Vietnam conflict was a disastrous period for the U. S. Army, which saw discipline, morale, and combat effectiveness plummet by the end of the war. The problem was recognized by the Secretary of Defense, Melvin R. Laird, who commissioned a study in 1970. The results were disseminated in 1973 by his successor, James Schlesinger. The Total Force Concept ("concept" later became "doctrine") stated that the National Guard and Reserve would be considered full partners with the Active Forces and others in all aspects of planning, programming, manning, equipping and employing forces.

General Creighton W. Abrams, Sr. was working quietly addressing the problem in the Pentagon during those years. He had faced the problems in the latter years of the Vietnam War, and eventually became Chief of Staff of the Army. His doctrine, which came to be called The Abrams Doctrine, stated that the United States should never again go to war without substantial use of the National Guard and Reserve. He then went on to build an Army that couldn't deploy without its Reserve Components. In fact,

100% of some required capabilities were exclusively in the Reserve Components.

The Office of the Secretary Defense (OSD) also initiated a Reserve Component Study in 1971 to determine ways to increase readiness. Twelve different tests were designed, many of them funded and implemented. One involved elements of the California National Guard who were destined to return to the division when reorganized in 1974. That test, dubbed OSD Test 3, was to determine if battalion level proficiency was attainable and maintainable if Reserve Component units were closely associated with and supported by Active Army units.

The test units selected to receive significant help from the 4th Infantry Division (Mechanized) were the 4th Battalion, 160th Infantry (M); the 2nd Battalion, 185th Armor; and the 2nd Battalion, 144th Field Artillery (155 SP). The control units to receive no help were the 2nd Battalion, 185th Infantry (M) (years later redesignated 1st Battalion, 184th Infantry); 1st Battalion, 185th Armor; and 1st Battalion, 180th Field Artillery of the Arizona National Guard.

The unit levels of proficiency were measured in 1972 in a series of Army Training Tests at Fort Irwin. The test battalions' weaknesses were addressed, primarily through the use of Mobile Training Teams from the 4th Division in eleven visits over the next year. The control battalions received no outside help.

The units were tested again in 1973 to determine the level of proficiency. It was found that the Active Army assistance was generally not a significant factor. All battalions improved, with control battalions improving as much as the test battalions due to competitive factors and the exceptionally high quality of the evaluation procedures. The units gained from 2 to 5.39 weeks of proficiency during the year. Most interesting, at the end of the evaluation it was found that no battalion would require more than seven additional weeks of training to achieve battalion level proficiency. That figure included four weeks of tank gunnery that would be required following mobilization.

The 40th Infantry Division returned as a mechanized infantry division on January 13, 1974 with its headquarters located in Long Beach. The division was reconstituted after the National Guard Bureau decided to move the authorization for a mechanized division (the 30th of Georgia, North Carolina, and South Carolina) to California, with an authorized strength of 14,700 soldiers. The 40th Infantry, 40th Armored, and 49th Infantry Brigades were dissolved (with the authorizations going to other states) to provide the trained troops. Major General Charles A. Ott. Jr. was designated to again command the division. Brigadier Generals Robert E. Johnson, Jr., commanding the 40th Infantry Brigade, and James T. Keltner, commanding the 49th Infantry Brigade, were named as Assistant Division Commanders.

Major General Thomas K. Turnage replaced Major General Ott in command of the division effective August 12, 1974. General Ott immediately left for a four year tour as Director of the Army National Guard, serving in the Pentagon.

General Turnage earned his commission in 1942 when he graduated from ROTC at Allen Military Academy. He served as an infantry platoon leader in the 97th Division during combat in Europe, and a company commander during occupation duties in Japan 1945-46. He joined the Fortieth Division while attending college following World War II. Activated with the division for the Korean War, he served as an Infantry Battalion Operations Officer and Executive Officer. He served at all levels of command and staff in the division, including Chief of Staff.

National Guard units were suffering the after effects of the Vietnam years. The Total Army was at a low ebb in morale and readiness, suffering from the backlash of drugs and "fragging" scandals, and the My Lai Massacre, as well as the general unpopularity of the Vietnam war. The quality of recruits in the Army and the National guard was slipping, and strength levels in the National Guard were to drop with the end of conscription in 1973.

General Turnage considered General Ott his mentor, having earlier been one of his subordinates for many years, and tried to emulate him in many ways. As a consequence, there was little if any change in command philosophy. There continued to be emphasis on training excellence, and combat readiness continued to improve. Considerable resources had to be diverted to improve strength.

One example of some of the innovative training conducted in 1974 was the 1-184th Infantry Battalion's participation in amphibious exercises in June of that year. Navy landing craft from the Amphibious School in Coronado, just outside of San Diego, landed the troops.

The strength of the division was 13,756 in 1975. For annual training that year, most of the division trained at either Camp Roberts or Fort Irwin. In addition the 240th Signal Battalion trained at Fort Lewis and Company E of the 540th Maintenance Battalion maintained divisional aircraft at the Los Alamitos Army Air Field. The division started taking Army Training Tests during the sixties. By 1975, twenty one units took the arduous test in just that one year. In addition, thirteen battalions plus the support command participated in command post or field training exercises. By this time, the division had stopped conducting an annual parade, an inspiring spectacle, but one that required a good deal of time and resources that detracted from other training and combat readiness.

Major General Robert E. Johnson, Jr. assumed command of the division on August 28, 1975, when General Turnage was called to Sacramento to serve as the Deputy Commanding General of the Army National Guard.

The division in 1976 had grown to 670 tracked vehicles stored in the equipment pools, primarily Camp Roberts and Fort Irwin. There were also 2180 wheeled vehicles and 65 aircraft in addition to 1222 major weapons systems. Annual training was conducted at the Camp Roberts/HLMR training complex and at Fort Irwin. Emphasis was on MOS, crew and squad training. There were live fire exercises. The armor units worked at transitioning into the M48A5 tank. The artillery was taking diagnostic Army Training and Evaluation Program (ARTEP) tests. Most of the division did their training in a field environment.

Major General James T. Keltner assumed command of the division from General Johnson on October 4th, 1976. General Keltner had joined the 36th Infantry Division of the Texas National Guard in 1940. He served with that unit and in the China-Burma-India Theater in World War II. Most of his service in the California National Guard was with the 49th Infantry Division while that division existed. When the 40th Division was reconstituted in 1974, he joined the division as Assistant Division Commander.

There continued to be an erosion of strength after the Vietnam era. Many troopers had enlisted to avoid the draft. By 1977, half of the units were experiencing serious strength problems. There was great emphasis during General Keltner's tenure in eliminating the many non-participating soldiers, generally called "deadwood", and in maintaining strength. He also pushed for more reliance and confidence in noncommissioned officers at all levels. The annual division ball was reinstituted, a tradition that continues to this day, playing a role in improved esprit and camaraderie.

On November 7, 1977, General Turnage returned to command of the division. The situation had changed since he left the division. During his first tour, his emphasis was on training and readiness, with strength maintenance a secondary concern. Now he found a need to concentrate resources on improving declining strength, a problem still plaguing the National Guard nationwide under what came to be called the "Vietnam Syndrome."

In September 1978 there had been reports of weapons being hidden by prisoners on the grounds of the Tehachapi Corrections Facility in Southern California. There was even a report that a .38 caliber pistol had been hidden. As a result, the California Department of Corrections asked the National Guard for help in locating the weapons. General Turnage sent in the 132nd Engineers with eight mine detectors the night of September 12th and early morning the 13th. They started early that morning. They found no pistol, but did find numerous weapons including five homemade knives, one axe head, and several clubs including six bars or pipes.

Brigadier General Robert L. Meyer moved up to acting commander of the division on June 10, 1979. General Turnage shortly moved on to Washington, DC. There he served in a series of important assignments. These included work in the Office of Reserve Affairs, Department of Defense; serving as Director of Selective Service; and culminating his distinguished career as Administrator of Veterans Affairs.

General Meyer had served in World War II as an enlisted soldier with the 214th Field Artillery Group in Europe. He joined the 40th Infantry Division on the day it was activated in October 1946. Less than a year later, he received his commission as a Second Lieutenant in the Adjutant General Corps. He was activated with the division for the Korean War, serving as Chief of the Personnel Division. He served with the division until it was inactivated in 1968, later commanding the 40th Armored Brigade (Separate). When the division was reactivated in 1974, he commanded the First Brigade until being named Assistant Division Commander in September 11, 1974. He was officially named division commander on November 8, 1979, and was promoted to Major General the following January 24th.

Like his predecessors, General Meyer found strength to be his greatest problem when he assumed command. Recruiting was bringing soldiers in the front door, but they were going out the back door due to poor retention. This heavy turn-over in the junior enlisted ranks presented significant training challenges, and as many of these soldiers disappeared, some of their individual equipment disappeared with them. There also were shortages in schools money, impacting on training opportunities, especially for noncommissioned and newly commissioned officers.

General Meyer was even more frustrated by the shortages and incompatibility of equipment (compared to the Regular Army) which impacted on training. Unfortunately, the readiness reports were designed so that these equipment problems were not reflected up the chain.

During these years a conscious effort was made to reduce the age of organizational and major command commanders. Efforts were also focussed on improving the combat readiness of the division. There was steady progress in tests and evaluations, and elements of the division participated in logistical exercises at Fort Lee, Virginia, plus a series of command post and field training exercises.

Annual training in 1981 was the first year without any middle weekend. Tradition for decades had been that the middle weekend was used for inspections and a parade, followed by time off on Sunday. Several years before, the parade had been dropped in favor of additional training. That all changed in 1981, with both Saturday and Sunday midway through annual training devoted to increasing the combat readiness of the division.

The division in the post World War II years had almost always been oriented towards a role in the Far East. This mission orientation was often based on historical experience as much as any formal assignment. This changed for a very brief period when the division was told to prepare for a possible contingency in NATO. Senior commanders and staff flew to Germany for staff briefings and site surveys. The mission very quickly, however, returned to the division's traditional orientation towards Korea and the Far East.

General Meyer was moved to State Headquarters as Commander, State Area Command on November 8, 1981. His replacement was Brigadier General Anthony L. Palumbo. General Palumbo originally enlisted in the 37th Infantry Division, Ohio National Guard, and rose to the rank of Sergeant First Class before being commissioned in 1950. He was mobilized with the 37th in 1951, and served in combat during the Korean War as a Company

Commander in the 7th Infantry Division. He joined the Fortieth after the war, and rose to G-3. A full-time Guardsman, he served in various staff assignments in Sacramento and Washington, D.C. He commanded the 79th Support Center, Rear Area Operations, and served with Forces Command in Georgia, working on mobilization planning.

General Palumbo permanently changed the face of the division headquarters at Los Alamitos Armed Forces Reserve Center (formerly a Naval Air Station). He had a modern Emergency Operations Center built, and converted unused walls in much of the rest of the building to a museum. Each command of the division was given a portion of wall, where that command's colors (made by the wives) were hung, along with the unit's motto, a picture of the commander, and its history along with some artifacts.

The 40th Division was selected to participate in Exercise GALLANT EAGLE 82 at Fort Irwin in March and April 1982, acting as opposing forces against the 82nd Airborne Division. This was a test of the Rapid Deployment Joint Task Force (RD/JTF), fighting in a desert environment, and sponsored by the U.S. Readiness Command. The exercise, was scheduled for six days, and involved about 40,000 men and women of all four services operating in the Fort Irwin, Nellis AFB and Twenty-Nine Palms area.

A brigade of the 82nd Airborne loaded out on about thirty C-130 and sixty C-141 aircraft, arriving just after dawn on the morning of March 30th. The jump of the 82nd involved several problems. The most serious were the high winds in the area when they jumped, but the airborne soldiers also jumped without field jackets, and it was unusually cold that morning. Four soldiers were killed. One had a parachute malfunction, one landed on a piece of heavy equipment, and two were dragged across the rocky ground. More than sixty others were injured.

The 40th Medical Battalion treated casualties of the jump. The Commanding General of the 82nd, Major General Jim Lindsay, later issued a citation to the unit for their support of his sick and injured soldiers.

During the exercise itself, the 40th Division, acting as opposing forces, surprised planners with the speed of reaction to various maneuvers. The division was not only highly mobile due to its organic vehicles, but the division's troops were very familiar with Fort Irwin. The division also employed deception, including use of a warrant officer (Chief Warrant Officer Bill Hauger) who looked remarkably like the division commander.

The aggressive actions by the division were so disruptive that the umpires had to call a halt on at least two occasions to give the opposing forces time to reorganize themselves. The division received wide acclaim for its performance, which translated into more challenging assignments in future war plans.

The 1-149th Tank Battalion spent its Annual Training undergoing cold weather training at Camp Ripley, Minnesota. Other battalions, primarily infantry, were to take this arduous training over the years.

In 1983, the division performed annual training at both the Camp Roberts/Fort Hunter Liggett complex and at Fort Irwin. The extraordinary success of the division's brigade during Gallant Eagle '82 was the impetus that started the division planning for a large scale exercise in 1984.

One interesting mobilization exercise initiated by General Palumbo was to have each brigade attend annual training for the first week at Camp Roberts, conducting the personnel processing and other functions relating to Federal mobilization. They then loaded their tracked equipment on rail cars for shipment to Fort Irwin. The troops then convoyed to Fort Irwin where they unloaded their equipment and immediately deployed into a combat assault against an aggressor element.

Major General William J. Jefferds assumed command of the division on July 17, 1983 when General Palumbo was reassigned as the State Area Commander for California. General Jefferds, who had earned his civilian doctorate, was serving as Superintendent of the Alum Rock School District in San Jose. He had enlisted in the California National Guard, and was the first of a series of "post-war commanders" whose entire service was with the California National Guard. He served in all enlisted ranks through master sergeant before graduating as an infantry officer from the California Military Academy. He served at all levels of infantry command from platoon through brigade, and had graduated from the Army War College before being named an Assistant Division Commander in August, 1979.

General Jefferds' command philosophy centered on the four C's of Commitment, Competence, Courage and Candor espoused by Army Chief of Staff General John W. Vessey, Jr. He spent considerable energy in training leaders at all levels, with special emphasis on the Command Sergeants Major and their special relationship with their commanders and senior noncommissioned officers.

There was considerable pressure from the Active Army to keep the training level at the platoon level and below. General Jefferds fought that emphasis, and pushed training levels to the company, battalion and brigade level, with heavy emphasis on staff training at the battalion, brigade and division levels. This was based on his premise that the division could do the refresher squad and platoon level training during post-mobilization time but the coordination, synchronization, and complex staff and command training necessary to fight a division had to be done prior to mobilization. A prime example was the Nuclear Army Training and Evaluation Program (ARTEP). The senior Army leadership discouraged and lobbied against the division's artillery battalions taking this toughest of technical tests. The test involved speed and accuracy of fire; plus the transportation, handling, and firing of a simulated nuclear round. Nonetheless, the Guardsmen were up to the challenge, and all battalions passed.

The first unit of the division to conduct annual training in 1984 was 1-184th Infantry. That battalion took winter training in March at Camp Ripley, honing their winter survival and fighting skills. The wind chill factor occasionally took the temperature down to a minus 25 degrees.

Sunburst 1984 was a nine-day exercise during the summer of 1984 that included the entire division at once, located at Camp San Luis Obispo, Camp Roberts and Fort Hunter Liggett. The First and Second Brigades faced off in a force-on-force against the Third Brigade in a free play exercise with Active Army controllers. The value of the exercise was reinforced with multi-echelon training. Battalion commanders ensured that squad, platoon, company and battalion training were conducted simultaneously. Within the exercise, lane training was incorporated for battalion task forces at the company team level.

On August 1, 1985 the division was reorganized, losing a maneuver battalion (1-160th) and having a significant restructuring of the Division Support Command (DISCOM). Rather than having specialty battalions in the DISCOM (Medical Battalion, Maintenance Battalion, and a Supply and Transportation Battalion), Forward Support Battalions (FSB) were formed. Each of these FSBs had its own maintenance, supply, transportation and medical capabilities, and was designed to displace forward in close support of its assigned maneuver brigade. During this year the Aviation Brigade was also formed, giving the division a significant helicopter capability.

The division conducted annual training at Camp Roberts and Fort Hunter Liggett in June of 1986. While the bulk of the division's eleven maneuver battalions (the 40th had eleven, more than any other active or National Guard division) were there, two battalions trained elsewhere in 1986. The 1-184th Infantry had previously deployed overseas to participate in Team Spirit '86 in Korea, while the 2-159th Infantry conducted winter training at Camp Ripley, Minnesota the following February.

The division conducted field exercises with the First Brigade pitted against the Second Brigade. Emphasis was placed on night operations, changing task organizations in the middle of an operation, and a relief in place. In addition, the 49th Military Police Brigade was conducting a tactical "CORPS DEFENDER" exercise, training in the defense of corps rear areas in much of the same real estate.

Major General James D. Delk left his position as Military Executive of the Reserve Forces Policy Board in Washington and returned to the division as commander effective August 1, 1986. The actual change of command ceremony was conducted on Sunday, August 3rd. General Jefferds moved up to Sacramento as Deputy Adjutant General, Army. General Delk, also a U.S. Army War College graduate, had commanded through the mechanized infantry battalion level, and later served as Chief of Staff shortly after the division was mechanized.

In 1987, the division again sent a task force, built around the 2-160th Infantry, to participate in the Republic of Korea's Team Spirit '87. There they maneuvered as part of the Korean 92nd Regimental Combat Team.

During these years the 40th Division had a partnership arrangement with the 4th Mechanized Division out of Fort Carson, Colorado. They provided training teams and evaluators for all levels of training in the division. This valuable partnership program was part of the Active Army's CAPSTONE program. Each major command in the National Guard knew where they fit into war plans, who their wartime commander was, and was given an Active Army partner to assist with training.

The division transitioned to the M60A3 main battle tank during annual training in 1987. Many armor crewmen were sent to Gowan Field in Idaho where they underwent transition training. Division artillerymen also trained on the new Firefinder Radars, which almost instantly pinpointed the source of incoming artillery and mortar fire, and electronically transmitted the location to one of the division's fire direction centers. This was a bad year for forest fires. Many man days were expended in support of fire fighters in Northern California during the month of September.

TEAM SPIRIT '88 was particularly challenging for the division. In addition to the ROK Army, the exercise was to include both the 2nd Infantry Division, normally stationed in Korea, and the 25th Infantry out of Hawaii. This was to be an unusual TEAM SPIRIT exercise for a couple of reasons. One, the twelve previous Team Spirit exercises had been carefully scripted, ensuring a "safe" outcome through merely executing a preplanned scenario. TEAM SPIRIT '88, however, was to involve a free-play concept using a decentralized umpire system. The umpires were to determine fire support and assess battle damage based on relative combat power. Second, and just as revolutionary, the 40th Infantry Division was to provide all of the controller/umpires for the 2nd Infantry Division. This was the first time that National Guardsmen were to control and judge the efforts of active duty soldiers on such a large scale.

The 40th Division Commander sent Colonel George Gruner, a highly experienced brigade commander, with a small team to make advance preparations. In addition to the division commander, the division sent a total of four colonels, nine lieutenant colonels, fourteen majors, twenty-eight captains, twenty lieutenants, three warrant officers, eighty-seven noncommissioned officers, and twenty-three enlisted soldiers to perform the mission.

Colonel Gruner, in his after action report, reported:

"The Team Spirit maneuver would bring all the tensions of the changing alliance down to armed troops in the field. With about 25,000 soldiers, most in armored vehicles, in the area I was directly responsible for, the potential for incident was high. Back in '84, when we were not experiencing the discord of today, we had (over thirty) deaths (in Team Spirit exercises) resulting mostly from overzealousness on the part of commanders who wanted to gain recognition. In 1988's environment, both Koreans and Americans

*were making boasts about embarrassing each other and conse-
quently, taking chances and doing some dumb things. The success
of our effort is best gauged by the fact that the exercise overall
only had five deaths, and the one in our area was a blameless case
of a small child crawling under the wheels of an American Army
truck held up in traffic. The driver could not have known that the
child was there. Nonetheless, the police left the child's body lying
in the road for hours, for the benefit of the press and the maneuver
damage claim no doubt, and the soldier went into shock. There
were lots of close calls, but except for some isolated blows and
minor property damage, we kept the lid on (tightly). Our area had
the greatest potential for problems because we umpired the action
between the only US combat division stationed in Korea (the 2nd)
and the pride of the Korean army, the 20th Mechanized Infantry
Division. There is an unhealthy rivalry between the units, which is
evident from commander on down.*

*"The entire concept of having umpires this year was completely
new to the Team Spirit exercise, and the Korean military establishment either did not understand it or else tried deliberately to sabotage it. The Korean commanders at battalion and regimental level
claimed to know nothing about it or openly defied the rules of
engagement. The problems resulting from such reactions were
minimized by strong umpire presence, which we maintained contin-
uously forward between the forces in contact. Korean officers
would try to bluff us by running tanks or other vehicles right up
against our bodies, as if they were going to run over us, to see if
we would give up ground to them that they had not realistically
taken according to the rules. When that didn't work, they sometimes would try to push you backward with the vehicle itself. I
think all of us had the experience of standing chest against a tank
or other vehicle at least a couple of times. A regimental commander first threatened and then started to have one of our umpires buried by a bulldozer. I had some explosives deliberately
thrown close enough to me to drive rocks into my legs, and almost*

everyone got into some pushing and shoving. Sometimes we swore
and pushed back, but we never gave away ground, and we main-
tained control of the situation."

As division commander and senior controller at the time, the
author was called from one crisis like the above, to another. In one
they had a senior officer caught between two tanks, an extremely
dangerous situation which was elevated that evening at the nightly
controller's conference all the way up to Chief Controller (a Korean
Lieutenant General) level. That seemed to help over the next several days, but not much. Fortunately there were no serious injuries
from these games of "chicken" between tough, well-armed soldiers.

The performance of the soldiers of the division was described as
"superb." General Menetrey, the Commander-in-Chief for Korea,
sent a message to the Sixth Army commander stating he was
"impressed with the professionalism and dedication displayed by
soldiers of the 40th Mech Div." This was confirmed several months
later when the 40th Division was asked to provide controllers for
both the 2nd and the 25th Divisions in TEAM SPIRIT '89. The
division had to turn down that request, as it would take too many
of the division's leaders away from their troops. It was agreed that
some controllers would be provided on a volunteer basis.

Annual training in 1988 occurred with some troops training at
Fort Irwin, but most participating in the continuing series of
"SUNBURST" annual training exercises. Held at the Camp
Roberts-Fort Hunter Liggett complex, a large part of the division
trained while supported by combat support and service support
troops from several components under an umbrella exercise dubbed
"GOLDEN BEAR". An opposing force was established under the
assistant division commander, Brigadier General Daniel J.
Hernandez, to provide realistic opposition.

In 1988, the exercise was conducted in conjunction with a medical exercise called "WOUNDED WARRIOR"...the "casualties"
were air-lifted in Air National Guard C-130's and air ambulance

helicopters. The Navy and Marine Corps also participated in the exercise, with simulated casualties from the division evacuated to the U.S.S. Mount Vernon, which was anchored in Morro Bay harbor.

There was also a support exercise called "LASTING RESPONSE." The support exercise, planned by the 115th Area Support Group, conducted a rear area defense while hosting units and feeding replacement units into the system.

Many elements of the division were evaluated by soldiers from the 4th Mechanized Division at Fort Carson, Colorado. The 4th Division, still the 40th's training partner, sent 165 officers and men to work with the 40th Division. A total of 83 units were evaluated.

Counternarcotics efforts were initiated on October 23, 1988 with Border Ranger I. This effort involved the Sheriff's Departments of Imperial, Los Angeles, Orange, Riverside, San Bernardino and San Diego counties. Unfortunately, the operation ended tragically when a National Guard helicopter struck a power line near San Diego, crashing and killing the five sheriff's deputies and three crewmen aboard. Rather than slowing down any counter-drug efforts, the accident seemed to inspire all agencies to make sure they had not died in vain. Planning started almost immediately to launch an even larger effort.

In February 1989, the division initiated preparations for BORDER RANGER II. This involved planning for a multi-pronged interdiction effort with the U.S. Customs Service, and the same Sheriff's Departments that worked with the National Guard in 1988. The operation commenced May 2, 1989, and lasted for thirty days. Soldiers of the 40th Infantry Division and the 49th Military Police Brigade were deployed to land and sea ports of entry to search cargo. They operated hidden observation posts overlooking air strips and routes in which illegal narcotics were suspected of being transported.

During BORDER RANGER II, drug law enforcement officials confiscated more than twice the amount of illegal drugs that had been seized during the same month the previous year. More than $40 million dollars in illegal drugs were seized, as well as $102,000 in cash. They arrested 237 people on narcotics violations and 313 suspects for infractions ranging from outstanding warrants to possession of illegal weapons.

Having proven the value of using trained soldiers in assisting law enforcement, the program grew from there. Quickly there were about four hundred soldiers a day involved in the missions, most of them from the division.

The division continued to receive first-line equipment, including M1059 track-mounted smoke generators, H-60 Blackhawk helicopters, Fire Support Vehicles and Heavy Expanded Mobility Tactical Trucks. Battalion and brigade staffs were being trained using annual Army Training Battle Simulation System (ARTBASS) exercises. Administered by higher headquarters, such as I Corps out of Fort Lewis, ARTBASS exercises were highly sophisticated computer-driven simulations that fully stressed the staffs during a long weekend.

The division provided a great number of controller/umpires for TEAM SPIRIT '89 in Korea, as the division had in 1988. By the end of this exercise, most of the division's senior leadership had participated in this key exercise. This provided important leadership and tactical training in the area where the division was most expected to fight.

Interestingly, following TEAM SPIRIT, Major General Chung Jae Kyung of the ROK Army requested an opportunity to visit the headquarters of the division. The Director, Mobilization and Reserve Forces Bureau, he was interested in how the division trained its soldiers. He spent some time at the division headquarters at Los Alamitos, receiving a staff briefing and having many questions answered.

Train-up started for the Battle Command Training Program (BCTP) or "Warfighter" exercise during Spring 1989. This was an intensive training experience at the division level, culminating in a five day exercise in the field. The exercise was to be a computer-assisted exercise driven out of Fort Leavenworth. The train-up included sessions at Fort Leavenworth as well as training at home station.

The annual training in 1989 was similar to the previous year, with all of the time spent in the field conducting tactical training and exercises. There was one interesting group of visitors, sponsored by National Guard Bureau. They were military attaches out of Washington, including representatives from the Warsaw Pact. Flown out to observe the division in the field were attaches from Argentina, Egypt, France, Germany, Great Britain, Hungary, India, Iraq, Jordan, Mexico, the Netherlands, Poland, and Yugoslavia.

On October 1, 1989, Brigadier General Averill E. Hawkins moved up to assume command of the division, while General Delk replaced General Jefferds as Deputy Adjutant General, Army. General Hawkins was an infantry officer who had served at all levels of infantry command through brigade, and had served as both Assistant Division Commander for Maneuver, and Assistant Division Commander for Support.

The decade of the 1980's was a period when there was considerable investment in exercises of all kinds, as well as overseas training. The division sent command and staff elements to Fort Lewis, Korea and Japan each year. Large exercises were conducted by the division with its "Sunburst Series" and the state's Golden Bear exercises. The division was enjoying the fruits of President Ronald Reagan's increased emphasis on defense. Equipment was flowing into units faster than had ever occurred in peacetime, and training monies were significantly increased. Annual training by the mid-eighties included a minimum of ten days in the field. All battalions were required to undergo an external evaluation, similar to the old Army Training Test. All elements of the division were routinely making night displacements, including by echelon where necessary. Many units had even graduated to including river crossings during night displacements.

Annual Training in 1990 saw the division's first participation in a BCTP Warfighter. This was a highly stressful exercise conducted in the field at Camp Roberts and driven by computer simulations out of Fort Leavenworth, Kansas. The 1st Corps at Fort Lewis acted in their wartime role as senior headquarters to the division, with all elements of the division represented down to battalion level. The division had done its train-up under the close supervision of General Hawkins, who from the start had assumed responsibility for preparation in his previous role as Assistant Division Commander. He and his troops did a masterful job during the exercise. A message from the Sixth Army Commander, Lieutenant General William H. Harrison, to the Forces Command Commander on July 9, 1990 read in part:

"With the Battle Command Training Program (BCTP) Warfighter exercise for the 40th Infantry Division recently completed, I am receiving 'kudos' from many sources on the success of the exercise and the accomplishments of the division.

"All in all, the 40th ID performed magnificently during Warfighter - - a job well done by Averill Hawkins and the entire 40th ID. The accomplishments of the 40th ID during Warfighter were undoubtedly monumental and will ultimately contribute to the leader development and warfighting potential of the division."

The division was told by the Active Army's Chief Controller that the division performed better than any other National Guard division in previous such exercises. In fact, he stated that the division had performed better than many of the Regular Army divisions had up to that date. The 40th Infantry Division was also the first division to plan and conduct a river crossing during the exercise, a very complex maneuver.

When the Warfighter exercise was over, General Hawkins initiated a program called Operation GET WELL. This program was designed to bring administrative and logistical aspects of the division up to the high standards already demonstrated in the area of warfighting capability. Specific goals and time lines were established. Within six months the overall combat readiness of the division had improved significantly.

Iraqi President Saddam Hussein sent his armies rolling into Kuwait on August 2, 1990. For the first time since the Korean War, sizeable National Guard and Reserve forces were mobilized for combat in what became Operations DESERT SHIELD and DESERT STORM. The first alert notices went out before the month of August ended. Most of the units alerted were Combat Support and Combat Service Support. No National Guard divisions were mobilized, but about a hundred soldiers of the 40th Infantry Division (Mechanized) volunteered and served with other units being mobilized and deployed.

General Hawkins was promoted to Deputy Adjutant General, Army to fill a key vacancy in Sacramento effective May 1st, 1991. He was replaced by Brigadier General Daniel J. Hernandez, a soldier with an extraordinarily long career in the division. He enlisted when only fifteen, and was mobilized for Korea while a member of the 223rd Infantry. He had to leave the Guard then, and immediately reenlisted when the National Guard was reestablished following the war.

General Hernandez had a remarkable memory for technical details, coupled with a reputation as a "Soldier's General." Commissioned in the Medical Service Corps after serving as an enlisted man, he went on to command both infantry and Combat Service Support units.

The biggest challenge in decades faced the division in the Spring of 1992, when rioting broke out in South Central Los Angeles. The rioting started shortly after the Rodney King verdict was announced the afternoon of Wednesday, April 29, 1992. Unlike previous riots, rioting and looting continued into the next day. Unfortunately, even before calling for law enforcement mutual support, the National Guard was called in.

General Hernandez established his Crisis Action Center at Los Alamitos, and had dispatched his first elements early Thursday afternoon. Those initial Military Police elements were quickly followed by infantry and armor battalions. By Friday, the riots were under control. Much of the division had been mobilized by the second day, and was augmented by the 49th Military Police Brigade.

Even though the riots were over, and many Guardsmen were staged in armories waiting for missions, a decision was made by the mayor through the governor to call for Federal troops. This controversial decision was made without consultation with the Sheriff, Chief of Police, or National Guard commanders. At the very time some Guardsmen should have been sent home, Federal troops had to be committed to the streets to avoid political embarrassment, but were released after less than a week. In the meantime, some Guardsmen sat in their armories, inwardly fuming, for many days. It was a full month after the National Guard was mobilized before the last troops were released.

Discipline, especially fire discipline, had been exceptionally strong throughout the period the National Guard was on the streets of the Greater Los Angeles area. There had been literally hundreds of thousands of rounds issued, yet only twenty-two rounds were fired. No innocent people were injured by those bullets. The two that were struck were both habitual criminals. Just as important, no military personnel were injured by the many attacks of gang members.

That same year the division participated in the I Corps Warfighter Exercise at Fort Lewis. The division also sent battalions to the National Training Center at Fort Irwin to participate in various rotations. These training opportunities with the Active Army helped hone the division's combat skills. There were also several call-ups for fires, plus exercises in the event there were further riots in the Los Angeles area.

Brigadier General William F. Stewart assumed command of the division on August 8, 1993 when General Hernandez retired. General Stewart was a senior executive in Los Angeles County government. His ascension to command followed an unusual route, in that he was a lawyer and Judge Advocate General Corps officer who transitioned to combat arms. He eventually commanded both a mechanized infantry battalion and a maneuver brigade, and graduated from the U. S. Army War College, before being selected as Assistant Division Commander.

His most significant challenges occurred at 4:31 a.m. early on Monday morning, January 17, 1994. A devastating earthquake hit the Northridge area of the San Fernando Valley just northwest of Los Angeles. Freeway overpasses collapsed, and six hospitals were damaged, requiring about a thousand patients to be evacuated. Some buildings collapsed, including a police station, and fires broke out. A total of 58 deaths were attributed to the earthquake, and 1,484 people were hospitalized. The heaviest loss of life occurred in a three-story apartment house, where the top two stories collapsed the first floor.

The response by law enforcement, emergency crews and the military was impressive. Approximately 100 earthquake-related fires were put out by 9:00 a.m. Law enforcement quickly surveyed the damage, and civil authorities requested the National Guard set up tent cities to ease the plight of 30,000 people either displaced by damaged homes or psychologically traumatized and temporarily afraid to live in buildings. The 40th Infantry Division's Support Command quickly set up thirty tent cities, and with the help of the First Brigade and the 132nd Engineer Battalion, assisted with recovery efforts and established security over the next week.

Law enforcement personnel and the military found the amount of lawlessness to be extraordinarily low. The first night there were only a total of sixteen arrests for looting and burglary in the entire city, a total much lower than normal. More noteworthy, in a city which normally has several murders every night of the year, there was not a single murder for three days following the earthquake.

Annual training in 1995 was conducted at Camp Roberts and Fort Hunter Liggett, and was expected to be conducted at that training complex for the next several years. Training was conducted at the levels currently directed by Forces Command, focussed by maneuver units at the platoon level, and by support units at the company level.

Modern equipment continued to flow slowly into the divisions. The M1 Abrams tank started arriving in the division in February of 1996, with the last of the equipment scheduled to arrive by the end of 1997. Bradley fighting vehicles were scheduled to arrive in 1998-1999.

The organization of the division was again rapidly changing as the end of the century approached. September of 1995, the 1-188th Air Defense Artillery (ADA) Battalion of North Dakota was assigned to the division. In October, the 1-184th was converted to light infantry and lost to the enhanced, high-priority brigade in Hawaii. In September of 1996, an M1 Tank Battalion of the 163rd Armor of Montana was assigned to the division. In addition, the 1-139th Attack Helicopter Battalion from Missouri joined the division. The new Engineer Brigade of the division was programmed to be fully organized in 1997, with the 132nd, 578th, and 579th Engineer Battalions. Arizona was scheduled to provide an artillery battalion for the division. By that time, the 640th Military Intelligence Battalion (Cadre), was scheduled to be organized in California as the division's only cadre unit.

On May 5, 1996, Brigadier General Edmund C. Zysk was assigned as the Commanding General of the division. He served as an enlisted soldier in the Marine Corps before joining the California National Guard. He was commissioned in 1967, serving as an infantry platoon leader before attending the Army's Rotary Wing Flight School in 1970. He served in a series of aviation-related command slots before organizing and commanding the 40th's Aviation Brigade. He served in several positions in state headquarters, and played a key role in controlling the 1992 riots in Los Angeles.

General Zysk assumed command during a time of diminishing resources. To make best use of finite resources, training in the nineties was increasingly sophisticated and computer-assisted to make best use of limited training time. The ARTBASS computer-driven battle staff exercises for battalion maneuver units were supplemented by Brigade Battle Simulations (BBS) for non-maneuver units.

Brigades had formal Brigade Command Battle Staff Training (BCBST) once every three years. They traveled to Fort Leavenworth, Kansas for a one year train-up and evaluation. They returned to home stations for remedial training, and conducted a Brigade Battle Exercise (BBX). These were conducted with the battle staffs in their command vehicles reacting to a "world-class" opposing force in a computer-driven scenario. In effect, the brigades conducted a down-sized Warfighter, similar to the exercises conducted by the division.

Not surprisingly, senior officers of the division found over the years that command and coordination skills learned in command post exercises such as the Warfighter series were extremely valuable during sizeable domestic disturbances and natural diasters.

In February of 1997, the division held its annual Military Ball at the famous Hollywood Paladium, celebrating its eightieth anniversary. About 2000 division soldiers, past and present attended, along with their guests. Displays sponsored by the California Military Museum showed uniforms and artifacts from the division's past.

It was a fitting occasion for soldiers to reflect on the division's long history, and honor those who had served in at least five wars. They couldn't help but look back on the division's lengthy heritage with great pride.

APPENDIX 1

GLOSSARY

A-20	Douglas "Havoc" 2-engine Attack Bomber. World War II
AA or AAA	AntiAircraft or AntiAircraft Artillery. Now Air Defense Artillery (ADA).
AC	Assistant Chief (of Staff) or Active Component (Regular Army)
ACS	Assistant Chief of Staff
AD	Armored Division
ADA	Air Defense Artillery. Formerly AA or AAA.
AFAK	Armed Forces Assistance to Korea. Unit-sponsored civil assistance to war-torn Korea and Koreans
ANACDUTRA	Annual Active Duty Training. The annual training period, usually two weeks, and usually performed in the Summer, by National Guard units. (See AFT and AT)
AFT	Annual Field Training. Same meaning as ANACDUTRA.
AGO	Adjutant General's Office
APO	Army Post Office
ARTBASS	Army Training Battle Simulation System. A computer-assisted training program for battalion and brigade commanders and staffs. Introduced in the 1980's.
ARTEP	Army Training and Evaluation Program (Post Korea War era)

AT	Annual Training. Same meaning as ANACDUTRA.
AW	Automatic Weapons
B-24	Consolidated "Liberator" heavy bomber, 4-engined, World War II
B-25	North American "Mitchell" medium bomber, 2 engines, World War II
B-26	Martin Marauder medium bomber, 2 engines, World War II
BAR	Browning Automatic Rifle. The standard squad automatic weapon, calibre .306, until after the Korean War.
BBX	Brigade Battle Exercise. A computer-assisted exercise for non-maneuver staffs.
BCBST	Brigade Command Battle Staff Training. A computer-assisted and driven series of training evaluations and exercises.
BCTP	Battle Command Training Program. Also called "Warfighter." A computer driven training exercise for higher level commanders and staffs. Introduced in the 1980's.
BLT	Battalion Landing Team (for a sea-borne assault).
Bn	Battalion. A military unit, usually authorized about 500 to 1000 persons.
Brigade	A military headquarters controlling three or more battalions, plus supporting elements. See also RCT below.
Butai	Japanese. A force or group, usually named after the commander. Example: Kamii Butai.
C-119	Lockheed "Flying Boxcar" 2-engine transport. Heavily used during the Korean War.

Cav	Cavalry. Formerly horse soldiers, presently highly mobile troops especially organized for reconnaissance.
CAPSTONE	Army doctrine in the 1980's that called for Army reserve component units to be assigned specific wartime commands and areas of responsibility, plus training partnerships with Active Army commands.
CAS	Close Air Support
CBHL	Corps Beach Head Line
CP	Command Post
CCF	Chinese Communist Forces
CIC	Counter Intelligence Corps
CINCAFPAC	Command-in-Chief Army Forces, Pacific
CSLO	Camp San Luis Obispo. National Guard training camp near San Luis Obispo, California.
DBHL	Division Beach Head Line
DISCOM	Division Support Command
Div	Division. A large military formation of from 10,000 to 25,000 persons.
DUKW	An amphibious vehicle based on a 2½ ton chassis. Pronounced "Duck."
F4U	Chance Vought "Corsair" fighter aircraft w/gull wings flown by Navy and Marine pilots. World War II
FA	Field Artillery.
FDC	Fire Direction Center. The center controlling the fires of a mortar or artillery unit.
FO	Forward Observer, or Field Order
FSB	Forward Support Battalion
FTC	Field Training Center
GI	Government Issue

G1, G2 etc	The General Staff found at Division and Higher Headquarters. The G1 is the Adjutant, The G2 is the Intelligence Officer, The G3 is the Operations Officer (and Training Officer in peacetime), the G4 is the Logistics Officer, the G5 was the Plans Officer through World War II, and the Civil Affairs Officer thereafter.
GO	General Order, or less frequently, General Officer
HBT	Herringbone Twill. The material used to make fatigue (utility) uniforms in the World War II and Korean War era.
HHC	Headquarters and Headquarters Company
HLMR	Hunter Liggett Military Reservation (in California). Now Fort Hunter Liggett
HQ or HQS	Headquarters
ID	Infantry Division
IIB	Independent Infantry Battalion (Japanese)
Inf	Infantry
I & R	Intelligence & Reconnaissance. Each regiment had an I & R Platoon in World War II and through the Korean War
KATUSA	Korean Augmentation Troops, U. S. Army. Korean soldiers who fought beside American soldiers in American units.
KCOMZ	Korean Communications Zone. The geographical area just behind the combat zone.
Kempei Tai	Japanese Secret Police (40th ID faced the Kempei Tai during their occupation of Korea, 1945-6)
KIA	Killed In Action
KSC	Korean Service Corps. Korean laborers who carried food, ammunition and other materials

	for American units, especially in rugged terrain.
L-4	Light, 2-place, "Cub" aircraft used for liaison and artillery observation.
L-5	Similar to the L-4, but a later model
LCI	Landing Craft, Infantry
LCM	Landing Craft, Mechanized
LCP	Landing Craft, Personnel
LCVP	Landing Craft, Vehicle and Personnel
LCT	Landing Craft, Tank
LSD	Landing Ship, Dock
LST	Landing Ship, Tank
LVT	Landing Vehicle, Tracked. Normally armed with a .50 calibre machine gun.
M-7	Self-propelled 105mm artillery, also called the "Priest" because of a pulpit-like portion of the hull. World War II and Korea
M-10	Tank destroyer, with a 3" gun on a tracked platform. World War II and Korea
MASH	Mobile Army Surgical Hospital
MC	Medical Corps, or Military Cross (a British decoration).
MIA	Missing In Action.
MLR	Main Line of Resistance.
Mort	Mortar
MOS	Military Occupational Specialty. An alphanumeric designator describing a soldier's job. For instance, 11B is the MOS for an infantryman.
MP	Military Police
MSR	Main Supply Route
OD	Officer of the Day, or Olive Drab. Olive Drab was the color most vehicles were painted in World War II and Korea. The

	term "OD, or OD's" also applies to the winter service uniform of that color worn by troops during the same era.
OP	Observation Post
OPLR	Outpost Line of Resistance. A series of positions in front of the Main Line of Resistance (MLR) used to provide warning of the enemy's approach and deceive him as to the true location of the MLR.
OSD	Office of the Secretary of Defense.
P-38	Lockheed "Lightning" two-engined fighter, World War II
PBY	Consolidated "Catalina" amphibian aircraft with two engines, World War II
POW	Prisoner(s) of War
PCT	Parachute Combat Team (Regiment). An airborne regiment with its supporting arms so it can operate independently.
PT	Patrol Torpedo (boat). Fast attack and liaison craft armed with torpedoes and .50 cal machine guns.
RCT	Regimental Combat Team. An infantry regiment with its supporting arms so it can operate independently. Consists (as a minimum) of the infantry battalions, an artillery battalion, an engineer company, and needed support troops.
Regt	Regiment. An organization normally consisting of three or more battalions.
ROAD	Reorganization Objective Army Divisions. An Army reorganization of the early 1960's to increase flexibility, with a fixed base common to all divisions, but varying

	numbers and types of infantry and armor elements depending on its mission.
ROCAD	Reorganization Objective Current Armored Divisions
ROK	Republic of Korea. Pronounced "rock," the term came to mean both the nation, or an individual soldier from that nation.
S1, S2 etc	The Special Staff found at Brigade/Regiment and lower Headquarters. The S1 is the Personnel and Administration Officer, or Adjutant, the S2 is the Intelligence Officer, the S3 is the Operations Officer (and Training Officer in peacetime), the S4 is the Logistics Officer, the S5 was the Plans Officer through World War II, and the Civil Affairs Officer later.
Sep	Separate
SFPE	San Francisco Port of Embarkation
Sig	Signal
SOP	Standing Operating Procedures, until about 1950. Then the term evolved into Standard Operating Procedures, although the meaning did not change. The former is still used occasionally to this day.
Sqdn	Squadron. In the Army, equivalent in size to a battalion.
SRF	Selected Reserve Force. Units designated in the 1960's to receive additional resources and training time so they could deploy quickly if needed.
Trp	Troop. A cavalry unit equivalent to a company.
U.S.S.	United States Ship

WD	War Department. The predecessor to the Department of Defense.
WIA	Wounded In Action.

APPENDIX 2

CHRONOLOGY

<u>World War I Years</u>

7 May 15	British Liner Lusitania sunk by German submarine with loss of over 1000 lives, including 124 Americans
28 Feb 17	President announces Secret Service intercepted secret letter from German Foreign Minister urging Mexico and Japan join Germany in war against the United States
26 Mar 17	National Guard mobilized, ordered to train and actively recruit
2 Apr 17	President announces need for declaration of war
6 Apr 17	Congress declares war on Germany
5 Aug 17	Entire National Guard federalized
25 Aug 17	40th Division ordered organized
16 Sep 17	40th Division organized at Camp Kearny, CA
26 Jul 18	40th Division left Camp Kearny, temporarily at Camp Mills, NY
9 Aug 18	40th Division sailed from U.S., travels thru England
22 Aug 18	40th Division asgd as 6th Depot (Replacement) Division in France
24 Aug 18	40th Division arrives La Guerche, France, traveling thru Cherbourg
31 Aug 18	All 40th Division troops in Europe
2 Nov 18	40th Division leaves La Guerche (Cher), France
4 Nov 18	40th Division arrives Revigny (Meuse), France
11 Nov 18	Armistice signed
6 Jan 19	40th Division left Revigny (Meuse), France
8 Jan 19	40th Division arrived Castres (Gironde), France
19 Feb 19	40th Division left Castres (Gironde), France
20 Mar 19	40th Division arrived Camp Stoneman, California

Jan-May 19	Elements of the 40th Division demobilized in various sites

Between the Wars

4 May 26	The War Department grants authority to reorganize the 40th Division
18 Jun 26	40th ID Hqs established in Berkeley
24-26 Nov 27	Folsom Prison Riots
10 Mar 33	Long Beach earthquake
6 Aug 33	40th ID artillery converted from horse drawn to motorized
5 Jul 34	40th ID elements activated for longshoremens' strike in San Francisco
1 Oct 37	40th ID Hqs moved to Los Angeles (federally recognized 18 Oct 37)
2-4 Mar 38	Disastrous floods in Southern California

World War II Years

10 Feb 41	Company C 194th Tank Bn Inducted (formerly 40th ID Tank Company)
3 Mar 41	40th ID Inducted into Federal service
Aug 41	40th ID participates in large maneuvers in SW Washington State
29 Sep 41	159th Infantry Regiment detached and assigned to the 7th ID
Oct 41	Division maneuvers at HLMR under III Corps
7 Dec 41	Japanese attack Pearl Harbor. 40th ID immediately deploys to provide security
18 Feb 42	40th ID reorganized from square to triangular division
28 Feb 42	Japanese submarine shells Bankline Oil Refinery near Santa Barbara, California. This is the first attack of the war on the U.S. mainland.
22 Apr 42	40th ID moved to Ft Lewis for Advanced Training
14 Jun 42	184th Infantry detached and assigned to the Western Defense Command
8 Jul 42	40th ID starts move to Hawaii (completed early Oct 42)

1 Sep 42	108th Infantry from the 27th ID joins the 40th ID as the third regiment
20 Dec 43	40th ID leaves for Guadalcanal
4 Jan 44	40th ID debarks at Guadalcanal
25 Mar 44	40th ID transferred to General MacArthur's command, then to XIV Corps
23 Apr 44	Elements of the 40th ID relieve 1st Marine Division on New Britain. Balance of the Division lands over the next several days
27 Nov 44	40th ID relieved from its mission on New Britain
9 Jan 45	40th ID invades Luzon, P.I.
21 Feb 45	40th ID transferred to XI Corps, commanded by MG Charles P. Hall
2 Mar 45	40th ID relieved by 43rd Division. Transferred to Eighth Army, commanded by LTG Robert L. Eichelberger
8 Mar 45	108th RCT sails from Luzon to Leyte, relieves 164th Infantry of Americal Division
18 Mar 45	185th RCT reinforced by 2-160th invades Panay
22 Mar 45	Company G 2-185th secures Inampulugan Island. 2-160th amphibious patrol secures Guimaras Island
29 Mar 45	185th lands on Negros Island, Occidental Province.
7 Apr 46	2-108th (reinforced) lands on Masbate, starting three week campaign to secure island
10 May 45	108th RCT lands at Macajalar Bay on Mindanao as part of X Corps
15-18 Jun 45	40th ID elements return from Negros to Panay
14 Aug 45	Japan accepts unconditional surrender terms
16 Aug 45	Japanese Imperial Headquarters announces cessation of hostilities
2 Sep 45	Official signing of surrender document aboard USS Missouri in Tokyo Bay
15 Sep 45	40th ID Advance Party arrives at Inchon
1 Oct 45	185th Inf CP opened at Taegu
2 Oct 45	160th Inf closes at Pusan. CP established
7 Oct 45	108th Inf established CP, occupies Andong, Yongdok, and other cities
8 Oct 45	Division Artillery established CP at Chinhae
7 Apr 46	40th ID inactivated at Camp Stoneman, California

THE FORTIETH DIVISION

Post World War II

14 Oct 46	40th ID reorganized and federally recognized at Los Angeles

Korean War Years

25 Jun 50	North Korea invades South Korea
27 Jun 50	President Truman orders US air and naval forces to help repel North Koreans
30 Jun 50	President Truman authorizes General MacArthur to send ground forces to Korea
5 Jul 50	US troops fight their first engagement in Korea
7 Jul 50	UN Security Council authorizes use of UN flag in Korea
1 Aug 50	40th ID receives telephonic alert for induction
1 Sep 50	40th ID activated for Korea. Advance party departs for Camp Cooke
15 Sep 50	All 40th ID troops are at Camp Cooke. Prepare to receive fillers
6 Nov 50	40th ID recruit training commences
26 Dec 50	LTG Matthew B. Ridgway arrives to take command of all UN ground forces in Korea
24 Feb 51	40th ID receives alert orders for movement to Japan
28 Mar 51	40th ID Advance Party leaves for Japan
29 Mar 51	40th ID Main Body departs for Japan
10 Apr 51	40th ID advance elements arrive in Japan. Division given mission of defending No. Honshu while training
11 Apr 51	GEN MacArthur relieved of command
12 Apr 51	GEN Ridgway replaces GEN MacArthur. GEN James A. Van Fleet assumes command of forces in Korea
10 Jul 51	First meeting between UN and North Korean-Chinese delegations held at Kaesong
4 Aug 51	40th ID rear detachment arrives in Japan after training at Camp Cooke
15 Aug 51	Far East Air Forces start "Operation STRANGLE"
23 Aug 51	Communists suspend armistice negotiations

13 Sep 51	UN begins attack on Heartbreak Ridge
25 Oct 51	Armistice talks resumed as delegates meet for twenty-seventh plenary session
18 Dec 51	Both sides exchange prisoner lists. UN held 132,474 Red prisoners. Communist list had 11,559 names
22 Dec 51	40th ID alerted for move to Korea to relieve 24th ID
26 Dec 51	40th ID Advance Party departs for ROK
6 Jan 52	First ship departs Japan for Korea with first elements of the 40th ID Main Body (the bulk of the first echelon sailed 7 Jan)
11 Jan 52	40th ID first echelon landed at Inchon
13 Jan 52	143rd FA fired first round in anger when SFC Gary Ducat of 143rd pulled lanyard on 105mm howitzer
19 Jan 52	160th Inf completed relief of 19th Inf Regt (24th US ID)
20 Jan 52	40th ID's first loss was SFC Kenneth Kaiser Jr. of 160th killed by mortar fragments near Kumsong
22 Jan 52	40th ID assigned Eighth US Army when 2nd echelon landed Inchon this date
24 Jan 52	Korean truce negotiations stalemated
28 Jan 52	223rd Inf completed relief of 21st Inf (24th US ID)
10 Feb 52	224th Inf relieved 5th RCT (24th US ID)
Mar 52	The 40th ID: Had a daily average of 19,436 organic and 7,858 attached troops to support. Moved the Division CP from Ascom City (near Seoul) to the Chunchon area
22 Mar 52	160th Infantry relieved by 1st ROK Regiment
28 Mar 52	Relief of 224th Infantry by 7th ROK Regiment completed
29 Mar 52	Relief of 223rd Infantry by 2nd ROK Infantry completed
Apr 52	40th ID: Six B-29's dropped 210 500lb bombs in the division sector resulting in 34 secondary explosions and one large fire. Construction and occupation of all installations was completed by the end of the month. Enemy probes of the division's lines increased during the month, especially towards the end of the month. There were a total of 3636 enemy mortar and artillery rounds impacting in April.

1 Apr 52	40th ID completed relief of 2nd ROK Div in Kumwha-Kumsong sector. 223rd on left, and 160th on right. 224th & 140th TK in reserve.
3 Apr 52	Boundary change between 40th & 2nd ID on left, 224th inserted left of 223rd.
6 Apr 52	40th ID assumed responsibility for portion of 2nd ID sector from CT665409 to CT699425
May 52	40th ID: Total of 29 missions (112 sorties) CAS during May. High levels of personnel turnover during the month. Fewer contacts initiated by the enemy during May. A total of 2722 enemy mortar and artillery rounds impacted during May.
7 May 52	Brigadier General Francis T. Dodd, Commander of UN Prisoner of War Camp Number One on Koje-do, is seized and held for seventy-eight hours by Communist prisoners
12 May 52	General Mark W. Clark takes over from General Ridgway as Supreme Commander
19 May 52	IX US Corps revised the 40th ID left boundary to the rear of the MLR and relieved the division of responsibility for the Kumwha Valley (then assumed by 7th US ID)
2 Jun 52	BG Cleland assumes command of 40th ID vice MG Daniel H. Hudelson at 0900 hours. COL Gordon B. Rogers arrives and assumes ADC duties vice BG Homer O. Eaton.
26-28 Jun	2nd ROK Div relieves 40th ID
30 Jun 52	40th ID (-) closed into Field Training Cmd #5 for training and rehabilitation while in IX Corps reserve. Divarty & 140th Tk remained in action under IX Corps control in spt 2nd ROK Div.
1 Jul 52	3-223rd Inf dispatched to Sangdong Mine Area to perform security mission
5 Jul 52	224th Inf attached to 2nd Log Command, left for Pusan to provide security for POW enclosures in that area
13 Jul 52	40th ID moved to new training area near Kapyong, resuming training and security missions
2 Sep 52	40th ID (NGUS) organized and federally recognized in Los Angeles

16 Oct 52	40th ID ordered to relieve the 25th US Div in the Paem-Ihyon-Ni sector
22 Oct 52	224th & 160th had relieved 27th and 14th Inf respectively, and CG, 40th ID assumed sector responsibility. 40th ID then passed to X Corps control, with 5th RCT attached. Deployed 160th on left, 224th center, and 5th RCT right. 223rd arrived a day later, placed in reserve. Div CP at Tokkol-Li.
31 Oct 52	5th RCT moved to 40th ID reserve after being relieved by 223rd
8 Jan 53	5th RCT relieved 223rd, which moved to division reserve
30 Jan 53	45th US Div assumed sector responsibility from 40th ID
31 Jan 53	40th ID in X US Corps reserve, with CP at Nambajchon
11 Feb 53	General Van Fleet turns over command of Eighth Army to Lieutenant General Maxwell D. Taylor
6 Mar 53	40th ID designated Eighth US Army reserve
27 Apr 53	CG, 40th ID accepted sector responsibility from 20th ROK Div at that time. 40th deployed across Ihyon-Ni-Kalbakkumi (Punchbowl) sector
10 Jul 53	20th ROK Div relieved 40th ID in Punchbowl area.
11 Jul 53	40th ID relieved 45th US Div in the Heartbreak Ridge-Sandbag Castle area, which extended from Paem to a point west of Ihyon-Ni. 223rd was deployed on Heartbreak Ridge to the left, while the 224th was in the Sandbag Castle sector to the right
27 Jul 53	En shelled friendly positions four hours with 4700 rounds of mortar and artillery. Few casualties and only slight damage. 40th Divarty countered with about 11,000 arty and mortar rounds. Ceasefire declared as armistice signed at Panmunjom
8 May 54	Final Review of 40th ID in ROK
19 Jun 54	Ceremony in San Francisco to celebrate return of 40th ID battle flags
30 Jun 54	40th ID (US) released from active Federal service and reverted to state control
1 Jul 54	40th ID reorganized and redesignated as 40th Armored Div

22 Jan 56	40th Signal Co responds to train wreck in L.A.
25-27 Jan 56	40th ID elements assist during floods in L.A. area
1 Jul 59	40th AD organized under "D" series TO&E under "ROCAD."
1 Jul 63	40th AD reorganized under "ROAD," changing combat commands to brigades
17-30 May 64	2-40th AD (+) participates in Exercise DESERT STRIKE at Fort Irwin
13-24 Aug 65	40th AD employed to control Watts Riots in L.A.
29 Jan 68	40th AD reorganized and redesignated as 40th Armored Brigade
13 Jan 74	40th ID (Mechanized) organized and federally recognized with Hqs in Long Beach
Apr 81	40th ID Hqs moved to Los Alamitos Armed Forces Reserve Center
Mar-Apr 82	40th ID (-) participates in Exercise GALLANT EAGLE '82 at Fort Irwin
Apr 86	1-184th Inf (+) participates in Exercise TEAM SPIRIT in the Republic of Korea
Apr 87	2-160th Inf (+) participates in Exercise TEAM SPIRIT in the Republic of Korea
Apr 88	40th ID provides controllers for 2 ID during Exercise TEAM SPIRIT (and over the next two years to a lesser degree)
23 Oct 88	Exercise BORDER RANGER I. Counter Drug efforts in conjunction with law enforcement end with disastrous crash of helicopter near Mexican border. Efforts are reorganized and continue for many years
Jun 90	40th ID participates in first BCTP Warfighter exercise at Camp Roberts.
Apr-May 92	40th ID employed to control L. A. Riots
17 Jan 94	Northridge Earthquake. 40th ID elements (primarily DISCOM) establish tent cities and provide security

APPENDIX 3

DIVISION COMMANDERS

MG Frederick S. Strong	5 Aug 17 - 2 Jun 19
MG David P. Barrows (1)	18 Jun 26 - 27 Jun 37
MG Walter P. Story	28 Jun 37 - 22 Jun 41
MG Ernest J. Dawley	23 Jun 41 - 15 Apr 42
MG Rapp Brush	16 Apr 42 - 21 Jul 45
BG Donald J. Myers	22 Jul 45 - 7 Apr 46
MG Harcourt Hervey (2)	15 Aug 46 - 1 Dec 47
MG Daniel H. Hudleson	2 Dec 47 - 1 Jun 52
MG Joseph P. Cleland	2 Jun 52 - 16 Apr 53
MG Ridgley Gaither	17 Apr 53 - 17 Jan 54
BG J. F. R. Seitz	18 Jan 54 - 4 Feb 54
BG William Bradley	5 Feb 54 - 30 Jun 54
MG Homer O. Eaton, Jr (3)	2 Sep 52 - 2 Jul 60
MG Charles O. Ott, Jr.	3 Jul 60 - 29 Jan 68
MG Charles O. Ott, Jr.	13 Jan 74 - 12 Aug 74
MG Thomas K. Turnage	12 Aug 74 - 28 Aug 75
MG Robert E. Johnson, Jr.	28 Aug 75 - 3 Oct 76
MG James T. Keltner	4 Oct 76 - 7 Nov 77
MG Thomas K. Turnage	7 Nov 77 - 9 Jun 79
BG Robert L Meyer (Acting) (4)	10 Jun 79 - 7 Nov 79
MG Robert L. Meyer	8 Nov 79 - 9 Nov 81
MG Anthony L. Palumbo	9 Nov 81 - 17 Jul 83
MG William J. Jefferds	17 Jul 83 - 1 Aug 86
MG James D. Delk	1 Aug 86 - 1 Oct 89
MG Averill E. Hawkins	1 Oct 89 - 1 May 91
MG Daniel J. Hernandez	1 May 91 - 8 Aug 93

MG William Stewart   8 Aug 93 - 5 May 96
MG Edmund C. Zysk   5 May 96 -

(1) MG Barrows took a nine month leave of absence, departing for Germany immediately after annual training in 1933, returning on 10 April 1934. BG Story temporarily assumed command in his absence.

(2) Not federally recognized as a Major General

(3) There were two 40th Infantry Divisions for a time during the Korean War. The Fortieth Infantry Division (NGUS) was reconstituted in California effective 2 Sep 1952 composed primarily of troops rotated back from Korea. The 40th U.S. Infantry Division was relieved from active Federal service effective 30 Jun 54, although the colors were passed during a ceremony 19 June 1954 in San Francisco.

(4) For administrative reasons (shortage of Major General slots), BG Anthony L. Palumbo was on state orders as division commander, even though BG Robert L. Meyer was on division orders as acting commander and actually functioned in that role.

APPENDIX 4

ORGANIZATION OF THE 40TH DIVISION

World War I

Div Hq Troop	79th Inf Bde	80th Inf Bde	65th FA Bde	115th Train Hq & MP
115th Fld Sig Bn	157th Inf	159th Inf	143rd FA Regt	115th Supply Train
115th Engrs	158th Inf	160th Inf	144th FA Regt	115th Ammo Train
143rd MG Bn	144th MG Bn	145th MG Bn	145th FA Regt	115th Engr Train
			115th TM Btry	115th Sanitary Train

(The division did not exist from demobilization in 1919 until organized again 18 June 1926, although many traditional elements of the division existed in the interim)

1930

Hq Co	79th Inf Bde	80th Inf Bde	143rd FA Regt	40th Spec Hqs Trp
40th Tank Co	159th Inf Regt	160th Inf Regt	115th Ammo Trn	115th Med Regt
40th Sig Co	184th Inf Regt	185th Inf Regt		40th QM Train
40th Div Aviation	115th Mtrcycle Co			

1939

Div Hq	HQ 79th Inf Bde	HQ 80th Inf Bde	HHB 65th FA Bde	HHD Spt Troops
40th MP Co	159th Inf	160th Inf	143rd FA Bn	115th Engr Bn
40th Sig Co	184th Inf	185th Inf	145th FA Bn	115th Med Regt
40th Tank Co			222nd FA Bn	115th QM Regt
40th Div Avn				115th Ord Co
115th Obsn Sqdn				

World War II

Hq Co	108th Inf	HHB Divarty	HQ Special Troops
MP Plat	160th Inf	143rd FA Bn	115th Engr Bn
40th Recon Troop	185th Inf	164th FA Bn	115th Med Bn
40th Sig Co		213th FA Bn	740th Ord Co
40th Counter Intell Det		222nd FA Bn	40th QM Co

1953

Hq Co	160th Inf	HHB Divarty	115th Med Bn
40th MP Co	223rd Inf	143rd FA Bn	740th Ord Co
40th Recon Trp	224th Inf	625th FA Bn	40th QM Co
40th Sig Co		980th FA Bn	578th Engr Bn
140th Tank Bn		981st FA Bn	
		140th AAA Bn	

1954 (Armored Division)

Hq Co	Cbt Cmd A,B,C	133rd Tk Bn	HHB Divarty	Hq Train & Band
40th MP Co	160th Armd Inf	134th Tk Bn	143rd FA Bn	40th Armd QM Bn
40th Sig Co	161st Armd Inf	139th Tk Bn	214th FA Bn	40th Armd Med Bn
132nd Engr Bn	223rd Armd Inf	140th Tk Bn	215th FA Bn	40th Armd Ord Bn
111th Recon Bn	224th Armd Inf		225th FA Bn	
140th Repl Co			217th AAA Bn	

1959 (Armored Division)

Hq Co	Cbt Cmd A,B,C	1-185th Tk	HHB Divarty	Hq Train & Band
40th MP Co	1-160th ARB	2-185th Tk	1-144th (Rkt)	40th Armd QM Bn
240th Sig Bn	2-160th ARB	4-185th Tk	2-144th FA	40th Armd Med Bn
132nd Engr Bn	3-160th ARB	5-185th Tk	3-144th FA	40th Armd Ord Bn
3-185 Recon Bn	4-160th ARB	6-185th Tk*	4-144th FA	540th Admin Co
140th Avn Co		7-185th Tk*		
		(*added 27 Apr 62)		

1966 (Armored Division)

Hq Co	Hq 1/2/3 Bdes	1-185th AR	HHB Divarty	Hq Div Spt Cmd
40th MP Co	1-111th Cav	2-185th AR	1-144th (Rkt)	40th Med Bn
140th Avn Bn	1-160th Inf	3-185th AR	2-144th FA	40th Maint Bn
240th Sig Bn	2-160th Inf	4-185th AR	3-144th FA	40th S & T Bn
132nd Engr Bn	3-160th Inf	5-185th AR	4-144th FA	540th Admin Co
1-18th Cav	4-160th Inf	6-185th AR	5-144th FA	

1979 (Mechanized Infantry Division)

Hq Co	Hq 1/2/3 Bdes	2-159th Inf	HHB Divarty	Hq Div Spt Cmd
40th MP Co	1-149th Armor	1-160th Inf	1-143rd FA	40th S & T Bn
40th Avn Bn	1-185th Armor	2-160th Inf	1-144th FA	40th Med Bn
240th Sig Bn	2-185th Armor	3-160th Inf	2-144th FA	540th Maint Bn
132nd Engr Bn	3-185th Armor	4-160th Inf	3-144th FA	40th AG Co
1-18th Cav Sqdn		1-184th Inf	F-144th (TA)	40th Fin Co

1987 (Mechanized Infantry Division)

Hq Co	Hq 1/2/3 Bdes	2-159th Inf	HHB Divarty	Hq Div Spt Comd
40th MP Co	Hq Avn Bde	2-160th Inf	1-143rd FA	40th Spt Bn
240th Sig Bn	1-149th Armor	3-160th Inf	1-144th FA	240th Spt Bn
132nd Engr Bn	1-185th Armor	4-160th Inf	2-144th FA	340th Spt Bn
1-18th Cav Sqdn	2-185th Armor	1-184th Inf	3-144th FA	540th Main Spt Bn
D/E/F 140th Avn	3-185th Armor	1-140th Avn	F-144th (TA)	
40th Div Band	1-221st Armor			

(The 140th MI Bn of the USAR was assigned to the 40th Division, the 8-40th Armor Bn of the USAR had a training association, and the 4-200 ADA Bn of the New Mexico National Guard was affiliated with the division)

CAMPAIGN DECORATIONS AND CREDITS AWARDED TO THE 40TH DIVISION

CAMPAIGN PARTICIPATION CREDIT:

World War I
    Streamer without inscription

World War II
    Bismarck Archipelago
    Luzon (with arrowhead)
    Southern Philippines

Korean War
    Second Korean Winter
    Korea, Summer-Fall 1952
    Third Korean Winter
    Korea, Summer 1953

DECORATIONS:

World War II:

Division: The Presidential Unit Citation, Streamer embroidered 17 October 1944 to 4 July 1945 (DA GO 47, 1950)

Units: Distinguished Unit Citation, 40th Reconnaissance Troop for January 9 to April 25, 1945, action in Southern Philippine Islands

Distinguished Unit Citation, Company I, 160th Infantry Regiment, for February 15, 1945 action on Luzon.

Korean War:

Division: Republic of Korea Presidential Unit Citation, Streamer embroidered Korea 1952-1954 (DA GO 50, 1954)

Units: Distinguished Unit Citation, 140th Tank Battalion, for June 1-8 and July 16-18, 1953 action vicinity Nojonp-Yong.

Meritorious Unit Commendation, 40th QM Company, for service August 15, 1953 to January 31, 1954.

CITATIONS:

Distinguished Unit Citation: GO #66, War Department 10 August 1945

16. *The 40th Cavalry Reconnaissance Troop (Mechanized)* is cited for outstanding performance of duty in action against the enemy. On 9 January 1945 the troop landed with the leading elements at Lingayen and before night fell, by using amphibious tractors, crossed the Calmay and Agno Rivers and probed enemy positions in Salasa and Labrador. Given the special mission of reconnoitering to Dasol Bay on the China Sea Coast, the troop slashed through enemy resistance at Alaminos and patrolled the Dasol Bay shore from Egia to Santa Cruz. Turning south, the troop continued reconnaissance to Camiling and Tarlac. Thrusting beyond Bamban the *40th Cavalry Reconnaissance Troop (Mechanized)*, making a number of enemy contacts, on 24 January reconnoitered Mabalacat, Dau, the barriers to the east, and dashed into Clark Field. A week later a platoon was dispatched to Guagua and preceding infantry troops entered Dinalupihan, northeast anchor of Bataan Peninsula. On landing at Tigbauan, Panay, 18 March 1945, elements of the troop were dispatched north and northeast to Alimodian and Santa Barbara Airfields, which were reached before nightfall. In a sharp engagement at Pavia, the enemy force was disorganized and broken into small groups which withdrew up the Tigon River.

More than ninety enemy dead were left in this encounter. The troop sought enemy contacts to the extremities of the island, to Unidos on the northwest and Estancia to the northeast. On reaching the shore of Negros at Pulupandan, elements of the troop searched La Carlota and Pontevedra to the south. On 30 March, at the end of the encounter with the enemy in the vicinity of Atipuluan, the troop captured five Japanese and counted 114 killed, while losing only one of its own killed and three wounded. On 2 April, Silay, Alicanta, and Malago air strips were reconnoitered, and on the next day Victorias and Manaplas on the north coast were reached. By 7 April, a permanent bivouac was established at Fabrica, and the troop was reaching east to Escalante and later south to San Carlos. On 25 April reconnaissance was extended to Dumuguete on the southeast coast where, next day, contact was established with an infantry combat team which had just landed. In all, the troop killed 292 of the enemy and captured twenty. The volume of intelligence obtained of the enemy situation, terrain, avenues of approach, and conditions of roads, bridges and trails was of inestimable value to the division commander, and the speed, dash, boldness and combat effectiveness displayed by the *40th Cavalry Reconnaissance Troop (Mechanized)* were inspiring to the officers and men of the division.

Distinguished Unit Citation: GO #68, War Department 14 August 1945

18. *Company I, 160th Infantry Regiment,* is cited for outstanding performance of duty in action against the enemy. On 15 February 1945, in the Zambales Mountain Range, Luzon, P. I., *Company I* was given the mission to attack and secure a commanding hill approximately 1,800 yards to the front, referred to as Objective Hill. The company advanced approximately 1,000 yards encountering heavy enemy small-arms fire and knee-mortar fire, then pushed forward until they reached a ridge paralleling their front, approximately 300 yards short of and below their objective. Here they were subjected to fire from their front, both flanks and rear. The remaining distance was open country and the terrain necessitated a steep climb of over 400 feet, the last 50 feet being almost straight up with only one approach for men in single file. With the enemy in a commanding position, with excellent fields of fire and superior observation, the decision was to make a night assault. At 0400 hours, 16 February 1945, the company under cover of darkness succeeded in getting one platoon of men on the hill and inside the enemy's positions. At that time the enemy detected their presence and, after a short but severe close-in fight, retreated off the hill to positions some 30 yards down the reverse slope in a bamboo draw. The balance of the company, in single file, scaled the cliff and joined the platoon already there. At dawn they were subjected to heavy enemy

fire from the front and flanks and broke up a counterattack from the left front. Running short of ammunition, without water or rations, suffering considerable casualties, the aid men killed, and without plasma or morphine for the wounded, the company held its position. Every attempt by carrying parties to resupply them all that day and the following night failed to get through to the company because of enemy action. The next day attempts to supply by air-drops were unsuccessful because of the hard rocky hilltop, the steep cliffs on three sides, and the nearness of the enemy on the fourth side. As a result, only one box was recovered and it consisted of machine gun ammunition and four canteens of water. Although completely exhausted and without food and water for over 36 hours, the company maintained control of the hill until 0130 hours, 18 February 1945, when another company was able to relieve them. Upon the relief, the largest part of the litter bearers was made up of *Company I* men, and to transport the wounded it was necessary to tie them to the litter and lower them by rope. The terrain was so difficult that from 8 to 10 men were required per litter. In the accomplishment of the assigned mission, overcoming the extreme hardships and suffering 39 casualties out of 96 men, *Company I, 160th Infantry Regiment*, displayed courage, determination, and a unit spirit by teamwork and the will to win despite all obstacles, and maintained their high morale and esprit de corps to the end of their mission.

ROK Presidential Unit Citation: GO #50 DA, Wash DC 30 Jun 54-
    REPUBLIC OF KOREA PRESIDENTIAL UNIT CITATION awarded by citation dated 27 July 1953, by Syngman Rhee, President of the Republic of Korea, for exceptionally meritorious service to the Republic of Korea during the period 22 January 1952 to 15 January 1954, inclusive, with citation as follows:

The 40th United States Infantry Division arrived in Korea in January 1952 and assumed control of the Kumwha sector on the central front. Consolidating their positions along the entire line assigned to them, the troops of this Division maintained the security of a broad segment of the battle area and successfully contained the enemy. On 30 June 1952, the Division was relieved on position by the 2d Republic of Korea Army Division with artillery elements of the division remaining on position in support of the Korean troops. Intermittently assigned to reserve and to front line positions, the Division continually rendered active support to various Republic of Korea units and made evident its superior combat and training proficiency.
    On 27 April 1953, the Division received the responsibility of defending part of the main line of resistance along the northern rim of the Punch Bowl and later was assigned to protect the Heartbreak Ridge sector. Division units such

as 143rd and 981st Field Artillery Battalion, and many others continued with their mission of supporting the 12th Republic of Korea Army Division. During the entire campaign, the Division displayed superb solidarity and combat effectiveness in performing the many vital duties assigned to it and exhibited outstanding resoluteness in its training and supporting of Republic of Korea forces. The individual concern of all members of the Division in aiding their Korean comrades-in-arms and the consistent efficiency prominent throughout the Division's service in Korea reflect great credit on the Division, the United States Army, and the entire United Nations forces.

Distinguished Unit Citation to 140th Tank Battalion. GO #56 DA, Wash, DC dated 20 July 1954. Citation as follows:

The 140th Tank Battalion, 40th Infantry Division, is cited for outstanding performance of duty and extraordinary heroism in action against the enemy in the vicinity of Nojonp-Yong, Korea during the period 1 to 8 June and 16 to 18 July 1953. Committed to direct support of the 12th Republic of Korea Army Division, the battalion had been manning tank positions in four vitally strategic hills. On the night of 1 June the enemy began preparatory fires followed by a large scale attack on one of the hills and succeeded in displacing infantry elements. However, the tank platoon located in that sector refused to leave its positions and continued valiant efforts in denying the enemy its objective. That night another platoon moved up under the supporting fires of Company B and Company C to aid the beleaguered unit, and the following morning they were reinforced by an additional platoon.

Fierce action continued throughout the remainder of 2 June with the tankers resolutely refusing to withdraw. With tanks spearheading the infantry, a counterattack was launched on the morning of 3 June and although it did not clear the hill it permitted the besieged tanks to be replaced with others which, supported by the balance of the battalion tanks, denied the enemy access to the crest.

On 5 June, Company A, which was in reserve 56 miles to the rear, was alerted and moved in an excellently coordinated forced march and arrived in an exceedingly short time to relieve Company B. That evening the hostile force began concentrated attacks on two adjacent hills and gained a few friendly outposts, however, the infantry, inspired by the tankers' valiant stand, counter-attacked and hurled the enemy from these positions. In the remaining days, from 6 to 8 June the battalion continued devastating fire against hostile positions, sealing off approach routes and permitting friendly lines to be reconsolidated. Fierce as these actions were, it was realized that they were but a prelude to a more massive attack to seize the entire hill complex and clear the way to the south.

On the night of 16 July the foe commenced battalion-size attacks against two of the hill positions. The combined tank, artillery, and infantry fires, particularly flanking fire from the tanks which the aggressor had not anticipated, destroyed one battalion and so decimated the others that it only made minor gains. The following night small diversionary actions were attempted and on the morning of 18 July they began a regimental size attack against another sector. Here the aggressiveness, esprit de corps, and prowess of the defenders succeeded in wreaking havoc among the hostile force. The superb gallantry of the tankers displayed in both phases of this action paved the way for a stiffened defense and better coordination and as a result the attacking enemy division was completely demoralized and ceased to be an effective striking force.

The heroism and courage exhibited by the members of this unit in denying the enemy a vitally strategic area reflect great credit on themselves, their organization and the military service of the United States. (GO 285, HQs, Eighth U.S. Army, 10 May 1954)

Meritorious Unit Commendation to 740th Ordnance Bn, 40th Inf Div. GO #95 DA, Washington, DC dated 1953. Citation as follows:

The 740th Ordnance Battalion, 40th Infantry Division is cited for exceptionally meritorious conduct in the performance of outstanding service in support of combat operations in Korea during the period 27 January to 27 July 1953. The battalion efficiently provided maintenance, supply, ammunition and instruction-inspection services to the 40th Infantry Division. Although reorganized from a company to a battalion and operating with only 80 percent of its authorized strength, the unit effectively overcame obstacles of treacherous roads and mountain passes, adverse weather and frequent exposure to enemy fire in competently performing its duties. During much of the time, the battalion achieved a zero backlog in its shops, either evacuating or repairing all unserviceable material on the same day that it was received. In order to increase its effectiveness in a sector where infantry regiments on the line were separated by an extremely high mountain, the unit operated twice the number of ammunition offices than is normal and thereby maintained a constant flow of ammunition to the front. The unit conducted a superior instruction-inspection service and materially increased the combat efficiency of all troops in the area. The 740th Ordnance Battalion, 40th Infantry Division, displayed such outstanding devotion to duty in the performance of exceptionally difficult tasks as to set it apart from and above other units with similar missions. The initiative, ability, and esprit de corps exhibited by members of this battalion reflect great credit upon themselves and the military service. (GO 967, HQs Eighth U.S. Army, 28 October 1953

Meritorious Unit Commendation to 40th QM Co, 40th Inf Div (Same GO as 140th Tank Bn). The citation reads as follows:

The 40th Quartermaster Company, 40th Infantry Division, is cited for exceptionally meritorious conduct in the performance of outstanding services in support of combat operations in Korea during the period 1 August 1953 to 31 January 1954. Serving all units of the 40th Infantry Division, this company continued its normal functions without interruption or decrease in efficiency during three complete moves made by the division.

In addition to handling a prodigious amount of Class II and IV items, receipt, storage, and distribution of over 560 tons of winter clothing and equipment was effected and 5,000 quartermaster items were expeditiously repaired and returned to service, thereby saving the United States Government thousands of dollars in replacement stock. Over 22,000 tons of rations were provided and handled with superior protection and accountability and 35,000 tons of petroleum, oil and lubricants were expeditiously delivered to motor pools and supply points, assuring an adequate supply for transportation and heating unit consumption.

The three Quartermaster Truck Platoons provided excellent transportation facilities during Division moves and daily operations, traveling thousands of miles every month over hazardous terrain and under adverse weather conditions. The provision of laundry and shower facilities and the production of more than three servings of ice cream each week for assigned and attached personnel were high among the many contributing factors in the maintenance of morale throughout the division.

The 40th Quartermaster Company displayed such outstanding devotion to duty in the performance of exceptionally difficult tasks as to set it above and apart from other units with similar missions. The initiative, ability, and esprit de corps exhibited by the members of this unit throughout the entire period reflect great credit on themselves and the military service of the United States. (GO #333, HQS, Eighth U.S. Army, 28 May 1954).

Sergeant David B. Bleak of Medical Company, 223ʳᵈ Infantry Regiment just prior to earning the Medal of Honor in Korea. (Photo: Mrs. David B. Bleak)

MEDAL OF HONOR CITATIONS

World War II:

STAFF SERGEANT JOHN C. SJOGREN
Company I, 160th Infantry Regiment, 40th Infantry Division. Vicinity of San Jose Hacienda, Negros, Philippine Islands, 23 May 1945. GO. Nr. 97, 1 November 1945. The citation reads:

Staff Sergeant Sjogren led an attack against a high precipitous ridge defended by a company of enemy riflemen, who were entrenched in spider holes and supported by well-concealed pillboxes housing automatic weapons with interlocking bands of fire. The terrain was such that only one squad could advance at a time; and from a knoll atop a ridge a pillbox covered the only approach with automatic fire. Against this enemy stronghold, Staff Sergeant Sjogren led the first squad to open the assault. Deploying his men, he moved forward and hurling grenades when he saw his next in command, at the opposite flank, was gravely wounded. Without hesitation he crossed twenty yards of exposed terrain in the face of enemy fire and exploding dynamite charges, moved the man to cover and administered first aid. He then worked his way forward and, advancing directly into the enemy fire, killed eight Japanese in spider holes guarding the approach to the pillbox. Crawling to within a few feet of the pillbox while his men concentrated their bullets on the fire port, he began dropping grenades through the narrow firing slit. The enemy immediately threw two or three of these unexploded grenades out, and fragments from one wounded him in the hand and back. However, by hurling grenades through the embrasure faster than the enemy could return them, he succeeded in destroying the occupants. Despite his wounds, he directed his squad to follow him in a systematic attack on the remaining positions, which he eliminated in like manner, taking tremendous risks, overcoming bitter resistance, and never hesitating in his relentless advance. To silence one of the pillboxes, he wrenched a light machine gun out through the embrasure as it was firing before blowing up the occupants with hand grenades. During this action, Staff Sergeant Sjogren, by his heroic bravery, aggressiveness, and skill as a soldier, singlehandedly killed forty-three enemy soldiers and destroyed nine pillboxes, thereby paving the way for his company's successful advance.

The Korean War:

SERGEANT DAVID B. BLEAK
Medical Company, 223rd Infantry Regiment, 40th Infantry Division. Vicinity of Minari-gol, Korea, 14 June 1952. GO. Nr. 83, 2 November 1953. The citation reads:

Sergeant Bleak, a member of the medical company, distinguished himself by conspicuous gallantry and indomitable courage above and beyond the call of duty in action against the enemy. As a medical aidman, he volunteered to accompany a reconnaissance patrol committed to engage the enemy and capture a prisoner for interrogation. Forging up the rugged slope of the key terrain, the group was subjected to intense automatic weapons and small arms fire and suffered several casualties. After administering to the wounded, he continued to advance with the patrol. Nearing the military crest of the hill, while attempting to cross the fire-swept area to attend the wounded, he came under hostile fire from a small group of the enemy concealed in a trench. Entering the trench he closed with the enemy, killed two with bare hands and a third with his trench knife. Moving from the emplacement, he saw a concussion grenade fall in front of a companion and, quickly shifting his position, shielded the man from the impact of the blast. Later, while ministering to the wounded, he was struck by a hostile bullet but, despite the wound, he undertook to evacuate a wounded comrade. As he moved down the hill with his heavy burden, he was attacked by two enemy soldiers with fixed bayonets. Closing with the aggressors, he grabbed them and smacked their heads together, then carried his helpless comrade down the hill to safety. Sergeant Bleak's dauntless courage and intrepid actions reflect utmost credit upon himself and are in keeping with the honored traditions of the military service.

CORPORAL GILBERT G. COLLIER (Died of Wounds)

(Later Sergeant) Company F, 223rd Infantry Regiment, 40th Infantry Division. Vicinity of Tutayon, Korea, 19-20 July 1953. GO. Nr. 3, 12 January 1955. The citation reads:

Corporal Collier, a member of Company F, distinguished himself by conspicuous gallantry and indomitable courage above and beyond the call of duty in action against the enemy. Corporal Collier was point man and assistant leader of a combat patrol committed to make contact with the enemy. As the patrol moved forward through the darkness, he and his commanding officer slipped and fell from a steep 60-foot cliff and were injured. Incapacitated by a badly sprained ankle which prevented immediate movement, the officer ordered the patrol to return to the safety of friendly lines. Although suffering from a painful back injury, Corporal Collier elected to remain with his leader, and before daylight they managed to crawl back up and over the mountainous terrain to the opposite valley where they concealed themselves in the brush until nightfall, then edged toward their company positions. Shortly after leaving the daylight retreat they were ambushed and, in the ensuing fire fight, Corporal Collier killed two hostile soldiers, received painful wounds, and was separated from his companion. Then, ammunition expended, he closed in hand-to-hand combat with four attacking hostile infantrymen, killing, wounding, and routing the foe with his bayonet. He was mortally wounded during this action, but made a valiant attempt to reach and assist his leader in a desperate effort to save his comrade's life without regard for his own personal safety. Corporal Collier's unflinching courage, consummate devotion to duty, and gallant self-sacrifice reflect lasting glory upon himself and uphold the noble traditions of the military service.

CORPORAL CLIFTON T. SPEICHER (KIA)

Company F, 223rd Infantry Regiment, 40th Infantry Division. Vicinity Minari-gol, Korea, 14 June 1952. GO. Nr. 65, 19 August 1953. The citation reads:

Corporal Speicher distinguished himself by conspicuous gallantry and indomitable courage above and beyond the call of duty in action against the enemy. While participating in an assault to secure a key terrain feature, Corporal Speicher's squad was pinned down by withering small-arms, mortar, and machine gun fire. Although already wounded, he left the comparative safety of his position, and made a daring charge against the machine gun emplacement. Within ten yards of the goal, he was again wounded by small arms fire but continued on, entered the bunker, killed two hostile soldiers with his rifle, a third with his bayonet, and silenced the machine gun. Inspired by this incredible display of valor, the men quickly moved up and completed the mission. Dazed and shaken, he walked to the foot of the hill where he collapsed and died. Corporal Speicher's consummate sacrifice and unflinching devotion to duty reflect lasting glory upon himself and uphold the noble traditions of the military service.

DIVISIONAL ELEMENTS THAT FOUGHT ELSEWHERE DURING WORLD WAR II

Divisional Tank Company

As conflict began spreading around the world, the first unit to be activated was the divisional tank company. Tank Companies from all of the divisions were being withdrawn to form provisional tank battalions. The 40th Tank Company of Salinas was redesignated, with its 107 men becoming the nucleus of Company C, 194th Tank Battalion effective September 1, 1940.

Company C, 194th Tank Battalion left for the Philippines on September 28, 1941, having been told they would be there for five months in support of American and Filipino forces. The atmosphere quickly changed when the Japanese attacked Pearl Harbor. The tankers were assigned to battle positions in the vicinity of Clark Field and Fort Stotsenburg when the Japanese landed on the island of Luzon three days after Pearl Harbor. National Guard tank units were the first armored units of our army to be engaged in combat in World War II.

During the fight against the Japanese invaders of the Philippines, the 194th was part of the Provisional Tank Group which consisted of the 192nd Tank Battalion (Light), 194th Tank Battalion (Light), and the 17th Ordnance Company (Armored). The Tank Group was awarded battle honors (GO #101 dated March 9, 1942):

> "for outstanding performance of duty in action during the defense of the Philippines. Organized late in November 1941, it took battle positions on December 1st in the vicinity of Clark Field and Fort Stotsenburg, from which it fought a notable action in the defense of these critical points in the initial hostile attack. In the course of the

withdrawal into Bataan, its units were constantly in the field, covering the supporting four divisions of the North Luzon Force, and two of the South Luzon Force, its elements operating initially 150 miles apart. This unit contributed most vitally in all stages and under extraordinary handicaps to the protraction of operations and the successful withdrawal. Its units were the last out of both North and South Luzon and the last into the Bataan Peninsula, on 7 January 1942."

The tankers were among the last to withdraw into the Bataan Peninsula, and participated in the infamous Bataan Death March. Only forty-seven members of the unit made it back to Salinas after the war.

159th Infantry Regiment

The National Guard divisions were converted to triangular divisions, giving up two of their four regiments, and receiving one regiment from another division. The 159th Infantry Regiment was detached from the division on September 29, 1941, joining the 7th Division in their desert training for the African Campaign. The regiment was converted to a motorized regiment. In one of those decisions that boggle the minds of civilians (and most soldiers), the 7th was then sent to Alaska to assist in defending the Aleutians.

When the campaign started to recapture the Aleutians, it was decided to invade Attu before Kiska. At that time, Kiska was considered a tougher nut to crack.

The 17th and 32nd Infantry Regiments of the 7th Division invaded Attu in May of 1943. Several thousand Japanese and American troops were killed or wounded in the first three weeks of fighting. The 159th replaced the 17th Infantry on Attu as the garrison force effective July 9, 1943. It was originally intended to then have the 159th participate in the invasion of Kiska, but plans were changed when it was decided to have the 159th garrison Attu. The regiment was transferred to the Alaskan Department on August 23, 1943, and remained on Attu until August 9, 1944.

The regiment, no longer motorized, then traveled to Camp Swift, Texas. There they became a part of 4th U.S. Army.

Personnel and equipment of its three battalions were transferred to other combat units, and a reconstituted 159th Infantry Regiment was sent to the European Theater of Operations.

They embarked from Camp Kilmer, New Jersey, landing in France on March 18, 1945. They replaced a regiment of the 106th Infantry Division, the division that had been so terribly decimated during the Battle of the Bulge. The 159th entered Germany on April 25, 1945. The regiment is authorized two World War II Campaign Streamers, for the Aleutians and for Northern France.

184th Infantry Regiment

The Aleutian Islands stretched between Japan and Alaska, and were a constant concern to strategic planners. They could be used as stepping stones by invaders, and initially there were too few troops to properly garrison our "Northern Frontier." Reconnaissance told planners that Kiska was more heavily defended by the Japanese than Attu, so the decision was made to recapture Attu first.

The 7th Division was selected to recapture Attu. When the National Guard converted to triangular divisions, the 7th Division was advised they would be receiving the 184th Infantry Regiment, formerly part of the 40th.

Captain Ralph Lui was a National Guardsman on active duty as an artilleryman with the 7th Infantry Division. There were very few reservists in Regular Army divisions when the war started, so discussions about National Guardsmen and reservists were very frank in his presence. When officers in the 7th Division heard the 184th was going to be replacing the 159th, Lui heard comments such as "Oh, Oh! Another National Guard outfit!" He didn't let anyone know he was from the Sacramento area. He prayed to himself, "Dear God, please have them do a good job."

In organizing for the invasion of Kiska, the 184th Infantry Regiment was part of the 9th Amphibian Force. This task force was commanded by Colonel Curtis D. O'Sullivan, the 184th's

Regimental Commander. The Kiska Task Force, scheduled to land on Kiska August 15, 1943, consisted of:

9th Amphibian Force:	184th Infantry Regiment
	87th Mountain Infantry
9th Canadian Brigade units:	22nd Royal Canadian Infantry
	24th Royal Canadian Artillery
7th Division Units:	57th Field Artillery
	31st Field Artillery
	13th Combat Engineers
	17th Infantry (in reserve)
Alaskan Defense Cmd Units:	104th Combat Engineers
	110th Heavy Construction Engineers

The commanders and staffs were handicapped by the fact they had inadequate maps. The same had applied during the campaign on Attu. What few maps they had provided adequate information for the coast line, but almost no information on the interior. Nonetheless, planning proceeded using what little hard information they had.

The 184th attacked Kiska Island at 6:21 a.m. on August 15, 1943. There was considerable apprehension when they landed, based on the Attu experience. There Japanese soldiers had bayoneted American wounded in aid stations. Then and later the Japanese fought fanatically, and sometimes exhibited behavior bizarre enough to make witnesses wonder if they were drunk or drugged. Regardless of expectations, the 184th was not opposed when they landed. This was fortunate, because weather conditions precluded air support of the landing.

Colonel O'Sullivan's operations report for August 17, 1943 read:

"Achieving complete surprise, our troops landed on the southwest
portion of Kiska Island, 15 August, at a point 7 miles west of Kiska
Harbor. A second landing was made 16 August on the northwest side
5 miles northwest of the harbor area. Both landings were unopposed
and our troops are driving rapidly inland toward the eastern shore
where the principal installations at Gertrude Cove and Kiska Harbor
are located. The southern force of 9,000 men has reached the east
shore one mile east of Gertrude Cove encountering little opposition.
The northern force 7,000 troops is moving toward Kiska Harbor from
the west and north, attempting to confine the Japs to the east central
portion of the 22 mile-long island. Hurriedly abandoned trenches,
one with hot coffee in it, tents and ammunition were taken by our
southern force west of Gertrude Cove. Low visibility is hampering
operations."

Colonel O'Sullivan's Intelligence Officer reported on August
18th:

" No enemy forces have been found on Kiska after searches of the
central portions of the island from the lake area 3 miles north of Kiska
harbor to over 6 miles south of the harbor, 17 August. The main camp
area Gertrude and Reynard Coves, Conquer Point, Salmon Lagoon,
the airfield and pass west of the main camp to the west coast have
been occupied by our troops. Canadian troops, operating with our
forces, reported the seaplane base vacant, apparently deserted 4 or 5
days. It is increasingly apparent enemy strength has lately been
sharply reduced below prior estimates of 6,100 to 7,700 enemy troops.
It is still a possibility the Japs have withdrawn to the north to the
Volcano area, or to the southern end of the island to terrain now being
scouted by our forces Many buildings in Gertrude Cove were found
wrecked and foxholes lately abandoned. Two 75mm field guns, one of
which was smashed, and one flak gun have been captured. The Navy
reported sighting a Jap biplane 4.0 miles southwest of Attu."

The operations report for August 19th read:

"Further evidence of the Jap evacuation of Kiska prior to our landing
was found 18 August as our troops pushed patrols toward the north
and south section of the island without contacting the enemy.
Hampered by the heavy fog, our troops pushed into South Head, the

401

Volcano area, and toward Vega Point and Cape St. Stephen. Little Kiska was found to have been hastily evacuated about ten days ago. The Japs had removed firing mechanisms from three 6 inch seacoast guns, which were otherwise intact with ammunition. The buildings, riddled from fire of our strafing planes, contained clothing and food. Our forces now occupy Gertrude Cove and the main camp area. No anti-submarine net was found in Kiska Harbor where a sunken ship was found with masts above the surface. The last entry in the log of the operator at the seaplane base power plant was 23 July. One of our destroyers was damaged by an underwater explosion in Conquer Bay. The grave of a P-40 pilot, shot down over Kiska 24 July, was found near the main camp with the following marker: 'Here sleeps a gallant young hero of the skies who lost happiness and youth for his homeland.'"

The Intelligence Officer's report on August 19th added two additional pieces of information. A Japanese medium bomber had been spotted 400 miles south of Attu. The other was that two Japanese dogs were all that was found in the main camp area on Kiska. The worst the troops had to face, no Japanese remaining on the island, were "Williwaws," the violent wind storms found in that part of the world.

The regiment shipped to Hawaii for further amphibious training in preparation for landings in the South Pacific. The regiment trained, starting in September, for the rest of 1943. The weather cooperated, and the troops enjoyed the islands as much as anyone can during wartime.

The little islets around Kwajalein had been neutralized by air and naval strikes by late January 1944. The landings on Kwajalein were set for February 1st. The 184th, still commanded by Colonel O'Sullivan, was given the job of seizing the southern portion of the island, along with the 32nd Infantry Regiment. The crescent-shaped island was a half mile wide and three miles long, with the 184th to land at Red Beach 1 on the inner southwest tip, and the 32nd to hit Red Beach 2 on the outer crescent.

The beachhead was secure within an hour, but it took four days of intensive and close fighting to reduce the hundreds of fortified shelters, so strong that point blank artillery fire often failed to penetrate them. At the end of the first day, the 184th had lost 10 killed and 13 wounded. The fighting was all but over by the end of the fourth day.

Elements of the regiment went on to assist in securing neighboring islands. In all the regiment lost 65 of the total 177 Americans killed, and 400 wounded while killing 2000 and capturing 137 Japanese.

Later in February the regiment returned to the Hawaiian Islands for rest and reequipping. The rain was warm, and as the troops who had been in Kiska noted, vertical rather than horizontal. The division remained in the islands for most of 1944, training while providing for the defense of Hawaii.

The 184th then fought on Leyte, making an assault landing on the left of the XXIV Corps on October 20, 1944. The regiment met and beat 52 identified Japanese organizations, although they received a great deal of assistance from the guerrillas.

The 184th, now commanded by Colonel Roy A. Green, invaded Okinawa on D-Day, 1 April 1945. The campaign was hard fought, with two American, and several Japanese generals killed in combat. The regiment participated in 91 days of intensive fighting, much of it in torrents of rain and subsequent mud.

The 184th arrived in Korea for occupation duty September 8, 1945. The 40th Division was also assigned to occupation duty in Korea, so this brought the regiment as close to its "home" division as it was to serve prior to rejoining the division many years later. The 184th served until it was inactivated on January 19, 1946, with the regimental colors sent home.

No story of the 184th in World War II would be complete without mentioning the Patrick R. Burke Memorial Bell. The story of the bell is a strange mixture of fact and fiction to this day.

The bell was mounted on a miniature locomotive in San Francisco's Fleishhacker Park, very close to where the regiment was bivouacked waiting to be shipped out to join the 7th Division early in World War II. The troops were irritated at having to hear the bell, as they sat wondering if each day might be their last in the United States. Finally, one morning, in a very dense fog, the bell disappeared. Because the troops were bivouacked so close to the scene of the crime, they were the obvious suspects.

Quite a commotion erupted from City Hall regarding the theft, and a reward of $25 was offered, no questions asked. There was no reaction, and the regiment got sailing orders for Kiska, so the bell was quickly forgotten.

The seas were rough during the voyage to Kiska. Tension was extremely high as each member of the regiment was repeatedly reminded of his particular role during the assault. The troops then replayed those roles in their heads.

Aircraft had flown over during the pre-invasion bombing and shelling of Kiska, although weather on August 15th precluded close air support during the actual landings. The troops were understandably tense as they went over the side into the landing craft for their first exposure to combat. Their stomachs were nauseous from the rough seas, hands were clammy, and their mouths were dry. The tension was broken somewhat when the troops heard the peal of the tiny bell they had stolen from the little locomotive in San Francisco. Someone laughed, and the troops relaxed ever so slightly as they went ashore. No one knew that the Japanese had already withdrawn from Kiska several days before.

The regimental officers had heard the bell, and as soon as the 184th had reached their initial objectives, the regimental commander ordered a search for the bell. It remained hidden.

The next combat stop for the regiment was Kwajalein. Here the landing was not only opposed, it was bloody. The bell again pealed shortly after the landing, and raised the spirits of the troops. However, the bell stopped ringing for a while when its guardian,

Private First Class Pat Burke of Sacramento, fell mortally wounded and passed it on to a comrade.

The regiment made other landings at Okinawa and Leyte, and the bell was again pealed. However, as always, the bell remained hidden as the regiment headed for home following the war.

After the war, the Assistant City Editor of the Sacramento Bee dug up the story of the bell, and located its custodian. He brought the matter to the attention of San Francisco's Mayor Elmer Robinson. The mayor had the city Department of Recreation and Parks declare the bell surplus, and "technically" ordered it returned to the purchasing agent, Harold Jones. Jones then offered it for sale to the highest bidder. With the knowledge that Jones could not deliver the bell, a past commander of the Veterans of Foreign Wars, offered the sole bid. He purchased the bell, and then transferred title to the mayor in one of a series of stratagems to gain the desired end. At that point, the current custodian of the bell, Warrant Officer Glenn Gwinn from Battery B, 636th Field Artillery in Woodland identified himself.

Warrant Officer Glenn Gwinn had carried the bell when a private in Company A, 184th Infantry. He later became the full time administrator in the Woodland unit. The name of its first custodian was engraved on the bell, and it was proudly displayed in the regiment's Sacramento armory, ready for use if the regiment were ever sent into battle again. Unfortunately, the bell later disappeared.

Field Artillery Organizations

The 144th Field Artillery Regiment formed Headquarters and Headquarters Battery, 144th Field Artillery Group, and the 980th (Bakersfield) and 981st (Santa Barbara) Field Artillery Battalions. The 980th was credited with an amphibious assault landing in Normandy. Both battalions won battle honors for the Normandy, Northern France, Ardennes, Rhineland and Central Europe campaigns. The 981st, while attached to the 9th Infantry Division in Belgium, was awarded the Belgian Croix de Guerre.

Battery B of the 144th Field Artillery Regiment had been converted to Battery B, 858th Field Artillery Battalion. The 858th Field Artillery Battalion was attached to the 4th Infantry Division, and landed with VII Corps at Utah Beach on D-Day. Headquarters and Headquarters Battery of V Corps Artillery, formerly the 76th Artillery Brigade of California, also landed on D-Day.

The 145th Field Artillery Regiment went to Hawaii. Units were disbanded and reorganized into the 213th and 145th Field Artillery Battalions. The 213th fought with the 40th Division on Guadalcanal, New Britain, and in the Philippines. The 145th fought on Saipan, Tinian, the Philippines, and Okinawa.

APPENDIX 8

OPERATIONS MEMORANDUM
FOR THE OCCUPATION OF KOREA

CONFIDENTIAL

Headquarters, 40th Infantry Division
APO 40

OPERATIONS MEMORANDUM   16 October 1945
NUMBER 13

Processing of Evacuees Both Military and Civilian
Prior to Movement to Japan

Operations Memorandum Number 12, this headquarters, subject as above, dated 7 October 1945, is hereby rescinded and the following substituted therefore:

1. In the processing of evacuees both military and civilian prior to evacuation from Korea to Japan careful investigation will be made to insure that the following is complied with:

a. *Money permitted to be carried to Japan:*

(1) Commissioned Japanese Army and Navy Officers returning to Japan may carry out a maximum of 500 yen. Other grades and enlisted men may carry out a maximum of 250 yen.

(a) Currency in excess of such amounts will be taken up by Japanese Army and Navy Finance Officers and turned over to the American Finance Officer against bulk receipts. This money will be deposited in the Bank of Chosen to the credit of "Special Accounts, Japanese Armed Forces Personal Fund."

(b) All Japanese Military unit funds and funds in the hands of Finance Officers will be turned over to the American Finance Officer to be deposited in the Bank of Chosen to the credit of "Special Accounts, Japanese Military Funds." Receipts will be given and records kept showing the name of the unit, its Korean location, and the amount and description of the fund.

(c) The Japanese Army will perform all clerical work in connection with the above.

(d) When funds are turned over they will be segregated as to type and bundled in even hundreds. They will be accompanied by itemized accounts in duplicate showing source.

(2) Japanese civilians, regardless of age, may carry out a maximum of 1,000 yen per person.

(a) Excess currency will be taken up against individual receipts and records maintained containing name, Korean address, proposed address in Japan, amount and description.

(b) Currency, when confiscated, together with pertinent records, will be turned in to the Finance Officer.

(3) Bank of Chosen notes will not be taken out. If the Bank of Japan notes are not available for exchange, Bank of Thailand or Bank of Chosen notes may be carried out to the limits set forth above.

b. *Jewelry and Securities*:

(1) Civilian and military personnel will not be permitted to carry out gold, silver, jewelry, securities, financial instruments, or other property except wearing apparel and personal possessions of value only to the owner.

(a) Japanese military and civilian evacuees will be permitted to retain watches, personal jewelry, and similar trinkets obviously not loot.

(b) All negotiable instruments including Bank Pass Books, will be taken up and a receipt given to the owner.

(2) All such property in excess of the personal allowance will be confiscated. A receipt will be given showing the description of the article, name of its owner, the owner's Korean address, prospective Japanese Address, and any information which may be used to identify the article.

c. *Cameras*:

All Japanese military and civilian evacuees will be permitted to retain personal cameras obviously not loot.

d. *Supplies*:

Troops will be permitted to retain ten (10) days medical and office supplies and rations for demobilization purposes.

e. *Flags*:

(1) All Japanese battle flags, colors and standards of company and larger units will be surrendered upon departure from Korea.

(2) Individual battle flags of value only to the owner may be carried out.

f. *Arms*:

(1) No arms of any description, including swords and sabers, will be taken by the evacuees.

(2) Swords and sabers which are confiscated will be tagged with the description of the article and identification of the owner.

(a) All swords which belong to Japanese General Officers or which appear to have considerable monetary value or historical background will be segregated and held. Commanders will be prepared to receive swords from Japanese Officers who desire their swords appraised for the above purposes. These swords will be tagged with the owner's name, address, and with history of sword if available. Receipts for such swords will be issued to respective Japanese Officers.

g. *Miscellaneous:*

(1) Japanese military and civilian evacuees will take out only what they can carry individually, subject to the foregoing restrictions, except that:

(a) Baggage for Japanese Officers, in addition to authorized military equipment, will be limited to the following: General Officers, two (2) pieces--all other officers one (1) piece. Officer baggage will be of the small wicker type baggage carrier or similar size (sic).

(2) All KEMPEI TAI and former Japanese Prisoner-of-War Camp Guards will be moved to Japan when processed and released by C. I. C.

(3) Japanese military organizational records will be screened for intelligence information, but may be retained for demobilization purposes.

(4) Insignia, Medals, and Service Ribbons may be carried out by Japanese military personnel.

(5) Rosters of Japanese troops will be prepared in duplicate by the Japanese for use upon embarkation, Japanese troops will be checked off by roster. Both copies of rosters will be retained for file.

2. Japanese troops being evacuated from Ports of Embarkation to Japan will be permitted to retain only the following articles of clothing and equipment; all other articles brought to the Port will be confiscated by processing troops of the U. S. Army:

a. *Clothing and Equipment:*

Article:	Amount
Shirts, cotton, Khaki	2
Underwear	2
Sox, cotton, pair	2
Cap, cloth, Khaki, peaked	1
Trousers, drill, long pair	2
Tunic, Drill	2
Shoes, rubber, split toe, pair	1

Shoes, leather, pair	1
Mess Tin	1
Belt, Leather	1
Water Bottle	1
First Aid Field Dressing	1
Pack	1
Haversack	1
Hold-all Canvas	1
Blanket	2
Overcoat	1
Raincoat	1
Leggings, wrap around, or 1 pair leather puttees	1
Uniform, wool	1
Cap, wool	1
Toilet, set	1
Underwear, set, wool	1
Gloves, pair	1

b. Miscellaneous

Article:	*Amount*
Fountain Pen	1
Pencils	3
Writing Pad	1
Bottle of Ink	1
Reading Material (Books, Magazines)	5
Candles, Dozen	1
Condoms, Dozen	1
Cigarettes, Cartons	2
Postal Stamps, Box	1

MYERS

Brig. Gen.

Official:
WILSON
G-3

APPENDIX 9

SOURCES

Collections:

The California Military Museum, Sacramento, California.
Extensive collection of research materiel. 1992-1996.

California State Library, Sacramento, California. Older California
National Guard histories published by the Office of the
Adjutant General. 1993.

The Center for Military History, Washington, D.C. Unit
histories. 1995.

The Eichelberger Papers, Special Collections Library, Duke
University, Durham, North Carolina. January, 1996.

National Archives, Washington, D.C. Metropolitan Area: Various
records and material from the downtown, College Park, and
Suitland branches of the National Archives. 1995-1996.

U. S. Army Military History Institute, Carlisle Barracks,
Pennsylvania. Various collections and living histories.
1992-1994.

Individuals:

Agnew, Richard S., Texas . Officer in Company F, 223rd Inf.
Earned DSC in July 1953 with Corporal Collier, who
earned MoH.

Bass, Silas W., California. Major. Provided information on 160th
and 223rd Regiments 1934 thru 1949.

Beattie, Jim, California. Corporal in Company A, 223rd RCT Dec
51-Aug 52.

Belknap, Arthur L., California. Colonel. Served as commander,
Company E, 224th Infantry in Korea.

Berebitsky, Bill., California. Military Historian. Wrote a history on National Guard units in Korea. Exchanged information.

Berry, Robert W., California. Officer on division staff. Former Public Information Officer of the Division in Korea.

Bloom, Seymour, California. Corporal. Mortarman who served in Company M, 224th Infantry in Korea.

Camozzi, Ken, California. Military historian who provided lead to General Brush's former aide-de-camp. Provided some archival material, and processed photos.

Carranza, Jesus (Jess), California. SSG thru Colonel, 1948 through seventies in the 40th Division (primarily the 160th Infantry).

Cleland, Mrs. Joseph P., Florida. Widow of MG Cleland.

Collins, James J., New York. Member of Battery B, 980th Field Artillery in Korea.

Conklin, Roy W., Connecticutt. Colonel. Wrote :Cease Fire," history of the latter months of the 223rd Infantry in Korea.

Couch, Neil P., Ohio. Sergeant First Class. Served as corporal in Company C, 160th Infantry in Korea.

DeRosa, Anthony (Tony) F., New York. Sergeant First Class. Served as corporal in Company C, 160th Infantry in Korea.

Fette, Richard C., Ohio. President of the 223rd Infantry Regiment Association. Provided information and leads.

Gale, Al, San Diego. Artillery Officer. Provided information on rescue of British Mosquito pilot in Korea, May 1952.

Gorrell, Otmer (Ron), Colorado. Major. Medic with the 224th Infantry in Korea, and commissioned after the war. Provided much information and rosters.

Gregoire, Paula Hendrick, California. Father was Sergeant David L. Hendrick,   Battery B, 164th Field Artillery. Provided personal letters relating to WWII.

Gruner, George R., California. Brigadier General. Provided information on Team Spirit exercise in Korea.

Gustafson, David A., California. Colonel. Military historian and member of the 40th Division. Provided much information.

Hamilton, William G., California. Colonel. Military historian and former member of the 184th Infantry. Provided a great deal of information.

Hanks, H. S. (Stan), Vermont. Artillery officer. Served as artillery observer with the 625th Field Artillery Battalion. Provided information on the Collier MoH incident.

Hansen, Robert W., California. Corporal. Served with both the 108th and 185th Infantry in World War II. Provided information on the sinking of the Warhawk and Major Norman E. Thrall, 108th Bn commander who was killed..

Hardy, Willard J., Florida. Captain in Company C, 160th Infantry in Korea, retired as a Major.

Hawkins, Averill E., California. Major General. Former commander of the division.

Hess, David A, Pennsylvania. Sergeant First Class. Member of Company C, 160th Infantry in Korea.

Holzgang, A. O., California. Lieutenant Colonel. Finance Officer of the division in WWII and Korea.

Hunt, Donald E., California. Brigadier General. Military historian who provided many historical extracts and recollections.

Jacobs, Bruce, Virginia. Major General. Military Historian. Provided information regarding service by National Guard divisions in World War I as related by Major General Ellard A. Walsh to the National Guard Association in 1947.

Jefferds, William J., California. Major General. Former commander of the division.

Johnson, Richard J., California. Brigadier General (Air Force). Warrant officer in Company F, 223rd Infantry who provided newspaper clippings and other information.

Keltner, James T., California. Major General. Former commander of the division.

Kondratiuk, Leonid, Washington, DC. Lieutenant Colonel. Military historian for the National Guard Bureau. Provided unit histories, citations, and other information.

Lavenberg, William H., California. Chief Warrant Officer. Ordnance officer who provided information and photos on Korea.

Lawson, Thomas O., California. Major General. Served in the division in both World War II and Korea. Provided much information, including his personal diaries.

Lauber, John H., Kansas. Member of Battery C, 164th Field Artillery. Provided information, especially about the fight for Clark Field in the Philippines.

Lown, Edward., New York. Former member of the division PIO section, and active in the 40th Infantry Division Association. Provided much information and many photos over the years.

Lui, Ralph, California. Captain. Guardsman who served with the 7th Infantry Division in early World War II. Provided information on the 159th and 184th Infantry in the Aleutians.

McClanahan, Donald D., California. Brigadier General. Military historian and author. Provided information on Korean War and more recent years.

Miller, Don, Ohio. Corporal. Member of Company C, 160th Infantry in Korea.

Moore, Donald N., California. Major General. Provided much information and several artifacts, which were sent on to the California Military Museum.

Mulkern, James A. (Jim), Arizona. Artilleryman with the 145th Field Artillery. Provided pre-World War II anecdotes.

Munyon, Robert W., California. Captain. Aide-de-camp to General Brush throughout World War II. Provided a great deal of first-hand information and many photographs.

Meyer, Robert L., California. Major General. Former commander of the division.

Orton, George W., Virginia. Brigadier General. Former commander of Company G, 160th Infantry in Korea.

O'Sullivan, Curtis H., Jr, California. Brigadier General. Military historian who provided much pre-World War II information.

Ott, Charles O. Jr., California. Major General. Served as artilleryman with the division in combat, and later as division commander.

Palumbo, Anthony L., California. Major General. Former division commander who later retired as a state lieutenant general.

Popp, Henry, New Jersey. Colonel. Commanded Cannon Company of the 108th Infantry in World War II.

Portante, Guido J. Jr., California. Brigadier General. Assistant Division Commander of the division. Provided recent history.

Rangel, Rodney R., California. Sergeant First Class. Provided history of the 1-18th Cavalry.

Reece, Donald P., California. Colonel. Provided newspaper clippings and artifacts from World War II and Korea.

Reilley, Dale R., California. Mortarman with the Heavy Mortar Company, 224th Infantry in Korea. Wrote "The Korean War - An Odyssey (1950-1953) about the unit. Active with their veterans organization. Provided much information.

Rogers, Robert H., California. First Lieutenant. Served as the 40th Division Psychological Warfare Officer in 1952. Provided PsyWar information (now in California Military Museum).

Sadecki, Don, Illinois. Served in Company A, 160th Infantry in Korea 1952-1953. Provided information, especially about Camp Drake, Japan, and photos.

Schneider, Raymond G., California. Served with Company F, 160th Infantry.

Shea, Leonard P., Massachusetts. Platoon Sergeant. Served with Company F, 223rd Infantry. Provided details on Collier MoH incident.

Strom, Edward J., California. Sergeant Major. Served with both the 980th FA and division headquarters in Korea.

Sultzbaugh, Sid, Ohio. Sergeant. Secretary of the Association of 40th Division Korean War Veterans. Former member of Company C, 160th Infantry who provided information regarding Heartbreak Ridge & Koje-do.

Taylor, Edwin B., California. Major General. Served with the 184th through the Attu campaign. Then with 7th Division. Provided information regarding the early years of World War II.

Tolputt, W. P. R. (Peter), Hampshire, England. First Lieutenant. British artillery observer who was rescued by troops of 224th Infantry in Korea.

Turnage, Thomas K., California. Major General. Served in combat with an infantry battalion in Korea. Later served as division commander.

Van Goor, Jacob A., California. Lieutenant Colonel. Division G-3 in 1995 who provided recent history.

Wagner, Richard C., Nevada. Lieutenant. Served with Company F, 223rd Infantry during the combat when both Sergeant Bleak and Corporal Speicher won the Medal of Honor.

Weber. Harry., California. TSgt. Army Air Corps crewman in World War II who provided information on largest bombing raid on Luzon up to that time. (In support of the 40th Division)

Zehr, Norman R., Colorado. Pilot with the 40th Aviation Company in Korea. Provided a great deal of material, plus an exceptional bibliography on the Korean War years.

APPENDIX 10

BIBLIOGRAPHY

Anonymous. *California National Guard State Emergencies, 1903-1960*. Military Department, State of California, Sacramento, 1961.

Anonymous. *Complete Roster Fortieth Division, Camp Kearny, California,* November 15, 1917. Camp Kearney: J. Milledge and W. B. Tyler, c. 1917.

Anonymous. *40th Infantry Division Years of World War II, 7 Dec 1941 to 7 Apr 1946*, Baton Rouge: Army and Navy Publishing Company, 1947.

Anonymous. *Fortieth in Review*. Tokyo: Dai Nippon Printing Co., 1952.

Anonymous. *Historical and Pictorial Review, 40th Infantry Division, Army of the United States, Camp San Luis Obispo, California, 1941*. Baton Rouge: Army and Navy Publishing Co., 1941.

Anonymous. *The Nation's National Guard*. Washington, DC: National Guard Association of the United States, 1954

Anonymous. Unpublished document: *One Hundred Eighty Fifth RCT in World War II*. Mimeographed history by the regiment, 168 pp., Unpublished, undated.

Berebitsky, Bill. *A Very Long Weekend. The Army National Guard in Korea 1950-1953*. Story of the forty-three Army Guard units that served in Korea. 1996

Black, Robert W. *Rangers in Korea*. New York: Ivy Books, 1989.

Breckinridge, Henry et al. *History of the Fortieth (Sunshine) Division*. Los Angeles: C. S. Hutson and Co., 1920.

Conklin, Roy W.. *Cease Fire*. Self-published history of 223rd Infantry Regiment during last six months of the Korean War. Litchfield, CT.

Delk, James D. *Fires & Furies*: The Los Angeles Riots. Palm Springs: ETC Publications, 1995.

Diminyatz, Kerry L. *The 40th Infantry Division in the Korean Conflict: The Employment of the California National Guard in an Undeclared War*. A Masters Thesis submitted to Sonoma State University May 4, 1990. Unpublished.

Eichelberger, Robert L., and MacKaye, Milton. *Our Jungle Road to Tokyo*. New York: Viking Press, 1950.

Hackworth, David H. and Sherman, Julie. *About Face (The Odyssey of an American Warrior)*. New York: Simon and Schuster, 1989.

Hermes, Walter G. *Truce Tent and Fighting Front*. United States Army in the Korean War. Washington: Government Printing Office, 1966.

Hogan, John J. *I Am Not Alone* (From the Letters of Combat Infantryman - 184th), Washington: MacKinac Press, 1947.

Kreidberg, Lieutenant Colonel Marvin A. and Henry, First Lieutenant Merton G. *History of Military Mobilization in the United States 1775-1945*, DA Pamphlet 20-212 dated June 1955. Washington: Government Printing Office, 1955.

Luvaas, Jay. *Dear Miss Em*, General Eichelberger's War in the Pacific, 1942-1945. Westport, CT: Greenwood Press, 1972.

Marshall, GEN George C. *Report on the Army, July 1, 1939 to June 30, 1943*. Washington, DC. The Infantry Journal: 1943.

Marshall, S. L. A. *Island Victory*, Washington: The Infantry Journal, 1945.

McCreedy, William W. *Sunburst Saga* (A Story of the 160th Infantry Regiment). Louisville, KY: The Bishop's Press, 1947.

Pershing, GA John J. *My Experiences in the World War.* New York: Frederick A. Stokes Co: 1931

Reilley, Dale R. *A Korean War Odyssey* (An unpublished but comprehensive history, with emphasis on the Heavy Mortar Company, 224th Infantry). Fillmore, CA, 1993

Ridgway, Matthew B. *The Korean War.* Garden City, New York: Doubleday and Co., 1967.

Smith, Robert R. *Triumph in the Philippines.* United States Army in World War II. Washington: Government Printing Office, 1963.

Summers, COL Harry G. Jr. *On Strategy: The Vietnam War in Context.* Carlisle Barracks, Pennsylvania. Strategic Studies Institute: 1981

Swanner, Charles D. *The Story of Company L "Santa Ana's Own,"* Claremont, California: Fraser Press, 1958.

U.S. Army. (657th Engineer Topographical Battalion) *40th Infantry Division in the Philippines.* 1945.

U. S. Army. *Official Record of the United States' Part in the Great War.* Washington: Government Printing Office. Undated.

U. S. Army. *Order of Battle of the United States Land Forces in the World War (1917-1919).* Several Volumes, Washington: Government Printing Office, 1948-9.

U. S. Army. *Staff Study of Japanese Operations on Negros Island.* Compiled by the 10th Information and Historical Service, Eighth Army, using papers captured by the 40th Division from the Japanese 170th IIB. 1946.

U. S. Army. *Staff Study of Japanese Operations on Panay Island.* Compiled by the 10th Information and Historical Service, Eighth Army, using papers surrendered by the Japanese and interrogations. Those interrogated included LTC

Shigekatsu Aritomi, 77th Infantry Brigade (Kono Unit);
LTC Kiyuoshi Suzuki, 2nd Air Division; and 1LT Komei
Fujitomi, 174th IIB.

U. S. Army. *United States Army in the World War (1917-1919).*
Several Volumes. Washington: Government Printing
Office, 1948.

Williams, Mary H. *Chronology, 1941-1945. United States Army
in World War II.* Washington: Government Printing
Office, 1960.

INDEX

422

THE FIGHTING FORTIETH

This book covers the history of the 40th Division from the time it was organized 1917 for World War I, up to the late 1990's. The narrative includes peacetime activities of the division as well as chronicling the combat of the division through three wars. Actions in which soldiers of the division earned the Medal of Honor are particularly detailed.

The Fighting Fortieth reflects almost eight years of research at the National Archives in both Suitland and College Park, Maryland; the Army's Military History Institute at Carlisle Barracks, Pennsylvania, the Center for Military History in Washington, DC; as well as the California Military Museum in Sacramento, California. The research effort included interviewing dozens of veterans from both World War II and Korea.

THE AUTHOR -

Major General Delk retired in August 1992 from the National Guard after more than 42 years of military service, including over 23 years of active duty. He rose to the rank of Sergeant First Class as an enlisted soldier in tank units before graduating from Officer Candidate School. He later had almost eighteen years of command, culminating with command of the 40th Infantry Division (Mechanized).

His decorations include the Defense Distinguished Service Medal, the Army Distinguished Service Medal, and the Legion of Merit.

COVER PHOTO -

The cover photo shows infantrymen of the 185th Infantry Regimental Combat Team taking cover behind tanks while advancing on Panay shortly after the assault landing. The photo was salvaged from the camera of Lieutenant Robert Fields, who was killed by a sniper's bullet immediately after this photo was taken on March 18, 1945.

(Source: National Archives)

"The soldier is the Army. No army is better than its soldiers. The soldier is also a citizen. In fact, the highest obligation and privilege of citizenship is that of bearing arms for one's country. Hence it is a proud privilege to be a soldier – a good soldier. Anyone, in any walk of life, who is content with mediocrity is untrue to himself and the American tradition. To be a good soldier a man must have discipline, self-respect, pride in his unit and in his country, a high sense of duty and obligation to his comrades and his superiors, and self-confidence, borne of demonstrated ability."

General George S. Patton, Jr.,
War As I Knew It, 1947